General Editor: A. Slaven

THE UNIVERSITY OF GLASGOW: 1451–1996

By

A. L. Brown and Michael Moss

UNIVERSITY, CITY AND STATE:

The University of Glasgow since 1870

By

Michael Moss, J. Forbes Munro and Richard H. Trainor

University, City and State: The University of Glasgow since 1870

Michael Moss, J. Forbes Munro
and
Richard H. Trainor

Edinburgh University Press
for
the University of Glasgow

Edinburgh University Press
22 George Square, Edinburgh EH8 9LF

Typeset in Times by
Pioneer Associates, Perthshire
Printed by
The Bath Press, Glasgow

CIP Data for this book is available from the British Library

ISBN 0 7486 1323 4

Foreword by the Principal

This volume records the major events that have shaped the University of Glasgow over the years and brought the University to its current status of excellence. As it prepares to celebrate its 550th anniversary in 2001, the University of Glasgow is a dynamic and vibrant institution.

The five years since the publication of the short history *The University of Glasgow 1451–1996* have been characterised by a keen spirit of cooperation. During this time the University has made a number of significant alliances, nationally and internationally.

In March 1997, the University became a founder member of Universitas 21, an international association of broad-based, research-intensive universities committed to working together to enhance their status and capabilities.

Recognising the undoubted benefits of collaboration, the Universities of Glasgow and Strathclyde, in September 1998, launched the Synergy initiative through which the two largest universities in the City of Glasgow recognise each other as 'preferred partners' in research.

Seven months later, 1 April 1999 marks the date of the merger of the University with St Andrew's College. Within its newly established Faculty of Education, the University has assumed the role of training teachers for Catholic schools in Scotland, returning full circle to the roots of its foundation by Pope Nicholas V at St Peter's in Rome on 7 January 1451.

In October 1999, the first students were admitted to Crichton Campus of the University in Dumfries. The BA (Liberal Arts) degree, which the University will confer upon students of the Crichton Campus, owes its origins to the Scottish ordinary (general) degree. The Crichton model, its roots therefore firmly in the traditions of Scottish education, again embodies the spirit of cooperation: the Crichton Campus will be shared by students of the Universities of Glasgow and Paisley alongside those from Bell College. Each of these major events in the history of the University of Glasgow has presented challenges and rewards in equal measure.

Through contributing to these recent developments and in my more general rôle as Principal it gives me great pleasure to have played a part in the shaping of its history.

Graeme J. Davies

General Editor's Preface

Writing the history of a great and ancient university is not an easy matter, especially since whole or partial histories of the University of Glasgow have been written on at least nine previous occasions. This new history, however, has a special purpose. It marks the 11th Jubilee of the University, half a millennium of teaching, scholarship and community involvement, which has transformed the University from a local College into a notable, international institution distinguished in both its research and teaching. It is also the opportunity for the University to look forward to the new millennium.

Celebrating our 11th Jubilee by producing this new history has involved more people, and more contributions from individuals, than can possibly be acknowledged here. The first steps in planning this volume were taken as early as 1992 when a small Publications Advisory Group was established comprising John Gillespie, Lesley Richmond, Michael Moss, and Tony Slaven as Convener, with Eileen Reynolds beginning her long involvement as Clerk. That small group reported to the new 2001 Committee chaired by Vice-Principal James Armour and successively by Vice-Principals Drummond Bone and Malcolm McLeod. The Publications Advisory Group developed a proposal that we could best present the long history of the University by approaching it in two stages. For although there had been many earlier histories, none had attempted to present an outline history of general interest. On this occasion the plan was to produce two companion volumes: the first to be a shorter, scholarly but popular account of the history of the University over its 550 years, and the second to be a more detailed volume, set in the comparative context of the history of other universities in Scotland and beyond, focusing on the modern University on its new site at Gilmorehill. The plan was agreed and A. L. Brown and Michael Moss were appointed as authors for the first volume, *The University of Glasgow: 1451–1996,* which was published in 1996 to lay the foundation for this later volume.

Laying the foundations for this more ambitious volume also involved exchanging views with the General Council, and promoting awareness of the initiative through the *University Newsletter* and the graduate magazine *Avenue*. In a more focused way the background and context were explored in depth by mounting a series of 2001 Seminars in 1995–6, 1996–7 and 1997–8. Michael Moss, Eileen Reynolds, Tony Slaven and Rick Trainor organised no fewer than twenty-nine seminars, with invited speakers from all over Britain encouraging wide-ranging discussion and debate. These covered topics as varied as The Undergraduate Curriculum, The Development of Scientific Research, Medical Education, Women in the University, The University and the City, Student Politics, University Governance, The University and the Wider World, Sport, Cultural Outreach, Religion in the University, and much more. We owe a particular debt of thanks to the many individuals from outside institutions as well as from the University of Glasgow who participated so willingly in these seminars which provided a rich seam of information and opinion to fire the imagination and enthusiasm of the authors.

Planning this volume, *University, City and State: The University of Glasgow since 1870*, with three authors rather than a single author was also a deliberate policy designed to make the enormous scope of the modern history of the University manageable and capable of being written by those with special interests in the three main chronological periods in which the volume has been constructed. While the authors have conferred and commented on the entire volume, each author has had primary responsibility for a particular section: Richard H. Trainor for Part I, J. Forbes Munro for Part II and Michael S. Moss for Part III. Professor Munro deserves special mention, assuming his responsibilities later than the other authors when Dr Dan Greenstein, the original author for the middle section, had to withdraw upon taking up a new appointment in London. Forbes Munro wishes to thank Dr Dan Greenstein personally for sharing his research notes with him. Professor Trainor would like to thank Dr Mark Freeman (assisted latterly by Ms Jacqueline Kearney) for highly skilled, highly productive research assistance. In addition to the General Editor and his fellow authors he would like to thank the following for references and suggestions: Dr Marguerite Dupree, Dr Andrew Hull, Dr Campbell Lloyd, Professor Andrew Skinner, Dr Judy Wakeling and Professor Rex Whitehead. Michael Moss especially wishes to thank James McCargow, Sir Charles Wilson, Sir Alwyn Williams and Sir William Kerr Fraser. Lesley Richmond and the staff of the University Archives were particularly helpful in tracing material and selecting illustrations. The collaboration of three authors has worked well and has now produced this fine volume as a companion to the outline history, making a set that will serve the University well for a considerable time to come.

As General Editor I would wish to record my own thanks to the authors for their unfailing involvement with the progress of writing and revision, and for cheerfully putting up with reminders, meetings, and suggestions designed to keep to ever tighter timetables. I would especially like to thank Eileen Reynolds who has been a constant support over this very long period of planning and writing. On behalf of the authors I extend warm thanks to all the members of the initial Publications Advisory Group and to the 2001 Committee for their support in what has been a long and challenging period of piloting the research and writing to a successful conclusion. Much of the early fact-finding for the authors and the seminar presenters was researched by Archie Leitch, while Dr Ian Anderson contributed significantly in the compilation of data. We gratefully acknowledge their assistance. Finally the working relationship with Edinburgh University Press has been congenial and supportive.

The publication of this volume is not only a tribute to 550 years of great achievement which has made the University of Glasgow known and respected throughout the world where its graduates – more than 100,000 – serve communities and countries in every continent; it also marks the strength and ambition of this great University as it enters the new millennium. Being involved in the writing of this history of my own University has been a privilege and the reading of it has been a fascination. I am sure it will be long enjoyed by many others who have been part of that history, and who will be part of it in the years ahead.

Tony Slaven
General Editor

Contents

List of Illustrations

[Illustrations are all taken from sources in Glasgow University Archives and Special Collections, with the exception of the following: 2.2 (*The University of Glasgow Old and New*), 3.2 (J. Coutts, *A History of the University of Glasgow*, 1909), and 4.1/4.3 (J. L. Story, *Later Reminiscences*, 1913)]

Glasgow City Centre*

*See Key on page xviii

Plan of Glasgow University Gilmorehill Campus*

*See Key on page xviii

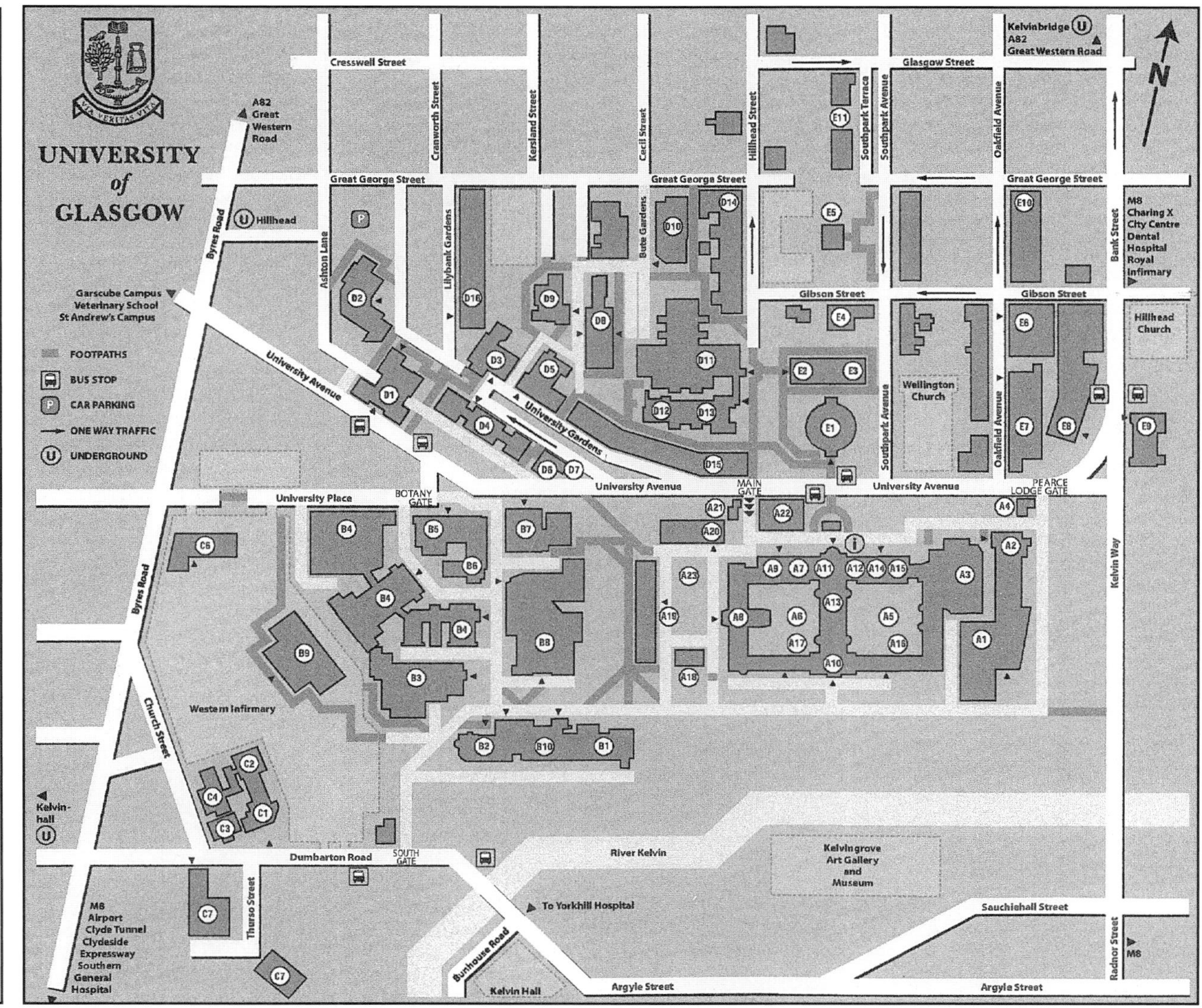

Key to Glasgow City Centre map

1. Provand's Lordship
2. Glasgow Cathedral
3. Tolbooth Steeple
4. Tron Steeple/Tron Theatre
5. Hutchesons' Hospital Hall
6. Trades House
7. City Chambers
8. Greater Glasgow Tourist Information Centre
9. Stirling Library
10. Willow Tearoom
11. Mitchell Library
12. Art Gallery and Museum Kelvingrove
13. Hunterian Museum and Art Gallery
14. People's Palace
15. Tenement House
16. Third Eye Centre
17. City Halls/ Ticket Centre
18. Citizen's Theatre
19. King's Theatre
20. Mitchell Theatre
21. Pavilion Theatre
22. Theatre Royal
23. Glasgow School of Art
24. Kelvin Hall Int. Sports Arena and Transport Museum
25. Henry Wood Hall
26. Riverboat Departures
27. RSAMD
28. Princes Square
29. 'Barras' Market
30. P. S. Waverley Departures
31. Glasgow International Concert Hall
32. Stock Exchange
33. Merchants House
34. Glasgow's Glasgow
35. McLellan Galleries
36. Templetons Carpet Factory
37. Glasgow Film Theatre
38. Scotland Street School
39. Glasgow University Visitor Centre
40. Dome of Discovery

Key to Glasgow University Gilmorehill Campus plan

Building	Grid
Accommodation Service	D14
Adam Smith Building	D8
Adult and Continuing Education	E10
Anderson College	C1
Archives and Business Records	C7
Joseph Black Building	B4
Bower Building	B7
Boyd Orr Building	D1
Bute Hall	A13
Careers Service	D15
Chapel	A8
Chaplaincy Centre	A19
College Club	A9
Computing Service	A2
Concert Hall	A12
Conference and Visitor Services	A20
Davidson Building	B1
Dining Rooms	A9
East Quadrangle	A5
Estates and Buildings	B6
Florentine House	E4
Gardiner Institute	C6
George Service House	D7
Graham Kerr Building	B3
Gregory Building	D2
Hetherington Building	D10
Hetherington House	D6
The Hub	E2
Human Anatomy	A3
Hunter Halls	A14
Hunterian Art Gallery	D12
Hunterian Museum	A15
James Watt Building	A1
John McIntyre Building	A22
Joseph Black Building	B4
Kelvin Building	B8
Kelvin Gallery	A7
Graham Kerr Building	B3
Library	D11
Lilybank Gardens	D16
Lilybank House	D9
John McIntyre Building	A22
The Mackintosh House	D13
Main Building	A10
Main Gatehouse	A21
Mathematics Building	D4
Modern Languages	D5
Officers' Training Corps	B5
Pearce Lodge	A4
Principal's Lodging	A18
Queen Margaret Union	D3
Rankine Building	E7
Reading Room	E1
Refectory	E3
Registry: Enquiry Office	A17
Robertson Building	C2
Senate Room	A17
Student Recruitment and Admissions Service	A20
George Service House	D7
Adam Smith Building	D8
Southpark House	E5
The Square	A23
Stair Building	A19
Stevenson Building	E6
Turnbull Hall	E11
University Offices	A16
University Union	E8
Virology Institute	C4
Visitor Centre	A11
James Watt Building	A1
West Medical Building	B2
West Quadrangle	A6
Western Lecture Theatre	B9
Wolfson Building	B10

Introduction

The origins of the University of Glasgow, like its subsequent development, make the institution an ideal subject of study in the context of relations with City and State. From the time of its foundation in 1451, the College of Glasgow was integral to the city of Glasgow, situated as it was halfway down the High Street between the ecclesiastical community clustered round the majestic Cathedral at the top and the burgeoning merchant community at the foot. The College, established to train men for the ministry, soon began to admit students whose vocations were entirely secular. At first these young men were the sons of noblemen and gentry; sons of merchants followed, mixed with a significant and growing minority of boys from more humble backgrounds.[1] Although never the 'toun's college' in the sense that the University of Edinburgh was,[2] the College of Glasgow provided access to higher learning for the young men of the city and the surrounding countryside without imposing the strict curriculum required for entry to the ministry. The ideas with which these young men were confronted at the College – by teachers such as John Mair and Andrew Melville and later Francis Hutcheson and Adam Smith – would shape their attitudes to the contemporary world. However, the link with the established Church also gave the College a direct relationship with the Scottish State. This link was supplemented in the eighteenth century by the creation of Regius chairs by the now British Crown. In an era of high politics, the College could not avoid engagement in faction, albeit mediated by successive Chancellors and Rectors. Long after the Reform Act of 1832, Regius appointments were a means of injecting new blood into a city notorious for its parochialism: many professors came from local families with deep connections with the fast expanding mercantile community.

The translation of the University to Gilmorehill in 1870 – a highly unusual migration for an ancient university – disturbed some of the intimacy of these relationships, particularly after the medical chairs moved from the Royal Infirmary to the Western Infirmary four years later. Gilmorehill was a leafy suburb distant from the city centre, too far away for the professors to be seen daily in the clubs and bars frequented by the leading citizens. Yet the move also broke the University's confinement not only to the deteriorating physical surroundings, but also to the often highly conservative official political and religious line of the College in the High Street. Set in the context of the turmoil of the immediately preceding decades, 1870 – the defining moment in the University's long history – provides the formal starting point for our study, which revolves around the theme of the interplay between the University's own internal concerns, on the one hand, and local and national trends, on the other. However, there is another context in which the University of Glasgow must be seen. As one of Scotland's four ancient universities, and one of a relatively small group of institutions of higher learning which existed in Britain in the eighteenth and nineteenth centuries, its evolution forms a significant part of the larger story of the history of British, indeed European, universities as a whole.

Among the older British universities Glasgow was different, and had been for a long time. By the early nineteenth century it attracted some 1,500 students. This made it big in both Scottish and United Kingdom terms, not much smaller than Oxford or Cambridge (though with far fewer staff) and, though slightly smaller than Edinburgh, far larger than Aberdeen, St Andrews, Trinity College Dublin and the nascent Durham. Unlike many of the older foundations, Glasgow found itself in a prosperous mercantile and later industrial city and region with a rapidly growing middle-class population from which to draw its students and, as importantly, from which to raise money. Another unusual feature of Glasgow was its proximity to Ulster: Glasgow had become the university of Irish Presbyterianism, a presence which imposed its own constraints but which also provided some insulation from the hard-line attitudes of the Church of Scotland. Partly as a result, a streak of radicalism – often eclipsed in official pronouncements but evident during the crises of the American War of Independence, the French Revolution and the rising of the United Irishmen – could frequently be found in the University, distancing it from the State. Yet despite such distinctiveness Glasgow resembled in important ways other United Kingdom universities, notably in its increasing fascination with German intellectual fashions. Also, like the much later foundations of Queen's Belfast and Liverpool, Glasgow's urban base knew largely buoyant affluence in the nineteenth century followed by predominant economic adversity in the twentieth.[3] Thus the interactions between the particularities of the University, on the one hand, and the features that it shared with many universities in Britain and elsewhere, on the other, run as a thread through the volume.

The study of universities has become a major field of serious historical analysis during the last thirty years.[4] Boosted by the popularity of the 'new social history' and its rising concern with the upper as well as the lower echelons of society, university history has come to be seen as having significant implications for topics such as social mobility, women's history and the recruitment of elites.[5] Likewise, as university historians have increasingly directed their attention outside as well as within the walls of these institutions, higher education has become increasingly relevant to the history of the towns and cities in which the universities were situated, and thus to the history of urbanisation itself.[6] Indeed, as historians have rediscovered the significance of politics, economics and culture, and have realised the important role that universities and their graduates can play in each, higher education has begun to assume a significant role in national history, including the history of nation-building.[7] Meanwhile, the reinvigorated history of education has begun to integrate universities into wider historical debates.[8] Although much of what might be called the new university history has been general and comparative,[9] case studies of individual institutions relating their particular characteristics to national and international patterns have also made important contributions to the field.[10]

Unsurprisingly, given the antiquity of the Scottish system and its influence on developments in other countries, Scotland's higher education system has attracted a significant share of this recent attention. George Davie led the way with his distinctive analyses of the 'democratic intellect',[11] launching a debate about alleged anglicisation which still reverberates. There have also been important studies of the Scottish Enlightenment period with significant insights into the Scottish universities of the day and their leading professors.[12] For the period since the mid-nineteenth century the key work was R. D. Anderson's analytical survey of 1983, which placed Scotland's universities in the centre of debates about the history of Scottish education.[13] Anderson and others have followed this lead with further studies.[14] This work has been paralleled by detailed investigations of significant figures in the intellectual life of Scotland in the nineteenth century such as George Adam Smith, William Thomson (Lord Kelvin), Sir Joseph (Lord) Lister and James Clerk Maxwell.[15]

The University of Glasgow, the second oldest of the Scottish universities and in the modern period the most socially diverse, has attracted significant recent scholarship, particularly for the early modern and Enlightenment periods[16] and, for more recent decades, with regard to particular themes such as community relations, finance, medicine, student recruitment and the role of women.[17] Yet, with the significant exception of the recent short history by A. L. Brown and Michael Moss, no major survey of the University's history has appeared for almost half a century.[18] This volume is the first scholarly history of the institution focusing on the period since the mid-nineteenth century, when upheavals in the Scottish universities generally, and the University's move from the High Street to Gilmorehill, arguably transformed the institution and brought it into the emerging modern international system of higher education. Indeed, despite the upsurge of interest in Scottish university history, this is the first recent comprehensive study of an ancient Scottish university in the modern period.

In order to understand the institution in the round, and to maximise the general relevance of the study, we have attempted – while paying due attention to the often highly particular circumstances of the University – to relate our evidence and interpretations to wider patterns. Thus, while this volume is the study of an institution, it aims to be more than an institutional history. Accordingly, while the book is deeply rooted in the records of the University, it has also delved into sources (notably the local press) related to the city and to evidence generated by Scottish and national sources such as memoirs and parliamentary investigations.

Yet in writing the history of any major institution, much of the focus must inevitably be on the organisation itself – its purpose, its structures, its policies, its personalities and its achievements. This in turn implies a necessary degree of inward orientation, so as to be able to understand how the institution functions over time, how its various parts fit together – or alternatively fail to do so – and what inner strengths and resources it may have to draw on to survive. Our study therefore has the day-to-day workings of the University of Glasgow at the forefront of its concern. Simply to tell the story of how the University fared since it made the transition from the High Street to Gilmorehill requires a complicated narrative, because the University itself was and is a complex organisation. Both one of the oldest and one of the largest of the British universities, it undertook the task of advancing and disseminating knowledge across a wide range of academic disciplines and a large cross-section of professional educational requirements. The tensions arising from the differing demands of its various academic components, as well as the problems of finding adequate capital to support the extent of their endeavours, have therefore constantly engaged the attention of those charged with providing management and leadership for the institution. We have attempted to identify the broad patterns which emerged from these processes of internal interaction in terms of various stages in curricular innovation and reform, and of the broad directions of initiatives in scholarship and research – notably the impact of German humanistic and laboratory-based research in the later nineteenth century and the emergence of new disciplines and sub-disciplines, such as biblical criticism, nuclear physics and applied economics, after the Second World War. Key figures who contributed to institutional innovation and change, or alternatively represented forces of conservatism, loom large, though they may not fully represent the many individuals, both among the staff and within the student body, who contributed to the scholarly, cultural, artistic, athletic and social life of the large and diverse University community that congregated in and around Gilmorehill.[19]

The salient features of the academic and support staff of the University were their dramatic growth in numbers over time from the hundred or so of 1870 to the more than five thousand of 2000,[20] the increasing diversity of academic subject areas of which they were practitioners, and a relative flattening of career structures as the ratio of professorial to non-professorial posts declined. Year by year, but more rapidly in the post-1945 decades, these changes among the skilled and articulate people working in the University presented challenges to the cohesion of the institution itself. Despite attempts to provide focal points for staff interaction and communication – notably in the College Club established by Sir Donald MacAlister in 1919, and in the *University Gazette* created in the 1940s, followed by the *University Newsletter* in the mid-1970s – men and women whose first loyalties were to their disciplines and their departments were not always aware of, much less involved in, the policy-making issues and processes at the centre. This was particularly true within the ranks of the more junior lecturing staff, which increased proportionately over time, and of the technicians and the short-term contract research staff whose numbers have risen rapidly in recent decades with the development of the University's research profile. Female staff, too, whose numbers increased only slowly over time, frequently believed themselves to be marginalised within the academic body. For successive Principals, therefore, as well as for the Court and the Senate, a constant issue has been how to evolve internal systems of governance which take account of changes in the size and composition of staff, as well as to provide appropriate middle-level organisational structures for a growing and diversifying institution. The creation of new departments and faculties throughout the period, reforms in the composition of Senate at intervals since the First World War, and the introduction of planning-units in the 1990s, have all played a part in this evolving process, and generated much short-term discontent in the by-going. Thus it may be doubted whether the University has always successfully combined the bottom-up collegial ideal of academic participation with the top-down requirements of financial and managerial responsibility. The long persistence of professorial prerogatives at Glasgow may have made this set of problems particularly intractable there (though probably no more so than at other ancient Scottish universities), but in broad outline the University shared such difficulties with other large higher education institutions throughout the Western world.

The student body also expanded greatly in numbers (see Statistical Appendix, Figure 1) and diversity of interest. By comparison with academic and support staff, however, the students enjoyed a semi-autonomous position within the University. Admittedly they shared the lecture hall and, subsequently, the laboratory and the library with their teachers; still later, though relatively rarely, the two groups met in the formal setting of the committee room. We have tried to reflect that shared experience of teaching and learning, and take account of the student voice in matters relating to curriculum, study facilities and the quality of educational provision. However, the students also enjoyed a substantial social, cultural, political and recreational life revolving around their own institutions and organisations – the two unions, the Students' Representative Council, the Athletic Club, the Rectorship, the student press, and the various clubs and societies. Succeeding generations of undergraduates enjoyed a lifestyle in and near Gilmorehill of which most senior members of the

University caught only occasional glimpses. Such activities were affected by the non-residential character of a large part of the student population. A constant theme of student life on Gilmorehill was the dichotomy between the 'corporate lifers', who made the University the focal point for their social and cultural activities, and the 'nine-to-fivers', who commuted daily into Gilmorehill for their classes and took their recreation in the evenings and weekends away from the University environment. The corporate lifers, although perhaps in a minority, were vocal in demanding material assistance from the University authorities for a range of student welfare needs, and for the upkeep of the main student institutions. This group also threw up leaders who made a name for themselves in student affairs, and subsequently in wider public life.[21] We have been able within our pages to take some account of the nature and outcome of the interaction between the student body and the University, but have been constrained by lack of space from doing justice to the rich texture of its student life.

The phenomenon of the 'student-as-commuter' was one of the many ways that the University of Glasgow was marked by being for a long time the only, and thereafter still the largest, university in a great industrial and commercial city. For although the University was in some senses an entity unto itself, continuously wrapped up in its own internal affairs, it was also a relatively open institution, subject to ideas and influences from outside. However much some of its members might wish it, the University could never be an 'ivory tower', insulated by wealth, prestige and power from wider social, political and economic circumstances. Two sources of external influence – the city of Glasgow and the government of the United Kingdom – were of particular significance in its story, and provide us with the title for the book: 'University, City and State'. By 'City' we do not mean the Corporation of the City of Glasgow, its policies and the local authority politics that swirled around it, although these were not without significance for the University. Ours is a rather broader concept, which embraces the other institutions of higher and further education within the city boundaries, the local business community which supported the University financially, the local professions and their governing bodies which demanded attention to their educational needs, and the wider Glasgow public, from the sizeable numbers who sent their sons and daughters to study on Gilmorehill to those whose only involvement with the University was to put a few coppers in a collecting can on Charities' Day. Our concept of 'City' also includes the idea of 'city-as-region', for Glasgow was the throbbing (and later the dysfunctional) heart of the wider economic region of industrial West-Central Scotland, which extended from the iron-and-steel towns of North Lanarkshire to the shipyards of the Lower Clyde and the coalfields of Ayrshire, as well as various points in between.[22] Its location at the centre of Scotland's most industrialised, and most highly urbanised, city-region, containing some two-fifths of the entire Scottish population, marked the University of Glasgow out from the other ancient Scottish universities with which it otherwise shared so much – not least in the way that it drew the greater part of its student population from within thirty miles of Gilmorehill itself, and shared the ups and downs in the fortunes of the West of Scotland economy. Processes of interaction with the local economic and social environment, shaping the history of the University and to a lesser extent that of Glasgow and its environs,[23] are to be found in the chapters which follow.

An equally powerful influence on the University was exerted by national government. This operated at two levels. First came legislation and policies which transformed the constitutions of the Scottish universities, and prodded and nudged them into serving the perceived educational needs both of Scotland as a whole and of the wider world, especially the Empire and Commonwealth. How to define and maintain a relationship between the independent universities, on the one hand, and – on the other – the government agencies (especially the Scottish Education Department) which were responsible for primary and secondary education in Scotland, emerged as a continuing theme in the history of educational policy and practice. Second, at a British or United Kingdom level, the growing tendency for universities (earlier in Scotland than in England or Ireland) to rely on Treasury funding for their financial support opened the University of Glasgow, along with all the others, to the influence of government ideas about the appropriate role of universities within national policies and priorities. For most of the time, this power was exercised at second hand, through the light touch of a relatively benign, if not always generous, Treasury and University Grants Committee.[24] However, by the late twentieth century, when the level of financial reliance on the state had reached heights undreamed of in 1870, and the University like others had entered into an era of mass higher education, the directives of national government became the driving force behind the bulk of institutional activity. Such subordination to higher authority meant conflict, partly because historically Scotland's participation rates were significantly higher than those in England: Glasgow and Edinburgh, in particular, remained relatively large in UK terms and aspired to budgets which matched their bulk.

The three-way interplay between the University, the City and the State followed no linear pattern. During late Victorian and Edwardian times, which were generally very prosperous in Glasgow, the relationship with the city and region was the more dominant. The University, like other voluntary bodies, relied financially on the generosity of the local business community and enjoyed a high degree of intimacy with the Liberal (later Liberal Unionist) political elite which ran local government in Glasgow and the rest of West Central Scotland. For many years the professors of Gilmorehill played a significant role in the life of the City. Principal John Caird was a legendary preacher whose published works reached a wide audience, and Professor Sir

Henry Jones was not only a leading political thinker but contributed in a practical way to politics in Glasgow and beyond. Moreover, many of the University's academics had close involvements in industry, often in the region. The institution's close relationships with the City were symbolised by regular 'town-and-gown' dinners, and by the fact that distinguished visitors to Glasgow usually obtained both the freedom of the City and an honorary degree from the University. The University was also well connected to Scotland more generally: while increasingly well linked to British and imperial elites and to international scholarship, Glasgow remained in ethos and student (if not staff) recruitment very largely a Scottish university, showing only gradual signs of 'anglicisation' even in its curriculum. Meanwhile, the State's demands were muted, and by late twentieth-century standards only a modest level of central funds flowed into the University's coffers, although the principals regularly asked for more.

The First World War bound the University even more tightly to Glasgow, as the institution's students and graduates – heavily represented in the casualty-prone junior officer corps – constituted, as in universities elsewhere, a disproportionate share of the city's dead. However, between the wars both the City and the State failed the University – the former because of the especially troubled regional economy and the latter because of systemic financial neglect of the Scottish universities in general and Glasgow in particular as universities in England were developed more vigorously. There was also the erosion of the informal alliance with the local political elite: the rise of the Labour Party in the West of Scotland brought to power in local government men most of whom had little personal experience of university education and who were largely indifferent to the role and requirements of the University, particularly in the face of the pressing employment, housing and welfare needs of their constituents. Although a large proportion of its graduates pursued their careers in Western Scotland, the University came to be seen as elitist, concerned with training men and – in substantial numbers, especially in teaching – women for the professions and not for trade and industry. Whatever the efforts of those such as William R. Scott in Political Economy or Edward Cathcart in Physiology to address the mounting problems of the region, the grandeur of the buildings on lofty Gilmorehill betrayed their intent.

The election of Sir Daniel Macaulay Stevenson, a coal merchant and former Liberal Lord Provost, as Chancellor of the University in 1933, in the same year that the Labour Party took sole control of Glasgow City Chambers, represented the last act of the alliance between the senior figures in the University and the former Liberal business and political elite. However, the University was diverted from the necessity of forging close ties with the new political establishment in city and region by the demands of the Second World War and the post-war settlement, which ushered in a period of generous funding of universities by the State. The influence of London-based policies and connections became dominant, and for much of the period after the War the University was almost totally preoccupied with the growing power of the State. The same was true of the City: sliding inexorably into multiple deprivation on an unparalleled scale, it came to depend increasingly on government support to sustain its flagging fortunes. As the wealth of the region declined relative to the rest of Britain so dependency on the State increased. Politics remained part of university life, but it was increasingly trivial, preoccupied with detail rather than grand gesture. Not surprisingly perhaps, with the same paymaster the University and the City drifted apart. Many city fathers and a number of local businessmen came to view the Royal Technical College (RTC) in the city centre as the natural successor of the College in the High Street, providing practical training to meet the needs of Glasgow's industries. Although the University never completely forgot its local roots in its service to a still predominantly regional student population, its central vision increasingly became that of achieving national status and recognition, especially through research in the fields of natural science, medicine and the social sciences.

This phase of generous State support for the University, obviating the need to build new bridges to local institutions and organisations, or refurbish older ones, lasted until the mid-1970s. By that time the economy of the city and region was once again in decline; the University, enjoying only weak connections with local authority structures, had become an efficient vehicle for the out-migration of educated and talented manpower. Only after a reconstruction of higher education, which saw the RTC become the University of Strathclyde, and a more painful reconstruction of the local economy, which witnessed the almost total eclipse of its traditional industries, did the University and the City rediscover the importance of a secure relationship for their mutual advantage. Thus from the mid-1980s, having found itself bereft of strong local support in confronting the full force of the Thatcher government's demands that it should do more with less, the University managed to revive its local and regional alliances as part of a regeneration of university, city and region alike. Having reforged these links, the University's combination of intense regional ties with strong Scottish, UK and international connections seemed to provide it with an important advantage for the future.

Thus, while reflecting many of the trends which affected other Scottish and British universities – and participating vigorously in the Scottish, the British and the international university scenes – the University of Glasgow during the last century and a half has experienced in a particularly vivid way the interdependence of higher education with national budgets and local fortunes. For much of the period Glasgow was unusually dependent on the public purse and on the changing higher education policies of governments. Yet even more than most Scottish universities, much more than the English 'provincials' and of course far more than Oxbridge, Glasgow retained even to the end of the twentieth century a strong local recruitment base. Also, the University's other ties to local and regional communities – assets in good times, occasionally liabilities in bad – appeared equal to those of any other Scottish university and stronger than those which most English civic universities have had since 1914.[25] In the early twenty-first century, as government encourages ties to the commercial and voluntary sectors of the kind which seemed unnecessary distractions to British universities for a third of a century after 1945, the University of Glasgow finds its relations with City and State moving in tandem. In this respect, as in many others since the mid-nineteenth century, the University seems to combine unusual features with emerging aspects of the British university system as a whole.

M.M., J.F.M., R.H.T.

Notes and References

1. R. D. Anderson, *Universities and Elites in Britain since 1800* (Cambridge, 1995), 25.
2. T. Bender, 'Introduction', in Bender (ed.), *The University and the City: From Medieval Origins to the Present* (Oxford, 1988), 7.
3. See T. W. Moody and J. C. Beckett, *Queen's Belfast 1845–1949: the History of a University* (London, 1959); T. Kelly, *For Advancement of Learning: the University of Liverpool 1881–1981* (Liverpool, 1981).
4. See for instance the emergence of the journal *History of Universities* and the lively Studium electronic bulletin board. For examples of serious scholarship in the earlier period, see W. R. Ward, *Victorian Oxford* (London, 1965) and J. P. C. Roach, 'Victorian Universities and the National Intelligentsia', *Victorian Studies*, 3 (1959–60).
5. L. Stone (ed.), *The University in Society*, 2 vols (London, 1975); C. Dyhouse, *No Distinction of Sex? Women in British Universities 1870–1939* (London, 1995); Anderson, *Universities and Elites*.
6. Bender, *University and City*; R. C. Whiting (ed.), *Oxford: Studies in the History of a University Town since 1800* (Manchester, 1993).
7. M. Sanderson, *The Universities and British Industry, 1850–1970* (London, 1972), 'The English Civic Universities and the "Industrial Spirit", 1870–1914', *Historical Research*, 61 (1988), and *Education and Economic Decline in Britain, 1870 to the 1990s* (Cambridge, 1999); R. Soffer, 'The Modern University and National Values 1850–1930', *Historical Research*, 60 (1987); M. J. Wiener, *English Culture and the Decline of the Industrial Spirit 1850–1980* (Cambridge, 1980); H. Perkin, *The Rise of Professional Society: England since 1880* (London, 1980).
8. R. Lowe, *Education in the Post-War Years: A Social History* (London, 1988); W. D. Rubinstein, 'Education and the Social Origins of British Elites, 1880–1970', *Past & Present*, 112 (1986); R. D. Anderson, *Scottish Education since the Reformation* (Dundee, 1997). Cf. important works in the sociological tradition such as A. H. Halsey, *The Decline of Donnish Dominion: the British Academic Professions in the 20th Century* (Oxford, 1992).

9. E.g. K. H. Jarausch (ed.), *The Transformation of Higher Learning* (Chicago, 1983); F. K. Ringer, 'The Education of Elites in Modern Europe', *History of Education Quarterly*, 18 (1978); S. Rothblatt, *The Modern University and its Discontents: The Fate of Newman's Legacies in Britain and America* (Cambridge, 1997).
10. E.g. C. N. L. Brooke, *A History of the University of Cambridge, vol. 3, 1750–1870* (Cambridge, 1997); A. J. Engel, *From Clergyman to Don: The Rise of the Academic Profession in Nineteenth-Century Oxford* (Oxford, 1983); B. H. Harrison (ed.), *The History of the University of Oxford*, vol. viii, *The Twentieth Century* (Oxford, 1994); N. B. Harte, *The University of London 1836–1986* (London, 1986); S. Rothblatt, *The Revolution of the Dons: Cambridge and Society in Victorian England* (Cambridge, 1968); J. G. Williams, *The University College of North Wales: Foundations 1884–1927* (Cardiff, 1985).
11. G. Davie, *The Democratic Intellect: Scotland and her Universities in the Nineteenth Century* (Edinburgh, 1961) and *The Crisis of the Democratic Intellect: The Problem of Generalism and Specialisation in Twentieth Century Scotland* (Edinburgh, 1986).
12. E.g. R. L. Emerson, *Professors, Patronage and Politics: The Scottish Universities in the Eighteenth Century* (Aberdeen, 1992); N. T. Phillipson, 'Commerce and Culture: Edinburgh, Edinburgh University and the Scottish Enlightenment', in Bender, *University and City*; L. Rosner, *Medical Education in the Age of Improvement: Edinburgh Students and Apprentices 1760–1826* (Edinburgh, 1991); A. S. Skinner, 'Economics and History: The Scottish Enlightenment', *Scottish Journal of Political Economy*, 12 (1965); M. A. Stewart, *Studies in the Philosophy of the Scottish Enlightenment* (Oxford, 1990).
13. R. D. Anderson, *Education and Opportunity in Victorian Scotland: Schools and Universities* (Oxford, 1983).
14. R. D. Anderson, *The Student Community at Aberdeen, 1860–1939* (Aberdeen, 1988); J. Butt, *John Anderson's Legacy: The University of Strathclyde and its Antecedents, 1796–1996* (East Linton, 1996); J. Carter and D. J. Withrington (eds), *Scottish Universities: Distinctiveness and Diversity* (Edinburgh, 1983); J. D. Hargreaves with A. Forbes, *Aberdeen University, 1945–1981: Regional Roles and National Needs* (Aberdeen, 1989); I. G. Hutchison, *The University and the State: The Case of Aberdeen* (Aberdeen, 1993); L. Moore, *Bajanellas and Semilinas: Aberdeen University and the Education of Women, 1860–1920* (Aberdeen, 1991). For slightly earlier works see D. Southgate, *University Education in Dundee: A Centenary History* (Edinburgh, 1982); and G. Donaldson (ed.), *Four Centuries: Edinburgh University Life 1583–1983* (Edinburgh, 1983).
15. C. W. Smith and M. N. Wise, *Energy and Empire: A Biographical Study of Lord Kelvin* (Cambridge, 1989); R. B. Fisher, *Joseph Lister* (New York, 1977).
16. J. Kirk and J. Durkan, *The University of Glasgow 1451–1577* (Glasgow, 1977); A. Hook and R. B. Sher (eds), *The Glasgow Enlightenment* (East Linton, 1995); A. Skinner, *A System of Social Science: Papers Relating to Adam Smith*, 2nd edn (Oxford, 1996); D. A. Dow and M. S. Moss, 'The Medical Curriculum

at Glasgow in the early 19th century', *History of Universities*, 7 (1988).

17. W. Alexander, *First Ladies of Medicine* (Glasgow, 1987); J. Bradley, M. A. Crowther and M. Dupree, 'Mobility and Selection in Scottish University Medical Education, 1858–1886', *Medical History*, 40 (1996); A. Hull and J. Geyer-Kordesch, *The Shaping of the Medical Profession: A History of the Royal College of Physicians and Surgeons of Glasgow, 1858–1999* (London, 1999); C. F. Lloyd, 'Relationships between Scottish Universities and their Communities, c.1858–1914' (Ph.D., University of Glasgow, 1993); P. L. Robertson, 'The Finances of the University of Glasgow before 1914', *Higher Education Quarterly*, 16 (1976) and 'The Development of an Urban University: Glasgow 1860–1914', *History of Education Quarterly*, 30 (1990). There is also much about the University in Anderson, *Education and Opportunity*.
18. J. D. Mackie, *The University of Glasgow, 1451–1951: A Short History* (Glasgow, 1954) devoted relatively little attention to the post-1800 period. Cf. A. L. Brown and M. Moss, *The University of Glasgow, 1451–1996* (Edinburgh, 1996).
19. Some of these areas have already been covered in more detailed studies such as: R. B. Neilson (ed.), *Fortuna Domus* (Glasgow, 1951); R. Y. Thomson (ed.), *A Faculty for Science: A Unified Diversity: A Century of Science in the University of Glasgow* (Glasgow, 1993); R. O. MacKenna, *Glasgow University Athletic Club: The Story of the First Hundred Years* (Glasgow 1981); C. Oakley, *Union Ygorra: The Story of the Glasgow University Student over the last 60 Years* (Glasgow, 1950).
20. Statistical Appendix, Figure 7, shows the equally impressive increase of academic staff.
21. J. Wakeling, 'University Women: Origins, Experiences and Destinations at Glasgow University, 1939–1987' (Ph.D., University of Glasgow, 1998) has a wide-ranging treatment of student life among both males and females.
22. S. G. Checkland, *The Upas Tree: Glasgow 1875–1975: A Study in Growth and Contraction* (Glasgow, 1975); A. Slaven, *The Development of the West of Scotland 1750–1960* (London, 1975).
23. For the more dramatic impact of other British universities on smaller urban environments see R. C. Whiting, 'Introduction', and A. C. Howe, 'Intellect and Civic Responsibility: Dons and Citizens in Nineteenth-Century Oxford', in Whiting, *Oxford*. For the general development of Glasgow in this period see, for example, W. H. Fraser and I. Maver (eds), *Glasgow Vol. II 1830 to 1912* (Manchester, 1996), and A. Gibb, *Glasgow: The Making of the City* (London, 1983).
24. C. H. Shinn, *Paying the Piper: The Development of the University Grants Committee 1919–1946* (Lewes, 1986); M. Shattock, *The University Grants Committee and the Management of British Universities* (Buckingham, 1994).
25. Cf. D. R. Jones, *The Origins of Civic Universities: Manchester, Leeds and Liverpool* (London, 1988).

PART I

From the Mid-Nineteenth Century to 1914

CHAPTER ONE

'Black College' to Gilmorehill

Throughout the nineteenth century, and beyond,[1] the city of Glasgow did much to shape the fortunes of its university.[2] Like its area of settlement, Glasgow's population grew extremely quickly, advancing from less than 100,000 in 1801 to more than 300,000 at mid-century and to almost 800,000 by 1901 – fuelled at first by textiles and latterly by shipbuilding. Even for the prosperous this dynamism could be treacherous, as many Glasgow worthies discovered during the massive local failures of the Western, and City of Glasgow, Banks respectively in 1857 and 1878. Yet overall the city's increasingly mercantile and industrial middle class was expanding rapidly in numbers and in resources; the publicly prominent elite largely drawn from this middle class became significantly more numerous but remained well off. During the century there was a marked upsurge of Liberalism, and of allegiance to presbyterian churches other than the Church of Scotland, both among Glasgow's population as a whole and its elite in particular. All of these developments were challenges to a long-established university, located in the decreasingly fashionable High Street of the city (see Map, p. xvi), with firm roots in the Established Church and in the Tory Party. Some of these challenges would fade, but the need to satisfy the increasingly numerous and self-conscious urban middle class would not.[3]

Of course, the University had some substantial advantages in its relations with the city. The University's antiquity and fame were major civic assets, as the automatic coupling of great university occasions – notably the rectorial installations of famous politicians – with key civic events implied. In the decades preceding 1870 the city fêted Macaulay and Palmerston, for example, on the same days that the University honoured them. Macaulay exploited the occasion to flatter both the locality and the University:

> In the whole kingdom we shall find no district in which the progress of trade, of manufactures, of wealth, and of the arts of life, has been more rapid than in Clydesdale. Your University has partaken largely of the prosperity of this city and of the surrounding region . . . We now speak

> the language of humility when we say that the University of Glasgow need not fear a comparison with the University of Bologna.[4]

Underlying such sentiments was a long-established official relationship between town and gown. For example, the Lord Provost and magistrates attended the funerals of principals 'in their official capacity'.[5]

Yet there were also major difficulties – political, professional and more general – in relations between town and gown. By the early nineteenth century University officials had a deeply ingrained instinct against political innovation – in line with the sympathies which had led the institution to confer an honorary degree on the Duke of Cumberland in 1745. Thus in 1831 only strong popular pressure induced the University to put candles in its windows in supposed sympathy with local enthusiasm for parliamentary reform.[6] In professional terms, the situation was not so fraught as in Edinburgh, where the long-established rights of the Town Council, and the claims of the Royal College of Physicians and the Royal College of Surgeons, put the University firmly on the defensive. Yet in Glasgow the University engaged in a lengthy, acrimonious and expensive dispute with the Faculty of Physicians and Surgeons, which until 1850 denied those who had qualified only through the University's Master of Surgery degree the right to practise surgery within the area of the Faculty's jurisdiction.[7] There were also more general mutual resentments, like the earlier feelings of many Glaswegians that the professors lived too grandly in their houses in the College. Similarly, there was no hint of deference in those local inhabitants who prosecuted the University's chaplain, James Mylne, in 1815 for a supposedly seditious sermon.

In many ways Glasgow's difficulties were symptomatic of the problems that each of Scotland's universities had in relating to the wider society in a time of rapid political and social transition. In Scotland, as in Britain as a whole, universities had to shift from serving the landed and older professional elites to paying greater attention to urban industrial society, especially its professional element.[8] During the second quarter of the nineteenth century the Scottish tradition of state intervention in universities was reinforced by rising middle-class enthusiasm for efficiency, accountability and a curriculum relevant to meritocratic examinations – and by decreasing tolerance for the apparently closed and selfish academic structures inherited from the past. There were also strong reform impulses from within the universities as some academics attempted to free their institutions from denominational and political impediments to talent and to rid their classrooms of boys whose poor preparation lowered the level of the teaching and learning experience. As Robert Anderson has put it, 'University reformers were not concerned only with the curriculum, or with such matters as the universities' relation to the professions and the schools, but also with the internal constitutions of the universities and with bringing them out of the shadow of clericalism and under the sway of public opinion.'[9] For the universities were viewed as under the thumb of the Tory Party and of the 'Moderate' party in the Church of Scotland. Attacks – and defences – received wide publicity in the Scottish press.

In addition to the strains engendered by the very unusual juxtaposition of an early Renaissance university and a major centre of industrialisation and urbanisation,[10] the University of Glasgow's particularly sharp dose of mid-nineteenth-century controversy derived from the institution's internal governing arrangements. Although drastically reformed during the Reformation and again in 1727, they were antiquated by the early nineteenth century, after decades during which the University suffered either from extremely strong rule by the Principal[11] or from internal bickering among professors. By the 1820s Glasgow's controversies focused on the professoriate. The government established several new 'Regius' chairs against the wishes of the existing professors; the latter, as members of 'Faculty', from which the new Regius professors were excluded, used the College's resources to the material as well as the constitutional disadvantage of the newcomers. This discrimination helped to inspire a tempestuous reform campaign which – in the eyes of its targets – violated 'alike the rules of courtesy and the laws of truth'.[12]

Moreover, the traditionally strong position of the Church of Scotland ('the Kirk') within the University was being challenged, partly from evangelical forces within the Kirk, partly from those who found clerical control – especially when it was linked to Toryism – a threat to the academic autonomy of those who differed. Religious tension became particularly sharp at Glasgow, in part because of the strongly clerical approach adopted by Duncan Macfarlan, Principal from 1823 to 1857.[13]

Having resolutely defended the *status quo* of the University against the hostile commissioners of 1826–30 (see below, p. 26), Macfarlan and his allies within the College remained unrepentant.[14] Macfarlan's conservatism was many-faceted, including a defence of the University's calendar and curriculum as well as of the distinction between 'Faculty' and Regius professors. Yet a fundamental aspect of the Principal's stance was to protect the role of the Kirk both within the University and beyond. Indeed, as Minister of the 'High Kirk' (Glasgow Cathedral) – a post he controversially combined with the principalship – and as Moderator of the General Assembly during the Disruption of the Church of Scotland in 1843, Macfarlan at times seemed more a combative Churchman than the University's head. When he welcomed the Queen to the University in 1849, for example, he had already greeted her earlier in the day in his High Kirk capacity. For Macfarlan the distinction between Kirk and University was artificial. He made this assumption explicit in his blunt 1843 sermon on religious tests for university professors – an issue sharpened by the secession of the Free Church from the Church of Scotland.[15] For Macfarlan, the dangers abolition posed to Kirk and Crown loomed as

1.1 *Duncan Macfarlan, Principal 1823–57.*

large as the perils to universities themselves. Moreover, in defending the tests, Macfarlan – in sharp contrast to some of his successors – was willing to criticise both local government and fellow protestant churches such as the Episcopalians.[16] Furthermore, Macfarlan rejected meritocratic arguments, justifying a retrospective view that before statutory university reform in 1858 'there was not quite the same feeling as now exists that the success of the University depends on choosing the best men that can possibly be obtained for the places'.[17]

Nonetheless, the old regime within the University was in decline well before 1858. Even on the issue of religious tests, a less stringent regime (except for professors of divinity), recommended by the Senate over Macfarlan's opposition in 1843, became law ten years later. Likewise in 1855, against the Principal's wishes once more, Glasgow proved more liberal than the other Scottish universities in its attitude to Kirk exclusivity regarding the Bachelor of Divinity. These defeats on religious issues paralleled a rising Whig presence among Glasgow's professoriate; the 1840s were a turning point in terms of the internal balance of power.[18]

Macfarlan's stout allegiance to the Kirk – and to the Conservative Party – had worsened tensions within the College and prejudiced its standing in the city. Yet such damage was limited by the persisting prestige of his university office – and the appealing nature of his personality. Macfarlan was 'genial, courteous and fair-minded, and could maintain his own views firmly and forcibly without offending his opponents'.[19] While some found him 'stiff and formal', others thought this 'old-fashioned dignity and reserve' excusable because he was 'social and hospitable'.[20] Also, he was famed for his work among the poor. Thus he 'stood high in the esteem of the citizens of Glasgow, and no public function was considered complete unless Principal Macfarlan was present'.[21] As a result, in 1842, on the fiftieth anniversary of his ordination, Macfarlan received a testimonial dinner, unparalleled for a Glasgow clergyman, attended by 'three hundred gentlemen, including men of rank and influence, and the *elite* of the citizens'.[22] As late as 1856 a journalist opined that 'No inhabitant of Glasgow has greater influence in the city than Principal Macfarlan' who – at the age of 84 – 'still retain[ed] much vigour of body and mind'.[23] On the day of his elaborate funeral in 1857, 'Every window along the route was filled with spectators, crowds lined the foot-pavements, and on a large open space . . . many hundreds of people were collected'.[24]

Given the turbulent constitutional, political and religious context of the University in the early Victorian period, its practical operations were surprisingly straightforward and – despite marked areas of anachronism and weakness – dynamic. Student numbers are difficult to calculate: even more than later in the century, students might be seriously involved in the University without being formally enrolled. Yet those officially on the books in 1861 numbered 1,140 – almost half the total of 1914 – on an upward trend, albeit still below the level of 1800. The students came mainly from Western Scotland, but there was much diversity, both within the rest of Britain and beyond; English dissenters and Irish presbyterians, in particular, were attracted by the absence of formal religious tests for students at the time of entrance. Socially, by the 1840s a significant shift had occurred from landed, and toward urban industrial, backgrounds; while as much as a third of the latter may have been from humble homes, many were from the middle class. Similarly, in the 1860s perhaps a quarter of Glasgow's students were 'working-class'; the bulk

1.2
W. J. Macquorn Rankine, Professor of Civil Engineering 1855–72.

of the rest came from comfortable urban middle-class homes. Age at entry averaged 15 or 16, so that much of the preliminary instruction at the University might have been delivered in schools instead: although there were voluntary preliminary examinations, the College did not require either formal qualifications or entrance examinations.[25] In marked contrast to Oxbridge, Glasgow – like other Scottish universities – did not house its students. In combination with the absence of informal social space within the College, scattered residences meant, in the words of James Bryce (a student in the 1850s), 'the want of opportunities for social intercourse among the students'.[26]

Still, the latter had a periodic communal outlet in the rectorial elections. Also, students played an increasingly organised form of football in the college grounds, and at mid-century societies – especially political clubs – began to develop. Moreover, students 'formed groups or circles that met in each other's houses or lodgings and discussed all sorts of questions . . . Friendships were formed which lasted through life'.[27]

Glasgow's professoriate was also undergoing major change in the mid-nineteenth century. Traditionally inbred, the professors' origins were increasingly diverse, as demonstrated by the American Henry Rogers (Natural History, 1857–66), the foremost structural geologist of his era. Also, at least in the case of Allen Thomson (Anatomy, 1848–77), a leading microscopical anatomist, extremely close connections with the Scottish professoriate (he was the grandson of a Glasgow professor, and the son of an Edinburgh professor) were no barrier to merit. A key appointment – ironically open to charges of nepotism, as his father was already a Glasgow professor – was that of William Thomson (Natural Philosophy, 1846–98), the future Lord Kelvin, who had liberal political instincts and an innovative approach to laboratory science both in teaching and research. Another major change was the increasing disciplinary diversity of the professoriate. Early nineteenth-century Regius foundations had encompassed subjects such as forensic medicine and chemistry, followed in 1840 by the novel foundation of civil engineering, filled from 1855 by the eminent W. J. Macquorn Rankine, who excelled in basic science and in practical applications alike. Yet the 'old' and the 'new' professoriate coexisted uneasily in these decades, helping to account for extremely bitter disputes such as those relating to the income and teaching arrangements of the famous William Hooker (Botany, 1820–41).[28]

The mid-nineteenth century was also a transitional period in terms of the attitudes of the professoriate to the city around it. The new recruits, in particular, were not aloof. Thus professors and students responded quickly to the Volunteer craze of 1859, organising companies headed by Macquorn Rankine and William Thomson. The Faculty had the good sense to subscribe £105 in 1854 to the Patriotic Fund associated with the Crimean War; in the same year the University showed sensible opportunism in conferring an honorary degree on David Livingstone.[29] Also, there was already a tradition of popular lectures to local citizens, notably through John Pringle Nichol (Practical Astronomy, 1836–59). Yet there was still a sense of 'the neighbouring city', in which some professors would not attend civic feasts, public meetings or – in extreme cases – even dinner parties.[30]

With regard to the originality of the early Victorian professoriate, there was great variation. In philosophy, Glasgow professors achieved little serious scholarship throughout the first half of the nineteenth century; a number of other disciplines did no better. Yet there were already some 'stars', notably Hooker, Kelvin, Rankine and Joseph Lister (Surgery, 1860–9), who 'conceived

1.3 *Joseph Lister, Professor of Surgery 1860–9.*

and brought forth' his crucial innovation of antisepsis during his time in Glasgow.[31] A number of other professors made substantial contributions to their subjects, especially John Burns (Surgery, 1815–50), Robert Grant (Astronomy, 1859–92) and the classical professors William Ramsay (Humanity [Latin], 1831–63) and Edmund Lushington (Greek, 1838–75), who 'vastly outshone their contemporaries in the other Universities', though Lushington published little.[32] While even this delicate balance largely depended on more recent appointments, the College was up-to-date enough overall to play a major role in hosting the British Association during its visit to Glasgow in 1840.[33]

Mid-nineteenth-century teaching at Glasgow already had many of the features which would characterise the regime half a century later. During a twenty-week session which extended from November to March, professors usually lectured five days each week – giving supplementary classes and (in many cases) setting written exercises for large classes, often without the help of assistants. For that half of the year, then, Macfarlan only slightly exaggerated when he referred to the 'unceasing toil' and the 'comparatively humble duties' of Scottish professors.[34] The quality of the teaching, as of the original

1.4 *Edmund Lushington, Professor of Greek 1838–75.*

investigations, was highly variable. Thus, while 'every student' of Lushington 'had a fair chance' and was 'guided, assisted, and enabled to do his best and make progress',[35] Hugh Blackburn (Mathematics, 1849–79), who was hard of hearing, could not control his class and Robert 'Logic Bob' Buchanan (1827–64) used the same lectures year after year. Still, Buchanan's students 'learned to think' through his skilful use of the Socratic method,[36] and Bryce found much to admire, even from the perspective of his later Oxford experiences, in many of his Glasgow professors, notably Ramsay. In this youthful period Kelvin struck one of Bryce's contemporaries as an 'enthusiastic and

1.5 *Hugh Blackburn, Professor of Mathematics 1849–79.*

inspiring teacher',[37] who did not rely on notes and supplemented the factual material that a textbook could provide, thereby evoking a 'living interest' in science. Allen Thomson led a modernisation of medical teaching, lecturing clearly and precisely, bringing an awareness of histology to dissection by students and removing the skeletons of criminals which had been suspended from the roof of the anatomy classroom.[38] While the surviving accounts are biased toward enthusiastic students,[39] their very positive responses to the teaching they received is striking. Bryce recalled that – spurred on by a system of public recitations and of prizes voted by the students – 'nearly the whole class' had a keen desire to learn, prompting 'incessant' discussion of the courses outside class hours. What was almost entirely lacking in this system was either 'personal social touch between the students and the professors' or any professorial concern for the students' life outside class.[40]

With regard to the curriculum many casual students were highly selective. But at Glasgow, as elsewhere in Scotland in the early nineteenth century, the 'regular' students – i.e. those who formally matriculated and were eligible for degrees – were meant to follow a fixed curriculum in a set sequence, with equal emphasis given in Arts to classics, philosophy and the combination of mathematics and physics (natural philosophy). Glasgow's Arts curriculum had been reviewed in 1826, and it made early provision for science. Also, the College was moving cautiously in this period from its traditional reliance on the sometimes perfunctory oral examinations in the venerable Blackstone chair at the start of the session to a system of formal written examinations. Still, oral examination in class, supplemented by written exercises and essays, remained central to the class work which was assessed independently of the degree examinations. Graduations remained uncommon, especially in Arts. Outside medicine, degrees had little value; instead the certificate of attendance was crucial, even for intending ministers. Thus, while the annual conferment of degrees was a low-key internal affair, the prize-giving each May was a festive occasion attended by professors, students and the public. The many students who did not aspire to a degree could, therefore, participate not only in the classes but in the central ceremonials of the College. This breadth of local involvement had significance in terms of the University's role in the city: in the 1850s 'most of the prominent business men of Glasgow had either passed through the Arts curriculum or had attended the Philosophy classes during two or three sessions'.[41]

The mid-nineteenth-century University, then, had many points of academic strength and development as well as of weakness and inertia. Apart from its internal disputes, the University's chief problem was how to relate to the frequent, increasingly intrusive attention of a government which – reinforced by local advocates of Reform – was prone to magnify the faults, and underestimate the ongoing improvements, of the institution.

The Royal Commission on the Scottish Universities of 1826–30, which adopted an especially hostile approach towards Glasgow, had sounded a loud warning signal. The Commission alleged the selfishness of the Principal and the Faculty in shortening the session and increasing fees – at a time when fees constituted the income of the professors – and their foolishness in selling valuable parcels of land for slight returns. Yet the Commissioners found no corruption. Also, they had to concede that the University's building decisions had been sound and that it had undertaken significant reforms of its teaching and examining practices. Although the city's MPs pressed for change, and while the University was the subject of yet another commission in the later 1830s, the key recommendations of the period – notably the proposal for a University Court which would check academic bodies such as Glasgow's Faculty – lay dormant for a time.[42]

Government intervention in the University of Glasgow's affairs sprang to life again with the passing of the 1858 Act, which had strong roots in pressure from graduates who felt they had neither rights nor influence in their universities. Glasgow-based societies of graduates were active from the late 1840s, notably the Graduates Association led by James Bryce's eponymous schoolmaster father, who saw the movement as, in its political dimension, 'a sort of counterpoise to the popular element'.[43] The Scottish Literary Institute also attracted influential advocates of reform, notably the Glasgow publisher Dr W. G. Blackie.[44] There was a countervailing force, mainly from the aged Macfarlan and his dwindling band of conservative professorial allies. The bill was modified as a result of representations from the Scottish universities, including Glasgow, which sent a deputation. Indeed, the intervention of the University's Chancellor, the Duke of Montrose, who was sympathetic to the conservative faction in the College, nearly stripped the bill of key clauses abolishing the distinction between types of Glasgow professors and opening the principalship to laymen.[45] Yet the core of the bill survived.

The legislation had important immediate effects on Glasgow, though it did not turn the institution upside down. The abolition of the distinction between Faculty and Regius professors was a major step, especially for the medical chairs, though it only took effect after a rearguard action – which included omitting the Regius professors from the new Principal's induction! – was crushed by the Court of Session. The Commissioners appointed under the 1858 Act, who made ordinances, were now a major force in university affairs. For years the Commissioners interfered even in small matters such as the arrangements for a temporary keeper of the Hunterian Museum. Yet their academic actions in regard to Glasgow were fairly minor – the creation of three chairs (English Literature, Conveyancing and Biblical Criticism) and the replacement of the BA by a new MA which was very similar to that produced by the Faculty in 1826.[46] Also, in collaboration with two other Scottish universities, Glasgow managed to suppress the proposal for a national university.[47]

More important for the University, both in the short and the long term, were the new parts of its constitution, the Court and the General Council. The 1858 Act attempted, as Campbell Lloyd has written, to 'produce more openness and greater accountability without allowing any individual or group' to have 'sole authority'.[48] Its principal mechanism was the Court, which – including (among others) the Principal and representatives from the Senate and the new General Council of graduates – would handle appointments (other than Regius chairs) and suspensions of professors while supervising, and serving as a court of appeal for, the Senate. The latter would retain its primary financial jurisdiction as well as its academic powers. The General Council gave graduates an assembly and thus for the first time an established role in university affairs, even though it could meet only twice a year, had only a consultative function and (until 1868) anomalously excluded holders of degrees in law and divinity. The introduction of the General Council brought immediate and enduring benefit to the academics by providing partial immunity from the argument that the universities were self-governing reactionary institutions and by establishing a channel for communication between the University and the wider community.[49] Yet the Council was a volatile body, particularly in these early years, making frequent representations to the Court on a range of issues stretching from the efficiency of the summer session to the representation of the universities in Parliament. Thus in 1865, for example, the General Council pressed the Senate and Court on graduates' access to the Hunterian Museum, the nature of the Arts curriculum and the ability of the Council to know what the Court was doing. The latter, while resisting some of the more ambitious demands of the Council, adopted a more conciliatory attitude toward it than did the Edinburgh Court.[50] Similarly, the Glasgow Court had a generally harmonious relationship with the Senate, which met much more often, had a much more elaborate system of committees, dealt with much more business and was in this period the more important body.[51]

It was fortunate for the viability of the post-1858 system at Glasgow that the Crown appointed a new Principal just as the Act was going through. The choice was made quickly after Macfarlan's death, supposedly to circumvent the 1858 Act's abolition of the requirement to select a clergyman of the Established Church. Yet while Thomas Barclay (1792–1873, Principal 1858–73) was a son of the manse and was a parish minister at the time of his appointment, he differed from his predecessor in many important respects. Barclay was a Shetlander and, as an Aberdeen graduate, had no previous association with the University. Also, the new Principal had had a successful secular career – as a reporter for *The Times* – before taking up the ministry. Moreover, Barclay had been a progressive in Kirk disputes. Crucially, as Principal he 'took little part in ecclesiastical politics', believing that his new role entailed a stance of public objectivity regarding public controversies.[52]

Thus Barclay (who did not hold a church living while he was Principal) focused his attention on the University and helped to calm it. Admittedly the new Principal was not an academic: evidently his appointment resulted from having impressed the politician Sir Henry Holland with his skill not only as a preacher but also as a boatman during a perilous outing off Shetland! Still, Barclay had claims to expertise, particularly in Northern European languages. Also, while not good at keeping students in order, Barclay was very popular among them. More importantly, whether because or in spite of his somewhat fearsome appearance, he 'managed his colleagues with great dexterity'.[53] Although his 'somewhat brusque manner . . . and his lion-like growls at anything that displeased him' put some people off, his 'unpretending simplicity of character, his humorous directness of utterance, and his geniality and kindliness

1.6 *Thomas Barclay, Principal 1858–73.*

of nature, endeared him to his colleagues'.[54] In marked contrast to Macfarlan, Barclay prized liberty of thought and expression and so proved very tolerant of differences of opinion within the University.[55] Yet he was no cipher, for he 'thoroughly understood how to conduct a business meeting, kept it well in hand and was an adept in deciding points of order'.[56] He presided successfully over the new Court (as deputy for the Rector) and (as deputy for the Chancellor and the Rector) the General Council, defusing a crisis over a petition to Parliament from the latter with the quip: 'Gentlemen, you need not give yourselves so much trouble . . . as the House of Commons will never read it'.[57] Barclay also did much to reconcile the 'old thirteen' Faculty professors to the new authority of the Senate. Thus, by the end of Barclay's principalship, his successor thought of the Senate as – in marked contrast to earlier decades – 'a harmonious body'.[58]

Yet in his final illness-plagued years Barclay played little part in the affairs of the city (where he had never been so active as Macfarlan), and he became less active even in the University. Indeed, twenty years of bronchial complaints had forced him to spend part of each winter abroad. Latterly Barclay had yielded considerable influence to a capable group of senior professors. Still, in many ways Barclay had been an ideal choice to preside over the University's transition from a faction-filled city centre college steeped in tradition to a more harmonious suburban university starting to concern itself with international standards of excellence.

The biggest problem – though it masked the largest opportunity – of the newly reformed University was its physical plant and location. The seventeenth-century complex of buildings had been reinforced by early nineteenth-century additions and renovations, notably the Hunterian Museum and Hamilton Building, which featured a new Common Hall and several classrooms, including dissecting rooms. The enlarged complex was in many respects a well-loved and serviceable set of buildings, notably the Fore Hall, which served both as a professorial common room and as a place for academic meetings. The classrooms were large, adequately heated and lighted, and there was a well-stocked reading room heavily used by students between lectures.[59] Yet further improvements proved necessary as early as 1824, and the increasing number of chairs and students during the mid-century period put the teaching accommodation under ever greater pressure. The rapidly accelerating sense of crisis arose not so much from these internal problems – the University had handled these more than once before on its High Street site, which still contained much vacant land – as from a growing belief by the 1850s that the neighbourhood of the College was unsuitable both for students and for the 'Faculty' professors who lived with their families in Professors' Court. In part this perception arose from the unpleasant air pollution from the factories which had grown up nearby. More seriously, there was also the peril

1.7 *Old College, Frontispiece, c. 1870.*

1.8 *Old College, Inner Court, c. 1870.*

1.9 *Old College, interior of Hunterian Museum, c. 1870.*

of disease, notably the typhus and cholera which killed the elder Professor Thomson and other professors and their relatives during the 1840s.[60]

In addition, there was an important social dimension to the case for removal. Advocates of the move emphasised the extent to which the area around the College was inhabited by social undesirables: their presence menaced the family life of the professors and deterred enrolment by students from the city's well-off families, who increasingly resided far from the High Street, especially in the expanding West End. Static enrolments from the city reinforced these worries. Yet there was also an opportunistic element to the drive for removal. The interest of railway companies in the High Street site made it possible to contemplate the radical innovation of a change from a site which the University had occupied for centuries. The prospect of these resources, in turn, caused influential people within the University to exaggerate, at the margin, the negative features of the High Street; athough no longer fashionable, it was still prosperous in the 1850s, its flats inhabited by 'physicians in small practice, teachers and tradespeople'.[61] In fact, a strong underlying motivation for the removal was the chance not just for the resident professors but for the whole University to associate itself with the most prosperous groups and the most progressive forces in the city, thereby shedding the negative, unfashionable connotations that the institution had acquired in previous decades.

Underpinned in these various ways, the consensus in favour of a move grew rapidly. By the mid-1840s, when the first railway-financed removal scheme was mooted, the resident Faculty professors strongly favoured a move. That scheme having collapsed in the late 1840s due to a change of strategy by the company, the idea was given a major boost by an 1859 report by the Commissioners which, *inter alia*, agreed with the University's worries about desertion by the most respectable families of Glasgow. By 1860 the prospective move had the strong support of the General Council, which noted that the High Street area was 'one of the last places in the city which one would now propose for professors to reside in, or for students to frequent'.[62] While pointing out that the expansion of the College had outstripped its buildings, the Council observed that 'owing to the progress of the city westward, the present buildings are no longer conveniently situated for those classes of society in Glasgow who are most interested in the University', 'the middle and upper

1.10 *Old College, Fore Hall, c. 1870.*

1.11 *Old College, Professors' Court, c. 1870.*

classes'. Noting that a move west would also gratify the desire for an additional hospital, the Council concluded – in apparently unconscious irony regarding the statement in the same report that the University 'opens its doors to all classes of the community without distinction' – that the prospective move would 'bring University education more generally within the reach of those citizens who are in the best condition and circumstances to avail themselves of it'.[63] While at first the Regius professors had been sceptical about the move, the 1858 Act, and the growing dissatisfaction of the medical professors with the Royal Infirmary, gained new recruits for the cause. By the time of the removal there was also strong support within the city's middle class. This reflected not only Gilmorehill's location in the dynamic, fashionable West End but also a perception that the civic isolation as well as the declining surroundings of the High Street location had made the 'old black college in High Street' 'to a large extent isolated from the general life of the city'.[64]

The major problem, of course, was money. The project could not be financed from the University's own resources: the interim cost estimate of £266,000

1.12 *Old College, High Street entrance, c. 1870.*

dwarfed the University's annual budget in the 1860s of under £12,000. Moreover, the net result of the financial changes made during the 'age of reform' was to reduce the University's income relative to its commitments. Even with compensation of £12,000 from the aborted 1840s scheme and the offer of £100,000 from the Glasgow Union Railway Company for the High Street site, there was a major shortfall.[65]

Government assistance filled a substantial part of the gap. While there had been a University deputation to London as early as 1853, the University again pressed its case in the more propitious atmosphere following the 1858 Act. A joint deputation from the city and the University, supplemented by Glasgow's two MPs, met the Prime Minister, Lord Derby, and the Chancellor of the Exchequer, Disraeli. The sequel was a very substantial government pledge of £120,000. Yet this left a large fund-raising requirement, which was in any case a government stipulation. Also, the amount that had to be raised was constantly rising as the estimated cost of the project increased. An additional government pledge of £21,400 in 1864 was again contingent on further fund-raising.

With the aid of graduates and of sympathetic forces in the city, the University mounted a large, complex fund-raising campaign which managed to raise the massive sum of £113,000 by 1868; by 1876 this had grown to £159,000 raised from Scotland out of the total cost of £428,000, including the Western Infirmary.[66] Apart from the sheer scale of the money required, the University had to overcome lingering resentments concerning, for example, its denominational associations and reach the significant number of graduates who lived outside Glasgow. There was a Committee for Obtaining Subscriptions (chaired by the Principal and, after a public meeting, including key figures such as the sheriff Sir Archibald Alison), a Joint Subscription Committee and a Joint Building Committee, including as members city notables such as the textile magnate Archibald Orr Ewing. Within these bodies the key figures were Professor Allen Thomson, whose brother had masterminded the scheme of the 1840s, and the department store owner James A. Campbell.[67] These committees met frequently over a long period, and elaborate efforts were made to involve the public of the city and its surrounding area, using arguments appropriate to people who were not graduates as well as those who were. Thomson, convener of the Committee for the Purchase of the Site, for many months could be seen, with his colleague Anderson Kirkwood, 'hurrying through the streets of Glasgow on their way to the offices of business men . . . from whom they hoped to obtain support'.[68]

Who gave? Michael Sanderson has argued that only a small proportion of Glasgow firms subscribed, and that much of the money came from a few very rich people. Certainly there were large contributions, especially if the later gifts for the University's main meeting halls are taken into account. Yet Campbell Lloyd has demonstrated that not only did almost 95 per cent of the

1.13 *Allen Thomson, Professor of Anatomy 1848–77.*

subscribers donate less than £1,000: these subscribers supplied nearly fifty per cent of the money. In terms of occupations, the 'mercantile' interest raised almost half the total, with significant though much smaller shares for such groups as professionals – and even university professors! Also, a broad group of men from industry and commerce played important roles as canvassers in the fund-raising campaign. Moreover, the campaign attracted significant civic contributions – £10,000 from the Corporation, £1,000 from the Merchants' House and £2,875 from the Trades House (including the various 'Incorporations'). Thus the fund-raising drive drew upon, but also strengthened, the University's improving ties not only with its graduates but also with the broader public.[69]

The planning and construction of the Gilmorehill buildings, and of the adjoining hospital, were massive undertakings. Inevitably there was a mushrooming of committees. In 1864 the University controversially awarded the architectural commission to the English virtuoso Sir George Gilbert Scott, arguably the only person capable of carrying out a project of the required magnitude.[70] The building committee then peppered Scott with advice, drawing on the 1846 plans and on statements made by each of the professors. The design was approved, after various amendments, in March 1866.

The project necessitated the levelling of the top of Gilmorehill. Construction of the building began in earnest in April 1867. It proceeded quickly, aided by as many as 1,000 workmen. Yet there were delays due to the unexpected discovery of a coal seam, a prolonged strike (which caused considerable controversy in the local press) and repeated crises about escalating costs. As a result, from autumn 1869 works were focused on those items which would be necessary to begin the academic session 1870–1 on the new site. Thus the buildings were still incomplete when they were turned over to the University in the summer of 1870; the Principal's Lodging, for example, could not be furnished for another two years. Yet the actual removal process went surprisingly smoothly: not a single book was lost from the Library.

The progress of the project attracted enormous interest, which peaked at the stone-laying by the Prince and Princess of Wales in October 1868. The city observed the day as a holiday 'and an immense concourse of people was attracted to the City and the neighbourhood of the University'. The first great event, in the city centre, was the conferring of the freedom of the city on the Prince and Princess – in the presence of, among many other dignitaries, the University's Lord Rector. After a heartily cheered procession through the heavily decorated route to Gilmorehill, the Prince of Wales and his companion, Prince John of Glucksburg, received honorary degrees in the presence of the Glasgow professors, the principals of the other Scottish universities, the Lord Provost and other local dignitaries – who had places of honour in the subsequent outdoor ceremony, as did the resident foreign consuls. The stone-laying took place in front of a crowd of some 20,000 spectators, including 'the City and County authorities in the West of Scotland, representatives from the whole Public Institutions of the City, Subscribers to the new buildings, and Students and others connected with the University'.[71] But the crowd 'was so great as to be, to a certain extent, beyond . . . control'. The stands nearly collapsed, and the 'aristocracy and well-to-do classes of Glasgow' found many of their places taken by 'boys, servants, workmen about the place, and so forth'.[72] Nonetheless the actual foundation-laying proved very decorous. Prominent parts in the ceremony were accorded to the architect and, significantly, to the lay chair of the subscribers' committee; the names of the subscribers were buried with other souvenirs inside the foundation stone; and the University's address to the Prince suggested that the subscribers to the building had eclipsed the generosity of previous ages.[73] Links to local institutions were evident in the Clydesdale Bank's giving notes for the bottle buried under the foundation stone, though the local trades had with few exceptions declined a late invitation to take part. Lunch at the home of the Lord Provost followed the ceremony, and on departing the Prince expressed his gratitude for the invitation from 'the city and University of Glasgow'. A civic banquet hosted by the Lord Provost, and attended by the Principal, rounded off the day. The aftermath, too, was pleasant: subscriptions of 100 guineas from the Prince of Wales and £500 from his mother.

Given such a boost, the transition from the High Street to Gilmorehill took place in a celebratory atmosphere. On 29 April 1870, when the session closed, the students gathered in the Common Hall; the Senate left on 29 July, a day before the railway took over the site (and a year later than originally agreed). In a significant symbol of the new governing structure and outward outlook of the University, the farewell dinner combined members of the Senate, Court and General Council and friends of the University, culminating in 'Auld Lang Syne'.[74] Thus, as a result of the removal itself, the mode of the fund-raising and the inclusive nature of the surrounding rituals, the University departed for Gilmorehill more united – and more positively connected to the elites of its city and region – than at any time in its modern history.

Notes and References

1. For earlier general accounts of the University in the period from the mid-nineteenth century to 1914 see: J. Coutts, *A History of the University of Glasgow: From its Foundation in 1451 to 1909* (Glasgow, 1909); J. D. Mackie, *The University of Glasgow 1451-1951: A Short History* (Glasgow, 1954); and A. L. Brown and M. Moss, *The University of Glasgow 1451–1996* (Edinburgh, 1996). For important more specialised work see, among others: C. F. Lloyd, 'Relationships between Scottish Universities and their Communities c.1858–1914' (PhD thesis, University of Glasgow, 1993); P. L. Robertson, 'The Finances of the University of Glasgow before 1914', *Higher Education Quarterly*, 16 (1976), 449–78 and 'The Development of an Urban University: Glasgow 1860–1914', *History of Education Quarterly*, 30 (1990), 47–78; and R. D. Anderson, *Education and Opportunity in Victorian Scotland: Schools and Universities* (Oxford, 1983).
2. With regard to the terms 'College' and 'University' – for consistency this chapter will generally use the latter: while the distinction between the two was central to the early nineteenth-century battle about Regius professors, after 1858 there was in effect no difference, as Glasgow (unlike Oxbridge and St Andrews) had only a single college.
3. N. J. Morgan and R. H. Trainor, 'The Dominant Classes', in W. H. Fraser and R. J. Morris (eds), *People and Society in Scotland II 1830–1914* (Edinburgh, 1990), 103–37; R. H. Trainor, 'The Elite' and S. Nenadic, 'The Victorian Middle Classes', in W. H. Fraser and I. Maver (eds), *Glasgow Volume II 1830*

to 1912 (Manchester, 1996), 227–64 and 265–99; Anderson, *Education and Opportunity*, 324.

4. J. Tweed, *Biographical Sketches of the Honourable The Lord Provosts of Glasgow* (Glasgow, 1883), 118. (The Papal Bull of 1451 which established the University had modelled it on Bologna.)
5. *Lord Provosts*, 180 (quote), 291.
6. Coutts, *University*, 396.
7. A. Hull and J. Geyer-Kordesch, *The Shaping of the Medical Profession: A History of the Royal College of Physicians and Surgeons of Glasgow, 1858–1999* (London, 1999), modifying Coutts, *University*, 547–54; C. F. Lloyd, 'The Search for Legitimacy: Universities, Medical Licensing Bodies and Governance in Glasgow and Edinburgh from the late eighteenth to the late nineteenth centuries', in R. J. Morris and R. H. Trainor (eds), *Urban Governance: Britain and Beyond since 1750* (Aldershot, 2000), 198–210.
8. K. H. Jarausch (ed.), *The Transformation of Higher Learning, 1860–1930* (Chicago, 1983); R. D. Anderson, *Universities and Elites in Britain since 1800* (Cambridge, 1995), 1, 4.
9. Anderson, *Education and Opportunity*, 27, and cf. 31–2, 49.
10. Cf. Robertson, 'Development', 48.
11. In Glasgow, as in other Scottish universities, the Principal is the effective head of the University, guiding its affairs and – as Vice-Chancellor – conferring degrees in the absence of the Chancellor (theoretically senior to the Principal but in practice largely ceremonial).
12. 'Observations by the Principal and Professors of Glasgow College, on Schemes of Reform . . .' (2nd edn, Glasgow, 1837), 36. Cf. Robertson, 'Finances', Table III.
13. Born a son of the manse in Drymen (where the University's Chancellor the Duke of Montrose – a key intermediary between University and Crown in the appointment of principals – was a parishioner) in 1771, Macfarlan spent eight years as a student at the College before succeeding his father in 1792. A King's Chaplain for Scotland from 1815, he was Moderator of the General Assembly four years later. Meanwhile, despite being disappointed in an early bid for a chair, he received the University's D.D. in 1806 and was Dean of Faculties from 1810 (J. MacLehose, *Memoirs and Portraits of One Hundred Glasgow Men* (Glasgow, 1886), [hereafter OHGM], 189–90; DNB).
14. 'Observations by the Principal and Professors'.
15. The tests required all new professors to 'subscribe' to the Kirk's Westminster Confession.
16. D. Macfarlan, 'University Tests in Scotland' (Glasgow, 1846). Cf. Anderson, *Education and Opportunity*, 53; C. Smith and M. N. Wise, *Energy and Empire: A Biographical Study of Lord Kelvin* (Cambridge, 1989), 43.
17. Professor Sir William Thomson (later Lord Kelvin), R. C. Scottish Universities 1876 [hereafter R.C. 1876], III/II, 508, Q.10102.
18. Smith and Wise, *Energy and Empire*, 21, 28; Coutts, *University*, 419–21; Mackie, *University*, 261–2, 275.
19. D. Murray, *Memories of the Old College of Glasgow* (Glasgow, 1927), 288.
20. OHGM, 190.

21. Murray, *Old College*, 288.
22. *Lord Provosts*, 189.
23. *Fraser's Magazine*, May 1856, 517.
24. Murray, *Old College*, 290.
25. Anderson, *Education & Opportunity*, 150–1, 350; Anderson, *Scottish Education since the Reformation* (Dundee, 1997), 18. Cf. W. M. Mathew, 'The Origins and Occupations of Glasgow Students, 1740–1839', *Past and Present*, 33 (1966).
26. H. A. L. Fisher, *James Bryce (Viscount Bryce of Dechmont O.M.)* (London, 1927), 22.
27. Murray, *Old College*, 578; R. D. Anderson, 'Sport in the Scottish Universities, 1860–1939', *International Journal of the History of Sport*, 4 (1987), 178. These student lodgings could be fatal; James McCosh, a student in the 1820s, lost his cousin, his room-mate, to a contagious disease. W. M. Sloane (ed.), *The Life of James McCosh* (Edinburgh, 1896), 32
28. J. Walton, 'Natural History', University of Glasgow, *Fortuna Domus: . . . Lectures Delivered . . . in Commemoration of the Fifth Centenary* [hereafter FD] (Glasgow, 1952), 304; G. M. Wyburn, 'Anatomy', FD, 225; Smith and Wise, *Kelvin*, 117, 120, 130–1; *DNB* (Rankine); Coutts, *University*, 531–3.
29. Mackie, *University*, 308; Coutts, *University*, 415, 392; Murray, *Old College*, 268.
30. OHGM, 51–2, modified by Murray, *Old College*, 156.
31. C. F. W. Illingworth, 'Surgery', FD, 207–8 (quote); C. A. Campbell, 'Philosophy', FD, 113, 115.
32. Illingworth, 'Surgery', 205–6; C. J. Fordyce, 'Classics', FD, 37; *DNB* (Lushington).
33. Murray, *Old College*, 138.
34. Macfarlan, 'University Tests', 13.
35. Murray, *Old College*, 210–11.
36. Murray, *Old College*, 153.
37. Murray, *Old College*, 119, 121.
38. OHGM, 317–18; G. M. Wyburn, 'Anatomy', FD, 225.
39. For a dissenting voice, albeit one impressed with the system of regular examinations and written exercises, see Sloane, *McCosh*, 27–9.
40. Fisher, *Bryce*, 24–5, 22. Cf. Sloane, *McCosh*, 32.
41. Murray, *Old College*, 466 (quote), 85; Anderson, *Education and Opportunity*, 31, 34, 46; Mackie, *University*, 302–3, 306–7. Like other Scottish universities, Glasgow allowed presbyterian (and other) nonconformists to matriculate and follow an entire degree course – as would-be ministers of the pre-1843 secessionist churches and the post-1843 Free Kirk did – though religious scruples may have reinforced other factors in discouraging such students from proceeding to formal graduation in this period.
42. Mackie, *University*, 249, 251–2, 253–4, 255–6, 258–9, 268; Anderson, *Education and Opportunity*, 38–9; *Report on the Universities and Colleges of Scotland: II Report Relative to the University of Glasgow*; *Minutes of Evidence: Commissioners . . . University and College of Glasgow*, Principal Macfarlane [sic].

43. R.C. 1876 III/II 181, Q.8983. Cf. Anderson, *Education and Opportunity*, 65.
44. Anderson, *Education and Opportunity*, 63.
45. Coutts, *University*, 434.
46. Coutts, *University*, 435–6, 440, 569; Scottish Universities Commission, *General Report* (Edinburgh, 1863).
47. Cf. D. J. Withrington, 'The Idea of a National University in Scotland c.1820–1870', in J. J. Carter and D. J. Withrington (eds), *Scottish Universities: Distinctiveness and Diversity* (Edinburgh, 1983), 40–55.
48. Lloyd, 'Communities', 27. Cf. R. D. Anderson, 'Scottish University Professors, 1800–1939: Profile of an Elite', *Scottish Economic and Social History*, 7 (1987), 29.
49. Anderson, *Education and Opportunity*, 68.
50. Murray, *Old College*, 345–6; General Council Minutes [hereafter GCMN], 26 April and 1 November 1865; Lloyd, 'Communities', 104.
51. In contrast to the situation before the Act, when 'Faculty' (i.e. the Principal and those professors other than the Regius professors) ruled on most key decisions, after 1858 Senate was the unchallenged academic authority.
52. *Glasgow Herald* (hereafter GH), 24 February 1873 (quote); *DNB*.
53. Murray, *Old College*, 293.
54. E. Caird, 'Memoir of Principal Caird' [hereafter *Memoir*], in John Caird, *The Fundamental Ideas of Christianity . . .* (Glasgow, 1899), xcviii–xcix.
55. John Caird, '. . . The Very Rev. Thomas Barclay . . .' (Glasgow, 1873), 27–8.
56. Murray, *Old College*, 293. Cf. Mackie, *University*, 275 and praise from W. T. Gairdner, a colleague, 'Memories of College Life', in Students' Jubilee Celebrations Committee, *A Book of the Jubilee: in Commemoration of the Ninth Jubilee of the University of Glasgow* (Glasgow 1901), 49, 51, as gaining 'the respect and sympathy of us all' though 'no one, of course, will for a moment think of comparing Principal Barclay with his great successor'.
57. Murray, *Old College*, 294. The Rector, elected by the matriculated students after 1858, had the right to chair the Court and to make representations on behalf of students.
58. E. Caird, *Memoir*, c. Cf. Murray, *Old College*, 293.
59. Murray, *Old College*, 148, 165.
60. Smith and Wise, *Kelvin*, 136–7.
61. Murray, *Old College*, 3 (quote), 4 (quote), 5. For scepticism by Coutts concerning the necessity for a move see *University*, 424–5, 443 n. 1.
62. 'Reports on the Library, College Site, Graduation etc . . .', (1860) 6. Cf. 'Report of the buildings of Glasgow University', appendix to Report of the 1858 Commission, quoted Mackie, *University*, 266 and Coutts, *University*, 425.
63. 'Reports on the Library . . .', 6, 7.
64. *Who's Who in Glasgow in 1909*, 280 [hereafter WWG], 134; OHGM, 51; Cf. *Lord Provosts*, 80; Mackie, *University*, 280.
65. Robertson, 'Finances', 459, 471. Cf. Anderson, *Education and Opportunity*, 36.
66. Mackie, *University*, 285–6.
67. Later MP for the University's seat, Campbell was brother to the future Prime Minister, Sir Henry Campbell-Bannerman.

68. Murray, *Old College*, 246 (quote); Lloyd, 'Communities', 35, 209–10 and Table 6.3, 214–16.
69. Lloyd, 'Communities', 206–8 and Tables 1 and 6.2; 'University of Glasgow New Buildings: Report by the Chairman of the University Removal Committee . . .' (Glasgow, 1877), 41. Cf. Sanderson, *The Universities and British Industry 1850–1970* (London, 1972), 167–9.
70. James Macaulay, 'Sir George Gilbert Scott and the University of Glasgow' (paper, 2001 seminar, 11 December 1997). The architect, ironically, was of Scottish descent.
71. 'University of Glasgow New Buildings', 20.
72. *Glasgow Herald*, GH, 10 October 1868.
73. *Weekly Mail*, 10 October 1868.
74. Murray, *Old College*, 588.

CHAPTER TWO

OLD WINE IN A NEW BOTTLE? GILMOREHILL, 1870–84

The complex into which the University moved in the autumn of 1870 was gigantic by the standards of the day. Indeed, at 540 feet long it was the largest public structure built in Britain since the completion of the Houses of Parliament ten years earlier. Scott had surmounted a massive organisational task and had striven for serviceability, using modern materials and methods, as well as a fashionably neo-Gothic stylistic effect.[1]

In most respects he was triumphantly successful. The accommodation at Gilmorehill was much greater in extent than its counterpart at the High Street, roughly five times what had been available in the city centre. Each non-clinical professorial chair had 'a distinct classroom with its retiring-room, and, wherever necessary, all the suitable laboratories and apparatus-rooms', in contrast to the situation in the old buildings where 'several classes were required to meet in succession in the same apartment'.[2] There were twenty-five classrooms in all. The thirteen professors (the twelve 'Faculty' professors and the Principal) with the right to accommodation in the High Street retained it at Gilmorehill in spacious houses which, according to the well-born Allen Thomson, were 'suitable for persons of moderate income'![3] The apparently large and undeniably grand spaces for the library and museum also attracted much satisfaction.[4] Moreover, in a self-consciously modern touch, the building had a system for 'throwing fresh air in a more or less heated condition into the apartments of the building'.[5] Less clear at the time of the enthusiastic removal, though evident to professors and students soon thereafter, were shortcomings, some of which resulted from the extent to which the new accommodation had been patterned on the old. These problems included the absence of provision for small-group teaching, the shortage of accommodation for laboratory science, the lack of social spaces for professors and students – and, most seriously, the shortage of room for expansion. Ironically, the new site, shorn of the land sold to the city for the new 'West End Park' and the area set aside for the Western Infirmary, had twenty-one acres, five fewer than on the High Street.[6] For the moment, however, the sheer modern grandeur of the building, and the salubrious nature of its superb hilltop site, dominated impressions.[7]

2.1 *University Buildings at Gilmorehill, c. 1892, after the completion of the tower, spire and Bute Hall.*

The opening ceremony of the building, on 7 November 1870, was triumphantly positive. The Chancellor, the Duke of Montrose, presided in the lower hall of the museum which, until the Bute Hall was opened in the 1880s, had to double as a place of assembly. Members of the public attended, as did the students, and the platform party included the Marquess of Bute, the Lord Justice-General, the Lord Dean of Guild, the Lord Provosts of Glasgow and Edinburgh, the Provosts of Partick and Hillhead, and a range of other dignitaries including the Principal of Edinburgh University. Having noted that the buildings were raised 'partly by assistance from the national exchequer, but much more by the very grand subscriptions by the citizens of Glasgow', Montrose bluntly alluded to the University's escape from 'the wretched population which infested the neighbourhood' of the Old College.[8] There followed an inaugural address by Professor Lushington and comments by – among others – Lord President Inglis (a key figure in the 1858 Act and Commission and an ex-Glasgow student), the MP for the Universities of Glasgow and Aberdeen, Principal Barclay, Archibald Orr Ewing and Allen Thomson.[9] That evening, the subscribers were the hosts for a dinner – held,

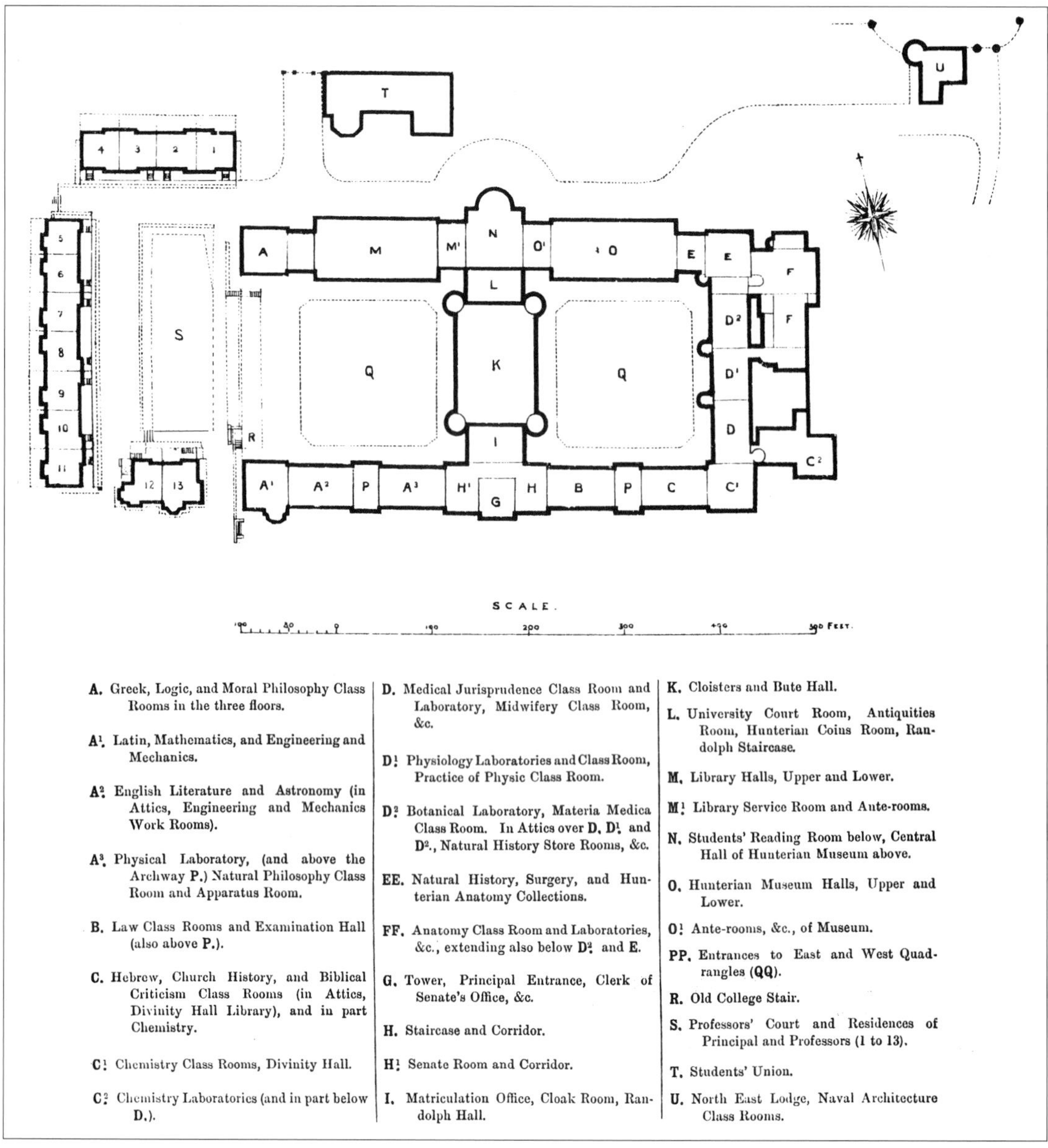

2.2 *Diagram of layout of New Buildings at Gilmorehill.*

significantly, in the Corporation Galleries – for the Principal and professors, with the Lord Provost in the chair and various sheriffs and MPs in attendance. A far less happy example of town-gown relations occurred two nights later when a torchlight procession of students from the Old College to Gilmorehill was disrupted by rowdy local youths.[10] Yet there was strong civic approval for the new buildings. As the *Glasgow Herald* commented, 'Learning in the fifteenth century was the appanage of a caste. In the nineteenth the State replaces the Church, and the munificence of the great city which has grown round the knees of the University, exceeds the munificence of the State itself'.[11] Thus, the University and the city congratulated each other on the splendid fruits of their collaboration.

Moving into Gilmorehill, the University combined an intense desire to profit from the modernity of its new buildings with a strong sense of tradition and underlying assumptions of educational continuity.[12] In an opening lecture the divinity professor and future Principal John Caird was pleased that the spirit of the Old College was being brought to Gilmorehill, but his address also emphasised the most recent aspects of the University's life, particularly the need for a scientific approach to knowledge.[13] Still, there was no clear anticipation that the academic life of the University would alter radically, except in its practical arrangements. The assumption – symbolised by the incorporation into the perimeter of the building of the old Lion and Unicorn staircase – was that the new and the old would coexist happily. Implicit, too, was a belief that the process of removal, in addition to linking the University more closely to the city, would help to knit together the University's factions, both within and beyond the Senate.

A key figure in translating into reality these aspirations for harmonious progress was John Caird (1820–98), professor of divinity from 1862 and Principal from 1873 until his death. Like Macfarlan and Barclay, Caird was a minister of the Kirk. However, he was not a son of the manse: his father had been a Greenock shipbuilder. Also, while Caird won his initial, and most enduring, fame as a spectacularly popular yet thoughtful preacher, he was much more a scholar, and infinitely more an academic, than his two immediate predecessors. Following a brilliant undergraduate career with spells as minister at increasingly fashionable churches, Caird made a deep impression as professor on a generation of divinity students, including those he welcomed from the Free Church and other denominations. Also, having served as an influential professor prior to his election, Caird was comparatively well equipped to take up the duties of Principal. Perhaps most importantly, whereas Barclay's appointment evidently had been a surprise to the University, Caird's selection by the Crown followed a unanimous petition from the Senate – an enormous asset in the difficult quarter century which lay ahead.[14]

Caird's approach to religion significantly influenced his principalship. Having learned German while a parish minister in order to keep pace with the latest theological thinking, Caird was – like his even more scholarly brother, the philosopher Edward (see below, pp. 55, 58–61) – a neo-Hegelian Idealist. The consequence of this approach for John Caird was a liberal, developmental view of Christianity which emphasised the superiority of ethics over dogma, and the compatibility of Christianity with reason, and thus with science. Moreover, he was 'almost indifferent to the causes of disagreement between

2.3 *John Caird, Professor of Divinity 1862–73, Principal 1873–98.*

the main denominations'.[15] At first, this approach aroused sharp criticism from more orthodox Scottish protestants, notably when Caird persuaded the University in 1868 to give an honorary degree to John McLeod Campbell, who had been expelled from the ministry in the 1830s for theological heterodoxy. Yet, as his own approach mellowed, and as the trend of Scottish thinking moved in his direction, Caird became a revered figure at a time when religion featured very prominently both in public and private discourse. Like Barclay, as principal Caird kept out of ecclesiastical politics, repeatedly refusing nomination as Moderator to the General Assembly, for example.[16]

For John Caird religion – understood in his flexible, practical, almost unsectarian way – was fundamental to a University. Indeed, even before his principalship, he responded to the move to Gilmorehill by 'reviving' University chapel services and superintending the arrangements by which preachers of many denominations – including, controversially, the Scottish Episcopalians – were invited. For Caird it was important to bring students together 'independently of the special communion to which they might belong'.[17] During his principalship Caird continued not only with his theological scholarship but also with his regular sermons to the University community, including large numbers of students, in the Museum Hall and, later, the Bute Hall on subjects such as 'Truth and Freedom' and 'The Guilt and Guiltlessness of Unbelief'.[18] This approach to religion helped to provide the University with a useful middle way, during decades of tumult in Scotland and Britain more generally regarding religious orthodoxy, between hidebound versions of the latter, on the one hand, and the increasingly prevalent scepticism of many intellectuals on the other. As implied by his lecture 'A Plea for a Scientific Theology', Caird did much to reconcile the university as a place of pursuit of scientific truth with the university as a place where nondogmatic Christian religion could flourish. In large part because of this approach – which resembled that of the influential President of Princeton, the Scotsman and ex-Glasgow College student James McCosh (1811–94) – during the final quarter of the nineteenth century Glasgow kept its own religious, and related cultural, divisions to a minimum.[19]

Meanwhile, Caird's tolerant but serious approach to religion found its parallel in his vision of the university, which he urged – evidently with some success – on student and professor alike. Disseminated during his address to the students at the start of each session and through the remarks he made at graduation ceremonies, these views included a broad conception both of academic study and of the University's role in society. Both were founded on his optimistic assessment of human capacities and his strong, religiously-based sense of duty toward his fellow men. Yet this knowledge was to be approached in a systematic way. For Caird, 'the peculiar function of a University [is] to teach *Science*, or the universal element in human knowledge'.[20] Such learning was neither impractical nor impersonal:

> Much of the mere information which the student acquires here may fade away from his mind, but what is not lost is the training to keenness and accuracy of his powers of observation, the practiced ability to see what the facts really are, to grasp their meaning, appreciate their value, discern them in the light of their relation to other facts and phenomena, weigh the force of evidence for conflicting interpretations of them. Now, here

> we have a result which only the guidance of a living instructor can supply, and which is of inestimable value as a preparation for the future work and conduct of life.[21]

Caird urged liberal education as countering vocational narrowness, notably in alerting individuals to the 'important social duties which lie outside of every man's professional work'.[22] Thus, for Caird, a liberal education equipped students not only to earn a living but to improve society. This was a powerful apologia for an institution which provided much general, 'impractical' teaching in a city and a country characterised at the time both by hard-headed private enterprise and conspicuous public-spiritedness.

Caird's personality, like his ideas, was almost ideally suited to a Glasgow principal of his era. Within the University his 'remoteness and shy diffidence, which . . . kept him so much to himself', his lack of 'superficial bonhomie', added to his authority.[23] Yet Caird 'never lost his temper'.[24] He had close friends among the professoriate, especially Duncan Weir (Oriental Languages, 1850–76; and Clerk of Senate, 1855–76), John Nichol (English Language and Literature, 1862–99), John Veitch (Logic and Rhetoric, 1864–94) and, above all, his brother Edward (Moral Philosophy, 1866–94), who 'was in constant, and, during the session, almost daily communication with him, for a period of twenty-eight years . . . on subjects of philosophy, theology, or University affairs'.[25] Meanwhile, John Caird's quiet authority, his 'unassuming personal worth, and most lovable character', his 'entire absence of self-seeking' gave him great influence over his fellow professors more generally.[26] Though small of stature, he was a great figure within the University. His 'quiet dignity, his urbanity, his modest, shy courtesy' towards students induced quiet when he addressed them, in marked contrast to the Glasgow tradition of disrupting public occasions.[27]

While viewing himself as unprepared for the principalship, and while detaching himself from most Senate business during his years as professor, Caird had a significant role in the latter stages of Barclay's principalship both as the Principal's confidant and in fund-raising for the Gilmorehill buildings, when his persuasiveness was used 'to the uttermost'.[28] Caird evidently settled quickly to his new duties. Aided perhaps by his early experience in business, Caird had a 'rare business capacity, presiding over meetings with tact, urbanity and judgment'. What Caird particularly lacked preparation for was the financial side of the post, which inspired 'constant' visits to Greenock to consult his successful businessman brother.[29]

Caird was a conciliator. As Principal, 'constantly appealed to by all parties', he 'had often to mediate between them'. His marked emphasis on fairness and toleration helped considerably in this process.[30] He was not by nature a controversialist, and he devoted great effort to preventing the recurrence of the sorts of bitter disputes among professors which had plagued the University earlier in the century. Thus, while he gave firm and prominent backing to the higher education of women, even on that issue he allowed others – notably his brother Edward – largely to make the running when differences of view surfaced in the Senate. His admiring biographer only slightly exaggerated in remarking that he 'seemed to be the common denominator through whom both sides in every controversy became conscious of a unity of purpose'.[31]

At times Caird struck observers as patient 'almost to a fault'. Yet for all his moderation Caird faced up to difficult issues – and people. Thus as Principal he stood up to the attacks made on the Senate before the 1889 Act (see below, pp. 54–5).[32] His courage and determination were evident when he encouraged the tempestuous Andrew Buchanan (Institutes of Medicine, 1839–76) to retire once he lost touch with advances in his subject – and lost control of his class.

2.4 *Andrew Buchanan, Professor of the Institutes of Medicine 1839–76.*

Caird was revered locally as a great figure in the Scottish Church, and in Scottish life more generally, who was closely associated with the city. This high standing was assisted by the fact that, like Barclay, Caird studiously avoided public controversy. Less well suited to interaction with the city's secular worthies were the Principal's almost reclusive habits. He avoided public speaking, other than preaching, outside the University. Also, 'In a drawing-room or a social gathering he was never really a success'. He displayed a 'courtly but heavy solemnity which always gave to those who encountered him in social gatherings the somewhat depressing sensation that they were in the presence of a walking cathedral'! While Mrs Caird kept the Principal's shyness in check, they seldom entertained outside the University.[33] Nonetheless, Caird felt good relations with the city to be of great importance, and he was on friendly terms with many key businessmen and municipal leaders. The Principal was very courteous, and he attended 'important public occasions' when he 'might be counted upon to speak wisely and well'.[34] Thus the city liked and respected John 'as an honour and glory to the town'.[35] In any event, within the University Caird's solemnity and austerity were more assets than liabilities. Even his moments of embarrassment added to an almost legendary prestige. For example, it was fondly recalled that when, during a University sermon, he 'burst out into a magnificent peroration ending with a wild crescendo shout of "Light, light, give us more light!"', the Bedellus turned up the gas.[36]

The University needed an effective personal approach by the Principal during the early Gilmorehill years, not only because of the institution's troubled recent past but also because the University had a very slight administrative structure. During this period the University's finances were managed by lawyers in the city centre, and the unpaid secretary of Court was also a lawyer there; the only full-time administrators were the assistant secretary of Court and the registrar. There was not even an office for the Principal: Caird conducted his work from his study in Professors' Square, where he had retained his original house as professor of divinity.[37]

Another aspect of the Principal's importance was his role in the complex system of government bequeathed to the University by the 1858 Act and Commissioners. The Principal was the only individual with permanent places on both Senate and Court,[38] and Caird made clear that his role on the latter was not merely as the spokesman for the Senate. Because he saw the Principal as representing the University as a whole, he felt the need to mediate among the various constitutional bodies. In a period when the notion of a full-time, non-teaching principal was still somewhat controversial, Caird's allies emphasised that there was much for him to do in a University 'where the professors have very large classes to manage, where there is an immense amount of small details of business which somebody must attend to, and where there is often somebody wanted to represent the University and consult with other people'.[39] Usually Caird was present for the whole of the meetings of Senate and Court, which often lasted 'several hours', and was prepared across the whole range of the business discussed. In Senate, he curbed 'digression or desultory talk', bringing to bear 'a quick appreciation of whatever might be urged on either side, impartiality, unfailing courtesy, and geniality'.[40] In Court he took a particularly strong lead regarding professorial appointments, which he thought crucial to the welfare of the institution. Caird also made strenuous efforts to retain professors who were in danger of being lured elsewhere. While he did not usually chair committees, the Principal frequently attended them. Those who took him for granted found themselves sternly, if quietly, rebuked.[41] Thus Caird was influential though he sometimes found himself on the losing side of Senate votes.

For the Court the early Gilmorehill years were a transitional period. Its early membership was dominated by aristocratic, clerical and legal interests, but by about 1880 industrialists and merchants became more numerous, albeit within a pattern of continuing strength for the Church of Scotland and, to a lesser extent, the Conservative Party.[42] A particularly contentious part of the Court's business was the appointment of professors. As in the other Scottish Courts, members were subjected to considerable pressure, notably when advocates of a Glasgow candidate had tried to deny Lister his chair. In particular, there was a constant risk that the intense rivalry between the Church of Scotland and the Free Church, strongly felt in the General Council in these years, would spill over into chair decisions. To judge from repeated accusations made before the 1876 Royal Commission, the Court sometimes proved susceptible to local and partisan rather than professional considerations. This situation annoyed many Glasgow professors, who unsuccessfully pressed for special panels of senators, along the lines of late twentieth-century appointment committees, which would advise the Court concerning the professional suitability of applicants.

With the exception of the self-interested and extreme Andrew Buchanan,[43] critics of the Glasgow Court usually called for it to show more rather than less resolve. Even allowing for the narrow scope of its powers regarding resources, the Court was passive in financial matters during these years. Yet it proved more energetic in dealing with other universities and in recognising outside courses, even though prior to 1889 Glasgow was significantly less active and less cosmopolitan in this respect than was Edinburgh. The Court was also vigorous, if impotent, in noting the many restrictions on its authority by the Commissioners, even on matters as detailed as the date on which an assistant's appointment would expire.[44] Moreover, at least occasionally the Court proved diligent in investigating breakdowns of academic effectiveness such as the 'unseemly hootings and noises' which plagued the Physiology class in 1875 – a crisis which resulted in a reprimand to the class delivered by the Principal in person. Also, despite the fact that members represented various constituencies, the Court had acquired an esprit de corps by the 1870s.[45]

Nevertheless, during the 1870s and 1880s the Senate remained the University's foremost decision-making body. In 1875, for example, it met twenty-one times, covering a great many items of business, with an average of 17.5 of its twenty-eight members present at some time during a meeting. The Senate's continued primary control over resources necessitated several standing committees and guaranteed repeated discussions of important topics such as accounts, property, salaries, fee levels and arrangements for assistantships. Also, by the 1870s the faculties – Arts, Divinity, Law and Medicine – were active and influential, too much so for the taste of some senators. The system created by the 1858 Act, and the increasing calls for further legislation, also frequently involved senators in dealings with their counterparts in other Scottish universities. Moreover, despite the ambiguities created by the 1858 statute, there was continual cooperation between Senate and Court, notably on recognition questions and on appeals.[46]

The General Council enhanced its influence from 1868 when the University's graduates gained a parliamentary seat, held jointly with their counterparts from Aberdeen; this development dramatically increased the number of graduates who enrolled.[47] Yet, despite the transitional arrangements allowed by the 1858 Act for those long-time students who had never graduated, the General Council's membership was skewed toward particular occupations. In the mid-1870s, of the enrolled members from Glasgow and vicinity, only 13% were 'merchants' and 12% 'teachers etc'; the vast bulk were professionals, especially clergymen (31%) and doctors (28%).[48] There is no reason to suppose that the approximately two-thirds of the membership resident in Ireland, London and elsewhere had a different profile. John Caird, who construed narrowly the Council's right even to communicate, proved adept at presiding over and managing the Council's sometimes tempestuous meetings. While General Council committees played an active part in university government, they by no means always got their way. For example, during the early Gilmorehill period the Council agitated repeatedly for a broader choice of subjects, but ran up against the structures the Commissioners (cf. p. 26 above) had set up as well as the Senate's academic conservatism. Still, the Council was no cipher: in concert with its counterparts in the other Scottish universities Glasgow's General Council successfully pressed for a Royal Commission on the universities, which neither the Senate nor the Court desired.[49]

The 1876 Commission, a response to the perceived constitutional and curricular inadequacy of the 1858 Act and its commissioners, provided a forum for an extremely detailed exchange of views between the professoriate, representatives of the general councils and key politicians. While academics may have feared an inquisition, they were questioned – in marked contrast to the

1820s – with considerable respect and were given ample opportunity to present their own suggestions for improvement. The General Council representatives from Glasgow, as elsewhere, put forward sometimes sweeping proposals for curricular and constitutional reform, requesting in particular extra representation on the Court, greater flexibility in calling meetings and improved access to information about the University. Yet in the event the views of the Commission accorded more with those of John Caird and his professors. This outcome partly reflected the academics' increased popularity after the 1858 reforms; it also indicated that the general councils suffered politically from low attendance at meetings and domination by local graduates arguably unrepresentative of the broader membership. Also, the Council's desire for extra leverage was narrowly presented: it had no interest in 'popular' influence over the University, or even in representation for external notables such as the Lord Provost.[50] Thus the Commission rejected the idea of adding extra members to the Court, even with balanced additions from the General Council and the Senate, and it was content for the Senate to keep its control of academic property. Likewise, the professors' spirited defence of their workload and their teaching expertise helped to block the radicals' demands for three-term teaching and for the recognition of external lecturers in Arts subjects. While controversy about the need for further university reform continued, there was no immediate legislation either on these subjects or on other major points of discussion such as the call for a broader choice (especially in relation to natural sciences) for Arts students.

In terms of the actual rather than the ideal curriculum, the early Gilmorehill years were a time of consolidation rather than of sharp change. This was particularly true in Arts, whose students made up more than half the total during this period. Boards of Studies were introduced, and there was significant growth in honours – in a form which assumed private study and the prior completion of a general degree – albeit from a very low base.[51] Yet the great bulk of Arts students continued either to pursue classes which suited their interests or, if they intended graduating, followed the rather inflexible structure laid down in 1861. There was a broad consensus among Glasgow professors, including Kelvin, behind the objectives of 'liberal culture' underlying this framework, though there was also a desire, not confined to natural scientists, to permit students more scope for studying such subjects than the current structure allowed. Yet even Kelvin did not favour a separate science faculty or degree, and the Bachelor of Science introduced in 1872–3 in response to General Council agitation attracted few takers.[52] Edward Caird's approach, which treated all systematic knowledge as 'scientific', in the Humboldtian fashion, was preferred – reflecting the German influence on many Glasgow professors in this period. In Divinity, the pattern whereby students first studied Arts before proceeding to the divinity 'hall' was retained. On paper there was greater change in Law, but the two-year (later three-year) BL founded in 1878 was not very successful. The Glasgow legal curriculum, long constricted, still needed assistance from another university in the late 1870s, for example. Thus, although from the 1850s the upper branches of the legal profession required entrants to be graduates, even in the 1870s Glasgow confined its law teaching mainly to the Scots Law and conveyancing lectures that all would-be solicitors had to attend. These lectures were given early (on Gilmorehill) and late (in the city centre) to accommodate apprentices working in city law firms.[53] It was in Medicine, still attracting a high proportion of the institution's students, that the 1870s and 1880s saw marked academic changes, some of which had their origins in the 1858 Medical Act and subsequent interactions among commissioners, the GMC, the medical colleges, the universities and the hospitals. In 1871 students had to complete four years and pass three (from 1877, four) professional examinations for a medical degree, though only a year had to be spent at the University, making it possible to take attractive lectures in the extramural colleges. Fulfilling the University's requirements for the primary medical degree entitled students to take degrees in both medicine (MB) and surgery (CM), though students had to pay an extra fee – optional until 1881 – to the University for the surgery degrees. Yet there was instability in medical teaching arrangements, particularly on the clinical side, where relations with the hospitals, including the Western, were often fraught.[54]

The 1870s and 1880s were also decades of consolidation for the Glasgow professoriate. Even as their numbers gradually increased, their income continued to vary considerably; six professors earned more than £1,000 after expenses while seven had less than £400. Enthusiasm for fee rises reflected the Senate's view in 1875 that 'Professors seem to be about the only class who have not benefited by the continual rise of prices during this century'.[55] Fortunately for the professoriate, their incomes rose as student numbers increased between the mid-1870s and the mid-1880s. The Commissioners had augmented the salaries of various medical chairs, though for the clinicians income from private practice was more important. During the 1870s and 1880s bitter disputes among professors were largely confined to medical chairs, where the foundation of clinical posts created problems in the 1870s regarding the rights of their holders vis-à-vis the professors of medicine and surgery.[56] By the 1870s evidently little remained of the acrimony between the 'Faculty' professors and the holders of more recently founded chairs. For the resident professorial families there was frequent social interaction: 'Shut in by the same gates, able to get to each others' houses almost dry-shod in all weathers, occupied with the same interests, the little group of families met almost daily, and lifelong friends were made'. This intramural socialising included dinner parties, which the John Cairds sometimes attended.[57]

Unlike many of their predecessors on the High Street, the professors of the early Gilmorehill period had much to do with the city. They mixed socially with laymen. In 1877, for example, the Lord Provost invited Richard (Greek, 1875–89) and Caroline Jebb to dine in order to meet General and Mrs Ulysses Grant. Nor was there a perceived separation: even an incoming couple such as the Jebbs were not immune from the psychological effects of the failure of the City of Glasgow Bank in 1878.[58] The professors also sometimes were active in public life outside Gilmorehill. Political interventions usually focused on general issues such as the electoral franchise or particular educational topics such as Bible teaching in schools. The professors' broader public interventions were more diverse. The astronomer Grant daily supplied information about the correct time to the city and the port in return for civic generosity to his subject. More spectacularly, William Tennant Gairdner (Practice of Medicine, 1862–1900; knighted 1898) served the city from 1863 to 1872 on an unpaid, part-time basis as its first Medical Officer of Health. Reacting sympathetically to the acute social problems of Victorian Glasgow, other professors felt a strong commitment to social reform, notably Edward Caird, who campaigned tirelessly for various causes, especially widened access to higher education. Some professors also had significant national roles. Allen Thomson, for example, in addition to being 'one of the most active and influential citizens of Glasgow', was president of the British Association in 1876 and received an honorary doctorate from Oxford.[59]

In terms of their actual jobs, professors worked hard at lecturing and marking during the six-month session. In 1875, for instance, the newly arrived Richard Jebb reported that 'I get up at 7, have tea at 7.30, take a class from 8 to 9, breakfast at 9, take another class from 10 to 11, and a third from 2 to 3. As a rule I have to work three or four more hours a day preparing or looking over papers'.[60] In addition, while having an assistant who took the junior class, Jebb gave a well and prestigiously attended series of lectures open to the public. Sunday walks provided some relief, but professors, if they responded to the growing attention to research did so during the other half of the year when 'no one remained in the College'.[61] The six months were a significant 'carrot' in attempts to lure recruits from south of the Border such as the Cantabrian Jebb and to retain high-flying Scots such as Kelvin, who spent his summers in Cambridge and Largs.

Thus for many of Glasgow's professors during the early Gilmorehill years the months from April to October were not for holidays alone. As Hugh Blackburn recognised, 'Scotch University professorships, or certain of them, are endowed research appointments'; according to George Ramsay (Humanity, 1863–1906), the professors were 'anxious to advance their respective subjects'. The future Lord Kelvin, meanwhile, had already formulated the modern notion that research and teaching enrich each other.[62] Accordingly, quite a number of the Glasgow professors of the 1870s worked diligently during the spring and summer – allowing for one holiday to recover from the session and another to provide rest beforehand – on publications and other professional endeavours. Jebb produced extensive scholarly and popular works, campaigned for English schools of archaeology at Athens and Rome and helped to found a scholarly journal, meanwhile acquiring an honorary doctorate from Harvard.[63] John Nichol became one of the first serious scholars of American literature.[64] In philosophy, with John Veitch (the editor of Sir William Hamilton's works) and Edward Caird, 'Glasgow's philosophical fame probably stood as high as that of any University in any country'.[65] In science, where considerable research activity also took place, there was a growing recognition that the availability of assistants, and of equipment, was prerequisite to serious research.[66] In medicine, by the mid-1870s there was a consensus that professors in 'scientific' chairs – such as the eminent John Cleland, FRS (Anatomy, 1877–1909) – should spurn private practice so that they could research as well as teach,[67] while those in 'practical' (i.e. clinical) chairs could pursue private practice as well as teaching. In some instances

2.5 *John Nichol, Professor of English Language and Literature 1862–89.*

2.6
John Veitch, Professor of Logic and Rhetoric 1864–94.

even clinical professors sustained research, notably Gairdner who kept publishing and attained the presidency of the British Medical Association.[68]

Yet, during the early Gilmorehill years, teaching had primacy in Glasgow, as in other Scottish universities.[69] The professors gave nearly all the lectures. After the door was shut against latecomers, the lecture began with a prayer. Indeed, at Glasgow as elsewhere, lectures – at least in Arts subjects – were 'a sort of lay preaching', with a 'willingness to make connections between diverse subjects, an interest in general theories, and a tendency to make use of systematic classifications and abstract categories'.[70] Glasgow professors such as Veitch and Edward Caird believed strongly in the 'personal element' of teaching, which was 'necessarily distinctive'; they would have resisted any system in which the work of the class, verbal and written, was subordinate to examinations, especially if set by others.[71]

No doubt there was still much indifferent instruction. Despite his theories Veitch's hypercritical attitude, for example, alienated his students. Yet the

2.7 *Edward Caird, Professor of Moral Philosophy 1866–94.*

generally highly talented professors of this era treated their teaching, and especially their lectures, as the focal point of their working lives. Perhaps the most revered of the professors of the day was Edward Caird. A prize-winning product of both Glasgow and Oxford, Caird took his teaching very seriously, rewriting 'the whole substance' of his 120 lectures each year, devoting the entire autumn and winter to teaching and preparation. Caird's teaching methods may be taken as characteristic of the era in Arts subjects. Meeting the class daily at 8, he only occasionally looked at his notes as he expounded his subject, giving the impression of 'a great and good man saturated with much reflexion on the subjects that mean and matter most for humanity'. Then, during the second hour, he called on his students individually, coaxing those who feared the reactions of their peers. Alternatively, Caird would have the student authors read aloud the best essays, which had been painstakingly marked by him in advance. Although lacking eloquence, he was approachable, simple and sincere, with great impact on his students. Like many of his colleagues, Caird attended, and spoke at, annual class suppers, where he was the centre of attention.[72] Jebb had a more mixed record, perhaps more typical of the professors of his day. He was stern when confronted by lack of preparation,

2.8 *William Tennant Gairdner, Professor of the Practice of Medicine 1862–1900.*

and he lacked the common touch, particularly in dealing with local students from humble backgrounds, 'Glasgow Scotch not being among his accomplishments'. Yet Jebb 'grew in favour with his students from year to year'. He 'transform[ed] his audience into a class' and, in his renderings of Greek texts, 'not only did the thing, but created an ideal for us by doing it'. When he returned to his class after a serious illness the students made a presentation, with the Principal in the chair; later the students elected him president of the Glasgow Dialectic Society.[73]

In the sciences and medicine, lectures remained important. Yet Kelvin's earlier innovation of having students, like their German counterparts, carry out experiments rather than simply watch demonstrations spread to medicine when John McKendrick took up the physiology chair in 1876. There was also high-quality clinical teaching: Gairdner struck many as 'an exceptionally attractive lecturer, teaching the diagnosis of disease with singular thoroughness, and illuminating the subject . . . by means of a wide literary culture'.[74]

Students' responses to teaching depended, naturally, on what they were offered. Thus Kelvin's students, although they 'had a profound admiration for his genius . . . found that same genius rather trying, for its possessor used to get into a state of mathematical exaltation and soar to heights . . . where no ordinary mind could follow'.[75] John Caird's divinity students were more unambiguously positive:

> His coming to the Divinity Hall was truly a time of awakening among us. Whispered conversation, surreptitious reading of books and newspapers, once so common, now suddenly ceased . . . He did us an invaluable service in keeping us steadily at work. . . [through] the oral examination.[76]

As the students were subject to strict discipline regarding punctuality and recitation, they were disruptive when bored or confronted by a professor who could not keep order. Yet they responded in a strongly positive way to diligent, caring and – especially – inspiring teachers. Thus Edward Caird, though not an exciting speaker, was the object of strong adulation. One of the few occasions when he found it difficult to control the class came on a day when his students were excited by the news that their professor was to receive an honorary degree from St Andrews – a development of which the somewhat other-worldly Caird was unaware![77]

Good lectures inspired student discussion, informally or in student societies such as 'The Witenagemote' founded by students of Edward Caird. Also, a minority of students such as Henry Jones were strongly motivated by examinations and by the student-determined prizes – a custom which created a strong sense of identity for the class as a whole while rewarding merit in a way the professors generally approved.[78] Conscientious students found that they had to work very hard, including preparations for classes, oral examinations, exercises, essays and written class and degree examinations. Ramsay told the 1876 Commission that 'I never have known a year pass without students in my class breaking down in health . . . I find it necessary constantly to warn students against over-work, especially those engaged in other work besides their class-work . . . Our students work with a daily sense of competition before them'.[79]

Students, then, played a major role in determining the academic atmosphere of the University. During the early Gilmorehill years, when fees flowed directly to professors, they also had a major impact on their teachers' prosperity. As Table 2.1 indicates, there was a huge rise in student numbers during this period, from 1,279 in 1870 to 2,261 in 1884, especially during the years 1874–9; this boom, also characteristic of the other Scottish universities, persisted despite the city's financial crisis in 1878. Roughly four-fifths of the students

Table 2.1
Student Numbers, 1861–1913

Year	*Total*	*Year*	*Total*
1861	1140	1888	—
1862	1266	1889	2156
1863	1242	1890	2187
1864	1179	1891	2133
1865	1238	1892	2167
1866	1204	1893	2054
1867	1273	1894	1944
1868	1280	1895	1835
1869	1282	1896	1871
1870	1279	1897	1836
1871	1349	1898	1966
1872	1258	1899	2030
1873	1333	1900	2038
1874	1484	1901	2068
1875	1601	1902	2158
1876	1773	1903	2219
1877	2018	1904	2267
1878	2096	1905	2356
1879	2235	1906	2505
1880	2304	1907	2586
1881	2320	1908	2699
1882	2275	1909	2728
1883	2212	1910	2790
1884	2261	1911	2794
1885	2241	1912	2835
1886	2260	1913	2916
1887	2188		

Source: Anderson, *Education and Opportunity*, Appendix 1, 350, 354 were Scottish, with 13 per cent from England and Wales but only a small percentage from outside the UK. Within Scotland, almost two-thirds came from the West, but there were still substantial proportions from East Central Scotland, and from the Highlands and North; the latter group was vulnerable to condescension from fellow students.[80]

At Glasgow, as elsewhere, the expansion and reform of Scotland's secondary schools encouraged the campaign for university entrance examinations. Fought out publicly before the 1876 Commission, this battle pitted those who demanded better-prepared students against those who feared that such an examination would discourage poorer students and those of more mature years. Most of the contestants on both sides shared the assumption that Scottish schools did not prepare students adequately, especially in classical languages and in mathematics. Glasgow introduced its own entrance examination from 1883 because the University's attempts to promote a Scotland-wide scheme in 1875 and 1882 failed, perhaps because the institution had greater confidence than its counterparts that its key feeder schools could reach the desired standard. Yet the examination was applied only to entrants under seventeen, and throughout the 1860s, 1870s and 1880s the percentage entering Glasgow direct from primary schools remained high. For Medicine, too, lack of precise selectivity was the norm, apart from a requirement of prior general education.[81]

Educational origins had implications for social origins. As shown by Table 2.2, in 1880 just under a fifth of Glasgow's students came from professional homes, and a similar proportion, despite worries that businessmen saw no need for a lengthy university education for their sons, came from commercial and industrial backgrounds. The 'working-class' contingent was still relatively large – about a quarter – and the agricultural element remained sizeable at an eighth.[82] During this period the number of bursaries rose rapidly – a by-product, perhaps, of the perceived greater constitutional openness of the University after 1858.[83]

In Medicine, where there was a strong material incentive to graduate, money problems and failed exams – part of a deliberate weeding-out process – meant that about one-third of those who matriculated did not qualify; of those who did, a considerable minority obtained their qualification elsewhere, notably through the Faculty of Physicians and Surgeons of Glasgow, in relation to which the University, like its sister institutions, remained wary, albeit less so than before the 1858 Medical Act. Still, more students graduated at the University in Medicine than in Arts. Arts graduations were rising, and about an eighth of these graduates took honours. Yet only a small proportion – unusually low even by Scottish standards – of Arts students either completed the curriculum or graduated, in part because many students were working

Table 2.2
Father's Occupation of Matriculants, 1860–1910

	1860	*1870*	*1880*	*1890*	*1900*	*1905*	*1910*
Professional	29.2%	27.5%	18.1%	22.8%	24.7%	29.2%	26.7%
Commercial & Industrial	22.6%	26.8%	20.4%	23.3%	25.3%	23.0%	25.3%
Agricultural	11.9%	13.0%	12.5%	8.8%	5.2%	3.3%	2.7%
Intermediate	17.3%	15.9%	22.6%	17.1%	23.7%	20.6%	20.4%
Working-Class	19.0%	16.7%	26.4%	28.0%	21.1%	23.9%	24.9%

Notes

1. Excludes those not given, uncertain or dead. (2.3%, 15.8%, 10.5%, 15.0%, 2.0%, 0.9%, & 3.5% respectively).
2. Professional:
   Proprietors and gentlemen; ministers; doctors; lawyers; teachers; officers and officials; other professionals.
   Commercial and Industrial:
   Bankers etc; manufacturers etc; large traders; 'merchants'; managers and agents.
   Agricultural:
   Farmers; crofters and small farmers; factors etc.
   Intermediate:
   Small businesses; shopkeepers; clerks and minor officials.
   Working-Class:
   Artisans and skilled workers; policemen etc; labourers and farm servants; miners; domestic servants and gardeners.

Source: Recalculated from: Anderson, *Education and Opportunity*, Table 8.7, 310–11.

either during the term and/or in the vacations, whether in city offices, on farms or in Highland classrooms. Others, especially the younger students, still treated university courses as a form of secondary education beyond which they did not intend to progress. Yet a significant positive by-product of these patterns was the considerable number of young Glaswegians who, like the future Prime Minister Andrew Bonar Law during the 1870s, attended classes part-time for a year or more.[84]

Glasgow's students had little communal life, other than the camaraderie of the classroom, during the early Gilmorehill period. Most commuted from home, while others lived in lodgings of varying quality. On Gilmorehill the new buildings did not even provide a place for students to eat, and – as Henry Jones recalled – 'there was no Student's Union, nor any place within or connected with the university where students meet for social purposes'.[85] The only facility was a gymnasium, opened in 1872, as the result of a student initiative. There were societies, which Principal Caird did his best to encourage. Some had been established well before 1870, but there were also new ones such as the rugby club (1869) and football club (1873), and – in 1881 – Glasgow University Athletic Club (GUAC), which from the outset attempted to improve recreational facilities for students.[86] But while these institutions moved the collective life of the student body beyond the standards of mid-century, such provision was still very limited in comparison to later periods.

These shortcomings in services to students reflected the strained finances of the University. By the early years of the Gilmorehill period, annual deficits were accruing, in part because the new buildings had increased recurrent expenses. There was also the large burden of lingering debt on the buildings – a 'millstone about the neck of the University', in Nichol's words[87] – which the government thought should be paid off by selling the Hunterian coins and the Library's rare books. While Glasgow shared with other Scottish universities the problem that rises in professorial fee income did not accrue directly to the institution, it had the particular difficulty that its annual Government grant under the 1858 Act was well below Edinburgh's and, in relative terms, below those of the other two universities as well. Glasgow showed modest surpluses from the mid-1870s to the mid-1890s, but as various witnesses to the 1876 Commission made clear there was little extra cash for any purpose.[88]

While the critical issue of government finance to Glasgow and other Scottish universities remained unresolved, bequests of £45,000 raised by the

2.9 *The opening of the Bute Hall, 1884.*

Marquess of Bute and of £60,000 from the shipbuilder Charles Randolph allowed the University both to wipe out the remaining deficit and to complete those major parts of the new buildings which had not been erected in the 1870s.[89] Completed in 1882, the Bute and Randolph Halls, which had been modified by the original architect's sons George Gilbert and John Oldrid Scott, filled two important gaps. They provided the University with spaces for religious services, examinations and the like, while also giving the institution an appropriate place to host visitors from the town, which was developing its own magnificent City Chambers at this time for its ever more ambitious civic elite. As Allen Thomson had put the need fourteen years earlier, the University lacked 'the means of assembling and admitting a portion of the public within its own precincts on great ceremonial or other occasions'.[90] The festive opening of the Bute Hall in 1884 symbolised these dual functions. Two thousand worthies, including many civic dignitaries and people drawn from outside the University staff, attended the opening conversazione. These guests were welcomed by the Principal and entertained by music and by objects on show in the library, the museum and the laboratories of Sir William Thomson.[91] Thus the occasion was more than the culmination of the building plans for Gilmorehill. It also represented a celebration of the 'entire sympathy which subsists between the city and the University', as Disraeli had noted when pleading for funds for this purpose in his rectorial address eleven years earlier.[92] By the mid-1880s any remaining doubts, in academic or lay minds, about the wisdom of the move from the High Street had evaporated.

Notes and References

1. Macaulay, 'Scott'. Cf. Brown and Moss, *University*, 47.
2. A. Thomson, 'Prefatory Note', *Introductory addresses delivered at the Opening of the University of Glasgow Session 1870–1* (Edinburgh, 1871), xix.
3. 'New Buildings', 37.
4. In the case of the Museum, unfortunately, the limits to the University's finances and competing priorities prevented systematic development of the assets, which the institution more than once attempted to deplete – C. H. Brock, 'Dr William Hunter's Museum, Glasgow University', *Journal of the Society for the Bibliography of Natural History*, 9 (1980), 408–9.
5. Thomson, 'Prefatory Note', xxiv.
6. 'New Buildings', 38, a comparison obscured in the facing map by displaying only part of the old grounds. The University sold the park ground, for which at the time there seemed no pressing academic need, in order to reduce the debt remaining from the removal.
7. There was similar satisfaction when the Western opened in 1874 after a separate subscription scheme. Until then, clinical teaching was carried on in the

Royal, with teacher and student transport to and from Gilmorehill classroom by means of omnibuses. Even after the end of this interlude there were problems: the University's increasing alliance with the Western Infirmary led to a breach with the Royal, which established its own medical college.

8. GH, 8 November 1870 (quote); Coutts, *University*, 445–6. The Lord Justice General was a senior Scottish judge; the Lord Dean of Guild was a major civic dignitary.
9. The Lord President was the most senior Scottish judge. The University parliamentary seats provided graduates, who had an additional vote for the purpose, with an advocate in Parliament.
10. Murray, *Old College*, 596–7; *Lord Provosts*, 274–5.
11. GH, 8 November 1870.
12. Cf. Brown and Moss, *University*, 31.
13. Caird, 'Introductory Address in the Faculty of Divinity', *Introductory Addresses*, 13–42.
14. It was also rumoured that the Queen, who had been greatly impressed by his preaching at Balmoral, favoured the appointment (GH, 1 August 1898).
15. E. Caird, *Memoir*, xv, xcvii (quote); J. Caird, 'The Unity of the Sciences' in *University Addresses* (Glasgow, 1898); G. Newlands, 'Religion in the University' (2001 seminar paper, University of Glasgow, 1997/98); H. Jones, 'Principal Caird' (Glasgow, 1898).
16. Cf. E. Caird, *Memoir*, lx–lxi; C. L. Warr, *Principal Caird* (Edinburgh 1926), 214–15.
17. E. Caird, *Memoir*, xcvi.
18. *University Sermons Preached before the University of Glasgow 1873–1898* (Glasgow, 1898). Cf. G. A. Gibson, *Life of Sir William Tennant Gairdner* (Glasgow, 1912), 467–8.
19. See J. D. Hoeveler, *James McCosh and the Scottish Intellectual Tradition: From Glasgow to Princeton* (Princeton, 1981); P. C. Kemeny, *Princeton in the Nation's Service: Religious Ideals and Educational Practice, 1868–1928* (New York, 1998), chs 1 and 2, which emphasises the philosophical and religious cautiousness of McCosh who, unlike John Caird, had joined the Free Church in 1843.
20. 'The Unity of The Sciences', 8 (emphasis in original). Cf. Caird, 'The Study of History', in *University Addresses*, 226, and Warr, *Principal Caird* (Edinburgh, 1926), 169.
21. 'The Personal Element in Teaching', in *University Addresses*, 364.
22. 'General and Professional Education', in *University Addresses*, 376.
23. Warr, *Principal Caird*, 164.
24. GH, 1 August 1898.
25. E. Caird, *Memoir*, lxiv–lxv (quote); Warr, *Principal Caird*, 201–2. The Clerk of Senate, an academic elected by the Senate to administer its affairs under the presidency of the Principal, often played a key role in University affairs in this period – as before and since.
26. Coutts, *University*, 447; Sir William Gairdner, in E. Caird, *Memoir*, cxxxv.
27. Warr, *Principal Caird*, 204.
28. Warr, *Principal Caird*, 192; E. Caird, *Memoir*, xciv; Mackie, *University*, 291 (also quoted by Lloyd, 'Communities').

29. Warr, *Principal Caird*, 196.
30. E. Caird, *Memoir*, cv.
31. Warr, *Principal Caird*, 197. As a conciliator he was complemented by Allen Thomson, whose 'tact and persuasiveness' made him very influential in the Senate, though not influential enough to persuade Arts professors of the need for extensive equipment in fields such as medicine (Gibson, *Gairdner*, 471, 473–4).
32. Jones, 'Caird', 12; E. Caird, *Memoir*, cvi.
33. Warr, *Principal Caird*, 170, 192, 203, 211.
34. GH, 1 August 1898. Cf. E. Caird, *Memoir*, cx.
35. J. H. Leckie, quoted in Warr, *Principal Caird*, 202.
36. D. M. Malloch, *The Book of Glasgow Anecdote* (London, 1913), 256.
37. Brown and Moss, *University*, 103; Warr, *Principal Caird*, 201.
38. Brown and Moss, *University*, 103.
39. E. Caird, R.C. 1876 III/II, 216 Q.9289.
40. Professor Dickson, quoted in E. Caird, *Memoir*, cxv, cxvi.
41. E. Caird, *Memoir*, cvii–cviii; Caird to Richard Jebb, 1 May 1889, in C. Jebb, *Life and Letters of Sir Richard Claverhouse Jebb O.M. Litt.D.* (Cambridge, 1907), 268.
42. Lloyd, 'Communities', 67, 70, 76.
43. 'The University Court of the University of Glasgow' (1876).
44. Caird, R.C. 1876 III/II 202, Q.9175; Lloyd, 'Relationships', 115, 122–3; Court Minutes (hereafter CMN), 14 July 1875.
45. CMN, 1 and 8 December 1875; Anderson Kirkwood, secretary of court, R.C. 1876 III/II 378 Q.10699.
46. For example, CMN, 26 May 1875, 22 July 1885. Faculties were groups of cognate departments which (under authority delegated by the Senate) supervised the admission, teaching and examining of students.
47. Anderson, *Education and Opportunity*; Lloyd, 'Communities'.
48. Calculated from figures in R.C. 1876 III/II, J. Cleland Burns, 154, Q.8703.
49. Professor Dickson, quoted in E. Caird, *Memoir*, cxv; J. Cleland Burns, R.C. 1876 III/II, 155 Q.8708; Lloyd, 'Communities', 56; Anderson, *Education and Opportunity*, 79–81; GCMN, 27 October 1875.
50. R.C. 1876 III/II, J. Cleland Burns, 157 Q.8710, 162 QQ.8733–5.
51. On the complex origins of the honours (i.e. more specialised) degree introduced by the 1858 Act, see G. E. Davie, *The Democratic Intellect: Scotland and her Universities in the Nineteenth Century* (Edinburgh, 1961), 41ff, 65–6, 69; Anderson, *Education and Opportunity*, 43–4, 71. Boards of Studies scrutinised proposals to establish new courses and amend existing ones.
52. R.C. 1876 III/II 305–27. The degrees offered in Science, Engineering and Law were all in the Arts Faculty.
53. Coutts, *University*, 453; Anderson, *Education and Opportunity*, 73.
54. Coutts, *University*, 570–5; Lloyd, 'Search for Legitimacy'; M. W. Dupree, 'The Development of Medical Education from 1870–1940' (2001 Seminar paper, 1 Feb. 1996), p. 8; Mackie, *University*, 273–4, 287.
55. SMN, 21 January 1875 (quote); Anderson, 'Professors', 35–6, table 2.
56. Coutts, *University*, 584–5; CMN, 1 and 8 December 1875; R.C. 1876 III/II, 468–85.

57. Jebb, *Life and Letters*, 202 (quote), 208.
58. Jebb, *Life and Letters*, 205 (Richard to Caroline Jebb), 20 September 1877; *ibid.*, 213.
59. *DNB*; OHGM, 317–20.
60. Jebb to Miss Horsley, 5 December 1875 (Jebb, *Life and Letters*, 194).
61. Jebb, *Life and Letters*, 181 (quote); Anderson, 'Professors', 36–7.
62. Edward Caird to Mary Sarah Talbot, 22 August 1893, in H. Jones and J. H. Muirhead, *The Life and Philosophy of Edward Caird* (Glasgow, 1921), 183; R.C. 1876 III/II, 140 Q.8631; R.C. 1876 II/1, 371, Q.2850; R.C. Scientific Instruction, 161, QQ.2669–2670.
63. Jebb, *Life and Letters*, 253 and *passim*.
64. Andrew Hook, 'Research in the Arts' (2001 Seminar paper, 22 Feb. 1996); *DNB*.
65. C. A. Campbell, 'Philosophy', FD 116 (quote), 17. It might have stood higher still if Veitch had not devoted much of his year and his writing to his native Peeblesshire (cf. *DNB*).
66. R.C. 1876 II/I, 225 Q.1748; III/II, 86 Q.3257; III/II, 262–6.
67. Dupree, 'Development', 9–10. Allen Thomson was a central figure in this development: see L. S. Jacyna (ed.), *A Tale of Three Cities: The Correspondence of William Sharpey and Allen Thomson* (London, 1989).
68. *DNB*.
69. R. D. Anderson, 'Ideas of the University in 19th century Scotland: Teaching Versus Research?', in M. Hewitt (ed.), *Scholarship in Victorian Britain* (Leeds, 1998), 1–13.
70. Anderson, *Education and Opportunity*, 32, 31 (quotes); Brown and Moss, *University*, 42.
71. Veitch, R.C. 1876 III/II 250 Q.9530; E. Caird 1876 III/II 222 Q.9351.
72. Jones and Muirhead, *Edward Caird*, 81–5, 112; Jones, *Old Memories*, 131–7; *DNB* (Veitch). For a laudatory account of Nichol's teaching, see Coutts, *University*, 447.
73. Malloch, *Glasgow Anecdote*, 260–1; H. Jones, *Old Memories* (London, [c.1923]) 127; Coutts, *University*, 447–8; Jebb, *Life and Letters*, 186–7, 214, 256.
74. *DNB* (quote); Smith and Wise, *Kelvin*; Dupree, 'Development', 9–10; Hull and Geyer-Kordesch, *Shaping the Medical Profession*, 27–9.
75. Malloch, *Glasgow Anecdote*, 265.
76. Dr Strong, quoted in E. Caird, *Memoir*, lxxi–lxxii.
77. Jones and Muirhead, *Edward Caird*, 80–5, 112.
78. E.g. R. Jebb, R.C.1876 III/II, 430, Q.11096.
79. R.C. 1876 II/I, 962, Q.7708.
80. Anderson, *Education and Opportunity*, 350, 252, 297–8, Table 8.1; Jones, *Old Memories*, 126.
81. Anderson, *Education and Opportunity*, 33–6, 97, 257, 305; Coutts, *University*; Dupree, 'Development', 7.
82. Anderson, *Education and Opportunity*, 310–11, Table 8.7, recalculating the percentages to allow for the exclusion of those classified as 'Not given, uncertain, dead'. The 'professional' and 'commercial and industrial' figures may be

slightly understated, as the closely-related 'intermediate' group seems surprisingly large (at 22.6%) compared to the 6.6% of Arts students 1866 (*Ibid.*, 150–1) and even perhaps the 15.9% and 17.1% of all students in 1870 and 1890 respectively.

83. For the various restrictions in eligibility which limited their impact on meritocratic recruitment, see Medicus, 'University Pamphlets III – Personal Experiences' (Glasgow, 1888), 1–16.
84. Dupree, 'Development', 7–8; J. Bradley, A. Crowther and M. Dupree, 'Mobility and Selection in Scottish University Medical Education, 1858–1886', *Medical History*, 40 (1996), 1–24; Hull and Geyer-Kordesch, *Shaping the Medical Profession*, ch.1; Anderson, *Education and Opportunity*, 74–7, 283–4; Ramsay, R.C. 1876 II/I 965–6 Q.7722. Cf. Mackie, *University*, 287; R. J. Q. Adams, *Bonar Law* (London, 1999), 9.
85. Jones, *Old Memories*, 149.
86. R. O. MacKenna, *Glasgow University Athletic Club: The Story of the First Hundred Years* (Glasgow, 1981), 14–15 and *passim.*
87. 1876 II/I, 487, Q.3780.
88. Mackie, *University*, 278, 286 n. 1; Hugh Blackburn, R. C. 1876 III/II, 138, Q.8623, 142, Q.8647. Glasgow's disadvantage regarding the grant may have been a knock-on effect of the particularly negative view of the institution formed by the commissioners of the 1820s.
89. With the completion of the spire, clock tower and Pearce Lodge (containing parts of the High Street building) in 1888, the original design was in effect complete.
90. 'Prefatory Note', *Introductory Addresses*, xxii.
91. GH, 2 February 1884.
92. 'Inaugural Address . . .' (2nd edn, London, 1873), 32 (quote), 34. The city's boundaries had been extended to include Gilmorehill in 1872.

CHAPTER THREE

ORIGINS OF TRANSFORMATION, 1884–98

The latter half of Caird's principalship was dominated by a second dose of government-led university reform. Already strong at the time of the 1876 commission, agitation for a further instalment of legislation became acute during the 1880s. Even semi-detached professors such as Richard Jebb were drawn into controversies concerning, in particular, the division of labour between schools and universities with respect to relatively young, comparatively poorly prepared prospective students. Glasgow's General Council, while worried about the financial impact of particular proposals, pressed hard for an additional university reform act which would include the transfer of the Senate's executive powers to the Court. Evidently the Council's active members were more concerned with, than impressed by, the vigour of Glasgow's Senate, which was critical of proposed legislation.[1] In 1885 the Senate met twenty-three times, covering a huge range of issues: more than half the senators attended a typical meeting, and the Principal and the Clerk of Senate were present at them all. Presumably the General Council paid more attention to the relative torpor of the body on which they were represented, the Court, which met only five times in the same year.

These were volatile years for the General Council. Radical elements, led in the 1880s by D. C. McVail's University Council Association of Glasgow, failed to obtain their goal of forcing on the University the recognition of extramural teaching in Arts and of affiliated institutions more generally. Edward Caird led the resistance, arguing for the diversification and deepening of teaching within the University. Aided latterly by a sympathetic pressure group, the Glasgow University Club, Caird succeeded in infiltrating the opposing group; he guided the business committee of the General Council (which he chaired during the frenetic years between 1884 and 1888) in rejecting the proposal for broad recognition, which was revived unsuccessfully in the 1890s.[2] Apparently a major reason for Caird's success, apart from his positive suggestion of additional junior teaching staff within the University, was his backing for the General Council's demands that the Court obtain more power and that the Council obtain more members on it – provided, Caird insisted, the Senate did also.

Caird's middle way became law. In Glasgow, as in the other Scottish universities, the 1889 Act dramatically increased the powers of the Court. Moving well beyond its previously merely supervisory powers, the Court now took control of resources from the Senate. For the first time, too, the Court could found new professorships – involving it in protracted negotiations such as those which led in the 1890s to the Adam Smith Chair of Political Economy – and appoint to these new chairs. The Court could now also select a third of the members of the committees which managed the University Library and the Hunterian Museum. In addition, the Court increasingly had to deal with outside bodies which, with regard to the geographical spread of recognition agreements, now duplicated Edinburgh's cosmopolitanism. Moreover, as the scope of university activity widened to include such issues as student unions, so did the agenda of the Court. Thus the Court's affairs quickly became much more complex and more voluminous, as a spate of committees indicated; by the eve of the First World War the business was longer still.[3]

1889 also brought significant changes to the composition and procedures of the Court. While the membership of the Rector, the Principal, and assessors for the Chancellor and the Rector remained unchanged, the Dean of Faculties lost his place, and both the Senate and the General Council now had four representatives rather than one (cf. pp. 26–7 above). Just as significantly, whereas between 1858 and 1889 only Edinburgh had had direct civic representation, Glasgow – like Aberdeen and St Andrews – now followed suit with seats both for the Lord Provost (the Scottish equivalent of the English Lord Mayor) and for an assessor of the Lord Provost, Magistrates and Council. This new formula influenced the profile of the membership, and the nature of the Court's links with the municipality, which was experiencing a period of prestigious activism in fields such as trams and parks during the 1880s and 1890s. While remaining centred on the wealthier sections of society, Court membership shifted between the 1889 Act and the First World War toward mercantile and industrial interests, toward links with other educational institutions, toward civic involvement and away from the Established Church. Local origins and Glasgow University educations predominated, but diversity was increasing. Also, as Campbell Lloyd has demonstrated, neither on the full Court nor on its committees (notably finance) were the lay members ciphers. Another sign of accessibility to outside influence was the Court's 1900 decision to open its meetings to reporters – except for in camera sessions, which dealt with appointments to committees and outside bodies – albeit many years after Edinburgh had done so.[4]

In addition to its extra seats on the Court, the General Council gained from the 1889 Act part of its long-standing wish for more flexibility: a special meeting could now be called on request from one per cent of the total number of members on the register. Meanwhile, the Senate reacted to its diminished powers by meeting less frequently in the early years after 1889. Nonetheless, the Senate remained involved in some 'resource' questions, notably the library and the fitness of professors to continue in their posts: while the Senate had fewer committees concerned with such matters than before 1889, there was a 'House' committee which looked after the academic buildings and, eventually, a joint committee with the Court dealing with observatories and laboratories. Likewise, the Senate had much residual academic business, including close attention to potential academic rivals to the University, notably the suggested law faculty attached to St Mungo's College.[5] Also, despite resentment in the Senate about diminished powers, it was in constant – and usually very harmonious – communication with the Court on a range of matters such as the level of endowments for new chairs.

In the longer term the greatest constitutional significance of the 1889 Act was the increasing importance of the Principal who, as significant salary rises implied, began to assume a strategic role.[6] As J. D. Mackie put it, the Principal 'came to enjoy the authority which comes to one who is Chairman of most of the important committees'.[7] Thus Caird attempted to mediate among the groups within the Senate which disagreed sharply on the Commissioners' ordinances and played a similar role in clashes between Senate, Court and General Council. Yet while he was straightforward in pressing on Court and Senate both extra-mural education and the university education of women, like his two successors Caird did not chair all the committees of either body. In fact, there was no drastic change after 1889 to the influence of Caird, who increasingly suffered anxiety and sleeplessness from his ever more complex duties. Later his brother, with John Caird in mind, wrote that a Scottish principal 'is a *primus inter pares*, and he can only act with effect if he gains their support and confidence'.[8] Indeed, in the short run the greater accretion of power was to the very long-serving (1876–1910) Clerk of Senate, William Stewart (Biblical Criticism, 1873–1910), who was for two decades also a senate assessor[9] on Court (and, for a time, convener of its powerful recognition committee), and with whom Caird collaborated on important decisions.[10]

Until 1898 a significant share of the power of the post-1889 system fell to the Commissioners established by the Act. They retained considerable authority regarding finances and constitutional matters, and were particularly charged to allow each University to permit women to graduate, to provide for a students' representative council (SRC) and to consider affiliated colleges. In addition, the Commissioners issued many ordinances which, for example, established fee funds, created a science faculty and instituted preliminary examinations. Thus, the Court spent much time in the 1890s composing, or reacting to, draft ordinances and conducting other business with the Commissioners. Also, Glasgow's autonomy was limited by a requirement that in order to enact an ordinance a university had to obtain approval of the Senates and General Councils of each of the other three universities as well as of the Commissioners and the Privy Council. This provision occasionally had teeth, as when the other universities – powerfully reinforced by Glasgow Corporation and by the University's own Senate – convinced the Commissioners to drop the Court's proposed ordinance allowing it to sell the Hunterian coins. Yet on most issues there was common cause among the universities. Interestingly, although the General Council regretted many of the decisions of the Commissioners, unlike the Senate they had confidence in the notion of a Court which would govern all the Scottish universities. Meanwhile, the universities were able to make their views known on the Commissioners' proposals and to take initiatives on their own ordinances. And from 1898, provided that they consulted the Senate and the General Council, and secured the agreements of the Courts of the other Scottish universities, the universities' proposed ordinances could go direct to the universities' committee of the Privy Council.[11]

The Commissioners' most important initiatives related to the curriculum. Following a plan very similar to Glasgow's proposals, the Commissioners decided that a very wide choice be available within the passes required for the Ordinary degree in Arts. With regard to honours, which had been little taken up, there would now be a distinct degree, with separate teaching.[12] In Science, where there was to be a separate faculty from 1893, a three-year degree superseded the 1875 B.Sc.; a similar degree in engineering was initiated in 1893.[13] In Law, a long-lasting eight-subject course for the LL.B. began, and the BL was upgraded.[14] Meanwhile, from 1892 the medical course was extended to five years, and the minimum hospital period was raised to three. The Commissioners also broadened the University's spread of subjects by establishing chairs in history and in pathology. Finally, the Commissioners set in place enabling provisions for postgraduate study, which Glasgow had been pursuing as early as 1885.[15]

Glasgow, like other Scottish universities, became more receptive to the loosening of curricular constraints as student numbers declined. Having reached 2,241 in 1885, from the following year they fell, to 1,836 in 1897, the low point of this era (cf. Table 2.1). A further initiative of the Commissioners had major effects on the student body in the medium term: the formal entrance qualifications introduced by all the Scottish universities in 1892. There were two paths open, either an entrance exam or a pass in the new school-leaving certificate. The controversial junior classes, opposed by the General Council, were relegated to preparation for the preliminary examination; they would wither away in the early years of the new century. Whether because of or in spite of such changes, by the 1890s (as shown in Table 3.1) degrees at Glasgow in any given year represented about one in nine of current students, a significant improvement on the 1870s.[16]

Table 3.1
Degrees Obtained as a Percentage of Matriculated Students

All Faculties	
1873–5	7.2%
1876–80	6.9%
1881–5	10.1%
1886–90	11.3%
1891–5	11.8%
1896–1900	11.3%
1901–5	14.4%
1906–10	16.9%
1911–14	17.1%

Notes: MDs excluded; MB, ChB etc. counted as one Degree; 1888 data missing; Percentages are averages of the percentages for individual years.
Sources: (degrees): University Calendars (GUL); (matriculated students): Anderson, *Education and Opportunity*, Appendix 1, 350, 354.

The slump in student numbers occurred despite the advent of women to the universities, reaching one-seventh of the Glasgow total in 1897. By British standards women came late to Glasgow, as to other Scottish universities.[17] Yet their recruitment became especially important as male enrolment lagged and as women became increasingly significant within a major growth market for the Scottish universities: trainee teachers. Thus Glasgow joined the other Scottish universities in compensating for initial caution toward women, who quickly made a major impact on the institutions.[18]

There were significant precedents in Glasgow of university-level education for women, and substantial support from apparently unlikely quarters such as the General Council. The first stage, originating in discussions at a dinner party in the University, were the lectures organised by Mrs Campbell (wife of J. A. – see p. 36 above) from the 1860s and provided, in part, by Glasgow professors. In 1877 came the Association for the Higher Education of Women, with Principal Caird – significantly – as president, and Janet Galloway as secretary, a post which she retained until 1909. Indeed, from the 1860s John and Edward Caird had campaigned fearlessly in the Senate for women's education, and Edward – along with professors such as Nichol, Veitch and Young – was among the lecturers in the phase which preceded the establishment of Queen Margaret College (QMC). Edward Caird was also among the first representatives on the College's governing board after the Senate, at first slowly and cautiously, began to warm to the idea of women's education from the late 1870s.[19]

Incorporated in 1883, QMC opened a year later, numbering many University professors and assistants among the lecturers. The College had a considerable boost from the 1888 visit of the Queen; more practical help came from the

3.1 *Janet Galloway, Secretary of Queen Margaret College 1893–1909.*

shipbuilding widow Isabella Elder's gift (worth £12,000) of North Park House and grounds, about half a mile north of Gilmorehill, on condition that the College itself raise an endowment.[20] Thus there was an appeal, particularly aimed at and pushed by women, on the eve of merger with the University. After initially aiming at affiliated status, QMC accepted absorption into the University, having stipulated that its buildings and endowment should be used for women. Principal Caird played a key role in the discussions. Students formally became part of the University in 1892; the first women graduates took their degrees (in medicine) in 1894, and an MA and a B.Sc. followed in 1895.

Yet the continued existence of QMC indicated that the integration of women into the University was a protracted and, in many respects, a contentious process. The General Council retained its enthusiasm, arguing for Queen Margaret students' access to first-year classes on Gilmorehill and for the right of QMC teachers to participate in university examinations. If the Senate

3.2 *Queen Margaret College.*

remained in some respects lukewarm, the Court pursued a variety of issues, notably the need to duplicate lectures caused by segregated classes. But uneasiness remained, reflected in the Court's instruction to its secretary in 1895 to warn the newly elected professor of logic that 'amongst other duties, he might be required to teach Women Students'![21] In the same year the Court rejected an eloquent appeal to appoint a woman graduate to the staff. During these years, and for some time thereafter, there was much educational and social segregation, at Glasgow as in Aberdeen and elsewhere.[22] There were separate 'QM' societies and, in many classes though not in honours, separate instruction. Also, the Western Infirmary remained closed to women medical students. These hesitations were controversial: the University had to cope with the demands of Isabella Elder that her condition of the separate and equal teaching of female and male students be met. As the number of female graduates rose rapidly, the question of postgraduate employment loomed. One comparatively bright spot was addressed by Coutts in 1909: 'Of the women who have graduated in Medicine not a few have obtained public appointments'. Yet while higher education for women at Glasgow also opened doors for them in teaching and social work, the variety of viable employment choices for the University's female graduates was limited, even in medicine.[23]

As in other Scottish universities, the corporate life of male students at Glasgow advanced rapidly during the 1880s and 1890s, though from a very low base. In the mid-1880s students lacked even a place to shelter from the wind; their strong, classroom-based common identity could find an outlet only in riotous collective behaviour, notably at rectorial elections and at graduations. Thus a persistent preoccupation of the Senate was disorderly behaviour by students – in particular at the 1884 rectorial installation of Edmund Lushington – such as the 'throwing of peas or other missiles, the interruption of business by unseemly noises, and all other forms of disturbance'.[24] Indeed, a major source of professorial enthusiasm for student organisations was the hope that they would channel youthful high spirits.

As Glasgow and the other Scottish universities were non-residential, improvements in student life had to meet the needs of day students, many of whom commuted significant distances. Accordingly, the movement for the desperately needed Union building progressed rapidly in the mid-1880s. With the support of the Principal, and aided by a substantial gift from a former student, the McIntyre Building was opened in 1888 and extended in 1893, providing premises for the new Union, the Students' Representative Council, student clubs and, perhaps most importantly, a student restaurant. The SRC did much to raise funds to equip the Union building and provide new sports facilities; the key event was the great bazaar of 1889.[25] The elaborate nature of this multi-stalled affair (complete with games, a theatre, a picture gallery and a wax works), and the extent of its support by the professoriate and their families, are evident in 'Glasgow University Students Union Bazaar News', which noted patronage by the Queen, Princess Louise, two peers (the Chancellor and the Rector) and the Principal and his wife. The goal, responding to English examples and attempting to make good a perceived traditional fault of the Scottish system, was the creation of a 'common or corporate life among the students' in 'their common pursuits and recreations'.[26]

Other aspects of student life also improved during the 1880s and 1890s. At least a minority of students had some social contact with the professors, notably in the Storys' lunch parties and 'at homes', during the period when the future Principal was a professor.[27] From 1889 the SRC published the weekly *Glasgow University Magazine* (GUM), which saw itself advancing the recent emergence of 'corporate life among the students'. This periodical portrayed lightheartedly a lively student existence – at least for the minority active in the SRC, the Union and the various clubs and societies which were proliferating at this time. The Dialectic Society, in particular, drew much attention and large audiences for debates on subjects such as the abolition of the monarchy (defeated in February 1889). Medical societies and functions were much in evidence, reflecting the Medical Faculty's significant proportion of the student body. There was also coverage of unruly classroom behaviour, job prospects, the alleged aloofness from students of Arts professors, literary activities, the

3.3 *Sketches of the disorder at the Rectorial installation of Edmund Lushington, 1884.*

perceived need for additional athletic facilities, the drift of recent graduates to study at Oxford, problems of mixing in classes across the gender line, the vitality of political clubs and rectorial disorders.

The ordinance for the SRC took effect from 1895, when the organisation was empowered to approach Senate and Court on various matters. The agendas of both Senate and Court quickly reflected this new relationship; for example, in 1895 the Library Committee lengthened the reading room's day by an hour after representations from the SRC.[28] True, the Senate repeatedly resisted requests for student representatives to attend their meetings, even for the discussion of particular items. Yet, the influence of the SRC was generally on the rise, not least as a vehicle of inter-university student collaboration, notably on curricular issues.

The teaching staff included ever more assistants and demonstrators. Since 1858 general funds had been spent on assistants in the main Arts classes, and fellowships provided teaching assistance, and a hint of a career structure, for a few aspiring academics such as Henry Jones. Also, by the 1880s there were stirrings of organisation among this group in the Association of Assistants to Professors; they drew support for a new graded structure from Edward Caird and the General Council. Yet, while in the late 1880s nineteen Glasgow chairs had assistants – with a range of duties including practical classes, 'text-book teaching' and examinations – at Glasgow as elsewhere their 'status, duties, and remuneration varied in a chaotic manner'.[29]

The professoriate remained central to the University in the late nineteenth century. Its last decade and a half brought increasing involvement by professors in the life of the city and region. Some of this activity was in partisan politics and thus by definition controversial. Yet the preferred outlet was Liberal Unionism, which was very fashionable in West Central Scotland, especially within the middle class. The Party attracted Glasgow academics as diverse as John Caird, Richard Jebb, and – most influentially – Kelvin, who became president of its West of Scotland association.[30] The even less divisive concept of 'civic duty' mobilised William Smart (Political Economy, 1896–1915), especially with regard to the housing of the poor; Edward Caird, notably in the Women's Protective and Provident League, out of which evolved the Glasgow Council for Women's Trades; and Henry Jones (Moral Philosophy, 1894–1922; knighted 1912), who joined with Sir James Bell, Lord Provost, to initiate a Glasgow Civic Society. Jones also lectured energetically to local audiences.[31] More formal teaching reached out into the community with the foundation of the Board for the Extension of University Teaching, authorised by the Court in 1887. Classes developed in various centres in Glasgow and beyond, though as elsewhere in Scotland the initiative proved premature, dying out in Glasgow by the mid-1890s.[32] The Settlement Movement had more sustained impact, again with support from Edward Caird and Henry

Jones. The Glasgow University Settlement Association, founded in 1886, was modelled on the Toynbee phenomenon in London; although the residential project faltered, Toynbee Hall in Cathedral Street provided improved leisure for the poor. Meanwhile, the Queen Margaret College Settlement, founded in 1897 at Anderston, was especially active in nursery schools and women's clinics. There was also an academic spin-off: the School of Social Study and Training, sponsored by the University though officially external to it.

The 1880s witnessed an increased emphasis on research by Glasgow professors, like their counterparts in other Scottish universities.[33] Teaching remained very important, and the grinding routine of lectures and classes played a part in losing some professors – notably Richard Jebb, Walter Raleigh (English Language and Literature, 1900–4), Richard Lodge (History, 1894–9) and Gilbert Murray (Greek, 1889–99) – to other universities, especially Edinburgh, Oxford and Cambridge. Yet Glasgow benefited in the interim, notably from A. C. Bradley (English Language and Literature, 1890–1900), arguably the greatest literary critic of his day. Also, exporting professors – or, as in the case of Archibald Bowman, who became professor of logic at Princeton in 1906, lecturers – to other universities was in itself a mark of esteem. Moreover, in addition to making professors out of Oxbridge college tutors, Glasgow imported professors from other institutions, especially St Andrews, Aberdeen, Liverpool, Birmingham, the Irish universities and Anderson's College and – in at least one instance (Ralph Stockman, Materia Medica, 1897–1937) – Edinburgh. Glasgow arguably gained more than it lost from the fact that, like other Scottish universities, increasingly it recruited professors from a British 'market'.[34]

In the humanities, while some of those who were significant researchers subsequently left the University, others who were active publishers in their subjects stayed on, notably: William Smart; Macneile Dixon (English, 1904–35); Robert Adamson (Logic and Rhetoric, 1885–1902), 'perhaps the greatest philosophical scholar of his time', although he did not publish much while he held the chair;[35] W. M. Gloag (Law, 1905–34), a distinguished, productive legal scholar; and Henry Jones who, though not original, was very prominent in his field. While Jones kept his afternoons for outdoor recreation, during term time he rose before six and devoted his long mornings to preparing and giving classes, seeing students, and marking papers. Also, 'In vacations he was never without some piece of writing to do'.[36] This was prudent: research was encouraged by groups such as the Scottish professors of philosophy who met twice a year for a philosophical discussion – and, of course, a dinner![37]

Key appointments led to an upsurge of science research from the 1880s, encouraged in part by the fact that assistants need no longer be paid from professors' personal resources.[38] Progress was not uniform, as Kelvin's disappointing though not fallow successor Andrew Gray (1898–1924) and the antiquarian John Ferguson (Chemistry, 1874–1915) proved. Yet, even in chemistry, Glasgow had a brilliant researcher, Frederick Soddy, as a lecturer. In many other scientific fields the professors made notable advances during this period. Kelvin was no longer in his prime, and his estrangement from the influential electromagnetic school associated with Maxwell at Cambridge helps to explain the deceleration of physics in Glasgow, but he continued to do important work.[39] Other highly productive scientists and engineers included Frederick Bower (Botany 1885–1925; FRS 1891), Archibald Barr (Civil Engineering and Mechanics, 1889–1913; FRS 1923), Sir John Graham Kerr (Zoology from 1902), John Gregory (Geology, 1904–29; FRS 1901), and Sir John Biles (Naval Architecture, 1891–1921). Bower led his field while building up a department with a worldwide reputation; Gregory published more than twenty books and 300 papers; and Biles published papers regularly for half a century and collected honorary degrees from Harvard and Yale. There were also major advances in medicine, especially by Sir William Macewen (Surgery 1892–1924; FRS 1895, knighted 1902), who significantly extended the range of surgery, especially of the bone and brain, through his practice and his writings and was regarded after Lister's death as Britain's foremost surgeon; Noel Paton (Physiology, 1906–28), a pioneer investigator of metabolism and nutrition whose research output ceased only shortly before his death; Murdoch Cameron (Midwifery and Obstetrics from 1894) and his successor Munro Kerr (from 1911); Joseph Coats (Pathology from 1895); John Glaister (Forensic Medicine from 1898); and Stockman.[40] Many of these scientific and medical researchers were leading figures in their respective professional associations, as Frederick Bower demonstrated by his frequent prominent role in scientific meetings. Such involvements dovetailed with the outreach of the institution as a whole, notably when the University entertained the British Medical Association when it met in Glasgow in 1888.

This increasing emphasis on research, and the tightening links with the city which also characterised the University in the last fifteen years of the century, were symbolised and advanced by the lionising of Kelvin. This process peaked in June 1896 when the University, in collaboration with the international scientific community and the city, celebrated the fiftieth anniversary of his taking up of the chair of natural philosophy. By this point in Kelvin's career he had attracted acclaim and wealth in quantities unprecedented for an academic, including his 1866 knighthood (which had prompted his being granted the freedom of the city) and his 1892 peerage.[41] These honours increased the University's prestige, particularly because virtually the whole of the winters of Kelvin's life had been spent in its precincts, because he declined offers to go elsewhere and because the title he chose linked him to the institution – which was to make him Chancellor in 1904 – and to the city.[42]

A long article in the *Herald* having celebrated his genius, his discoveries

3.4 *British Association Meeting, Section D (Biology), Edinburgh, 1892. Frederick Bower, Professor of Botany 1885–1925, is second from the left in the back row.*

and his practical inventions, there was a conversazione at the University in Kelvin's honour. The *Herald*'s report of that occasion, which attracted not only 'a long roll of eminent name[s] in various departments of science both at home and abroad' but also 'the most prominent citizens of Glasgow and the West of Scotland', captured the mutual congratulation of university, city, Kelvin and his fellow scientists. The 2,500 guests were met by the 'representatives of the University and the Corporation. On the right the members of senate wearing their academic robes, and on the left the Lord Provost and Magistrates in their robes of office formed parallel lines through which the company passed into the Bute Hall'.[43] Lord and Lady Kelvin received the guests from seats on a dais but later 'mixed freely' with the throng. Appropriately illuminated by specially fitted electric light, the guests spiced their conversations with musical entertainment and with visits to an exhibition of Kelvin's apparatus. The turnout of academics was large and diverse: 'the robes of most of the leading universities at home and abroad were worn'.[44] The American contingent, for example, included representatives of Columbia,

Johns Hopkins, Michigan, Pennsylvania and Princeton, whose delegate was Woodrow Wilson, later President both of his university and of the United States. Fittingly for a celebration of a teacher of so many Glasgow students, the latter acted as stewards and held their own celebratory meeting, complete with delegates from other universities, later in the evening.

At the honorary degree ceremony the next day, the Lord Provost was on the platform as, following the reading of a congratulatory message from the Prince of Wales, the representatives of the various universities and learned societies presented their addresses. The Glasgow Senate's own address captured the essence of the adulation: 'Your mathematical and experimental

3.5 *William Thomson, Baron Kelvin of Largs, Professor of Natural Philosophy 1846–98, Chancellor 1904–7.*

3.6 *Civic Banquet during the celebration of Lord Kelvin's jubilee, 1896.*

genius has unveiled the secrets of nature; your marvellous gift of utilising such discoveries has ministered in many ways to the happiness and dignity of human life.' There were also addresses from the General Council and from the SRCs of the various Scottish universities. After receiving his own honorary degree, in the absence of the ailing Principal Caird, Kelvin took the chair as senior professor and conferred the rest – awarded to distinguished scientists from many countries. Kelvin quipped that he had been rewarded 'for having enjoyed for 50 years the privilege of spending my time on the work most congenial to me and in the happiest of surroundings. (Applause).'[45]

That evening the Corporation gave Kelvin a banquet in the St Andrew's Hall. Kelvin, replying to a fulsome tribute from the presiding Lord Provost, expressed pleasure that the city and the University had joined to honour him. He could not forget that 'the happiness of Glasgow University both for students and professors is largely due to the friendly and genial city of Glasgow in the midst of which it lives. (Applause)'. He went on to praise the generosity of his fellow citizens 'in so largely helping to give [the University] its present beautiful site and buildings'.[46] Sir Joseph Lister, too, praised the cooperation between the University and the city. Only Gairdner, speaking for the University, perhaps struck a slightly sour note when he lauded Kelvin for being selflessly devoted to his work in the midst of a 'commercial' community – conveniently forgetting the riches Kelvin had accumulated for himself! But this was a nuance; the town-gown fêting of Kelvin had been a huge success. Thus, even in the largely academic context of these celebrations, whose emphasis reflected not only Kelvin's scholarly achievements but the increasing research thrust of the University more generally, the alliance between the city and the University held firm.

The Kelvin Jubilee indicated the University's broadening links, notably through mutual recognition of courses, to other universities and colleges, and the continued success of its graduates, especially in medicine, throughout the Empire.[47] Yet, for all this dynamism, by the later 1890s there were increasing, and in many respects justified, worries about the relative standing of the University. These problems were symbolised and partly caused by the decreasing vitality and the protracted final illness of Principal Caird. By the 1890s, arguably, his approach to higher education – rooted in the low-cost, lecture-centred, arts-dominated university of the early Gilmorehill era – had become slightly old-fashioned. In any event, after two decades in office, Caird became considerably less effective in his last years due to the departure for Oxford of his brother Edward in 1893[48] and, from 1895, a series of debilitating illnesses. His appearances beyond Gilmorehill, never numerous, became less frequent, and he became less decisive, occasionally betraying public signs of his diminishing grip. As Edward wrote in 1897, 'It is impossible but that there should be hot controversies and collisions between so many teachers, each set on his own subject, and moderating between them is apt to take a good deal out of any one whose nerves are not at their best'.[49] That year the Principal reluctantly gave notice of his intention to resign at the end of July 1898 – a deadline his death avoided by a single day. Even as early as 1873 *The Bailie* had been wrong to suggest that 'one of the nicest sinecures in the West of Scotland is the Principalship of Glasgow University'.[50] By the 1890s Caird had proven, to his own great cost, that his was an onerous and pivotal office. His personal stature and that of his position were revealed by his elaborate funeral at Greenock (where he died), which featured a huge procession, a major civic delegation from Glasgow and a wreath from the Queen.

Ironically, given this esteem and the extent of his generally highly successful labours on behalf of the University, Caird left an institution increasingly worried by the danger of being left behind. This anxiety focused on the English

3.7 *The Chemistry Laboratory, 1894.*

civic universities and, even more so, the German and American universities which had developed so rapidly in the preceding two decades. Falling student numbers and the rising costs of new chairs spread financial gloom. Some relief came from the acquisition of QMC, with its large endowments, and from an annual Treasury grant of £12,000. Yet the latter fell well short of need, especially as the University now had to pay for professorial pensions. The Treasury grant soon rose to £21,000, but the University's finances were only starting to improve.[51] Certainly Glasgow's resources seemed weak in relation to the perceived inadequacy of its physical plant, especially in terms of science buildings and equipment. Even before Caird's death there had been action on this front, resulting in the 1888 linking of Anderson's College of Medicine to the Western Infirmary and in projects, still incomplete in 1898, for new buildings in botany and engineering and for the extension of the premises of anatomy, surgery and chemistry. Also, a ten-year appeal for a new engineering laboratory, which attracted leading businessmen and civic leaders, had begun in 1894. Still, there was a feeling that Glasgow, like the other Scottish universities, was 'among the poorest in teaching power, equipment, and money'.[52] As the University neared the end of the century, therefore, it was with an increasing sense of crisis, centring on worries about competitors, domestic and foreign.

Notes and References

1. See Jebb, *Life and Letters*, 235–41; GCMN, 29 April 1885; SMN, 16 April 1885.
2. Jones and Muirhead, *Edward Caird*, 101–7; Anderson, *Education and Opportunity*, 261–3, 275.
3. CMN, 24 May, 11 July and 12 December 1895; Lloyd, 'Communities', 126–9, 132, 135–6.
4. Lloyd, 'Communities', 77–9, 82, 91–92, 130, 132–4, 162–3. Lay leverage was less marked in the English 'civics': see ibid., and D. R. Jones, *The Origins of Civic Universities: Manchester, Leeds and Liverpool* (London, 1988).
5. SMN, 21 February 1895.
6. Brown and Moss, *University*, 106; Anderson, 'Professors', 106; SMN, 30 April 1975.
7. Mackie, *University*, 290–1.
8. E. Caird, *Memoir*, cvi–cvii, cxii (quote); Warr, *Principal Caird*, 193, 198.
9. That is, a member of Senate elected by the latter to membership of Court for a fixed term.
10. R. T. Hutcheson and H. Conway, *The University of Glasgow 1920–1974* (Glasgow, 1997), 11; *Memoir of Robert Herbert Story D.D. LL.D.* by his daughters (Glasgow, 1909) [hereafter *Story's Daughters' Memoir*].
11. Robertson, 'Finances', 468; Mackie, *University*, 292–4; GCMN, 20 February and 3 April 1895; SMN, 7 February 1895.
12. Anderson, *Education and Opportunity*, 270–1 and cf. 358–61. For a highly critical account of the Commissioners' compromises, which allowed initial general education to coexist in a student's career with later honours specialisation, see Davie, *Democratic Intellect*, 76–80.
13. Cf. R. Y. Thomson, 'The History of the Faculty', in (ed.), *A Faculty for Science* (Glasgow, 1993), 7–12.
14. A. D. Gibb, 'Law', FD, 175; Walker, *School of Law*, 52–3.
15. SMN, 12 March 1885.
16. Anderson, *Education and Opportunity*, 252–3, 271–3, 283–4 (including Table 7.2), 350, 354. The improvement was especially rapid in Arts.
17. Anderson, *Scottish Education*, 37. Cf. C. Dyhouse, *No Distinction of Sex? Women in British Universities 1870–1939* (London, 1995).
18. For other Scottish universities, see Anderson, *Education and Opportunity*, 255–7.
19. Jones and Muirhead, *Edward Caird*, 96–101; cf. S. Hamilton, 'The first generation of university women', in G. Donaldson (ed.), *Four Centuries: Edinburgh University Life, 1583–1983* (Edinburgh, 1983); Mrs Campbell, 'The Rise of the Higher Education of Women Movement in Glasgow', in *Book of the*

Jubilee, 129; J. Geyer-Kordesch and R. Ferguson, *Blue Stockings, Black Gowns, White Coats* (Glasgow, 1994).
20. C. J. McAlpine, *The Lady of Claremont House: Isabella Elder: pioneer and philanthropist* (Glendaruel, 1997).
21. CMN, 13 June 1895.
22. L. Moore, *Bajanellas and Semilinas: Aberdeen University and the Education of Women 1860–1920* (Aberdeen, 1991); Anderson, *Scottish Education*, 37. For the ambivalent feelings about full integration experienced by many of the women associated with QMC, see H. M Nimmo, 'Some Real Notes and Recollections of Queen Margaret College Life', in *Book of the Jubilee*, 146–155, esp. 150.
23. Coutts, *History*, 459; cf. W. Alexander, *First Ladies of Medicine* (Glasgow, 1987); C. M. Kendall, 'Higher Education and the Emergence of the Professional Woman in Glasgow c.1890–1914', *History of Universities*, 10 (1991), 199–221. On the complex pattern whereby rising academic esteem coexisted with lingering academic and social separation, see C. D. Myers, '"Give her the apple and see what comes of it": University Coeducation in Britain and America c.1860–1940 (with special focus on the University of Glasgow . . . and the University of Wisconsin at Madison)', unpublished University of Strathclyde Ph.D. thesis, 1999, e.g. 233–4.
24. SMN, 23 April 1885. Cf. R. D. Anderson, *The Student Community at Aberdeen 1860–1939* (Aberdeen, 1988).
25. Brown and Moss, *University*, 53, 70, 71; C. A. Oakley, *Union Ygorra: The Story of the Glasgow University Student over the last sixty years* (Glasgow, 1950).
26. No. 1, 18 December 1889, 3.
27. *Story's Daughters' Memoir*, 228.
28. SMN, 7 February 1895.
29. Anderson, *Education and Opportunity*, 274 (cf. 264, 275); PP1888, lxxviii [Cd. 365] Parliamentary Return regarding assistants etc. in Scottish Universities, 29–31 of paper, 805–7 of volume.
30. Smith and Wise, *Kelvin*, 803–7.
31. WWG, 193; Jones and Muirhead, *Edward Caird*, 114–18; Anderson, *Education and Opportunity*, 333; H. J. W. Hetherington, *The Life and Letters of Henry Jones* (London, 1924), 88–90.
32. W. H. Marwick, 'The university extension movement in Scotland', *University of Edinburgh Journal*, 8 (1936/7), 227–34. Cf. R. Hamilton and J. Maclean, *Glasgow University Settlement: A Centennial History* (Glasgow, 1998), 20–34.
33. Anderson, 'Ideas of the University', 2.
34. Anderson, 'Professors', 42–5.
35. Hetherington, *Henry Jones*, 80.
36. *DNB* (Gloag); Walker, *School of Law*, 56–7; Hetherington, *Henry Jones*, 84.
37. Edward Caird to Mary Talbot, 5 January 1902, in Jones and Muirhead, *Edward Caird*, 236. While a number of pre-1914 humanities professors were not productive researchers, William Milligan was an example of a chairholder whose diverse teaching, administrative and outside involvements did not halt substantial scholarly achievement (*DNB*).

38. Brown and Moss, *University*, 94–5.
39. D. Wilson, 'Lord Kelvin: Sir William Thomson 1824–1907' (Glasgow, 1994), 6 and passim.
40. See, for example: Brown and Moss, *University*, 96; Coutts, *University*, 581–8; C. F. W. Illingworth, 'Surgery', FD, 210–11; M. A. Crowther and B. White, *On Soul and Conscience: The Medical Expert and Crime* (Aberdeen, 1988); Hull and Geyer-Kordesch, *Shaping the Medical Profession*, ch. 2.
41. He was also later made a privy councillor and one of the first members of the Order of Merit.
42. Cf. Smith and Wise, *Kelvin*, 809.
43. GH, 16 June 1896.
44. Ibid.
45. GH, 17 June 1896.
46. Ibid.
47. Cf. Lloyd, 'Communities', and 'Search for Legitimacy'.
48. Warr, *Principal Caird*, 201–2.
49. E. Caird to Mary Talbot, 13 January 1897, in Jones and Muirhead, *Edward Caird*, 217. Cf. GH, 1 August 1898; E. Caird, *Memoir*, cvii, cxxxvii.
50. No. 21.
51. Brown and Moss, *University*, 104; Mackie, *University*, 293–4; Coutts, *University*, 456; Robertson, 'Finances', 459.
52. GH, 14 January 1907, referring to earlier perceptions. Cf. Lloyd, 'Communities', 228–30. For parallel worries about the library see W. P. Dickson, 'The Glasgow University Library: A Plea for the increase of its resources' (Glasgow, 1889).

CHAPTER FOUR

THE ROOTS OF THE MODERN UNIVERSITY, 1898–1914

At first glance the new Principal seemed an unsuitable choice by the Crown to respond to the University's turn-of-the-century crisis; indeed, he appeared to be a reversion to an even earlier regime than Caird's, a kind of updated Macfarlan. Yet the Reverend Robert Herbert Story (1835–1907, Principal 1898–1907) was a largely modern figure in disputatious ecclesiastical disguise.

As a longtime parish minister who had become professor of ecclesiastical history at Glasgow in 1886,[1] Story brought to the office a heavy involvement in external disputes, especially the defence of the Church of Scotland. Moderator of the General Assembly in 1894, Story was 'the hardest of hitters' and 'emphatically a destructive disputant' in ecclesiastical battles.[2] While Story resembled his friend and predecessor Caird as a publishing scholar, Story – in marked contrast to Caird, and even to Barclay – retained many of his church involvements, notably his senior clerkship of the General Assembly, after his election as Principal and continued to push his controversial policies there. Also, while (like Caird and Barclay) he was a liberal within the Kirk, Story – though certainly no bigot[3] – was much less relaxed than Caird regarding the Church of Scotland's position vis-à-vis other denominations. Significantly, most of his close friends were fellow ministers of the Kirk.

Story also had a tendency to take unpopular academic stands. A well-publicised example was his refusal to approve Andrew Carnegie's emphasis on paying fees and his scheme's 'discrimination' against humanities subjects. For Story, the latter menaced the traditional curriculum, while the former risked giving students access to courses from which their social circumstances meant they could not profit. Story was at first so oblivious to the claims of the great philanthropist that, when the University gave Carnegie (along with many others) an honorary degree during the 1901 Jubilee, he was not among those invited to lunch in the Principal's Lodging. Likewise, as a determined defender of liberal education, and a settled opponent of 'cramming' for degree examinations, Story discouraged attempts by the Glasgow Chamber of Commerce to

4.1 *Robert Herbert Story, Professor of Ecclesiastical History 1886–98, Principal 1898–1907.*

press commercially relevant subjects on the University. For Story, the University's purpose was to instill high principles and to encourage its graduates to 'never cease to be students and learners still'.[4]

Story's personality also posed problems for his work inside and, especially, outside the University. He seemed to have touches of the 'aristocrat', of 'hauteur' and of 'unapproachability'; one observer spoke of the 'icy indifference, the cold reserve, the stately dignity with which he masked himself'.[5] Moreover, Story was not very popular with students, who prevented him from delivering his inaugural address; disaster doubled when in frustration Story lost his temper.

Nor did he relent: seven years later the Principal unsuccessfully opposed the SRC's proposal to hold a dance in the Bute Hall.[6]

Yet various features of Story's principalship helped to quell potential disputes within the University and to enhance his impact outside Gilmorehill. Despite the fears aroused at the time of his apppointment, and in part because of the cautions he received at that time from his fellow Unionist the Secretary for Scotland, Story felt that as Principal he had to rise above his own opinions and serve the University community as a whole. As he told a correspondent who wanted him to contribute to a religious periodical, 'My difficulty about *signing* an article is, that in the position of Principal one is expected to keep comparatively aloof from ecclesiastical or political questions'.[7] Likewise, evidently he suppressed public manifestations of his rampant Unionism, emphasising instead enthusiasm for the uncontroversial revival, in the context of the Boer War, of the University's role in the Volunteer movement. Thus Story hoped to insulate his principalship even from his continued ecclesiastical politicking. This was a difficult balancing act, but one which the less religiously charged atmosphere of the turn-of-the-century made possible in a way unthinkable at the start of Caird's principalship, when the Disruption of the Church of Scotland was still a raw wound. For, while keen to lead religious services in the Bute Hall on Sundays, when the Bedellus Lachlan Macpherson bore the mace with great panache, Story paradoxically had a more secular outlook on the University than Caird.

Also, although Story was more ambivalent than Caird had been about adapting the University to the practical interests of industry and commerce, he was more active than his predecessor in fostering contacts with influential people in the local community – and beyond. Even as professor Story had been outward looking, in his willingness to preach in various churches and to undertake such duties as opening bazaars, for example. This orientation increased once Story became Principal. For example, the Storys did much more entertaining than had the Cairds – using principals' week at Carnegie's Skibo Castle and return visits to chancellors and rectors – and mixed (if fleetingly) even with high society. For the first time the principalship became, to a significant degree, a husband/wife partnership in giving and receiving hospitality, albeit one that gave little recognition to the efforts of the female partner.[8] The Storys applied this approach to the university community as well as to outsiders, and to the two groups in combination. A major innovation of the Story regime was the 'at home' held twice a year in the Randolph Hall for all the staff of the University plus representatives of student societies. Key townspeople were also invited. The gatherings were lively, proving more to the taste of the sociable Mrs Story than of her husband. Also, Story appeared in public more often, and more actively, than the somewhat aloof Caird. Thus Story was in evidence on charitable occasions and at times of major disasters, when he 'gave eloquent expression to the feeling which pervaded

4.2 *Lachlan Macpherson, Janitor 1853–99, Bedellus 1862–99.*

the community'.[9] Likewise, the Storys exploited Royal visits – in 1903, when the King addressed the Principal 'with an air of ancient friendship' and a year later when they entertained Princess Louise to dinner to celebrate Lord Kelvin's installation as chancellor.[10] The Storys' social mission was inspired, in part, by a feeling that 'there has sometimes seemed to be a certain want of cordiality in the relations between the civic and the academic circles . . . the one too proud of its wealth, the other of its learning', that these problems were easing, and that the end of suspicions concerning professorial collection of fees and other supposed university abuses provided an opportunity to improve relations further.[11]

Crucially, Story perceived from the outset of his principalship the need for

4.3 *The Storys' Drawing Room, No. 13 Professors' Square.*

a revival of the University, and of Scottish higher education more generally, to meet the needs of Scottish students and to match international competition, notably from the United States. Revealing in his inaugural address concern about growing state control, Story appealed for a renewal of generosity of Glasgow benefactors, especially to found additional chairs in subjects universities such as Edinburgh already had. Concerned too about the effects of entrance examinations and curriculum changes, Story also called for a renewed emphasis on methods of education and the ideals that it served. While echoing Caird in affirming the compatibility of learning and religion, and while anticipating his successor in calling for a proper university chapel, Story put a new emphasis on the importance of research – valuable in itself and for its enrichment of teaching – and of research postgraduates.[12] In this way the former professor of divinity recognised the importance of the growth of research in science, engineering and medicine which had accelerated from the 1890s.[13]

This surprisingly modern manifesto underpinned Story's most important initiative, a campaign for new buildings and equipment. Inspired by the feeling that 'it was not conceivable that the ancient and honourable University of Glasgow could be content to fill a second place',[14] the Principal in 1900 launched the campaign with a series of articles in the *Glasgow Herald*, written by himself and various professors. These articles aroused resentment in the West of Scotland Technical College (which had a rival campaign underway) but evidently went down well in the city more generally. The series argued that methods of research and teaching, especially in the sciences, had altered substantially since the erection of the Gilmorehill buildings, and that the University had to adapt quickly in order to avoid falling irretrievably behind its competitors. While the University had broad intellectual aims in pursuing this agenda, it was suggested that overcoming the institution's competitive problems would also be good for the city's economy. Significantly, the series included an endorsing article by the Lord Provost.[15] Story was closely involved in the campaign, meeting and writing to potential donors and heading a promotional meeting in 1901. In addition to calling for new buildings and up-to-date equipment, the campaign targeted extra teaching staff (especially to continue the trend toward small classes, particularly for advanced students), a new reading room for students, an examination hall and the further substitution of electric for gas lighting.[16]

Although hampered by being launched during the Boer War, the campaign raised £75,000 during Story's principalship. In addition to a substantial donation from Glasgow Corporation it attracted large contributions from big businessmen, especially in shipping, shipbuilding and the iron and metal trades. In combination with the role of businessmen in planning the new engineering laboratory and in endowing chairs in naval architecture, political economy, geology and mining, these contributions marked an accelerating trend of business generosity toward the University. Reinforced by capital grants from the new Carnegie Trust (with whose chief Story latterly developed a rapport), the result of Story's campaign was a substantial number of new science and medical buildings: in Anatomy (1904), West Medical Building (1903–7), Natural Philosophy (1906) and the extension to the new engineering building (1908). There were also significant alterations in the main building which implied a modestly increased awareness of the need for a professional administration: the Clerk of Senate's room was converted into the Court Room, while new offices were constructed for him and for the Principal. An enduring legacy of the campaign was an equipment committee jointly organised by Senate and Court. Yet there was no sense of complacency, as it was reckoned that an additional £100,000 was still required, especially for the requirements of Arts.[17]

The need to revitalise the institution had been one of the themes underlying the University's celebration in 1901 of its Ninth Jubilee – which also provided an opportunity to advertise and strengthen links both to local interests and to

4.4 *West Medical Building (left foreground) and Natural Philosophy Building (centre foreground) under construction, 1905.*

the international academic community. Story gave a great deal of time to this series of events, as did student leaders, the Clerk of Senate and Mrs Story, who shook hands with over three thousand people on more than one occasion. Admittedly the Jubilee suffered from taking place soon after Victoria's death and from the King's being unable to attend. Also, as Glasgow was celebrating a jubilee rather than a centenary it had fewer events spread over fewer days than had Edinburgh at its 300th celebration seventeen years before. Yet the Glasgow event was a splendid example of lay and academic outreach that made a considerable impact, in part because it coincided with the city's 1901 international exhibition held nearby on the banks of the Kelvin.[18]

The dominant theme of the Jubilee was the University's status as a world institution, respected by major universities abroad as well as at home. With the flags of many countries decorating the Bute Hall, delegates attended from fifteen countries and four colonies or dependencies as well as from many parts of the United Kingdom. Academics attended from six German and twenty-eight American institutions, while the British universities, including the newest, Birmingham, were very well represented. Large numbers of these academic delegates, including Japanese representatives, received honorary degrees, and even more enjoyed excursions into Glasgow's scenic hinterland. Yet those honoured were not restricted to academics, as degrees for Carnegie and the Secretary for Scotland indicated. The University's graduates played an important part, enjoying a special reception. There was also strong acknowledgement of the University's interdependence with the city (now fully developed around the University), the central theme of the banquet that the Corporation gave to the University during the Jubilee. Paying tribute to the University's role in maintaining the intelligence and moral and spiritual force on which Glasgow's greatness rested, the Lord Provost offered the toast to the University. Not even Principal Story's introspective reply could dampen the occasion.

The Jubilee echoed Story's inaugural address in emphasising not only the University's many achievements but also its needs. Orations on James Watt, Adam Smith and William Hunter celebrated the institution's past glory, while

4.5 *Ninth Jubilee, 1901 – excursion down the Clyde.*

4.6 *View of the city looking north-east from Gilmorehill, 1905.*

the opening of the new Botany building in the presence of Hooker's son and the now ennobled Lister evoked both recent glories and the promise of the immediate future. Yet Kelvin did not let the audience forget the increasing need of the University for still more resources. Story played the same tune. This received a positive response in the local press – impressed, perhaps, by the 3,000 people who attended the conversazione and by the much larger numbers of Glaswegians who had witnessed the torchlight procession.[19]

The increasingly outward-looking tendency of the institution was reinforced when, in 1902, Story and Professor Raleigh launched a drive, strongly supported by the General Council, to strengthen links with graduates. In 1903 the General Council urged an annual Commemoration Day – an innovation for a Scottish university – on the day following the annual graduation, 'in order to maintain the connection of the graduates with their University'. The initiative also included attempts to establish local associations of graduates 'in places distant from Glasgow' and the furthering of 'class clubs' for graduates of individual faculties in particular years. The first 'commem' occurred in 1904 in a form followed, with minor adaptations, throughout the new century: a religious service; an oration (later dropped in favour of shorter speeches for each of the honorary graduates); the conferment of honorary degrees (including one on the American ambassador); and a banquet.[20] The University attached to the occasion an annual conversazione for graduates, at the suggestion of history professor (1899–1931) Dudley Medley. Also, by 1906 graduates' associations had been formed, in addition to the long-standing London club, in Newcastle, Leeds and Manchester. Admittedly the General Council remained less than deferential, particularly on issues such as the proposed commerce faculty and arrangements for admission. Interest in elections for the Council's assessors on the Court could be intense, notably in 1905 when the significant, and rapidly increasing, number of teacher members were excited about a pending education bill. Likewise, the Council played a part in the agitation in 1907 for more university reform, orientated this time to a desire for more autonomy for the individual institutions. Moreover, the Council's long-serving assessor on the Court, D. C. McVail, enlivened the latter, where he often found himself in a minority of one. Nonetheless, Story's and Raleigh's campaign had laid the foundations for a more continuously supportive role for the graduates.[21]

Commemoration's value for public relations was enhanced by a trend toward greater diversity of the honorary graduates – once dominated by clergymen – honoured on these occasions. Thus, while academics gained two-thirds of the non-divinity honours conferred between 1897 and 1914, a wide variety of other interests (including the artist James McNeil Whistler, though few businessmen) also benefited from a system in which lay members participated in the choices made. The honorary degree awarded in 1904 to the Lord Provost, Sir John Ure Primrose, epitomised the outward-looking nature of these occasions. Significantly, the Town Council presented him with his academic robes at a ceremony where he described the degree as an honour to the whole community. Toasts were given to 'the University and the City'; in such a setting disputes between town and gown seemed merely the 'quarrels of brothers'. The *Glasgow Herald* commented that the city was always 'amicable' with the University 'and never more so than at the present time'.[22] Such events contrasted sharply with memories of the High Street days when 'no entertainments were . . . given at which gentlemen in hoods and trenchers mingled with prosperous citizens and ladies in evening dress'.[23] The culmination of these events came in 1906 when the Lord Provost, presiding at the presentation of Story's portrait to the University, observed that the 'cordiality' between city and University had been 'much increased during recent years by the public spirit of their honoured guest'.[24]

Naturally Story's principalship included much routine activity as well as an unprecedented number of grand public occasions. Despite the initial suspicions of his friends, Story found himself very busy:

> He had no more lectures to prepare and deliver, it is true, but meetings multiplied, till sometimes nearly the whole day was consumed by them, and by necessary personal interviews with those who were involved in the various College problems. Holidays were not lengthened but curtailed, as the Principal had to be present on many occasions which the Professor could avoid. Correspondence also became a serious matter.

Public engagements also consumed 'several evenings in the week', usually including the need to make a speech at events which varied from bazaars to gatherings at the Faculty of Physicians and Surgeons. As a result, like many of his successors, Story found it impossible to attend all the special lectures on campus, though he enjoyed those he heard.[25] Fortunately Story had the support, notably in the building and graduate campaigns, of energetic professors such as Henry Jones, an influential senator who served a four-year term as assessor on the Court and, like a number of his professorial colleagues, was active on a large number of committees. During a crisis regarding adverse publicity in the local press, for example, Jones drafted a letter for Story, who was absorbed in other business, which the Principal signed without alteration.[26] Professor Jack helped too, as – even more so – did Stewart, the Clerk of Senate, Story's 'right hand'. Such support became increasingly important from about 1904 when Story's health began to fail. Thereafter, when ill, he held committee meetings in the Principal's Lodging, which served as his preferred office in any case. It was during this period of his physical decline that relationships between Story and his professorial colleagues noticeably warmed.[27]

Glasgow professors, like their counterparts in other Scottish universities, were flourishing in the years just prior to the First World War. As Robert Anderson has argued, they were significantly more 'professional' than in the 1850s, notably in terms of their self-perception and, through their assessors on the Court, control of appointments. Among other factors, the increasing salience of specialised research expertise gave professors rising influence over Courts formerly suspicious of their 'monopolistic' attitudes. There were more professors than ever before – thirty-six in 1914 compared to thirty-one in 1900 and eighteen in 1826 – who enjoyed a good standard of living, especially if they lived in the Square. Also, retirement at seventy, introduced from 1897, ended the degrading necessity for professors to petition the Court for a pension on the grounds of inability to carry out duties. The abolition of direct collection of fees in 1893, while it reduced top salaries, raised lower ones. There was considerable coherence within the professoriate, reflected in dinner parties, for example – apart from the occasional bitter quarrel such as that which divided the two professors of surgery, William Macewen and Robert Kennedy.[28]

The typical Glasgow professor of the 1900s was also much more externally oriented than his counterpart fifty or, less markedly, fifteen years before. Sir Henry Jones mixed extensively with the upper middle class outside the University, again especially at table: Jones used a dinner with local business friends to raise money for his class library, for instance. Also, there was a private 'College Club' which combined academics and men from the broader community, especially graduates living in Hillhead and vicinity. In addition, while some professors had few if any important involvements in local organisations, others played significant roles, as did their wives and daughters, notably in the Settlements and the Western Infirmary. Thus Dudley Medley was a key figure in the Territorials, the School Board and the Glasgow Athenaeum Commercial College. Some of these interventions were controversial, as in leadership of party political organisations by Robert Latta (Logic and Rhetoric from 1902), Sir Thomas McCall Anderson (Clinical Medicine, 1874–1900) and John Glaister. Yet the notably ecumenical James Cooper (Ecclesiastical History, 1898–1922) served both as a minister of the Kirk and as a trustee in a local Episcopal church! Also, many of these professors were key figures in their professions, as indicated by the massive medical dinner in 1906 held in honour of McCall Anderson's knighthood. In addition, a number of professors also played prominent roles in national affairs, notably William Smart, who served on the Poor Law Commission.[29]

The professors also remained a powerful elite within the University, monopolising the Senate and departmental headships. There was little social contact between professors and other staff, academic or (especially) administrative. Yet during the first decade and a half of the new century the number of assistants and lecturers increased significantly. Their salaries varied considerably – within and between categories – with, however, a marked inferiority to professorial remuneration. Also, they lacked any social facilities. Still, the foundations were laid for a career structure, notably after a 1913 report of the Principal and Deans committee which, recognising 'the real position they hold in the teaching staff of the University', felt it was appropriate to make 'more definite arrangements . . . regarding their appointment and promotion'.[30]

How did this diversification of the academic staff affect teaching? Coutts, while believing that the rank of the teacher made little difference to students, suggested that 'lecturers, who are shut out from the faculty, from the senate, and from direct representation on the University court, have not an equal opportunity to obtain favourable conditions for their teaching'.[31] Yet some of these young academics were people of very considerable talent, notably the great economic and social historian R. H. Tawney, who taught history at Glasgow before the Great War. In any event, the students clearly benefited from the marked reduction, which increasing numbers of assistants and lecturers made possible, of the student/teacher ratio even during the period 1900–14. In terms of expenditure, lecturers rather than assistants proved increasingly important in the twenty years preceding 1914. But it was the expansion of both categories, in preference to the relatively expensive professoriate, which made it possible for the University to 'diversify and modernize its curriculum so extensively in this brief period'.[32]

This diversification of the teaching staff facilitated the 1908 switch to a three-term teaching year and, crucially, the increased use of laboratory sessions on the science side and of seminars in Arts. For example, when Henry Jones acquired additional assistants, with whom he consulted closely, he introduced a fortnightly seminar element into the Ordinary (first year) class while reducing his previously onerous marking load. There was a clear division of labour: Jones largely taught his Ordinary class and Honours class, while leaving the Higher Ordinary (second level) class mainly to an assistant. The trend from the turn of the century was toward a more personal approach, notably in Jones's Honours class. Professors such as J. S. Phillimore (Greek, 1899–1906; Humanity, 1906–1926), Dudley Medley and William Gloag adopted a friendly attitude toward their students, learning their names quickly, inquiring about their plans and, increasingly, entertaining them. (Gloag invited his favourite students to alcoholic breakfasts, while Cooper gave elaborate dinners so that his future ministers would behave properly once in their parishes.)

Professors who participated fully in these trends received highly favourable student reactions. William Smart observed:

> how differently the men behave. They are all alert, because they are asked not to listen only, but to apply their intellects during class . . . Being made to find things out for themselves, they get rid of the idea that education means putting in instead of drawing out . . . And the effect on the teachers is not less happy. We are no longer limited to textbook courses. We have to meet men who are much nearer our own level, and we have to meet them round a table, with full right on their part of interruption, criticism, and inquiry.[33]

Some professors successfully cultivated a strong sense of 'fellow-feeling' between the staff, on the one hand, and students on the other, notably in Bower's Botany Department, where the excitement of research contributed to 'comradeship with dignity between teacher and taught'.[34] Some humanities professors such as Henry Jones also had a devoted and attentive following, responding to his eloquence, the freshness of his approach (leaving newly written notes largely unconsulted), his emphasis on applying moral criteria to contemporary issues, and his sense of fun. Nevertheless, much remained of the old system. As Robert Hutcheson has written:

> In Arts, tutorial work was minimal and confined to the higher and honours students. What was called a tutorial in the ordinary classes was really a meeting of a section of students to discuss performance in class

4.7 *Humanity Class, 1901–2, including John Phillimore, Professor of Humanity 1906–26 and of Greek 1899–1906. A. A. Bowman, Professor of Moral Philosophy 1927–36, is fourth from the left on the balcony above the Bedellus.*

> examinations, and for the return of essays. Honours students read their essays in the houses of their tutors.

Similarly, in medicine, while the student-staff ratio fell substantially in the 1890s, teaching methods remained much as before, though a conscientious extrovert such as Macewen could use operations and the Socratic method in ways that deeply impressed students. The latter retained a pragmatic attitude to classes, sharing information on the excitement (or otherwise) of lectures, the need (or not) to attend them to obtain class tickets, and the parts of the courses which loomed large in examinations.[35]

Like teaching methods, the curriculum was changing but not beyond recognition. With regard to the Ordinary degree in Arts, in 1908 Glasgow (after a failed attempt at concerted action by the various Scottish universities) grouped the large number of available options; the University specified that some work had to be at second level and that the three-term-long classes must have at least seventy-five meetings apart from tutorials and labs. This approach was intended to combat superficiality as well as to allow for more diverse teaching methods. Led by lectureships in French (1895), German (1899) and Italian (1902), as well as by the chairs in history and political economy, there was an increasing breadth of Arts subjects. Extension into the social sciences was assisted by the fund-raising efforts of Henry Jones and the generosity of wealthy citizens such as Sir Daniel Macaulay Stevenson. Also, many subjects could offer students increased depth of instruction. In political economy, for example, from 1898 the Ordinary Class was supplemented by an Honours Class, an assistant with special responsibility for social economics joined in 1907 and in 1911 a lecturer in economic history joined the staff. The 1908 reforms having reduced the number of subjects required at honours level, an increasing population of Arts graduates (21 per cent by 1913–14) achieved enough specialisation to graduate with honours degrees.[36]

Undergraduates in other faculties experienced similar developments. There was a significant increase in lecturers in Law, enriching its curriculum. Likewise, science extended its range – with a lectureship, then converted to a chair, in mining, for example. Postgraduate opportunities broadened, albeit from a very low base. For example, building on the public health 'Qualification' of 1876 and the Diploma of 1889 was the postgraduate B.Sc. of 1903; from 1891 Diploma classes were open to students taking courses with the Faculty of Physicians and Surgeons of Glasgow. More generally, the 1889 Commissioners had allowed for research students and research fellows. Yet despite the spectacular role-model of Kelvin's taking on these tasks on his retirement, takeup was slow, especially in Arts.[37]

There was more stability, but very considerable diversity, in the economic and social origins of the Glasgow students attracted to this increasingly rich curriculum. The most substantial change came in the economic sector of origin: 'industrial and commercial' backgrounds (of whatever class) had risen by 1901 to roughly two-thirds, well beyond the half of 1870 which in turn was sharply up on the early nineteenth century. Thus the University was increasingly well linked to its urban base. With regard to social origins, by 1910 about a quarter of Glasgow's students were working-class, only marginally higher than the fifth of 1860; what had changed in the intervening decades was that markedly fewer students now came from comfortable agricultural backgrounds, while significantly more came from urban middle-class homes – trends broadly representative of the Scottish universities as a whole. (See Table 2.2, p. 65 above.) Yet, unusually, the Glasgow manual students included men – less often women – whose fathers came from new industries such as the shipyards and engineering works.[38] Still, these tended to be skilled workers similar in some respects to the many lower-middle-class parents whose children attended Glasgow in these years. By the eve of the First World War, Law and Medical students were especially likely to be middle-class, with Divinity and, especially, Arts students (partly due to trainee teachers) more likely to be from humble backgrounds. The net result for Glasgow was an unusually wide version of Scotland's already especially broad social selection, albeit one probably shared with English 'civics'. As Macleod Malloch wrote in 1913, 'Few Universities present more varied types of student humanity than that of Glasgow. There one may behold the sons of the wealthy merchants of Glasgow, and likewise the sons of the people. Raw Highlanders from Mull and Skye rub shoulders with medical students from London'.[39]

Carnegie grants played a major part in maintaining this social diversity, especially in the face of rising fees. These grants were available to a significant number of students from 1901, benefiting for example half of the male and a third of the female medical students matriculating at Glasgow between 1906 and 1909. Carnegie grants filled gaps left by the previously rapidly increasing number of endowments for bursaries, which subsequently diminished. The rise in fees was substantial: up to between £12 and £17 a year on the eve of the First World War compared to about £9 in the 1860s, hitting those not in receipt of Carnegie grants. Yet overall the cost of education at Glasgow remained modest, especially in contrast to residential Oxbridge but even in comparison with northern 'civics' and Imperial College. As a result, the upward trend in student numbers not only recovered the ground lost in the slump of the late nineteenth century but went beyond previous peaks – from 1,966 (of whom 304 were women) in 1898 to 2,916 (of whom 662 were women) in 1913. (See Table 2.1, p. 63 above.) These trends, and the increasing recruitment of women, compensated for the effects of the entrance examination, particular problems in attracting legal and medical students, and the decline of the trend to send boys to universities to study Arts for a year or two without aiming at a degree.[40]

In a dramatic shift, graduation became the norm, notably for the two faculties whose students continued to dominate the University numerically: Arts and Medicine. (See Table 3.1, p. 76 above.) In the latter, not only did completions rise but the proportion qualifying through the University route also increased, perhaps because the extra-mural medical schools found it increasingly hard to compete with the University once its medically-related laboratories were upgraded and its students had preferential access to Carnegie grants. Still, the transformation in Arts was greater, as – reversing the position of the 1870s – in absolute terms Arts graduations exceeded those in Medicine in 1914. Improved teaching and pastoral care accounted for part of the change; so too did the advent of compulsory entrance examinations, the upsurge in teacher training, and a marked shift in the educational preparation of students. During these years there was a big movement toward secondary school backgrounds, including nearly all those who did not come through the pupil-teacher route. This trend, which achieved one of the goals of the reformers of the last quarter of the nineteenth century, was particularly marked at Glasgow due to the relatively rapid development of secondary schools in the city. Meanwhile, in many local firms, especially in law and accounting, the pattern of part-time, non-graduating students at the University persisted.[41]

How cohesive was this rapidly expanding student body? Students from Western Scotland rose from three-fifths to about three-quarters of the total, perhaps because Carnegie grants provided nothing for maintenance. Scottish students were especially prevalent in Arts and Law, but they rose as a proportion of the whole in Medicine as well. Improved university provision cut numbers from other parts of the United Kingdom (especially Ireland), but the proportion from overseas doubled to 10 per cent. The experience of overseas students was mixed, as Indian students discovered in 1913 when the University acquiesced as other students excluded them from a dance. The challenges of diversity were compounded by increasing numbers of Catholic and Jewish students, who formed their own associations.[42]

By the early twentieth century there was widespread concern about the campus activities even of the majority of Protestant Scottish students. The General Council fretted about overcrowding in the Union and perceived a need to foster athletics, residential hostels and advisers of study to promote 'public spirit and corporate sentiment'. University leaders worried about the 'traditional isolation of the Scottish student' and promoted improvements to recreation grounds and the Union. Others voiced concern about decreasing participation, for example, in the SRC. Student journalists decried a lack of student space on campus and lamented day-boys who identified little with the University, often – even after graduation – feeling closer to their former school. A prolonged regional economic downturn exacerbated these problems: many could not afford to use the Union, which had about 500 members (roughly a third of male students) in 1895.[43]

There was some amelioration in this situation before the War. Student activists helped, especially when O. H. Mavor (the future James Bridie) invented 'Daft Friday' in 1905.[44] The Union was extended in 1908 and gained the right to sell alcohol. There were new sports grounds at Bankhead (1906) and Westerlands (1912) and an Officers Training Corps (OTC) in 1908. For a small minority of men and women, halls of residence reinforced corporate life. The tradition of raucous collective enjoyment remained, especially on the occasion of the Rector's inaugural: 'with intervals of noisy outbursts, they paraded the streets all day in bizarre costumes'. In 1905, Liberal students painted the Conservative headquarters red during the night and, in the course of the campaign, twice wrecked their opponents' room. Problems persisted regarding rowdiness at solemn university occasions: 'Student humour' was 'conspicuous at graduation ceremonies'. Also, both Senate and Court concerned themselves with such student vices as 'smoking and spitting in the Quadrangle and Gateways'. Yet there was an increasingly strong partnership between the Court, the Senate and the SRC, notably with regard to appeal and discipline cases. More positively, just as students played active roles in great occasions such as the jubilees of 1896 and 1901, so University leaders and their families did much for major events which raised funds for student facilities.[45] Students plausibly rejected arguments that undergraduate life was better at Oxford and Cambridge: 'Because we do not all sleep in the same corridor, because we have our boots cleaned by a landlady instead of by a gyp or scout, are we therefore to be regarded as fit subjects for Milton's army of the damned?'[46]

What of the position of women, who constituted almost a quarter of the full-time students on the eve of war? By the time of Story's inaugural, their presence in the University was taken for granted. Positive symbolic steps included the conferring of an honorary degree on the Princess as well as the Prince of Wales in 1907 – a privilege not accorded her predecessor in 1868. This advance followed the award of honorary degrees at the 1901 Jubilee to three women who had played key roles in the development of female university education: Mrs Campbell of Tullichewan and Isabella Elder – leaders at Glasgow – and Emily Davies, founder of Girton College, Cambridge. Yet, despite mixing at social occasions and, increasingly, in student societies, doubts remained about how far women could be integrated into the everyday life of the University. In the years preceding 1914 the Senate was much concerned with issues of separate classes and buildings: the rising female student population began to make incursions onto the Gilmorehill campus. Also, while Janet Galloway received an honorary degree in 1906 with great fanfare (and the enthusiastic support of Principal Story), the male establishment remained ambivalent enough to decide in 1913 that the Mistress of QMC would be deemed equivalent, in University processions, only to a university lecturer![47]

Of at least equal importance to the student experience were the jobs which followed. Alterations in the curriculum combined with changes in Scottish society to shift substantially the career destinations of Glasgow graduates between the 1880s and the outbreak of the First World War. While medicine, for example, remained a popular destination, it was less so than in the 1880s. The opposite trend prevailed for science and engineering (fields in which Glasgow gave significantly more degrees than most other British universities by the eve of War) and, especially, for teaching (aspiring schoolteachers had become the biggest element in Glasgow's Arts Faculty by 1909). While science graduates gained jobs in industry, there was little penetration of commerce by Arts students, partly because only the more professionalised branches were interested in the University, except insofar as children of businessmen went there before turning to the family business. More prevalent, according to Robertson, was the movement into professional careers of children from business families: 'although the university came increasingly to supply the

4.8 *Mathematics and Natural Philosophy Party, 1907–8.*

technical education that a sophisticated industrial economy needed, its primary function was to provide a channel from industry and commerce into the professions of medicine, law, and teaching'.[48] Yet, such leakage may have been balanced, as Anderson argues, by shifts from professional to business families outside the university system altogether. Interestingly, by the eve of war, the Appointments Committee's rapid growth was being driven by local business employment as much as by the original target, the public sector; Glasgow students, it seems, seldom entered the Civil Service because of lack of appropriate family expectations. Still, the significant percentage of prewar graduates living outside Scotland but still in the UK suggests that Glasgow put its graduates into national elites as well as local ones.[49]

The appointment of a new Principal, Sir Donald MacAlister (1854–1934, Principal 1907–29) encouraged these changes in student life while taking a stage further the University's modernisation drive that Story had begun. Born in Perth the son of a publishers' agent, the young MacAlister had resided for a time in Aberdeen. However, the bulk of his brilliant schooling took place in Liverpool, and his equally outstanding student and academic career was at Cambridge, where he became a pivotal figure both in the medical school and at St John's College. By 1907, when the Government astonished MacAlister and the University by appointing him Principal, he was president of the General Medical Council (GMC) and an acknowledged virtuoso of academic administration. MacAlister's appointment, like those of his two immediate predecessors, drew added importance from the fact that the preceding

4.9 *Sir Donald MacAlister, Principal 1907–29, Chancellor 1929–34.*

Principal's effectiveness, both within the University and as its representative outside Gilmorehill, had been significantly reduced by illness in his final years. A vigorous fifty-three on appointment, MacAlister seemed set to make a significant impact on the University.[50]

MacAlister's was a key appointment in a number of other ways as well. He was very much a Scot by cultural identification, as he had demonstrated through study of Gaelic (among many other languages) as well as by frequent holidays north of the Border. Yet MacAlister had spent no significant part of his professional life in Scotland and had had no important involvement in its institutions, academic or otherwise. In many ways this was an ideal combination: he could not be criticised as an outsider, yet he carried a minimum of 'baggage'. This immunity applied especially to religion. MacAlister was a devout Presbyterian who believed that religion had a significant role to play in a university. This outlook minimised the jolt to the University posed by having its first-ever lay Principal succeed a man so closely identified with the Kirk as Story. Yet MacAlister was a member of the English Presbyterian Church with no ties in the Church of Scotland. Thus his appointment was the logical culmination of the progressive lessening of the Kirk's grip on the Scottish universities during the preceding seventy-five years, culminating in the 1889 Act's abolition of the remaining tests for professors. The appointment of MacAlister, then, guaranteed that there would be no repetition of the ironic situation whereby Story, despite efforts to emphasise his identity as Principal, was less well remembered as the latter than as a leading Churchman.[51] In practice, the new Principal held himself aloof from public entanglements not only in religious disputes but in party political conflicts as well.

MacAlister had to cope with a very demanding schedule. As his widow recalled ruefully, 'His days were crowded with engagements and appointments'. Within the University 'there were Senate meetings, Court meetings, all manner of other committees, countless interviews, enquiries to be made, consultations, questions to be answered'; beyond the University, he had a huge number of involvements, especially the GMC which required a weekly journey to London including two nights spent on the sleeper.[52] Curiously, MacAlister relied on extremely simple administrative arrangements. From the outset he preferred to work in his study in the Principal's Lodging, and after 1913 he gradually abandoned his office in the Gilbert Scott Building. Even more surprisingly, until 1913 (and to some extent thereafter) MacAlister handled his voluminous correspondence single-handed, dealing with 123 letters in an hour on one occasion. In a sense these were mere idiosyncrasies, but this punishing work pattern, for which Easters and summers spent at the seaside or in the Highlands could not fully compensate, arguably contributed to the Principal's increasing health problems. Moreover, MacAlister projected his old-fashioned work patterns onto an institution badly in need of an administrative shakeup, forbidding his colleagues to have secretaries, sternly correcting administrative subordinates, and failing to keep copies of his own letters which sometimes contradicted policies being pursued elsewhere in the University.[53]

Yet these work habits were more than outweighed by MacAlister's extraordinary facility in analysing problems, proposing solutions and obtaining consent to them. MacAlister was an extremely quick learner, adept at absorbing the intricacies of his new university as well as of institutions farther afield. He was also an outstanding draftsman. Moreover, he impressed his colleagues with his accessibility. Others noted MacAlister's 'habit of swift decision, his genius for concentrating on essentials, and for finding formulae to reconcile conflicting views and interests'. Thus he played a strong role in Court, where he was 'adept at pulling the strands of the debate together and producing a formula which was adopted unanimously'. Yet MacAlister was also determined to get his way; in the eyes of his opponents, he was a 'schemer'. Indeed his style had elements of the 'autocratic', and he was on poor terms with some of his colleagues.[54]

Nonetheless, the positive side of MacAlister's personality remained the dominant impression of his interactions with a variety of audiences. For example, he took special care to get on good terms with the students, addressing a social meeting in the Union on the day before his installation as Principal. Having emphasised his desire to 'uphold [the] honour and glory' of the University, MacAlister invited students to approach him as problems arose. Drawing on his experience as a Cambridge tutor, the new Principal won and retained friendly relations with the student body – in marked contrast to his predecessor. Significantly, one of the few occasions when MacAlister publicly rebuked students arose from antics during a prayer. More characteristic was the student presentation to MacAlister of a pendant (modelled on his Order of the Bath decoration) which he wore at graduations. Similarly, like Story, MacAlister also sought systematically to tighten the ties between the University and its alumni. Thus he enlarged the annual conversazione, regularly attended the London graduates' club and promoted similar organisations in other cities.[55]

Moreover, even more than Story, MacAlister sought to increase the University's impact on Glasgow and its region. As an acknowledged man of affairs, he had advantages over his clerical predecessors in relating to the local business community and other Scottish elites. It was felt that he 'brought more than a scholastic lustre'; 'his profound learning never held him aloof from work-a-day matters or the domestic politics of Senate or City'.[56] As the Clerk of the Trades House commented after his death: 'in one respect he was above all his predecessors in that he was essentially a man of the world and a very great man of affairs'.[57] Just as every movement within the University was public, 'the Principal was always in the public eye . . . He could not go to London even, or return thence, without a paragraph appearing [in the press] to note the fact'.[58] MacAlister and his wife – the daughter of a Cambridge professor – made extensive, and well publicised, excursions into Glasgow society, enduring 'almost embarrassing hospitality' in the form of 'an amazing spate of dinner-parties', including at least one with twenty-four courses! At the many public dinners '"a speech from the Principal" was almost a *sine qua non*'; fortunately MacAlister was highly skilled at public speaking.[59] MacAlister also skilfully exploited the overlap between university and civic events, as when the Rector and the Lord Provost joined him at the dedication of Lord Kelvin's statue in Kelvingrove Park. He also served on a variety of bodies in Glasgow, notably the Royal Technical College, the Commercial College, the Royal Infirmary and the Charity Organisation Society, and he was a man who took such affiliations seriously. Likewise, the Principal was made a justice of the peace, and a deputy lieutenant of Lanarkshire. MacAlister also defended municipal dignity, once forthrightly countering an attempt by students to spirit away the Lord Provost: 'He applied the stick across a part of the anatomy where the kidnappers felt it acutely, without suffering any permanent injury'![60] Thus, long before the splendid ceremony in 1924 when

4.10 *Unveiling of Lord Kelvin's statue, Kelvingrove Park, 1913. On the platform are the Rector, Lord Provost and Principal.*

MacAlister became the first Principal to receive the Freedom of Glasgow, he was a popular figure in civic life to an extent that none of his predecessors had managed. As an obituarist wrote, 'In the seven years that preceded the outbreak of war, he had, by his devotion to the cause of University education, made a bond between Town and Gown which, under his inspiration, became a thing of pride to all the citizens, revealing itself in a thousand ways in the relationships between the academical world and the busy life of the city'.[61] This was a considerable achievement given the demands for reform, and lack of confidence in university leadership, that filled the press as late as 1907. Therefore it was never said of MacAlister – as it was, in part erroneously, of Story – that he 'did not largely enter' into Glasgow's public life.[62] In the public arena, the forcefulness which distressed professors such as Henry Jones was an asset for MacAlister. Thus Professor Bower's complaint in Court about the outside encouragement of an academic post in 'civic and social subjects' was frustrated by the revelation that MacAlister had attended the meeting himself.[63]

Yet in no sense did MacAlister 'go native' in Glasgow: he became a key figure in wider Scottish circles, and he remained a member of UK, and international, elites – thereby helping to broaden the University's horizons in each respect. In addition to retaining a key role in the GMC, the Principal continued or took on responsibilities which linked the University in major ways to Scottish, British and wider elites on matters related to, but also beyond, medicine and academia. In medical matters, he played a major part in the revision of the British Pharmacopeia, chaired the medical consultative committee of the Scottish Board of Health and was a significant force in the development of the Highlands and Islands Medical Service Board. He was a member of the Carnegie United Kingdom Trust and of commissions on the Civil Service, the University of Wales and Queen's University Belfast. He also served as a governor of Imperial College. With regard to inter-university affairs, in addition to interacting with his fellow Scottish Principals at Carnegie's Skibo Castle and at other venues, MacAlister played a major part in the emergence of the Home Universities Committee, the Universities' Bureau of the British Empire (which later evolved into the Association of Commonwealth Universities) and the Committee of Vice Chancellors and Principals, which he chaired enthusiastically. It was characteristic of MacAlister's regime that in 1912 international delegates to the Universities of the Empire conference who were visiting Glasgow received honorary degrees.[64]

This cosmopolitan approach to academic life dovetailed with MacAlister's determination to lift further the University's research performance, partly by recruiting people adept at both research and teaching, partly by extending the spread of subjects, partly by pushing ahead with the building programme he had inherited, notably in Zoology. At the opening of the Natural Philosophy Building by the Prince and Princess of Wales in 1907 MacAlister rightly gave credit to Story. But on that occasion he launched an appeal for the Arts coinciding with the pending reform of the Arts degree and calling for additional chairs, smaller classes and improved buildings. Assisted by the proceeds of Story's equipment appeal, Carnegie institutional grants, a Treasury Grant from 1910–11 and the 1911 civic exhibition, the University managed to add the chair of Scottish History and Literature and lectureships in a variety of Arts subjects, drawing in part on benefactions which confidence in MacAlister helped to elicit. However, the War and subsequent economic problems long deferred many of MacAlister's aims, notably the combined scheme for a chapel and Arts buildings launched in June 1914.[65]

Even so, MacAlister had major academic achievements before 1914. The first of these related to his own profession, medicine. The Principal played a key role in reforging the University's links to the Royal Infirmary – a vital step in the expansion and rationalisation of the Medical Faculty – and in modernising clinical teaching. The largest of Glasgow's hospitals, and the site since 1889 of St Mungo's College, the Royal's rebuilding had by 1910 underlined the anomaly of the University's lack of a firm link since its clinical teaching, and chairs, had been shifted to the Western Infirmary in 1874. MacAlister chaired a special court committee on medical teaching at the Glasgow hospitals. With help from the Muirhead Trustees, the outcome was provision at the Royal for women students and, crucially, for four medical professors (in surgery, medicine, gynaecology and pathology). Facilitated by convenient vacancies in two chairs at the Western, they were transferred to the Royal to become the St Mungo Chair of Surgery and the Muirhead Chair of Medicine. In combination with new facilities there, MacAlister's aim was a 'clinical school of the first importance'. Establishing a pattern subsequently applied to other teaching hospitals in Glasgow, MacAlister's policies led to the appointment as honorary university lecturers of physicians and surgeons in the clinical wards. These changes substantially improved the number of clinical teachers and the size of clinical classes, helping to narrow a gap between Glasgow and English medical schools concerning the extent of active clinical experience for students. Similarly, just before the outbreak of war MacAlister played a key role in launching discussions between the University, the extra-mural schools and the Faculty of Physicians and Surgeons of Glasgow to consider a coordinated scheme of postgraduate medical education in the city. The improvement of Glasgow's medical school was a long-term project, but even by the early years of the War a significant positive change was evident, at least within the University.[66]

MacAlister also applied his formidable negotiating talents to the University's relationship with the Glasgow and West of Scotland Technical College – the descendant of Anderson's University which became, in 1912, the Royal Technical College (RTC). At one level, aided by their largely complementary curricula and by shared leaders like Sir William Copland, the

University and the College had, to use Kelvin's words, 'worked in perfect harmony'. Yet a combination of perceived superiority and worries about competition produced tensions evident in the University's successful legal challenge in the 1870s to its rival's use of the term 'University' and search for degree-granting powers. As the biographical directories of the city indicated, although inferior in fame to university professors (and jumping to university chairs if they had the chance), the Technical College's professors earned considerable respect in their own right. Also, the institution attracted increasing attention on festive occasions. As early as the 1863 city banquet for Lord Palmerston the president of the Andersonian University had an honoured place, and in 1903 the King laid the foundation stone of the Technical College's massive new building, for which the College had raised a substantial portion of the cost of £300,000 through an appeal. Moreover, at least in subjects such as chemistry, the University's rival sometimes proved more adept at forging links to local firms. By the time of MacAlister's appointment, shortly after a dispute concerning the University's re-equipment campaign revealed an unclear division of labour between the two institutions, the College's bulk and reputation required a systematic response from the University.[67]

Discussions on affiliation had their origins in the 1880s, when they were forwarded by Kelvin, a governor of the College. From 1889 Glasgow allowed the College's engineering diploma to exempt students from the first two years of the B.Sc., a provision which was taken up by many during the 1890s. The University prompted consideration of affiliation *per se*, starting with a Court committee in 1906 which delivered its preliminary report in 1908. MacAlister, a governor of the College from 1907, took charge of dealings personally, reaching an affiliation agreement in 1911 that resulted in an ordinance approved by the Privy Council in 1913. As a result, RTC students in specified fields could receive Glasgow degrees in applied science, supervised by joint boards and examiners. Students working for Glasgow degrees matriculated in the University and had access to the usual student facilities and activities. The curriculum could be followed on either campus, or on both. Yet these significant steps – followed shortly thereafter by even closer collaboration in chemistry – stopped well short of a merger, as both institutions seemed to prefer that they should. Likewise, partly on grounds of limiting the flow of students to the University, the arrangements extended only to the College's day students, disappointing a significant minority of Glasgow's General Council which feared discouragement to the 'earnest, diligent and able young man' who could only attend in the evenings. Looking back on these events in the 1930s, Principal Rait pronounced the agreement 'the most important step' the Court took under MacAlister before 1914 and attributed the result 'very largely . . . to his resourceful statesmanship'. It is difficult to disagree with either verdict, though the intervention of the War cut short the possibility that the College might evolve into a Faculty of the University.[68]

Thus by the outbreak of War MacAlister had placed his stamp on the University which had found a Principal tied to many of its traditions yet largely immune from most of its foibles. Unlike his predecessors, MacAlister had managed to master both the academic world and the public arena without becoming the prisoner of either.

What was the general situation of the University of Glasgow in 1914, and how had it changed from the years preceding the 1858 Act?

A major weakness, which would constrain the University's ability to react imaginatively to future difficulties, was its administrative structure. In 1914, in contrast to the other Scottish universities, 'there was no-one with overall responsibility for the administration', while on Gilmorehill the few full-time bureaucrats presided over a 'jungle' of rival offices.[69] Yet, as implied by the strength of MacAlister's position in relation to professors, lay members of Court and graduates, governance had become a major asset, in marked contrast to the internal rifts of the first half of the nineteenth century. The University's legitimacy – and, in significant ways, its efficiency, particularly through the thriving Court – had gained from the broadening of its constitution, especially from the infusion of key members of Glasgow's upper middle class and of its governing elite, during decades when those groups expanded rapidly in numbers and resources but did not lose their cohesion. Yet, in marked contrast to the fears of the professoriate before the Acts both of 1858 and of 1889, the General Council was more a talking shop than a parliament.[70] Meanwhile, the Senate – which through its assessors played a major role in the Court – remained a vigorous body, meeting twenty times in 1913, for example, with over half its members present at an average meeting. While having to defer to the significantly enhanced office of the Principal, the professors found themselves, for the first time in many decades, able to combine popularity with significant control of their own affairs.[71] Admittedly, by 1914 Glasgow, like other Scottish universities, had to submit regular plans to the Carnegie Trust and to the government in order to keep up the flow of grants on which depended hopes for remaining competitive in research.[72] Yet the detailed role of government in the universities was less intrusive, and more generous, on the eve of the First World War than it had been during long periods of the years since the 1820s.[73] Moreover, partly through the influence of government and bodies like the Carnegie Trust, the University was more tightly linked into a Scottish, a British and a world system of universities than ever before.[74]

Another notable success lay in the University's major outputs, its teaching and research. The curriculum of 1914 was much broader and more flexible than that of the 1850s,[75] and teaching methods had become more diverse without discarding the general excellence of the professorial lecture. The University now attracted significantly more students without having sacrificed either its strong middle-class base or its significant working-class clientele, and the numbers achieving degrees had risen very substantially since the mid-nineteenth century. Problems lurked within these achievements, particularly the relatively restricted penetration of honours, the very slow start on research degrees, and the major limitations to full, integrated student life, especially for women and other smaller minorities. Similarly, there were shortcomings in research, not least continuing difficulties – especially in relation to international competitors – in staff numbers and workloads and the quality of buildings and equipment. Particularly ominous was the University's heavy financial dependence on a combination of low fees, relatively large classes and comparatively small staff numbers.[76] Nonetheless, as in teaching, in research the trend had been distinctly upward in absolute terms. Even in comparative terms, Glasgow remained a leading university in many areas of research on the eve of the First World War.

It might be supposed that the University suffered from unfortunately distant relations with business and, in particular, with industry.[77] Yet physics and engineering professors – including Kelvin with his cable triumphs, Lewis Gordon (Brunel's assistant) with his major role in the Loch Katrine Scheme, Macquorn Rankine with his ties to shipbuilding, and Barr with his optical factory – had very strong business links. Also, as demonstrated repeatedly between the 1860s and the 1910s, businessmen made significant financial contributions to the University, whether by subscribing to appeals or by endowing chairs and lectureships. Arguably the ties should have been even closer during this heyday of the 'Second City of the Empire', and a more resolutely entrepreneurial approach by the University might well have tightened the relationship. Yet there were competing educational targets in Glasgow for business links, not least the RTC. Also, sometimes practical courses were offered but not well subscribed.[78] Moreover, in a city such as Glasgow where professional, commercial and industrial enterprises and elites were closely intertwined, the University's focus on professional careers, aided by the part-time teaching of leading medical men and distinguished lawyers, represented sensible concentration on the things it did well.[79] In 1900, of sixty-seven Scottish-born leading Glasgow businessmen, fourteen had been to Glasgow University, out of a total of twenty-six with university education. Like other Scottish universities, and more than the fledgling English civic universities, Glasgow successfully penetrated the education of its professional and business communities.[80] Moreover, as Campbell Lloyd has shown, the University had ever closer ties to another important regional 'business', the education sector, in relation to which a generally efficient division of labour had evolved.[81] Having shifted during the Victorian period away from its original rural base and having shed many even of its aristocratic associations, Glasgow (even more than the Northern English civic universities)[82] was tightly tied to a diverse range of middle-class groups in which business, broadly defined, played a key role.

Robert Anderson has suggested that, especially at Edinburgh, Scottish universities in the mid-nineteenth century approached the status of 'urban' universities, 'open to all comers, relying mainly on lectures, and serving as a tribune for the national intelligentsia. Nothing could be further from the residential and inward-looking universities of Oxford and Cambridge'.[83] The latter had their own virtues, of course, but the contrast was real, as the young Henry Jones discovered during his brief, unhappy excursion in the 1870s to Oxford, where the atmosphere seemed frivolous compared to Glasgow. During the period 1870 to 1914 Glasgow, like Edinburgh and the ancient English universities, on the whole managed to keep pace with new intellectual developments, including those in science. Yet it did so without losing strong reciprocal links with its country and, especially, its city. Indeed, as Campbell Lloyd has argued, Glasgow, even more than other Scottish universities, strengthened its links with its various 'communities' during the period between the 1858 Act and the outbreak of the First World War. Thus the longtime Clerk of Senate, William Stewart, did not allow his academic duties and administrative burdens to prevent his involvement on various educational bodies outside the University. Meanwhile, a majority of the significant minority of Glasgow's civic elite just before the War who had higher education experience had attended the University.[84]

By 1914 Glasgow University had achieved a 'virtuous circle': its successes boosted the prestige of the city, which in turn increased at least its symbolic support for the University.[85] Unifying rituals became more frequent, and certainly became more spectacular and more filled with mutually congratulatory rhetoric, during and after the move to Gilmorehill. The University played a major role in great civic occasions: its honorary degree was the focal point of the city's honouring of the war hero Lord Roberts in 1913, for example.[86] Whenever royalty came to the city – notably when visiting the various international exhibitions of the period – they tended at least to drive through the University and receive a loyal address. Nor were good relations confined to special occasions. Press coverage of the Scottish universities before 1914 tended to be neutral or positive, with criticism reserved for particular individuals, and embarrassing material was sometimes kept wholly or partly out of the press.[87] When complaints erupted, such as queries in 1899 regarding the Court's secrecy, or a 1914 difference of view between university and city which spilled over into the House of Lords, the underlying relationship was strong enough, by the early twentieth century, to withstand such disruptions. As a result, universities such as Glasgow stood much higher in public esteem, in the locality and beyond, than in the middle of the nineteenth century.[88] Arguably the University on Gilmorehill had become the greatest of all the great civic projects of Victorian and Edwardian Glasgow, a status implied by the city's willingness to make the University's new chair of Scottish History and Literature the chief beneficiary of its 1911 exhibition. For the citizens of

4.11 *Royal Party arriving at the 1901 Exhibition on Opening Day.*

early twentieth-century Glasgow, far less ambiguously than for their predecessors in the first half of the nineteenth century, the University was a source of pride combining both antiquity and progress.

How had this change come about? The University had moved its premises,[89] reformed its governance, shifted to meritocratic appointments, unified its professoriate, modernised its buildings and equipment, diversified its curriculum and student body, enhanced its international academic prestige, drastically increased its public involvements, shifted them from provocation to unification and increasingly included the city in its ever more splendid rituals. Meanwhile Glasgow, a boom city with massive social problems as well as great civic achievements, proved itself a locality hungry for the historical roots and intellectual respectability of an ancient but also a dynamic university arguably at the height of its international fame. Thus, the runaway growth, and the social, religious and political dynamism, of Victorian and Edwardian Glasgow had proven far more assets than liabilities for the University. What could not be foreseen in the spring of 1914, was how rapidly and fully this dynamism would go into reverse, with long-lasting negative consequences for the University.

Notes and References

1. Story had studied at Edinburgh, St Andrews and Heidelberg; he had a Glasgow connection in that his great-great-great-grandfather had been Principal!
2. GH, 14 January 1907. Cf. J. H. S. Burleigh, *A Church History of Scotland* (London, 1960), 399.
3. For example, he backed the controversial sending of a greeting to the Pope at the time of the 1901 Jubilee.
4. *Story's Daughters' Memoir*, 315 (quote), 344–5; J. L. Story [wife], *Later Reminiscences* (Glasgow, 1913), 331–2; Anderson, *Education and Opportunity*, 277–9.
5. Norman Maclean, in *Story's Daughters' Memoir*, 351.
6. Ibid., 308; GH, 21 October 1898; SMN, 7 December 1905.
7. Story to Rev. D. MacMillan, 7 October 1899, *Story's Daughters' Memoir*, 324 and 303, 357–8, 362; GUA, Story Papers, Balfour of Burleigh to Story, 22 June 1898.
8. Mrs Story got her revenge in her memoirs; see especially J. L. Story, *Later Reminiscences*, 336–7. Cf. Ibid., 309–15, 343–53; *Story's Daughters' Memoir*, 221, 228; Lloyd 'Communities', 274–5.
9. GH, 14 January 1907.
10. Story to Lady F. Balfour, 15 May 1903 in *Story's Daughters' Memoir*, 354 (quote) and 366–7; J. L. Story, *Later Reminiscences*, 333–6.
11. Story, GH, 19 March 1900. Cf. Story, 'Relation of Civic to Academic Life', in *Book of the Jubilee*, 3–8.
12. 'Inaugural Address . . .' (Glasgow, 1898).
13. This recognition seems odd given Story's aversion to a faculty of commerce. Yet for Story the latter evidently menaced academic independence in a way that laboratory research, even if boosted by donations from business for buildings and equipment, did not.
14. *Story's Daughters' Memoir*, 341.
15. GH, 19 March 1900–3 May 1900, esp. 19 and 29 March and 3 May.
16. 'The Extension and Better Equipment of the University of Glasgow' (1902).
17. Mackie, *University*, 291; Sanderson, *Universities and British Industry*, 169–70; Lloyd, 'Communities', 302; Robertson, 'Finances', 468, 471–3; 'Extension and Better Equipment', 4; J. Robb, *The Carnegie Trust for the Universities of Scotland 1901–1926* (Edinburgh, 1927), 51; GUA, Story Papers, Carnegie to Story, 28 May and 20 Aug. 1906.
18. For information on the Jubilee see *Record of the Ninth Jubilee of the University of Glasgow 1451–1901* (Glasgow, 1901) (hereafter *Jubilee*), and *Glasgow University Magazine*, 31 October 1901; for parallel accounts with similar positive emphases see Lloyd, 'Communities, 277–85, esp. 279 and Mackie, *University*, 291; J. L. Story, *Later Reminiscences*, 332. Compare Anderson, *Education and Opportunity*, 332.
19. *Jubilee*, passim; Brown and Moss, *University*, 106; Lloyd, 'Communities', 283.
20. *Story's Daughters' Memoir*, 361.
21. Hutcheson, *University*, 35; GH, 6 April 1905; GCMN, 12 April and 25 October 1905; WWG, 137.

22. GH, 24 and 30 June 1904; Lloyd, 'Communities', 268–71; General Council Report, April 1906; Anderson, *Education and Opportunity*, 332–3.
23. OHGM, 51.
24. *Story's Daughters' Memoir*, 377. Ironically the University only received a portrait because the collection for the project, undertaken within the Kirk, had produced enough money for two!
25. *Story's Daughters' Memoir*, 310 (quotes), 359 and cf. 321–2.
26. Hetherington, *Henry Jones*, 85–6, 110. The close collaboration between the Unionist Story and Jones, an ardent advanced Liberal, was indicative of the dampening down of political conflict in the University by this time.
27. J. L. Story, *Later Reminiscences*, 322 (quote), 361; *Story's Daughters' Memoir*, 363.
28. Anderson, 'Professors', 28, 33, 37–8, 43 and Table 3; Hutcheson, *University*, 60. For parallel professionalising in Oxbridge, see S. Rothblatt, *The Revolution of the Dons: Cambridge and Society in Victorian England* (Cambridge, 1968) and A. Engel, *From Clergyman to Don: The rise of the academic profession in nineteenth century Oxford* (Oxford, 1983).
29. Lloyd, 'Communities', 276–7; Hetherington, *Henry Jones*, 77 n. 1, 90–1; 'The College Club Glasgow' (1907); Mackie, *University*, 303; OHGM, 269–72; WWG, 47, 113–14; *DNB* (McCall Anderson); A. L. Macfie, 'Note on the Growth of Political Economy', FD, 130.
30. SMN, 6 February 1913; Hutcheson, *University*, 24, 30; Robertson, 'Finances', 470; Anderson, 'Professors', 38.
31. Coutts, *University*, 472.
32. Robertson, 'Finances', 467 (quote), 470; Lloyd, 'Communities', 185, Table 5.16.
33. GH, 30 April 1900 (quote); Hetherington, *Henry Jones*, 76, 79–80, 84; Hutcheson, *University*, 34, 37; A. Browning, 'History', FD, 52; *DNB* (Gloag). Smart's own students felt that he 'not only interests his classes, but makes them as enthusiastic as himself' (*Glasgow University Magazine* (hereafter GUM), 4 Dec. 1895).
34. *Jubilee*, 89.
35. Hetherington, *Henry Jones*, 73, 75, 78; C. A. Campbell, 'Philosophy', FD 118–19; Hutcheson, *University*, 29 (quote); Dupree, 'Development', Table 7; C. Duguid, *Macewen of Glasgow: A Recollection of the Chief* (Edinburgh, 1957); GUM, 25 April 1913.
36. Anderson, *Education and Opportunity*, 280–1 and 284, Table 7.2; Macfie, 'Political Economy', FD, 128; Hetherington, *Henry Jones*, 87.
37. Hull and Geyer-Kordesch, *Shaping the Medical Profession*, ch. 2; J. McEwen, 'The Role of the University of Glasgow in the changing tasks of Public Health', (2001 seminar, 19 March 1998); Coutts, *University*, 460; Walker, *School of Law*, 53–4.
38. On economic sector see Robertson, 'Development', 55; on social origin see Anderson, *Education and Opportunity*, 380–1 recalculating percentages to exclude those classified as 'Not given, uncertain, dead', and cf. 150–1; S. H. S. Patrick, 'A study of the social and geographical origins . . . of a sample of first year students at Glasgow University . . .' (Unpublished undergraduate

dissertation, Department of Economic History, University of Glasgow, 1990), 7; C. Logan, 'Women at Glasgow University: determination or predetermination?' (Unpublished undergraduate dissertation, Department of Economic History, University of Glasgow, 1986), 15, 61–4.
39. Malloch, *Glasgow Anecdote*, 245; Anderson, *Education and Opportunity*, 318–21, Table 8.11 and 339; *Universities and Elites*, 50.
40. Dupree, 'Development', 14; Lloyd, 'Communities', 236–8; Robertson, 'Finances', 474–5, and 'Development', 57 n. 17; Anderson, *Education and Opportunity*, 277.
41. Dupree, 'Development', 14 and Figure 3; Hull and Geyer-Kordesch, *Shaping the Medical Profession*, ch. 2; Anderson, *Education and Opportunity*, 305.
42. CMN, 13 February 1913; Robertson, 'Development', 74–6; Dupree, 'Development', 15; Anderson, *Education and Opportunity*, 294–8, Table 8.1; Brown and Moss, *University*, 73–4.
43. General Council Report, April 1906, 'Report by the Graduates' University Extension Committee', 57; R. S. Rait, in *Sir Donald MacAlister of Tarbert by his wife* (London, 1935), 346–8 [hereafter *MacAlister*]; Brown and Moss, *University*, 73, 88; GUM, 23 Jan. 1895 and 19 Feb. and 15 May 1913.
44. Parties and other student celebrations on the last day of the first term. For Mavor's irreverent, but generally positive, view of student life at Gilmorehill, see Bridie, *One Way of Living* (London, 1939), esp. 138–40.
45. J. L. Story, *Later Reminiscences*, 309, *Jubilee*, 74 and SMN, 21 December 1905 (quotes); GUM, 15 Nov. 1905; Brown and Moss, *University*, 73–4, 89; Anderson, *Education and Opportunity*, 328, 330.
46. GUM, 12 Nov. 1913.
47. SMN, 2 June 1913; Myers, 'Education', 240; O. Checkland, *Queen Margaret Union 1890–1980: Women in the University of Glasgow* (Glasgow, 1980); C. Logan, 'Women at Glasgow University', 32–3; PP 1913 [Cd. 6740], R.C. Civil Service, Appendix to 3rd Report, 212, Q.20423, D. J. M. Medley.
48. Robertson, 'Development', 48 (quote), 67–74 and Tables 8–10; Anderson, *Education and Opportunity*, 276, 279–80.
49. Anderson, *Universities and Elites*, 45, 26; *Education and Opportunity*, 326–7; SMN, 20 June 1913; Robertson, 'Development', 75–7 and Table 12; R.C. Civil Service, 205–12, 305–6.
50. MacAlister was knighted in 1908, became a baronet in 1924 and was elected Chancellor of the University in 1929 following his retirement as Principal; sources include *DNB*, *MacAlister* and GH, 16 January 1934.
51. GH, 14 January 1907.
52. *MacAlister*, 184–5.
53. *MacAlister*, 184; Hutcheson, *University*, 2–3; Brown and Moss, *University*, 108.
54. General Council Resolution, 30 October 1929, quoted by Rait in *MacAlister*, 363–4; Hutcheson, *University*, 28, 23 and 25 (quotes).
55. *MacAlister*, 175 (quote), 174, 237–8, 332.
56. Obituary, *MacAlister*, 177 (quote).
57. Harry Lumsden, GH, 16 January 1934.
58. *MacAlister*, 179.

59. *MacAlister*, 179 and 180 (quotes); Lloyd, 'Communities', 276.
60. *MacAlister*, 238 (quote), 186, 189.
61. GH, 16 January 1934.
62. GH, 14 January 1907.
63. CMN, 13 February 1913. For the increasing importance of the office of Principal to observers outside the University see Lloyd, 'Communities', 273–4.
64. *MacAlister*, 192.
65. *MacAlister*, 183, 323–6, 332–3, 345; GH, 30 April 1900 and 16 January 1934; Brown and Moss, *University*, 96–7.
66. *MacAlister*, 328 (quote) and 326–7, 329–30; Dupree, 'Development', 22–3; Hull and Geyer-Kordesch, *Shaping the Medical Profession*, ch. 2.
67. *Jubilee*, 55 (quote); WWG, 47–85 and passim; J. Butt, *John Anderson's Legacy: The University of Strathclyde and its Antecedents* (East Linton, 1996), 76–9; *Lord Provosts*, 209; Sanderson, *Universities and British Industry*, 170.
68. GCMN, 18 January 1913 and Rait in *MacAlister*, 332 (quote) and 330–1 (quotes); Brown and Moss, *University*, 107; Butt, *Legacy*, 99–100. Cf. Anderson, *Education and Opportunity*, 268 n. 35. Rait was the founding professor (1913–29) of Scottish History and Literature.
69. Hutcheson, *University*, 2, 9, 10 (quote).
70. Cf. Lloyd, 'Communities', 294; Morgan and Trainor, 'Dominant Classes', 105–17, 121–5 and Trainor, 'The Elite', 233–50.
71. Cf. Anderson, *Education and Opportunity*, 290, 293.
72. In 1907/8 state grants were down from the 37.9% of income they had constituted in the 1890s, but they remained substantial at 27.3% – Anderson, *Education and Opportunity*, 289, Table 7.4.
73. Cf. I. G. C. Hutchison, *The University and the State: The Case of Aberdeen 1860–1963* (Aberdeen, 1993), esp. 150–1.
74. Anderson, *Universities and Elites*, 13.
75. Cf. P. L. Robertson, 'Scottish Universities and Industry', *Scottish Economic and Social History*, 4 (1984), 39–55.
76. For the dominance of salaries in expenditure, and of fees in income, see: Anderson, *Education and Opportunity*, 285, Table 7.3 and 289, Table 7.4; Robertson, 'Finances', 465.
77. Sanderson, *Universities and British Industry*, 165, 167–73.
78. Robertson, 'Scottish Universities and Industry', 39–40; Lloyd, 'Communities', 154–5.
79. Morgan and Trainor, 'Dominant Classes'; Trainor, 'The Elite'; Lloyd, 'Communities', 302–3.
80. Sanderson, *Universities and British Industry*, 180; Anderson, *Universities and Elites*, 22.
81. Lloyd, 'Communities', 296–7, 301.
82. Cf. Jones, *Civic Universities*.
83. Anderson, *Education and Opportunity*, 34.
84. Lloyd, 'Communities', 314, Appendix 3.1 and passim; Trainor, 'The Elite', 244–5.
85. Lloyd, 'Communities', 300–1.
86. GH, 6 May 1913; on such rituals generally, see Lloyd, 'Communities', 303–4.

87. Lloyd, 'Communities', 285, 288, 289–90.
88. Lloyd, 'Communities', 305–6.
89. The move to Gilmorehill might have brought about isolation, but – as Story recognised – 'the city has followed the University' ('Relation of Civic to Academic Life', 7).

PART II

1914–51

CHAPTER FIVE

War and its Aftermath, 1914–20

The shots that rang round the world from Sarajevo echoed only distantly in the cloisters and grounds of Gilmorehill. The University, like the nation, was ill prepared for war. It had been touched in various ways, it is true, by the rise in international tensions which preceded the outbreak of hostilities. Nevertheless, when these tensions finally erupted in the summer of 1914 into a conflict between the Great Powers of Europe and their respective empires, it caught almost everyone in the University by surprise. The most pressing matters before the Principal and the University Court during those summer months were such long-standing and relatively mundane concerns as the plans for new buildings for Arts and Zoology and the rumbling row with the Corporation of Glasgow over proposed tramway lines down University Avenue and alongside Queen Margaret College. The students were on vacation and most of the staff had joined the annual exodus from Gilmorehill which occurred in the summer. The British declaration of war on 4 August was therefore virtually a bolt from the blue. Several members of staff, indeed, were on the Continent and found their return to Glasgow delayed by the closure of frontiers. Among them was the Principal, Sir Donald MacAlister, who had set off in late July, accompanied by his wife and niece, to convalesce from a recent illness by taking the waters at Bad-Ems in Germany. Following the outbreak of war, they were detained briefly by the police and then experienced a difficult set of train journeys across Germany, in the middle of that country's mobilisation and a time of heightened anti-foreign feeling, before returning, shaken but safe, to Scotland.[1] Some members of the teaching staff, however, were slower to return and were unavailable for the preliminary (or entrance) examinations and the degree examinations being conducted in September, while staff from other universities who acted as additional (external) examiners were similarly placed. Consequently, much ad hoc arranging had to be done to ensure the smooth running of the examination timetable.

The main challenge to the University's capacity to adapt to rapidly changing circumstances came from the mobilisation of manpower for the British armed forces. Several students rushed to join the colours as soon as war was declared, leading to special examinations and a graduation ceremony being hastily arranged for some of them.[2] The Officers' Training Corps, established under the Haldane Reforms of the Army in 1910, was at the sharp end of the recruitment process. At the beginning of the war it mustered some 400 men – 300 infantrymen under thirteen officers and 100 engineers under three officers – and by the end of October commissions had been granted to 170 serving and former cadets. However, students with no connection with the Corps also volunteered for military service during the excitement of these opening months of the conflict, as did a number of members of staff. Sir Donald played an active part in this recruitment process. Wearing his hat as President of the General Medical Council, he publicised the needs of the army for physicians and surgeons, and as Principal he took steps to encourage enlistment by staff. The Court decided at an early date that it would keep open the jobs of any of the non-academic employees who went on military service, and would continue to pay their wages less the army pay and allowances they received. It subsequently extended the same privileges to the teaching staff.[3] By February 1915, the University's Roll of Honour, which recorded the names of all those on military service, contained a total of 1,255 names – including 36 members of the academic staff, 20 other employees, 414 students and 520 graduates, together with certain other categories of people associated with the University. The great majority – 77 per cent of the total – had been commissioned as officers.[4] The University's greatest contribution to the war effort, it was clear, would be to supply and replenish the officer ranks of the armed services. It was a role it performed through another four, increasingly grim, years.

The 414 students who abandoned their studies to enter the war by February 1915, most of them into the 6th Battalion of the Cameron Highlanders for which Cameron of Locheil held a recruitment meeting in the University Union,[5] represented about fourteen per cent of the matriculated student body. Many were expressing personal convictions about patriotism and duty. But other pressures were also being brought to bear on young men to volunteer for the forces. An angry editorial in the student magazine, the *Glasgow University Magazine*, accused the professors, with 'their whiskered taunts', of being hand-in-glove with that 'band of stupid and inconsiderable little hussies,' who in the early weeks of August had 'conducted what they called a campaign in aid of recruiting' in Glasgow city centre.[6] This attack on professorial jingoism was published on 11 November, only one day before the Senate deliberated on the encouragement that should be given to students to equip themselves for the fray. The medical professors led the hawkish tendency, with a proposal from Professors Paton of Physiology and Glaister of Forensic Medicine that published examination lists should identify those students who were also undertaking military training, within the OTC or elsewhere, from those who were not (and thereby publicly identify the shirkers). This was defeated only by a counter-proposal to publish the names of those undertaking military

5.1 *The Officers' Training Corps at Summer Camp, 1914.*

training along with their studies separately from the examination lists, but on lists to appear on all noticeboards throughout the University. The message from the Senate to the undergraduates was further reinforced by the resolution from Professor Munro Kerr of Obstetrics and Gynaecology, which was passed on 9 December, that 'in the opinion of Senate the students in attendance upon the University should be invited to consider seriously the propriety of taking advantage of the opportunities offered for military training.'[7] Although the Senate's purpose was to encourage preparation for military service after graduation, rather than drive students immediately into the armed forces, some undoubtedly interpreted its actions as part of the wider campaign to promote an early enlistment, and there is evidence to suggest that the Senate's actions had the effect of dividing the student body into those openly preparing for war and the others, who avoided participation in student activities and concentrated on their studies.[8]

The female graduates and undergraduates too were swept up in the war and the preparations for war. The Scottish Women's Hospitals set up in France and Serbia recruited several women doctors and orderlies from the city hospitals, including Dr Louise McIlroy, the Assistant to the Professor of Obstetrics and Gynaecology at the Royal Infirmary. Part-time training for nursing in military hospitals was put in place in the Western and Royal Infirmaries in April 1915, attracting 36 women graduates and 68 undergraduates from

Queen Margaret College. For those, both men and women, who had neither the skills nor the temperament for military medicine and nursing, there were other outlets for voluntary wartime service – most notably in the booming munitions factories in and around Glasgow where the University's Appointments Committee placed some 400 part-time volunteers in 1914–15.[9]

As the war continued, and the stalemate on the Western Front was punctuated by periodic attempts to achieve an Allied breakthrough, the demands on the University's manpower rose inexorably. An upward shift in the recruitment

5.2 *Voluntary Nursing – Queen Margaret College students, 1915.*

process came in the late spring and early summer of 1915, when the draining away of the men of the pre-war Territorial battalions onto the battlefields of France and Belgium created a need for men to fill the ranks behind them. Consequently, on 21 June 1915, Senate entertained a motion that 'in view of the gravity of the situation and the urgent call of this City for 10,000 recruits for the Territorial Force Third Line, the Senatus make a public pronouncement urging students to give the question of military service their most serious consideration'. It agreed that an appeal for more volunteers should be attached to notices already issued by the Military Education Committee.[10] This caused some debate within the University, and more publicly, over whether senior medical students should respond to the appeal or not.[11] Continuing reliance on voluntary principles, however, proved incapable of fulfilling the demands for a greatly enlarged army for the Western Front, expressed by Kitchener in July 1915 as a need for a seventy division army, and a shift towards conscription came with the Derby Scheme of October 1915. The Senate duly announced that all Lecturers and Assistants of military age, except those who were qualified medical practitioners, were expected to offer themselves as recruits in army reserve B by 4 December 1915. Thereafter, as they were called up, the 'University authorities' would consider whether or not their services were considered indispensable to the University and exemption from military service might be claimed. Students who enlisted before 4 December – senior medical students were exempt – would also be transferred to Section B Army Reserve, whence they would be called up in groups, and it was hoped that many of them would be able to qualify for their 'class tickets' before they were called up for training.[12] These arrangements in turn were overtaken by the provisions of the Military Service Act of January 1916, which introduced compulsory service for all males between 18 and 41 years, with exemptions for those in essential occupations.

The effects of the national recruitment drive on the University community as a whole can be traced through the Roll of Honour, which recorded the names of all those who entered the armed services. This stood at 1,255 names in February 1915. It increased to 2,300 names (1,860 holding commissions) by October 1915, to 2,806 names by October 1916, to 3,172 names by October 1917 and to 3,363 names (2,650 holding commissioned rank) by October 1918. Most of these, however, were graduates whose absence at the war affected the University only indirectly, in its ability to maintain its links with and the support of its graduates. Much more serious was the migration of students and staff away from Gilmorehill itself. Of the student body, the number who had abandoned their studies to enter military service grew to 839 by October 1916. This, coupled with a reduction in the numbers of new entrants seeking places in the first year of degree courses, resulted in a dramatic decline in the number of students in attendance at classes. By 1916–17 the male student population was down to only forty per cent of its pre-war level, and although the number of women students gradually rose this barely compensated for the decline in the number of men. The fall in total student numbers – from 2,916 in 1913–14 to 1,662 in 1916–17, before recovering slightly to 1,921 in 1917–18 – was one of the most sudden changes that the University had faced in its long history, and certainly since the move to Gilmorehill. As a difficulty to be borne, it was matched only by the loss of staff to the war.

The numbers of non-academic employees in the forces peaked at fifty-four by October 1917, whereas the numbers of academic staff rose to fifty-five by October 1915 and remained relatively constant thereafter, indicating that most lecturers and assistants of appropriate age and levels of physical fitness had already volunteered for military service during the first year of the war, before the introduction of conscription. From October 1915 until the early months of 1919, therefore, roughly one quarter of the pre-war teaching staff was away at the conflict. Although student numbers fell faster than staff numbers, the requirements of the various curricula together with the needs of students still on course meant that the University could not reduce the range and diversity of its courses proportionately, and there were continuing problems for the Principal and professors in covering the work of a teaching staff depleted by military service. During the early months of the war, several refugee Belgian academics, principally from the University of Louvain, were employed to give lectures in their fields of study.[13] This, however, was more an attempt to offer short-term help to academics in distress than a serious effort to recruit new staff from the ranks of the refugees. New assistants were recruited to replace those away at the war from wherever qualified candidates could be found, and increasingly, as elsewhere in the economy, women obtained short-term opportunities from the absence of male applicants. The number of female assistants rose from four out of 58 in 1914–15 to six out of 52 in 1915–16 and to 11 out of 50 in 1917–18. Not all assistantships could be filled, however, and an even greater difficulty was experienced in replacing the more experienced lecturers who were on leave of absence for military and other purposes. Consequently, the pressures of teaching fell more heavily on those who remained behind.

The war affected the work of some departments more seriously than others. Engineering suffered from the departure of Professor J. D. Cormack in October 1915, to assume the post of Inspector of Contractors (Military Aeronautics) with the rank of Honorary Lt-Colonel, and from the fact that he took several of his staff with him. Fortunately, help was at hand in the shape of the recent association between the University and the Royal Technical College, and joint teaching arrangements for engineering were put in place. These became increasingly important as military and other wartime service drew heavily on the engineering staff of both institutions.[14] Similarly, in Naval Architecture Professor Biles had been fully engaged in war work since the opening of hostilities, leaving the task of teaching a diminishing band of students (none of them British) to Robb, his assistant. Robb left in turn in the spring of 1916, on temporary leave to assist in the construction of vessels for the Mesopotamia campaign, and when he was invalided home in November of that year, the few remaining students were told to take whatever relevant classes they could find in the Royal Technical College.[15] In Mining, the fall-off in student numbers was such that when the chair became vacant in 1917 it was decided to leave it unfilled, pending a post-war readjustment of teaching between the University and the College.[16] On the Arts side of the University, language teaching was also badly hit because of the prevailing practice of employing foreign nationals for this purpose. The two lecturers in French, Messieurs Martin and Pitoy, were both called up for the French army, although Pitoy was eventually invalided out and allowed to return to Glasgow early in 1917. Meanwhile, teaching went on with the assistance of retired staff and a series of temporary assistants, one of whom, Mme Valette, travelled to and from France every year until 1917–18, as a substitute for her husband who was also doing military service.

The needs of a government and economy at war also made other demands on the University's manpower. While the younger men served in the armed forces, their older colleagues were gradually drawn into an ever-widening range of government occupations or temporary duties. A. H. Charteris, Lecturer in International Law, assisted the Admiralty in the work of the Prize Court in London; Professor Rait of Scottish History was recruited for the War Trade Intelligence Department in 1916; S. H. Jones, Lecturer in Social Economics, joined the Ministry of Munitions; Professor Stevenson of Hebrew spent 1917–18 working for the Admiralty Intelligence Department in London; and Dr J. D. Falconer of Geography, who prior to his appointment had been a mineral surveyor in Northern Nigeria, was released by the University at the request of the Colonial Office to become an Assistant District Commissioner in that West African protectorate. Closer to home, Sir Henry Jones, Professor of Moral Philosophy, whose reputation in his native land made him an obvious target for a government seeking to recruit men of influence and intellect to the support of its policies in Wales, spent a good part of the war away from Glasgow. During 1914–15 he was engaged in a public speaking tour in support of the recruitment drive for the armed forces in Wales; in 1916 he was appointed to the Royal Commission on the Welsh university; and in October 1917 he was released by the University to undertake a lecture tour in the South Wales coalfield because his friend, Prime Minister Lloyd George, was greatly concerned about the spread of syndicalist views among the younger miners of South Wales and the threat of industrial action there, and believed that Jones 'has unusual gifts for dealing with this explosive material.'[17] Most of such wartime secondments came from the Arts side of the University, where the dwindling away of student numbers was most pronounced and from which it was therefore easier to release men for short periods of employment away from Gilmorehill.

A few individuals managed to combine continuing service to the University with new war-time responsibilities. Among them, Sir William Macewen, Professor of Surgery, was outstanding. On the outbreak of war, Macewen was commissioned as Surgeon-General in Scotland for the Royal Navy, with the rank of Surgeon Rear-Admiral, and thereafter took care of the medical and surgical needs of sailors of the fleet as well as the civilians in his own clinics. His greatest contribution to the 'Home Front' in the West of Scotland was undoubtedly his leading role in the establishment in 1916 of the Princess Louise Hospital for Limbless Soldiers and Sailors at Erskine in Renfrewshire. Here men cruelly maimed in the war were fitted with artificial limbs, many of them fashioned by craftsmen in the Clyde shipyards, and helped towards a re-entry into civilian occupations through employment in workshops where furniture and other items for sale were made.[18]

However, the predominant themes of patriotism and service running through the University's contribution to the war effort did not prevent the uglier face of the conflict from presenting itself from time to time. The national reaction against Germany and all things German first surfaced on Gilmorehill in the autumn of 1915, when the Assistant in German, Mr F. Broeker, was interned. Broeker had been in Glasgow since 1906, was married to a Scotswoman, had a young family, and had applied for naturalisation before the war broke out. Nevertheless, his German nationality marked him out as someone who could not remain at liberty.[19] Then in March 1916, following a request from the Secretary for Scotland, the Principal secured the agreement of Ludwig Becker that the latter would remove himself from the University Observatory, where he was the Director, and take paid leave from his Chair of Astronomy. Becker was a graduate of the University of Bonn who had attracted the attention of Lord Kelvin, with the result that he was appointed to the chair in Glasgow in 1893. Becker had been a naturalised British subject since 1892, but this did not prevent him from coming under suspicion of harbouring sympathies with the enemy, leading in turn to demands for his dismissal. When suspicions first surfaced in the House of Commons, in June 1915, that Becker was in a position to furnish weather reports helpful to the Germans, the Secretary for Scotland, Mackinnon Wood, vigorously defended him on the grounds that he had 'the most satisfactory assurances as to his loyalty' and that he lacked the means in the Observatory 'to enable him to make any effective forecasts or to communicate them if made.'[20] It is unclear what subsequently changed the Secretary for Scotland's mind about the dangers presented by Becker, or why Sir Donald MacAlister and Becker himself were prepared to yield to his pressure – although the fact that the chair of Astronomy was a Regius appointment undoubtedly had a part to play in this. Since there was no evidence of any impropriety on Becker's part, the action taken against him can

5.3 *Professor Ludwig Becker and students at the Observatory, 1915.*

only be understood as an indication of the intensity which anti-German hysteria had reached in Scotland by the early months of 1916. Becker spent the rest of the war cooling his heels, in retreat with his large family at a house in Crieff in Perthshire.[21]

With a staff complement greatly reduced by wartime needs and exigencies, the University did what it could to teach the students who remained behind. It cooperated with the other three Scottish universities in securing the passage through Parliament of the Scottish Universities (Emergency Powers) Act of July 1915. This gave greater autonomy to make more flexible arrangements for teaching and examining than was possible under the prevailing legislation. Collaboration with local higher education institutions was also pursued – in arrangements with the Free Church College, the West of Scotland Agricultural College and above all the Royal Technical College, which by 1917–18 was the sole provider in Glasgow of any instruction for University students in Engineering, Naval Architecture and Mining. The war indeed strengthened the bonds between the University and the Royal Technical College, one measure of this being the decision, which came out of a more general review of Chemistry within the University in 1916, to locate a department of Applied Chemistry in the RTC. Consequently, following the translation of Dr Cecil Desch, Lecturer in Metallurgical Chemistry, to a chair in the College in 1918, the University agreed to fund a University lectureship in the subject in the College, using endowment income for the purpose.[22]

Since over forty per cent of the University's income was normally derived from student fees, the large reduction in student numbers meant a severe squeeze on finances. Between the autumn of 1914 and the early months of 1918 the loss of fee income to the University stood at a total of £50,900.[23] Staff costs declined to a lesser extent, and meanwhile the other costs borne by the University rose year by year as shortages of such things as coal for heating and general wartime inflation ate into the University's funds. There were few alternative sources of additional income. Some payments of relatively small sums were made to the University and individual departments – principally Chemistry, Natural Philosophy and Engineering – by government departments, mainly the Admiralty, for research into steels, explosive substances and navigational or optical instruments associated with naval or military needs. This left the University at the mercy of the Treasury, whose annual grant normally provided about a third of the University's funds. The Treasury, it transpired from a joint approach from the four Scottish universities, was willing to assist through the introduction in 1915–16 of a system of annual supplementary grants which would partially compensate for the reduction of fee income, but in return it expected the universities to make 'every effort to meet the loss [of fee income] as far as possible by a rigid economy in expenditure.'[24] Such Treasury 'generosity' did not last for long – it made no further compensatory grants after 1915–16 and it froze the University's annual recurrent grant at the pre-war level of £24,680 per annum. Economies therefore had to be made to bridge the gap between an income that was greatly reduced in real terms and the day-to-day running needs of the University. The measures included the suspension of prizes and bursaries, cancellation of the annual Commemoration Day celebrations, cuts in spending on the library, the museum, and heating and lighting.

Sir Donald and the Court may even have taken some pride in their efforts to ensure that the University cut its cloth to suit its more limited means. In April 1916, when the University of Edinburgh learned that there would be no additional Treasury assistance for the coming financial year and wrote to suggest that the Scottish universities jointly approach the Carnegie Trust for the temporary use of monies standing to their credit with the Trust, the Court took the view that such action was 'not in the meantime necessary' and refused to collaborate.[25] The quinquennial Carnegie grants to the Scottish universities for capital projects had been earmarked in Glasgow to help pay for the proposed completion of the west side of the West Quadrangle, with a chapel and teaching and staff rooms for Arts, and for a new Zoology building on the ground between the Professors' Square and the Western Infirmary. By July 1915 it had become clear to the Court that any new construction would have to await the end of the war. The costs of this postponement fell particularly on the hard-pressed Department of Zoology which, uniquely, continued to have a problem of overcrowding. The Court promised to put a new Zoology building in hand 'as soon as circumstances permit' and in the meantime banked the Carnegie grants of £10,000 per annum as reserves to be drawn upon when better times returned.

By the winter of 1917–18, Gilmorehill was a cold and cheerless place – bereft of many of its students, their societies and clubs withering on the vine and the SRC elections lacking sufficient candidates. The teaching staff was down to the lowest point 'in numbers compatible with supplying the necessary avenues to a degree',[26] and economies in fuel, light and consumables reduced the effective working day. Looming over everything was a continuing uncertainty about the duration and outcome of the war. Within a largely comatose institution, only a few flickers of new life and vitality could be detected. Although the flow of financial support from the University's graduates and from the wider community of the city did not completely dry up with the outbreak of war, conditions often prevented an effective use of the funds. Thus Dr Gavin B. Tennent's bequest in 1914–15 for the establishment of a chair and a department of Opthalmology at the Western Infirmary, while generating a debate about the place of opthalmology in the medical curriculum and an agreement that the holder of the chair should focus on post-graduate work, could not be put into immediate effect because of difficulties in constructing an associated building at the Western.[27] Over time, however, as increased levels of taxation and national drives for investment in war loans bit into the personal incomes of potential donors, there was a slackening in the flow of gifts and benefactions coming forward.

During the early years of the war, bequests to the University from William Jacks, a local ironmaster, and a Robert Marshall of Grangehill became available to establish two new chairs in Modern Languages. These bequests came against a background of discussions the University had been having off and on since about 1903 with the Glasgow and West of Scotland College of Commerce and its backers in the business community, discussions which received further impetus from the formal association of the University and the Royal Technical College in 1913. Proposals for the development of commercial education in the city envisaged closer institutional links between the University and the College of Commerce and the introduction of joint teaching arrangements. The University would provide particularly the modern languages regarded as essential to the successful pursuit of business in an international economy. Despite strong support from within the General Council, opinion in both Court and Senate was divided over whether and how to become involved in education for a business career, and matters proceeded slowly. In 1914 a Court committee on 'Training for Commerce' had concluded that it was not practicable to establish a Faculty of Commerce, but that the University together with the College might institute a diploma in commerce.[28] The outbreak of war, however, postponed any practical moves in this direction, and thereafter complications over the terms of the bequests delayed the creation of the new chairs of modern languages.

The one new post to be created and filled in the University during the war years was a lectureship in Russian. This was linked to the discussions over commercial education, but also owed a great deal to happy circumstance. From time to time, opportunities presented themselves on Gilmorehill to express solidarity with Britain's allies in the great struggle with Germany. Thus in October 1914 the student body responded to the prevailing national sentiment by electing President Raymond Poincaré of the French Republic as their Rector, the first Frenchman to hold the post. Although hostilities postponed his installation, his election symbolised a commitment to the French alliance and the common struggle with Germany. Visits to the city and the University by separate parties of French parliamentarians and professors followed in 1916. However, this caused less of a stir than the arrival of members of the Russian Duma and Council of the Empire in May 1916. At a reception in the Bute Hall to welcome the Russian visitors, the Principal, who considered himself to be something of a linguist, was delighted to be told that his self-taught Russian was quite comprehensible. He also seized the opportunity to press on the city fathers and others the case for the introduction of teaching of Russian in the University. Consequently, a leading businessmen, Sir William Weir, offered £2,500 to fund a lectureship 'so long as the lecturer devotes a portion of his time to the Commercial College work on Russian', and his example was followed by the Lord Provost, Sir Thomas Dunlop, and others.[29] With these tangible expressions of wartime alliance and post-war commercial expectations in his pocket, Sir Donald moved more quickly to fill the post. Despite difficulties in communication with Russia, a candidate was found in the shape of Hugh Brennan, an Irishman attached to the British legation in St Petersburg, who was offered the lectureship early in 1917 and was allocated a small sum to purchase books to form the nucleus of a class library. After a long and difficult overland journey through Finland, Sweden and Norway, which took two months to complete, Brennan arrived in Glasgow in September 1917, just in time to take up his duties in the new academic year.

Brennan's arrival was a shaft of light illuminating a landscape darkened by the privations of war. It also coincided with a period of renewed pressure from the General Council for further consideration of the issues of commercial education and closer relations with the College of Commerce. The Business Committee of General Council initiated its own investigation into the possible introduction of a degree in commerce. What it had in mind appears to have been a Bachelor of Commerce degree which would provide professional training for a business career and which, like an LL.B. or BD, would be taken after completion of an MA. The sub-committee charged with the task had among its membership representatives of the Chamber of Commerce and the College, as well as local businessmen. Surprisingly perhaps, given its composition, it arrived at the conclusion that there was no need for either a Faculty of Commerce or a degree in commerce because most courses suitable for 'men employed in business' were already available within the Arts curriculum in the University, and these could be supplemented by courses on offer at the College. All that was really necessary was improved liaison between the University and the business community, via the Appointments Committee. However, it also recommended, and the Court agreed, that a joint advisory committee of the University and the College of Commerce be set up to promote the education of students preparing for a commercial career.[30] These steps fell considerably short of the hopes of the proponents of a University degree in commerce, including David Murray, a prominent city solicitor who was a General Council Assessor on the Court and who believed that such a degree was 'essential' to the University's future. To their chagrin, their counterparts in the city of Edinburgh experienced fewer obstacles, with the result that the University of Edinburgh introduced a B.Comm. degree in 1918. 'It seems extraordinary', Murray complained with some justice, 'that in a great commercial city such as Glasgow, where Adam Smith taught the principles of Political Economy subsequently embodied in *The Wealth of Nations* and where commercial questions have for generations been examined and discussed in reference to underlying principles, it should be suggested that professional training in subjects connected with commerce is unnecessary.'[31]

The discussions over commercial education that took place during the war years reflected the fact that there were continuing long-run debates about the University's relationship with the wider economy and society – in the city, the region and the nation – and how it should respond to changing needs. The war might cut across these debates; it might even lead to a postponement of any resolution; but it could not in itself completely still the discussion of these fundamental issues. One such long-standing strand of policy discussion was the nature and timing of the University's response to the demand for the education of emerging professions, of which the discussions over commercial education formed part. Another group whose needs were also beginning to receive some attention were those engaged in public service, including local government and social work, for whom the concept of a degree in civic and social study, that is essentially in social sciences, had been espoused by Professor Sir Henry Jones. This was looked at by the Senate in 1914, and was pressed once again by Jones in 1917,[32] but the University's inability to fund new posts for this purpose prevented any immediate action. Then there were the teachers, whose training requirements were met by the Scottish Education Department's training centres, but among whom there were aspirations for a professional degree. In the spring of 1915 the Faculty of Arts brought forward a proposal for an Honours degree in Education for those intending a career in teaching, but consultation with the Court and more especially the General Council, which had practising teachers among its members, elicited the advice that this would be less appropriate to the needs of the profession than the B.Ed. degree which was about to be introduced by the University of Edinburgh. This combined the study of educational theory and practice at a postgraduate level with further teacher training, and was regarded as being of a high standard.[33] The Faculty duly introduced such a degree in 1917, making opportunistic use for this purpose of such courses as already existed in the straitened wartime circumstances.

The rise of the teaching profession in Scotland, and in particular the growth in the numbers of secondary teachers, was part of a general expansion and improvement in the school system that presented the University, along with the rest of the Scottish universities, with a problem whose solution could not be postponed indefinitely. Prior to the war, the preliminary examinations run by the Scottish universities had gradually ceased to be the principal test of fitness for entry into higher education. Some three-quarters of those admitted to the University in 1911–12, for example, did so on the basis of exemption from the preliminary examinations granted on possession of the Scottish Education Department's School Leaving Certificate. The universities consequently feared that control over admissions was passing to the SED. They also had a need to revise the Ordinance on Preliminary Examinations, the provisions of which were now out of step with the actual teaching practices in the four institutions. Consequently, discussions had been taking place before the war with a view to creating a body capable of negotiating with the SED over entry standards and of continuing to administer preliminary examinations (which were entrance rather than bursary exams) in the interest of those coming from outside the Scottish state school system. Since no great financial issues were concerned, discussions over these matters continued during the war years, and came to a head in the autumn of 1917 when meetings of the four university principals with representatives of the SED and the Privy Council's University Committee agreed the principles underlying the reform of the arrangements along the interface between school and university. The schools, as the SED saw it, would be freed from the dead hand of the university preliminary examinations in developing their curricula, but the universities would be able to confer with the SED over the nature and purpose of the Leaving Certificate through a new Entrance Board, which would also run preliminary exams on behalf of the four universities. The universities retained the power to admit.[34] This agreement found expression in Ordinance No. 70 of 1918, which fortuitously put the Scottish Universities Entrance Board in place just in time for the post-war recovery in student admissions into higher education.

The first significant up-turn in new student matriculations in the University took place in the spring of 1918, although this was confined to the Medical Faculty. The previous decline in student numbers, as measured by the numbers of graduates from the various faculties (Figure 5.1), had been felt much more in the Faculties of Arts and Science than in Medicine, where the senior cohorts of students had continued with their studies much as before. By the beginning of 1918 national needs for qualified medical manpower indicated the necessity of also exempting junior medical students from military service, and the

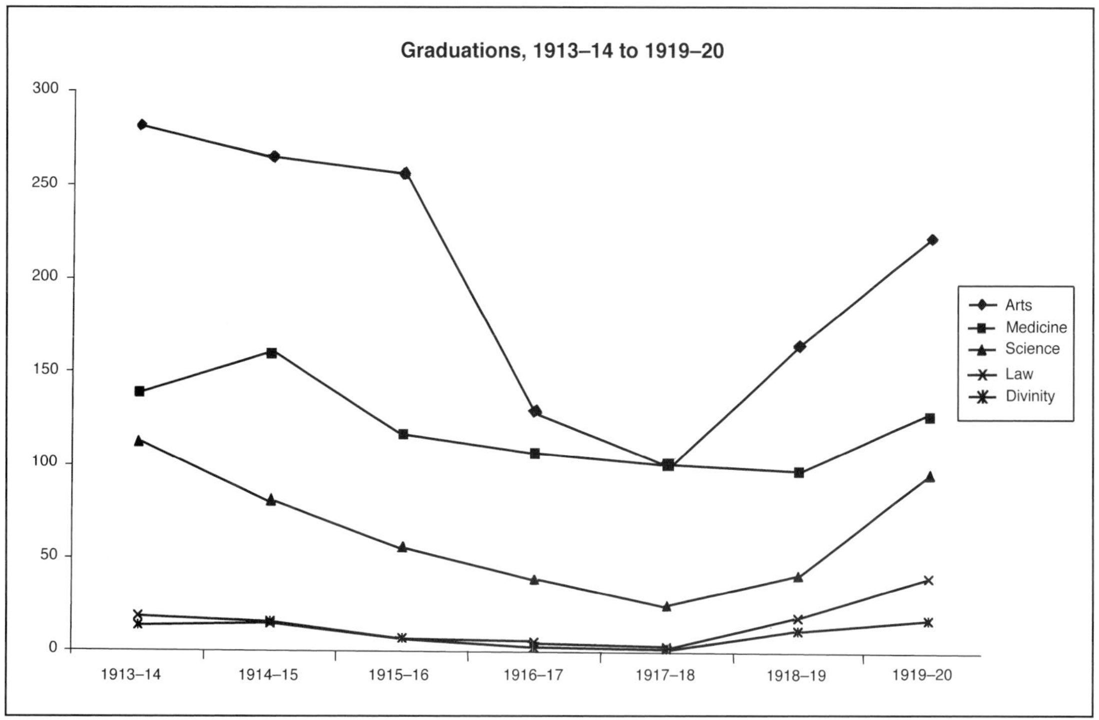

Figure 5.1

numbers of first year medical students consequently picked up. This turning tide of student numbers continued into the early months of 1918–19. It then grew into a veritable flood when, following the armistice in November 1918, students of all Faculties poured back into Gilmorehill from demobilisation, to compete for places with young men and women fresh out of school. In 1919–20, student numbers were already some 30 per cent above the levels of 1913–14, and a University which had had to adapt itself to a situation of too few students now found itself with too many.

The end of the war, coming almost as unexpectedly as its beginning, brought mixed moods of relief, rejoicing, a determination to secure a speedy return to normal, and abiding regrets at the great loss of life and limb which members of the University community had suffered in common with the rest of the nation. According to the Roll of Honour, 3,420 graduates, undergraduates and others associated with the University had been on military service, of whom 580 had been killed and over 700 were either wounded or still missing in action.[35] Sir Donald's first act following the close of hostilities was therefore to make known to the Court that 'with a view of setting up an abiding memorial of the service and sacrifice of the members of the University who have given their lives for the Country in the Great War, he had asked a few friends to join Lady MacAlister and himself in tendering to the University Court a sum amounting to some £14,000 and other valuable gifts, including the original bell of Greyfriars Church presented by Major John Garroway.'[36] A committee representing all sections of the University was established in February 1919, at the suggestion of the SRC, to arrange a suitable memorial. The Court also gave temporary financial assistance to the dependants of those employees who failed to return. The University, however, was as determined to celebrate the success of the survivors as to commemorate the dead. This it did in May 1919 with a special ceremony to confer an honorary degree on Field Marshal Haig. It was an event with a distinctly military tinge, attended by returning students and staff still in uniform as well as by other servicemen – but the dignity of the occasion was marred by the fact that the marshalling arrangements went wrong and students and members of the public ended up occupying the seats that should have been reserved for visiting luminaries.[37] The Rector, too, whose term in office had been extended by one year, contributed to the rejoicing and sense of Allied achievement by coming to Glasgow on 13 November 1919 for his much-postponed installation. M. Poincaré, who also conferred the Cross of the Commander of the Legion of Honour on Sir Donald MacAlister, must have been quite unprepared for the boisterousness of a rectorial installation – the hall 'was full of returned soldiers ready for any gaiety'[38] – and on his return to France he is said to have described Glasgow students as 'the most brutal in Europe'.[39]

On the whole, the academics and undergraduates returning to the University in 1919 and 1920 fitted themselves back into their former way of life without too much difficulty. Among the staff, some returned covered in glory and honours – like Professor Cormack of Engineering who, following his rise to become Director of Aircraft Supply and Equipment, came back to his old university as Brigadier-General J. D. Cormack, CMG, CBE. Others slipped back into their former posts quietly and with less fanfare. A few returned nursing physical disabilities or other long-term problems – such as J. S. Dunkerley, lecturer in proto-zoology, who 'returned badly crippled as a result of his wounds' and had to be given three months leave of absence to recover.[40] However, the most difficult staffing matter facing the Court as an employer was what to do with Professor Becker of Astronomy now that the war was over. An enquiry at the Scottish Office elicited the information that 'in view of the popular feeling that has been manifested' the Secretary for Scotland (now Robert Munro) expected the Court to retire Becker compulsorily. This the Court refused to do, on the grounds that the relevant legislation required 'sufficient cause shown', and 'Court is not aware of any fault committed by or even alleged against Professor Becker.' Nevertheless, the Court, on being pushed further by the Scottish Office to take action because of 'the reduction of his utility as a Professor through enemy associations', was willing to encourage Becker to retire voluntarily, especially once the Press got wind of the matter and wild stories began to appear about Becker having already 'retired to the Fatherland' on full salary. Becker was willing to go, but disagreement over the level of compensation to be paid dragged the matter into the early months of 1920 – when Becker's situation was once again the subject of questions in the House of Commons, and a petition from the Comrades of the Great War (Paisley Branch) to the University Court, which was also published in the Press, denounced his continued employment as 'a disgrace to the traditions of the University of Glasgow, a dishonour to our sacred dead, a slur on the abilities of the sons of our mighty empire, and an incentive to the present unrest in our national life.' Against such a background of continuing hostility towards those of German origin, an impasse developed between the University and the Scottish Office, each wanting the other to take decisive action. This was only broken when Becker himself forced the issue. In September 1920 he took up residence again in the house at the University Observatory and informed the Principal that he intended to return to his duties as Professor of Astronomy. The Court accepted the *fait accompli*, the Scottish Office quietly overlooked its earlier strictures against him, public agitation died away, and Becker resumed his membership of the academic community from which he had been excluded for so long and for no good reason.[41]

Some undergraduates returning to Gilmorehill from the dangers, difficulties and excitements of military service had trouble readjusting to their studies. This was particularly true of those who had been invalided out before the end of the war, such as the ex-serviceman medical student who admitted in verse:

> My brain has gone wool-gathering –
> The fire within me's dead.
> The Muse has cut acquaintance with my pen.[42]

Such effects of the war were happily more rare among the large number of young men who came roaring back from the Front in the spring and autumn of 1919, intent upon making up for lost time both academically and in their social life. Squeezing into lodgings wherever they could be found, and contributing no doubt to the acute scarcity of housing which was characteristic of

Glasgow in that year, they reinvigorated the University with their numbers, their youthful maturity and their enthusiasms. Student societies revived, the SRC recovered its energies, and dinners, dances and debates were the order of the day. The returning students also brought with them hopes and aspirations for better conditions, and gave a new impetus to improving student welfare. For the University, the main problem was finding the means to cope with the combined numbers of those returning to previously interrupted studies, of those who had delayed their entry to higher education until the end of the war and of those who were coming into first year classes straight from school now conscription had ended. The difficulties were partly related to staffing – although academics were also returning from their various wartime commitments elsewhere, staff:student ratios had fallen to unprecedented levels – but they mainly stemmed from shortages of teaching space. Even Lady MacAlister would later remember the years 1919 and 1920 chiefly for the constant stream of professors and lecturers who came to the door of the Principal's Lodging in despair over where they would be able to find accommodation for their classes.[43] Desperate needs called for desperate measures. Classes were shoehorned into whatever vacant corners could be deemed suitable as classroom or laboratories, and levels of overcrowding once confined to Zoology lectures became commonplace. Some professors took to repeating their lectures at several times in the course of the day, and a large part of the teaching of basic sciences to medical students was transferred to available space in the Royal Technical College and in Anderson's and St Mungo's Colleges (the independent extra-mural medical colleges).

The Medical Faculty was under the most intense pressure, more especially from ex-servicemen intent upon pursuing a medical degree with fees paid by the Government, and its professors were the loudest in their complaints about the Senate's inability to stem the tide. Attempts by the Clerk of Senate and the Registrar to regulate the new student intake having failed, Senate eventually agreed to impose a strict limit of 250 on the number of new students entering the Medical Faculty from April 1920. The number of women was limited to their proportion of the pre-war intake (roughly 30 per cent), and among the men first priority was given to ex-servicemen in accordance with their length of service.[44] Even so, this could not deal with the more pressing problem that the number of students seeking entry to clinical studies was predicted to rise from 600 in 1919 to over 1,150 by 1921 – which compelled the University to enter into arrangements with the Western and Royal Infirmaries to rationalise clinical teaching arrangements by placing limits on the size of individual classes, and to approach the Victoria Infirmary with a view to introducing clinical teaching there.[45] But the problems were by no means confined to Medicine. Faculties which before the war had accepted all qualified applicants were ill-prepared to cope with the postwar demand for places, such as the 200 qualified candidates who sought entry to the 120 places in Engineering in

1920, and from all sides, more particularly from the laboratory-based subjects, demands arose for more staff, accommodation and other facilities. It would take several years for the peak post-war intakes of students to work themselves through the system.

The needs and interests of the students were not the only pressing problems of the immediate post-war years. The academic staff too, and in particular the junior staff, were impatient to see an improvement in their terms and conditions. Such matters were being pressed with the Scottish universities before 1914 – as a result of the growth in the number of lecturers and assistants hired to support the professors and the emergence among them of a shared sense of academic professionalism – but a response to the concerns had been delayed by the national emergency. Pension rights were the first to be addressed, following an offer to the Scottish universities by the Carnegie Trust in 1917 to pay for the costs of most academic staff to join the FSSU scheme which had been established for the universities in England and Wales (exclusive of Oxford and Cambridge) in 1914. Within the University of Glasgow Court, however, the offer provoked a furious row. Two lay members of Court, Dr Murray, the Glasgow solicitor who favoured the introduction of a degree in commerce, and Sir William Lorimer, a local industrialist, objected to the proposal on various grounds, 'particularly that it involved joining an English institution and submitting to the jurisdiction of the English Courts,'[46] and tried to block Glasgow's participation in the scheme through the Court of Session. Behind-the-scenes negotiations eventually secured a *modus vivendi*, one part of which was the addition of several Scottish insurance companies to the FSSU's panel, and by December 1918 the Court was able to approve the appropriate ordinance. One of the first rewards for the academic staff in putting up with the rigours and deprivations of the war years was therefore the opportunity to participate for the first time in a contributory occupational pension scheme. This was a very significant improvement, more especially for lecturers and assistants who previously enjoyed no pension rights, but it still left issues relating to pay and status to be resolved. Because of wartime inflation, and despite the payment of a war-bonus, academic salaries had declined in real terms, and lecturing staff were discontented over how little part they played in the governance of the University by comparison with the professoriate.[47] A series of inter-university consultations on these matters culminated in a Scottish Universities Conference in Perth in January 1919, presided over by Sir Donald MacAlister, which agreed to introduce in all four institutions a more defined system of grades of service and salary structure for non-professorial staff. It also decided to introduce a new Universities (Scotland) Bill which would fix age-limits for the retirement of professors and staff, define the rights of lecturers to become members of Senate, the General Council and the Court, and make provision for supplementary pensions for lecturers who were too close to retirement to benefit from the new FSSU provisions.[48]

The mood in the Scottish universities in the heady optimistic months immediately following November 1918 was clearly to seize the occasion to introduce a new deal for the younger members of academic staff, who had borne the brunt of the war either though military service or through providing cover for those who were absent from Gilmorehill, and whose claims for greater recognition vis à vis the professoriate had been outstanding for some time. It was a mood that the government too seemed to catch, for in the spring of 1919 the University heard the results of a special financial enquiry (conducted by Sir William McCormick of the Carnegie Trust) that awarded it an annual grant of £48,000 for the year 1919–20, together with a special non-recurrent grant of £21,000. The latter was intended 'at once to restore the University, as far as possible, to its pre-war condition, implying expenses which have been deferred during the war on such services as repairs, books, apparatus and material'; while the increase in the annual grant was intended to address 'the most urgent question [which] relates to the remuneration of the members of the teaching staff and more particularly to the salaries of the lecturers and demonstrators.'[49] This timely infusion of new funding enabled the University to put in place for the first full post-war academic year a staffing complement comprising 22 full-time professors on salaries of £1,100–£1,200, 11 part-time professors (mainly in Medicine and Law) on salaries of £800, 52 full-time lecturers (in three grades) on salaries of £300–£600, 28 part-time lecturers (in Medicine and Law) on £120–£150, 29 full-time assistants on £200–£250, 11 part-time assistants on £50–£110 and 23 administrative staff on various salaries.[50] (For the first time, and reflecting the advances made by female staff during the war, one of the full-time lecturers was a woman – Theodora Keith, a third-grade lecturer in Economic History.) This attempt to reward and reinvigorate the teaching staff came none too soon, for between July and September 1919 no fewer than nine of the University's more experienced lecturers resigned to take up chairs at other universities, mainly elsewhere in the UK but also in such countries as Australia, Canada and France. It may be that this outflow was merely a normal turn-over in staff which had been delayed by war-time conditions; but it might equally be seen as evidence of some discontent with conditions in the University of Glasgow and a desire to seek new outlets for the exercise of talents now that other universities were filling chairs again. It was a slightly worrying sign that the University faced the post-war era without the services of some of the most experienced men from within its ranks.

By 1920, the University of Glasgow, like its sister universities in Scotland, had experienced six years of disruption and disturbance. Although its fundamental educational purposes were never seriously challenged, the enormous swings in student numbers, the absence of many of its best academic staff, and severe financial constraints were a serious test of its capacity to adapt and survive. This it did, but at what cost and with what results? On the face of it, one can find little evidence to suggest that the war shifted the University in new directions. The military and logistic requirements of the war had little impact on the University's research thrust and research potential, other than perhaps in the work done on gyroscopes by James Gray of Natural Philosophy (Physics). This indeed was one of the principal differences between Glasgow and many of the other British universities, where research and development in gases and explosives, as well as in glass-manufacturing techniques, dyestuffs, and aviation, not only enabled Britain to catch up in fields where Germany had formerly had an edge but laid the foundations for further post-war scientific advances.[51] Although the University's relatively limited participation in research activity reflected pre-war weaknesses – more especially in Chemistry – the need to harness science and technology to national goals, recognised by the wartime establishment of the new Department of Scientific and Industrial Research, largely passed by the University of Glasgow. On the teaching side, the courses on offer at the end of the war were essentially the same as those on offer at its beginning, and such innovations as occurred, including the introduction of the teaching of Russian language, tended to have their origins in policy debates which preceded the war, just as the closer working relations with the Royal Technical College, while reflecting wartime exigencies, were built on the foundations of a pre-war understanding. The educational services which the University provided were attuned primarily to the needs of professions – medicine, the church, the law, engineering, or teaching – which like the University itself were disturbed by but not significantly altered by the experience of war. There were therefore sound reasons for what seemed to be the prevailing belief within the walls of Gilmorehill – that the war was simply something to be endured, and that once it was over the task was to get back to business as usual as fast as possible.

But if the University was stirred rather than shaken by the First World War, the same was not necessarily true of Britain as a whole. In economics and in politics, the war proved to be something of a watershed – the time when Britain finally lost a leadership of the world economy that had been growing ever more precarious; an event during which the British economy lost many overseas markets it would have great difficulty in recovering; a period in British politics which saw the demise of the once-great Liberal Party, and the ideas which it espoused, and the emergence of a more overtly class-based politics. It behoved the University to recognise and take account of these changes. That it did not consciously appear to do so raises questions about leadership within the University during the war years, more especially about whether simply seeing the institution through its current difficulties was sufficient of itself. In 1916, Sir Donald MacAlister was offered the Principalship of the University of Edinburgh, and there was great rejoicing on Gilmorehill when he turned it down.[52] However, it was the University of Edinburgh, under its new Principal, Sir Alfred Ewing, rather than the University of Glasgow, under Principal MacAlister, which established a committee to consider the implications for itself of the eventual end of the war and how it should position itself for the world which would emerge. Such foresight was in marked contrast to the assumption of post-war 'business as usual' that underlay the University of Glasgow's entry into the decade of the 1920s.

Notes and References

1. *Sir Donald MacAlister of Tarbert, by His Wife* (London, 1935), 213–31.
2. Senate Minutes [hereafter Senate], 29 Oct. 1914.
3. Court Camera, 18 Sept. 1914 and Finance Committee, Court Camera, 27 Oct. 1914.
4. Report of Business Committee, General Council Annual Report, 28 April 1915.
5. C. A. Oakley, *Union Ygorra: The Story of the Glasgow University Student over the last Sixty Years* (Glasgow, 1951), 41.
6. *Glasgow University Magazine* [hereafter GUM], 27, 1 (11 Nov. 1914).
7. Senate, 12 Nov. and 9 Dec. 1914.
8. Editorial, GUM, 27, 8 (13 May 1915).
9. General Council Report, 27 Oct. 1915.
10. Senate, 21 June 1915.
11. *Glasgow Herald*, 29 June 1915, 12 d.
12. Senate 20 and 23 Nov. 1915.
13. Court Camera, 10 Dec. 1914, 7 Jan. and 11 Feb. 1915.
14. Court Camera, 7 Oct. 1815.
15. Court Camera, 11 Nov. 1915, 27 April and 9 Nov. 1916.
16. Court Camera, 8 Nov. 1917.
17. Court Camera, 4 Oct. 1917; for Sir Henry's wartime contributions to public life, see H. J. W. Hetherington, *The Life and Letters of Sir Henry Jones* (London, 1924), 120–41.
18. A. K. Bowman, *The Life and Teaching of Sir William Macewen: A Chapter in the History of Surgery* (London, 1942), 389–95.
19. Finance Committee, Court Camera, 3 Nov. 1915.
20. *Hansard*, LXXII, 3 June–2 July 1915, p. 1802 (30 June 1915).
21. Court Camera, 29 March 1916; Senate 17 Oct. 1935; *Hansard*, XCI, March 1917, p. 1311 (15 March 1917).
22. Court Camera, 16 July 1916, 3 Oct. 1918 and 24 April 1919.
23. Finance Committee, Court Camera, 29 May 1918.
24. Treasury Letter of 6 April 1915, in Court Camera, 21 April 1915.
25. Court Camera, 27 April 1916.
26. Report of Business Committee, General Council 31 Oct. 1917.
27. Court Camera, 11 March and 1 July 1915.
28. Court Camera Papers 50781, 1914.
29. Court Camera, 5 Oct. 1916.

30. General Council, 26 March 1918; Court Regular, 14 May 1918.
31. David Murray, LL.D, *Question of a Degree in Commerce: A Minority Report* (General Council, April 1918).
32. Senate, 22 March 1917.
33. Court Regular, 22 April 1915; General Council, 22 June and 27 Oct. 1915.
34. Court Camera, 4 Oct. and 13 Dec. 1917.
35. Business Committee Report, General Council, 29 Oct. 1919.
36. Court Camera, 12 Dec. 1918.
37. Senate 15 May 1919.
38. *Glasgow Herald*, 23 Oct. 1936, 12.
39. Anon, *The Curious Diversity. Glasgow University on Gilmorehill: the First Hundred Years* (Glasgow, 1970).
40. Court Camera, 11 Dec. 1919.
41. Correspondence and newspaper clippings in Professor Becker's File, University Archives M/6/1/564061; also Court Camera, various dates.
42. GUM, 28, 2 (6 Dec. 1916), 52. The anonymous writer may have been George Nairn Wilson, who had seen action at Gallipoli but was demobbed in 1915 suffering from shell-shock. He resumed his studies in the spring of 1916 but struggled academically and was declared medically unfit to be a student in 1919, compelling his withdrawal not only from the Medical Faculty but also from the editorship of *Glasgow University Magazine* to which he had been elected but had not yet taken up (GUM, 31, 3 (22 Oct. 1919), 19).
43. *Sir Donald MacAlister of Tarbert, by His Wife*, 234–5.
44. Senate, 4 Dec. 1919.
45. Court Camera, 24 April 1919.
46. Court Camera, 24 May 1918.
47. Senate's Resolutions on the Memorial from the Lecturing Staff (Court Camera, 4 July 1918) provide a useful summary of the grievances of the junior academics.
48. Court Camera, 13 Feb. 1919.
49. Letter from Secretary of State for Scotland, quoted in Court Camera, 24 April 1919.
50. Court Camera, 3 July 1919.
51. M. Sanderson, *The Universities and British Industry, 1850–1970* (London, 1972), 220–36.
52. *Sir Donald MacAlister of Tarbert, by His Wife*, 337–8; Court Camera, 27 April 1916.

CHAPTER SIX

THE POOR RELATIONS, 1920–36

The University emerged from the First World War more firmly part of a United Kingdom system of Higher Education than it had ever been before. The great reforms of the nineteenth century had created a distinctively Scottish university system, comprising four ancient institutions that were legally independent of each other but were linked by shared values and structures, as well as by a requirement to consult each other regularly and to act in consort. In the course of the twentieth century, however, this Scottish 'national' system of university education became subsumed in a larger complex of relationships embracing the more numerous, and more diverse, universities and colleges of England and Wales. This process of 'embedding' Scotland within a British system proceeded gradually. Before the war it had been fostered by the Annual Conferences of the Universities of Great Britain and Ireland, which were arranged by the Universities Bureau of the British Empire, and by the meetings of the Standing Committee of Vice-Chancellors and Principals (CVCP), which had been established through the same body. Sir Donald MacAlister, as Principal of the University of Glasgow, had played an active part in all of these organisations (cf. p. 115). After the war the process received a further boost from the participation of the Scottish universities in the FSSU pension scheme and above all from the establishment of the University Grants Committee. This agency, staffed largely by men from a university background, was put in place in 1919 to allocate the funds provided for higher education by central government and to serve as a buffer between the universities and the Treasury. It was created from a recognition of the important contribution made by the universities to the economic and social life of Britain, and from a concern for the financial difficulties that the universities had faced during and just after the war.[1] Although the UGC was a funding body rather than a planning agency, its policies and decisions, encapsulated within a system of quinquennial (five-yearly) visitations and grants, were capable of having a significant impact upon the fortunes of individual universities.

The foundation of the UGC reflected a tendency within political and governing circles (one very much in tune with the centralising processes set in train both by the war and a growing recognition of Britain's relative decline as an industrial power) to think in terms of a policy framework for higher education across Britain as a whole. Within this, the Scottish universities, Glasgow among them, became a sub-set of the UK system. One result was that the Scottish universities, which for so long had compared themselves with Oxford and Cambridge, now found themselves placed in a contextual relationship with newer institutions, including the federal University of Wales and more especially the English civic universities. The latter, which had risen in numbers, size and significance since the late nineteenth century, were emerging as competitors of the Scottish universities in the recruitment of high-quality academic staff, more especially in the fields of science and technology where they tended to pay higher salaries than in the arts. Now they were also competing with the Scottish universities in the attraction of UGC funds. Another consequence of the change was that for the first time statistics on the British universities began to be collected and published in a systematic way, enabling Glasgow and the other Scottish universities to be seen, and to see themselves, more clearly in the mirror of other institutions.

The UGC began this process itself, in the aftermath of its visitations in 1920 to all the universities and colleges under its care, by attempting an analysis of the comparative costs of university education and comparative levels of state support, at least among the bigger institutions. Its figures (Table 6.1) revealed a significant gap between the English civic universities on the one hand and the

Table 6.1
Costs and Grants: English Civic and Scottish Universities, 1920-21

	Cost per f/t student £	*Treasury Recurrent Grant per f/t student* £
Birmingham	55	21
Bristol	47	18
Leeds	66	22
Liverpool	65	19
Manchester	57	21
Sheffield	86	24
Aberdeen	41	21
Edinburgh	35	14
St Andrews	79	41
Glasgow	28	11

Source: UGC Return for 1920–1

Scottish universities (St Andrews excepted) on the other. In terms of costs per student (defined as total departmental expenditure per full-time student), Aberdeen, Edinburgh and Glasgow fell some way below the levels of the main English civic universities. Although this partly reflected size – both

Edinburgh and Glasgow, with over 4,000 full-time students each, were on a par with Oxford and were exceeded only by London and Cambridge in total numbers of students – it was also a product of historically less generous funding of Scottish universities by the state. In terms of Treasury grants per student in 1920–1 (Table 6.1), which were fixed at the comparative levels which the UGC inherited at its foundation, the Scottish universities (again St Andrews excepted) tended to do less well than the English civics. Glasgow did particularly badly – its Treasury grant of £11 per student was only half the level of support enjoyed by Birmingham, Leeds, Manchester or Sheffield. In presenting these figures, the UGC commented that there were 'questions which can profitably be asked' and that it intended to investigate 'the underlying causes of the differences'.[2]

In fact, the UGC did not go quite as far as it might have done in analysing the variations in income and expenditure between two of the principal groups of universities under its authority. On the income side, for example, the Treasury grant that it dispensed was only one source of government financial support to the universities. The University of Wales and many of the English civic universities also obtained grants from local government rates, whereas the Scottish universities, their origins predating the municipal pride of the late nineteenth century, obtained no such direct assistance from local government sources. Consequently, while the universities in England enjoyed an average contribution of 12.5 per cent of their income from local government grants, the only local authority contribution attributable to the Scottish universities (in the form of rates relief) amounted to only 8.2 per cent of their income. Only when total income is also taken into account does Glasgow's true position within the financial pecking order of the British university system really emerge (Table 6.2). The University of Glasgow, it is clear, had the lowest income per student of any of the British universities – institutions in comparable industrial cities in England had two or three times the £39 per head that was available to it. This in turn meant not only that Glasgow spent less on teaching each student but that, once the teaching costs had been met, as little as £11 per student remained to be spent on administration or to be invested in classrooms, books and equipment. Aberdeen and Edinburgh fared only a little better than Glasgow, but even so the staff and students of the University of Glasgow were unequivocally the poor relations among the British universities of 1920.

The University stood in such a relatively unfavourable position partly as a result of the post-war bulge in student numbers, which had raised staff-student ratios to an unprecedented 1: 22 in 1919–20. Consequently the resources available per student might be expected to improve once that particular cohort of students had graduated. More fundamentally, however, it shared with Aberdeen and Edinburgh a Scottish tradition of higher education in which students were educated in relatively large numbers and relatively inexpensively.

Table 6.2
Income and expenditures: English civic and Scottish universities, 1920–1

	Total Income per f/t student £	*Dept. Spend per f/t student* £	*Remainder* £
Birmingham	112	55	57
Bristol	78	47	31
Leeds	95	66	29
Liverpool	84	65	19
Manchester	79	57	22
Sheffield	121	86	35
Aberdeen	57	41	16
Edinburgh	51	35	16
St Andrews	131	79	52
Glasgow	39	28	11

Source: calculated from data in UGC Return for 1920–1.

The *University Handbook* of 1919 identified four distinctive principles of that tradition: 1. the essential unity of education, from elementary school to university; 2. equality of opportunity, offering access to university 'for the son of the crofter as for the son of the merchant prince'; 3. practical efficiency, emphasising the 'intellectual and moral capacity to deal successfully with the tasks of everyday life'; and 4. a stress on teaching capacity: 'The Scottish Universities were predominantly great lecturing corporations, though the large classes which were common were an accident rather than a necessary result of the system'.[3] Although employing the past tense, the writer was describing the current situation – for in the decade or so before the war, a combination of respect for university education, general improvements in secondary education and the activities of the Carnegie Trust (which paid the fees of approximately 50 per cent of the students entering Glasgow University) had resulted in a swelling demand for university education among the young men and women of Scotland. This demand, which the war had interrupted, was now being renewed. The higher participation rate in Scotland – in the early 1920s the Scottish participation rate, at one university student for every five hundred of the population, was twice that of England and Wales[4] – had as its price a system of teaching that emphasised large lecture classes and examination-based forms of assessment, that provided little in the way of small-group teaching or direct contact between staff and students, that left little room for scholarship and research other than what could be squeezed into the summer vacation, and that skewed expenditures on library and laboratory facilities towards the immediate needs of the student population. In that respect, the struggle which Glasgow (and no doubt Aberdeen and Edinburgh) had in coping with the post-war student bulge was merely a temporary exacerbation of a problem of dealing with expanding student numbers which had been present since the late 1890s.

It was a difficulty from which the University obtained little relief in the course of the 1920s and 1930s. Whatever thoughts the UGC may have had in 1920–1 about effecting greater equality in levels of support per student across the UK system, these quickly evaporated in the course of the depression of 1921–2 and the introduction of the Geddes Cuts, which reduced the size of the University Vote. They also withered in the face of protests from English universities that the UGC's concern with costs per student seemed to presage an intention to drive down costs towards those of the lower (i.e. Scottish) performers. At a time when there was considerable suspicion in university circles about the threat that the new agency posed to institutional autonomy,[5] the UGC clearly did not feel able to press matters to their conclusion. Instead, it seems to have settled for a policy of allocating government funds largely on the basis of inherited historical patterns, occasionally adjusting levels upwards to take account of further increases in student numbers in individual institutions (in as far as the total level of funds available to it permitted) but without altering the relative positions of the various universities. There was to be no shift of government resources towards the Scottish universities, more especially as Glasgow and Edinburgh were depicted by representatives of the English universities as institutions that had allowed themselves to over-expand at the expense of the quality of the educational experience of their students. Any additional public expenditure in the university sector would take place, if it were to take place at all, in England and Wales, which had under-provision of university places compared with Scotland.[6]

Nor did the numbers of students entering the University return to their pre-war levels. The post-war bulge peaked in 1922–3, when total matriculations (total student population) stood at 4,884 (Figure 6.1). Thereafter a down-turn in the total number of male students was partially off-set by a continuing rise in female matriculations, so that by the mid-twenties total student numbers were still some 50 per cent higher than on the eve of the war. There then followed a rapid recovery in male matriculations which, combined with constantly rising female numbers, meant that the student population peaked once again, at a total of 5,555, in 1929–30. In the process, Glasgow replaced Edinburgh as the largest of the Scottish universities. With the onset of the depression of the early thirties the tide of demand slackened – more so among females than among males – and total numbers declined once more. Even so, the 4,844 students attending the university in 1935–6 were only a few short of the 4,888 who had crowded Gilmorehill in the post-war peak year of 1923–4. Overall, therefore, the years between 1920 and 1936 represent a period of unprecedented pressure of student numbers on the resources and capacities of the University.

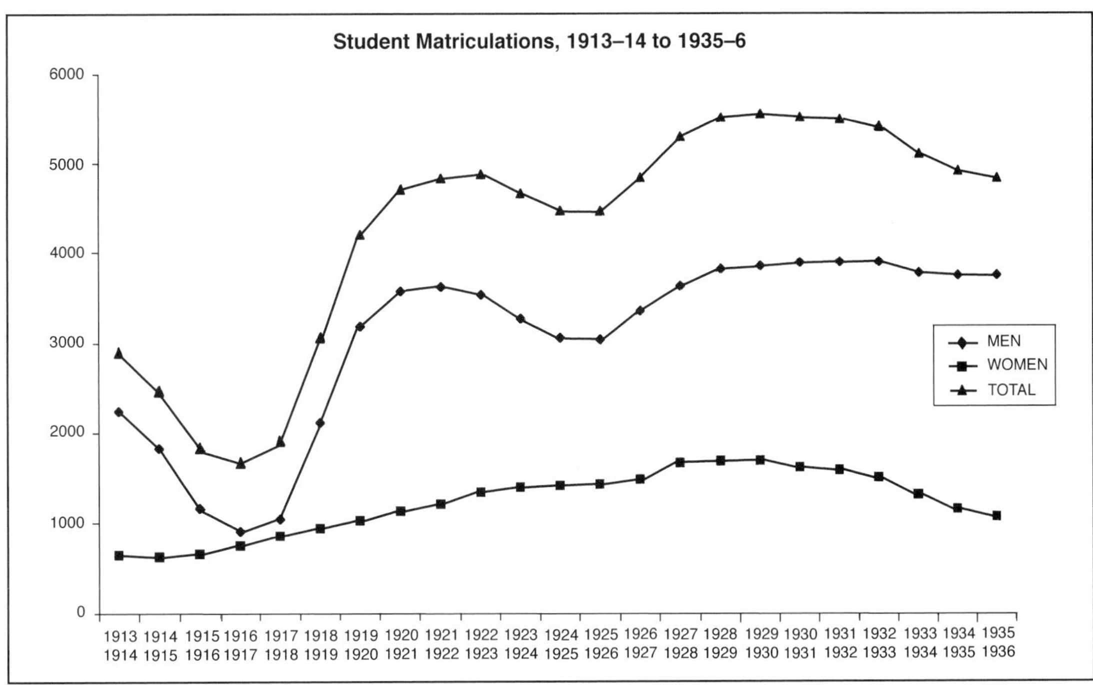

Figure 6.1

The expansion of student numbers in the later 1920s, and into the first year or two of the 1930s, had its roots in the interplay between three factors: first, the continuing expansion and improvement of the Scottish secondary school system under the aegis of the Scottish Education Department, with a consequent increase in the numbers of pupils leaving school with the Leaving Certificate that gave access to the Scottish universities; second, the rising rate of female participation in secondary and higher education; and third, the differential effects of the post-war cycles of economic expansion and contraction of employment prospects in the various professions. All of these combined to emphasise the attractions of school-teaching as a profession and the value of a degree as the passport to higher pay and better prospects within teaching. SED regulations about teaching qualifications, in particular those requiring a degree plus one year of training for teaching in secondary schools and denying entry to teaching in primary schools for males who were not graduates, drove students into Arts degrees as a preparation for teaching. Such pressures were to be found across Scotland – with the result that in the years 1927–9 more than half of the increase in Arts numbers within the British universities took place in Scotland – but they appear to have been especially acute in the West, for Glasgow alone accounted for some two-thirds of the Scottish increase.[7] The introduction by the Scottish local authorities, under the Education Act of 1918, of means-tested bursaries and awards for students entering higher education, supplementing the fees grants from the Carnegie Trust, was also important in encouraging students from modest family backgrounds to consider teaching as a future career. Even for those intent on teaching Science in schools the Faculty of Arts, with its broader curriculum, remained a natural home (new B.Sc. regulations in 1921 were designed to permit greater specialisation within an Honours degree and thereby equip the student for a career in industry and in scientific research). Consequently, the Arts Faculty, which in 1919–20 had fewer male students than either Medicine or Science, grew so quickly in numbers that by 1934–5 it had more male students than Medicine, Science and Engineering combined, and also contained eighty-seven per cent of the entire female student population of the University (Table 6.3). If the early twenties were a time of youthful enthusiasm for Medicine, Engineering and Science, born of the experience of war and an early post-war optimism about economic recovery and technical change, the later twenties and early thirties were a time of search for security in teaching, born out of the structural difficulties of the West of Scotland economy and the relatively generous funding of primary and secondary education by the Scottish Office vote.

Table 6.3
Matriculations by Faculty, selected years

	Arts Men	*Arts Wom*	*Divin Men*	*Divin Wom*	*Law Men*	*Law Wom*	*Med Men*	*Med Wom*	*Sci Men*	*Sci Wom*	*Eng Men*	*Eng Wom*
1914 1915	564		64		113		600		362			
1919 1920	601		53		176		1167		852			
1924 1925	801		9		228		775		411		529	
1929 1930	1594	1424	97	0	442	24	726	97	382	100	375	0
1934 1935	1633	1375	105	1	396	17	762	93	407	106	353	0

Note: the figures for women students by faculty before 1929–30 are not available

The University's emergence in the twenties as the largest of the Scottish universities (and the largest unitary, as distinct from collegially-organised, university in Britain) might be explained by the relative size of the population of the West of Scotland region from which it drew the greater bulk of its students. But it is more than likely that the influx of students was given an additional surge from two specific policies pursued by Sir Donald MacAlister and the Court in the early 1920s, policies that signalled very publicly that the University wished to be open and welcoming to students. The first of these related to the great row that took place in Scottish educational circles in 1920–4 over the powers of the universities to control the admission of pupils leaving the secondary schools. This followed the establishment of the Scottish Universities Entrance Board by Ordinance 70 of 1918, and was essentially a dispute between the Scottish Education Department and the teaching profession on the one hand and the universities and the remaining professions on the other. It contained lingering SED fears that the universities would use their Preliminary Exams to by-pass and undermine its Leaving Certificate, but at its heart was the issue of the prescription of Latin and Mathematics as prerequisites for entrance to the various faculties.[8] This row over entrance requirements has been interpreted by George Davie as yet another round in the long-standing debate over generalism versus specialism in Scottish education, and indeed as a focal point around which much of the intellectual history of Scotland in the 1920s is to be understood.[9] In Glasgow, the General Council, influenced no doubt by its teaching members, was in favour of a single, general test of fitness for entry, and interpreted any imposition of additional and specific faculty requirements as pressure by the universities on the schools for greater specialisation and streaming.[10] The Senate, for its part, agreed with the Senates of the other Scottish universities that Latin and Mathematics should be prerequisites for Arts students and Maths for Science students. However, the key debate in Senate, which took place on 1 March 1923, resulted in a relatively slim victory for the pro-Latin and Maths forces. The Court, taking account of the narrowness of the Senate vote, the views of the General Council, and the representations it had received from the Educational Institute of Scotland, decided to oppose that version of the draft regulations which imposed subject prerequisites.[11] This put it at odds not only with the Senate but also with the Courts of the three other universities, which had agreed with their Senates. Following an intervention by the Privy Council, which ruled out the proposed prerequisites on the grounds that they would take away from the schools the power to determine their own curricula, it was the SED, EIS and Glasgow Court and General Council position that held sway. The regulations under Section V of Ordinance 70 were finally agreed in 1925 and granted admission to the Scottish universities to all those completing a Group Leaving Certificate with passes (at least three at Higher and one at Lower level) in at least four subjects, including English, Maths or Science, and a foreign language.[12] This relatively liberal approach to entrance requirements by the Court almost certainly contributed to the substantial growth of numbers in the Faculty of Arts that followed immediately thereafter. It also left some lingering bitterness in the ranks of those inside and outside the University who favoured a narrower gate through which to enter Gilmorehill.

The second way in which the University stimulated a growth in student numbers was through the great efforts it made, with some considerable attendant local publicity, to improve facilities for the student body. These efforts were born out of the energy and initiatives of the post-war cohort of students as well as the determination of the Principal and members of the Senate that those who had returned from war should have their contributions recognised in a tangible way. Just as there was a public appeal for funds to build a Memorial Chapel in honour of those who fell, so too there would be fund-raising efforts for improved student welfare, including the introduction of student hostels, an extension of Union facilities, and an enlargement of the athletic grounds. (Behind the last objective lurked the understanding that the generation of young men who went to war in 1914–18 had been physically unfit, and that games and athletics constituted an important form of preparation for any future war, as well as 'equipping students for their life-work as citizens of the Empire'.)[13] A further consideration, which came into play from 1921–2 onwards, was encouragement from the UGC and the Treasury for universities to secure a larger proportion of their resources from local sources, a policy option into which the raising of funds for student facilities fitted quite easily.

Student enthusiasm for raising funds manifested itself after the war in two ways. In January 1920, the University's Infirmaries' Day was inaugurated, with the intention of raising funds for the city's hospitals. The origins were not entirely philanthropic – 'Processions such as those held on theatre nights were recognised as trouble-breeders' and someone 'had the bright idea that revelry and even rowdiness would be tolerated and approved by the Town if it was done in the name of charity, and particularly in the cause of the infirmaries'.[14] Nevertheless, by 1923, when it was decided to allocate part of the proceeds to the Lord Provost's unemployment fund, the public fun of the annual Charities Day had become a fixed landmark in the relations between Town and Gown. At the same time as Charities Day was being launched, however, the various fund-raising efforts of the main student organisations – the SRC for student residences to help alleviate the lodgings crisis, the two Unions to extend catering and social facilities to cope with the larger post-war numbers, and the Athletics Club for laying out playing fields and providing changing facilities at the Westerlands grounds which had been acquired in 1912 – were competing with each other for public support and getting in each other's way. At the SRC's suggestion, and with the backing of the Principal, these campaigns were transformed into a single public appeal by the University as a whole.[15] The Student Welfare Committee, which coordinated the appeal, was a large but energetic body of students and representatives of the General Council, Court and the Senate (the professors most actively involved included Bower of Botany, Medley of History, Cormack of Engineering and Henderson of Chemistry). Sir Donald threw himself into the project, calling on his wide network of contacts to secure extensive and high-profile public support for the appeal. The King and Queen agreed to be patrons and a General Committee of Patronage was established, comprising some 109 individuals, headed by the Chancellor, Lord Rosebery, and the new Rector, Bonar Law, who represented a cross-section of the 'great and the good' in Scottish society – from the aristocracy, through senior figures in the medical and legal professions and in the church, to Glasgow businessmen. One of the last, Leonard Gow, the shipowner, warned Sir Donald that the times were not propitious, since the economy had entered the post-war recession, and these circumstances do indeed appear to have somewhat blunted the appeal to the general public.

Although the total sums raised were £44,000 by April 1922, and £66,000 by October 1923, more than half of this latter figure came from only two sources – the Carnegie Trust, which contributed £15,000, and the UGC which provided £20,000 as a non-recurrent grant. The apex of the campaign, however, was a Grand Bazaar which was held in the grounds and buildings of Gilmorehill in November 1923, and raised a further £22,000.[16] This three-day event was a remarkable collaboration between students and staff, with Lady MacAlister and her friends well to the fore, and a great party spirit prevailed.[17] Also in attendance was the newly-installed Rector, Lord Birkenhead, 'who had the previous day delivered the address about winning glittering prizes that had aroused lively controversy.'[18] The sheer exuberance of the Bazaar, which brought the grand patrons of the appeal as well as the Glasgow public through the gates of Gilmorehill, was the high-water mark of an era of post-war self-confidence during which the University was still able to demonstrate an ability to finance its needs from local sources.

6.1 *Sir Donald MacAlister and Student Welfare – cartoon by O. H. Mavor (James Bridie).*

The money raised by the Student Welfare Committee (finally approaching £100,000 in all) was put to good use immediately, in refurbishing and furnishing two houses in the nearby Park Circus area of the city, which were gifted to the University in 1922–3 by Lord Maclay and Mr Laurence MacBrayne, for use as hostels for male students, and in purchasing the house at 1 University Gardens that was originally intended as a hall of residence but was then given over to the use of the Queen Margaret [Women's] Union. In 1926 a hostel for women students (Robertson Hall) was opened in Lilybank Terrace. At Westerlands, meanwhile, ground-levelling work which had gone on during the fund-raising campaign was followed by the laying out of additional pitches, the construction of six tennis courts, and the erection of a pavilion and grandstand building which was formally opened by the out-going Rector (Lord Birkenhead) in November 1926.[19] Dealing with the needs of the Men's Union took a little longer. Initially, it had been intended to extend and refurbish the Union building, which stood alongside the main entrance to the University from University Avenue, but in December 1923, Professor Bower of Botany, acting partly with the interests of his own department in mind, suggested that

6.2 *Rectorial Installation – Lord Birkenhead, 1923.*

the University should acquire the Union building for academic purposes, paying the students for this privilege and adding a grant from the Student Welfare Fund which would enable them to construct a new building on a different site.[20] The idea met with approval all round, and following the identification of an alternative site, at the southern end of University Avenue, on ground which had to be purchased and cleared of existing shops and houses, a competition to design a new building was held among the architecture firms in the city.[21] The new Union, in distinctive Scottish baronial style, was formally opened by the Rector, Stanley Baldwin, in December 1930, and the old building, refurbished at a cost of £7,000, was made over to the Queen Margaret Union in 1931 as a replacement for its smaller premises at 1 University Gardens.[22]

The substantial investment in new student facilities between 1922 and 1931 meant that the costs of running these enterprises also rose over time, with the result that student leaders were continually pressing the Court for further assistance. The Court dealt with this in two ways. First, in July 1925 it instituted a special University Students Fund, from which annual grants would be made to the Unions, to the Athletic Grounds and Pavilion, and to other student welfare organisations, and into which the Court would pay one quarter of the matriculation fees (enrolment rather than tuition fees) which were levied each year, together with income from certain endowments. When this in turn proved inadequate to meet the soaring costs of running Westerlands, it agreed to go along with a scheme, which had first been proposed in 1924 by the SRCs of the four Scottish universities and then had been taken up by Principal Ewing of Edinburgh University. This was that all the Scottish universities should introduce, by ordinance, an additional 10s 6d levy, to be paid as part of the Matriculation Fee but to be earmarked for Physical Welfare purposes. However, because the University of Aberdeen would not agree to a common approach, each of the others had to introduce their own ordinances – which Glasgow did in 1929.[23]

The student body now enjoyed a level of facilities considerably in excess of that available to the pre-war generation, and in some respects on a par with what was available anywhere else in Britain. The investment in student residences was relatively modest – by 1934–5 only 3.5 per cent of Glasgow students lived in halls, as compared with 13.9 per cent at Edinburgh or 24 per cent at St Andrews (and similar figures at English civic universities).[24] This in turn both reflected and further confirmed the essentially local or regional character of the university's teaching role, in which most students travelled to Gilmorehill on a daily basis from their homes within the Clydeside conurbation and returned there in the evening. The 'nine-till-five' syndrome and its centrifugal effects on the corporate life of the University were countered by the centripetal pull of improved Union and Athletic Club facilities. These latter, however, were not wholly successful in their task – in sports and athletics, more especially in such team games as rugby, the attraction of school F. P. [Former

6.3 *Charities Day, 1926.*

Pupils] clubs limited participation in Athletic Club activities and prevented Glasgow from being the force in inter-university competitions which its numbers might imply. There was also a strong undercurrent of dissatisfaction with the compulsory 10s 6d levy among the many students who participated in no sports at all. Similarly, only about half the student population could afford or could be bothered to pay the fee for membership in the two Unions.[25] Nevertheless, the new and enlarged facilities provided important focal points for student extra-curricular activities, and ensured that Gilmorehill was a place where friendships were made as well as classes attended. Thanks to the efforts of the Principal and several senior members of staff, among whom J. R. Peddie, the Adviser of Studies in Arts, was especially prominent, the University had put in place a range of facilities that were better able to cope with the catering, recreational and sporting needs of the large wave of student numbers which swept over it after 1925 than those which had existed in 1920.

However, these achievements – higher student numbers and improved student facilities – came at a price. Their origins and inspiration lay in the circumstances of the immediate post-war years, when confidence within the University was high and when many senior members of the University wished to commemorate the generation of students that had fought the war through the development of 'student-friendly' policies. But they came to fruition at a time when the national economy entered a relatively depressed period – the post-war slump of 1921–2 being followed by the deflationary policies designed to get Britain back on to the Gold Standard, and then only a few 'normal' years of trading in the international economy before the whole world slumped into the depression of 1929–33 – and when the economy of the West of Scotland, centred on shipbuilding and the heavy industries, began a long period of structural decline from the 'over-commitment' of the immediate pre-war and war years. Government tax-revenues and business profits were severely constrained after 1922, with the result that the University was unable to secure the levels of funding that would enable it to expand and improve on all fronts. Larger student numbers coupled with investment in better student facilities, which characterised the University in the later twenties and early thirties, put a strain on the University's finances at a time when mobilising external support was becoming increasingly difficult, and in turn resulted in a reduced capacity to invest in academic development through the recruitment of staff, the construction of new classrooms and laboratories and the promotion of research.

The struggle to raise capital costs for student facilities and to find running costs from the University's own revenues were not the root causes of the University's financial difficulties from the mid-twenties to the mid-thirties. Those lay elsewhere. Nevertheless, meeting these costs drew heavily on whatever declining stock of external funding was available to the University, and complicated its task of financing other aspects of its responsibilities. This is to be seen most clearly in comparing the University's capital development programme in the 1920s with that of Edinburgh University. While in Glasgow the emphasis was very much on buildings for student use and a Memorial Chapel – worthy projects in themselves but doing little to improve the University's capacities in teaching and research – Edinburgh was busy developing a new Science and Technology complex (King's Buildings) on a site at Liberton acquired for this purpose in 1919. The cluster included a new Chemistry building with many laboratories, Zoology and Animal Breeding and Research buildings funded by generous grants from the Rockefeller Foundation, and new buildings for Geology and Engineering funded by gifts and bequests from various private individuals. At the same time it also managed to invest in a new clinical medicine laboratory in the grounds of the Royal Infirmary, with a further grant from the Rockefeller Foundation.[26] Without neglecting the needs of students – new halls of residence were also built – Edinburgh conducted a development programme in the 1920s that reached out to international as well as local sources of financial support and which placed it within the mainstream of twentieth-century scientific research with its requirements for large laboratories and expensive equipment. By contrast, the only new buildings for teaching and research purposes that Glasgow University completed during the 1920s were the Zoology building (opened in 1923) and the western side of the West Quadrangle, containing staff rooms and classrooms for Arts as well as the Memorial Chapel, which was completed in 1929. Both were pre-war in their conception and (apart from the Chapel which was the subject of a public appeal addressed mainly to the University's graduates) were financed from reserves accumulated during the war together with additional non-recurrent grants made available by the UGC and the Carnegie Trust immediately after the war. Between 1922 (when the UGC effectively ceased to make non-recurrent grants and the Carnegie Trust agreed that the University could mortgage its claims on the next quinquennial round in order to complete the construction of the West Quad) and 1929 (when Sir Donald MacAlister handed over to his successor) no new projects for teaching and research buildings were introduced into the pipeline. This failure to attend to the future academic needs of the University appears to have stemmed from a combination of the countervailing attention that Sir Donald and the Court gave to the public appeals for student facilities and the Chapel and to the completion of the requisite buildings, and of hopes that before too long the national economic situation would improve and the UGC and Carnegie would come back into play as sources of capital funding. Consequently, by the time a new Principal took over in 1929 the moment for a public appeal for money for classrooms and laboratories had passed, Britain and the rest of the world entered the depression of the early thirties and financial support for university capital projects, from whatever sources, disappeared almost completely.

The years between 1922 and 1936 were essentially fallow years in the development of the University's physical plant, which failed to keep pace with the growth of student numbers, particularly on the Arts side, and failed to keep pace with national trends in investment in labs and equipment on the Science side. The symbol of these flagging capabilities, and of the dismal financial environment which gathered around the University in an ever darkening gloom, was the wooden building, of war-time vintage, which was erected in the east or 'medical' Quadrangle in 1920–1, at a cost of £4,000, to house a temporary laboratory for the Chemistry department. This edifice, incongruous amidst its solid sandstone surroundings, was so derided by the student body that it was the object of a notorious prank in November 1921 when some twenty students crept into the Quadrangle at night and painted it red.[27] Despite the very strong case that the newly-appointed Professor George Henderson had lodged with the Court in February 1920 for the provision of greatly expanded laboratory and equipment facilities for the Chemistry department,[28] and despite Sir Donald's successor, Principal Robert Rait, adopting the establishment of a 'Chemistry Institute' as his principal priority for capital investment, that wooden laboratory still stood there sadly in 1936, its paint peeling and its roof unsafe in a high wind.[29] It remained the only new investment undertaken by the University between 1920 and 1936 in what was one of the most important branches of the physical sciences, and one in which the University of Glasgow had already lagged behind in research terms for so long.

The University's financial difficulties after 1921–2 demonstrated themselves not only in an apparent inability to match its estates and buildings to current and future needs, but also in a struggle to meet its annual running costs. This is illustrated by the annual income and expenditure figures in Table 6.4. Although, with UGC help, the University recovered quickly from the financial deficits of the immediate post-war years and its income levels rose from 1920–1 onwards, peaking at £276,757 in 1931–2, this increase proved insufficient to cover the University's growing expenditures. For most of the mid-to-late 1920s the University ran at a deficit. Thereafter, the University managed to break even through the early 1930s, before a combination of further cuts in the UGC grant and a decline in tuition and other fees from the student body brought a return to financial deficit in the mid-1930s.

Table 6.4
University of Glasgow: Income and Expenditure, 1920–1 to 1935–6

	Total Income £	*Total Expenditure* £	*Balances* £
1920–1	175,904	191,331	-15,427
1921–2	199,702	190,646	9056
1922–3	208,809	208,167	642
1923–4	212,385	210,917	1468
1924–5	212,913	221,787	-8874
1925–6	227,672	232,252	-4580
1926–7	235,094	238,206	-3112
1927–8	241,968	246,932	-4964
1928–9	251,858	251,499	359
1929–30	256,476	260,933	-4457
1930–1	273,289	271,226	2063
1931–2	276,757	274,969	1788
1932–3	274,430	269,881	4549
1933–4	266,195	264,520	1675
1934–5	258,469	260,335	-1866
1935–6	257,875	263,356	-5481

Source: UGC returns for relevant dates.

The causes of this struggle to balance its books are to be found mainly on the income side. There were four principal sources of revenue. Two of these – Tuition Fees and Other Fees (principally matriculation and examination fees) – were linked to student numbers, and rose and declined as total student numbers changed. However, fees charged to students covered only a part – no more than about half – of the costs of teaching them, and the University's ability to function without a significant rise in fee levels depended upon the other two flows of income (Figure 6.2). The UGC (or parliamentary) grant was the larger and more important of these two streams, but it failed to keep pace with the growth in student numbers for most of the 1920s. This was partly because allocations were made on a catch-up basis once every five years, partly because the total funds available to the UGC – rising from £1 million per annum in 1920–1 to £1.5 million in 1925–6 – were constrained by limits on public expenditure, and partly because the UGC under Sir William McCormick was less than happy with the rapid rise in the numbers of Arts students in the University of Glasgow and refused to accept that money should follow the student. 'The measure of a University's performance is not the number of students to which it gives degrees,' the UGC said pointedly, 'but the number to which it gives a university education, with all which that term should imply. No one can, in fact, now seriously believe that mere numbers are any criterion of University strength, and, if the choice is to be made, a reduction in the numbers admitted to our University institutions is preferable to a reduction in the standard of education which they provide.'[30] However, a higher Treasury allocation to the UGC, coupled with McCormick's death in 1930, resulted in a slightly improved allocation of funds to the University in the quinquennium 1929–30 to 1934–5, thereby enabling it to return to the black once again. It rode the early years of the depression with somewhat greater ease than in the later 1920s, especially since student numbers, and therefore total costs, also began to fall (Table 6.4), and it was able to halt the drain on reserves which had been the hallmark of the later twenties. However, the University's position remained precarious, and when the government's financial difficulties resulting from the depression finally caught up with it and the other universities, in the shape of a reduction in the UGC recurrent grant from 1934–5 onwards, it returned to the red once more.

The University depended on the UGC grant to meet its teaching commitments partly because of a contraction in the flow of endowment funds to finance new teaching posts. (Aggregate figures for endowment income, rising from £31,175 per annum in 1920–1 to £48,022 in 1935–6 (Figure 6.2), are a poor guide to this process because they also contain funds for other purposes, including student bursaries, scholarships and prizes and, it would appear, money not yet expended on capital projects for which it was earmarked.) The record of individual bequests coming forward to Court to fund teaching posts reveals that there were three distinct phases in such activity. First, in the years 1919–21 there was quite a flurry of new investment, as both the University and the wider community attempted to return to the normality of the pre-war years. With endowments from the Carnegie Trust (which financed chairs in Mercantile Law and in Geology as well as several lectureships), from the

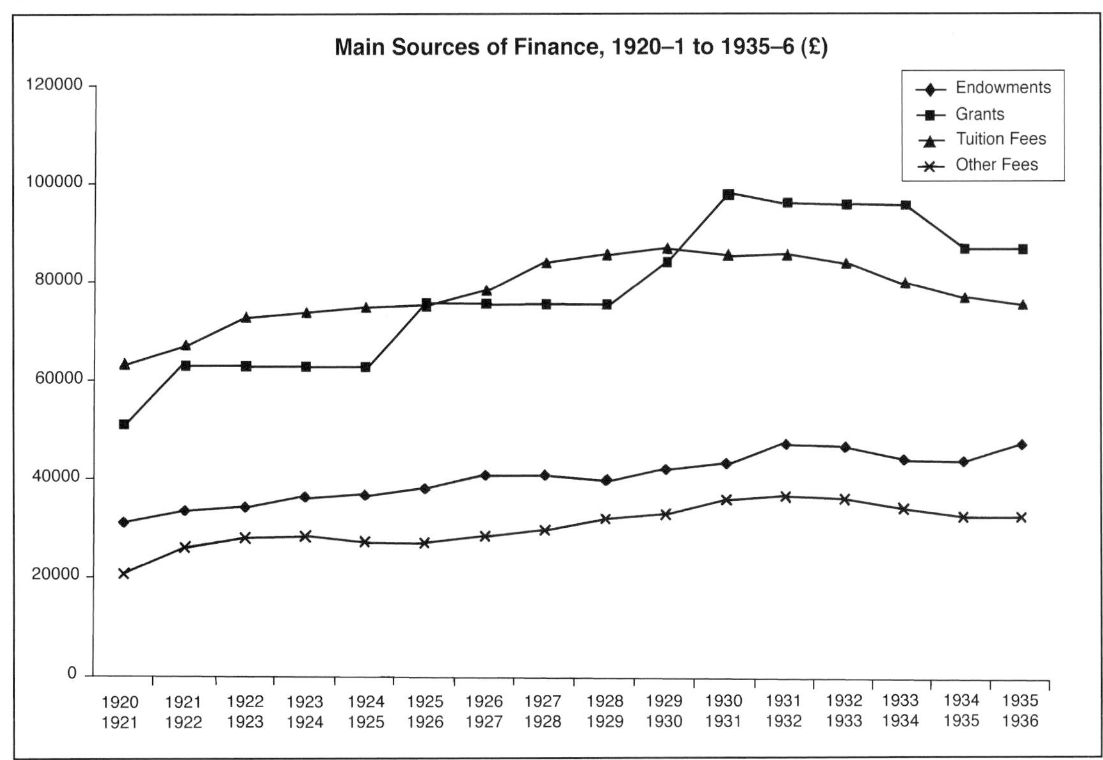

Figure 6.2

Institution of Engineers and Shipbuilders in Scotland (which in 1919 celebrated the centenary of James Watt's death with funds to endow chairs in Electrical Engineering and in Heat Engines) and from the wealthy individuals in the west of Scotland who gave their names to the Gardiner Chair of Chemistry, the Cargill Chair of Applied Physics, and the Stevenson Chairs in Citizenship, Spanish and Italian, the immediate post-war years were a time of revival and renewal, paralleling on the academic front the tide of external financial support for student welfare. From 1921–2, however, the waters receded. It may not have helped that the funding of the chairs in Spanish and Italian by Sir Daniel Macaulay Stevenson became surrounded by controversy, and brought the University some negative publicity. Stevenson, the scion of a local coal-exporting family, a long-serving Liberal member of Glasgow Corporation and a former Lord Provost, had it in mind to foster the links between the University and the College of Commerce by funding chairs whose holders would teach in both institutions. However, he surrounded his bequest with various restrictions, including an insistence that the tenure of the chairs should be for five years only – most probably because he suspected that the University or the professors would tend to forget the commitment to the College with the passage of time – and these brought him into conflict with members of the Court and of the Senate. The row over the Stevenson Chairs rumbled on through 1922–4, with Sir Daniel threatening more than once to withdraw from the entire project, until a compromise, in the shape of a Board of Selection to oversee the filling and subsequent activities of the chairs, brought about a peaceful resolution to the affair.[31]

Although such disagreement may have been discouraging to potential donors, the second phase, involving a perceptible slow-down in new bequests between 1922 and 1930, was brought about mainly by the general economic climate, which reduced the capacity of Glasgow's middle classes to support the University financially. Such new foundations as took place showed many of the characteristics of earlier developments. Thus in 1926 the Loudon Lectureship in Engineering Production and the Johnstone Smith Chair of Accountancy reaffirmed the links to business and the professions. The offer in 1927 from Sir Frederick Gardiner and W. G. Gardiner, two shipowning brothers, to found a Chair in Music in the University, conditional upon the establishment of an Academy of Music in Glasgow, was another example of the interest that many people outside the University had in linking its name and reputation to new developments in higher and further education within the city.[32] Once the Academy of Music and the Chair of Music were established in 1928, the Gardiner brothers, who had already funded a chair in Chemistry, came back to the University with an offer to fund a lectureship in the Pathology of Diseases of Infancy and Childhood in association with the Royal Hospital for Sick Children. None of these individual acts of generosity appear to have come about as a result of the University going out to seek funds for a need that it had identified itself. From about 1922 onwards the University seems to have been in a responsive rather than a proactive mode, living off the goodwill generated by earlier phases of active solicitation of funds, and relying on an ever diminishing band of active donors, including Stevenson and the Gardiner brothers. After 1930, when funds for a chair in Opthalmology became available, such sources of external support dried up altogether, and the University entered the third phase – one of a complete cessation in the attraction of private funds for the enlargement of the teaching body and the recruitment of the best talent available.

Private funding not only failed to keep pace with the growth of student numbers, but because it reflected the priority of donors it frequently did not provide help where it was most needed – which was in the Faculty of Arts. The University's staff-student ratio, which was at an already high level of 1:22 in 1920–1, rose to an even more unfavourable 1:28 in 1928–9, before recovering a little to 1:24 in 1935–6. The pressures on teaching staff that lay behind these figures, however, were much more acute in the classroom subjects than in the laboratory or clinical subjects, for student numbers in Medicine and Engineering both fell off after the early twenties and those in Science

6.4 *Sir Daniel Macaulay Stevenson, Benefactor and Chancellor from 1934.*

remained roughly stable. (The discrepancy between Arts and the rest of the University is best illustrated by the statistics of graduations with the three most popular degrees – Figure 6.3 – which clearly demonstrates how, in the course of the mid-twenties, the University was transformed into a predominantly Arts-based institution.) Arts departments did what they could to cope with the greater student numbers – large classes, such as those in History and English, were divided so that lectures could be delivered more than once in the day – but they struggled to maintain the quality of what they could provide, and by the late twenties there were signs of growing student discontent with what was on offer. Editorials in GUM of 1928–9 alleged that the University 'is overcrowded, unwieldy, aimless. Its staff is manifestly overworked; not half enough time is given to private [i.e. personal] tutorial work, and marking essays and papers is a task done with mechanical disgust' – or, more elegantly, that Gilmorehill was 'where the humanities are sparsely taught and studied perfunctorily, where technical proficiency is the achievement coveted by most of us, [and] learning is seldom the withdrawn and pensive lady adored by so many . . . She does not inspire; she exercises.'[33] By 1930, the annual conference of the SRCs of the Scottish universities was debating, at the instigation of the Glasgow delegation, the need for reform of teaching in Arts, so as to provide greater opportunities for contact between staff and students. Recognising that extra money for additional staff was likely to be in short supply, the conference focused on how student numbers might be limited.[34] Student leaders, it appears, were coming round to the view of the chairman of the UGC that the underfunded expansion of recent years had been disadvantageous, and that the University of Glasgow in particular should have been more selective in its entrance policies. Running parallel with these concerns was the belief held by some that 'more meant worse' – that the University was recruiting too many students who were poorly prepared and poorly motivated.[35] These views were a legacy of the passions aroused by the earlier debate over the Scottish universities' entrance requirements, with those who had been on the losing side of the argument remaining free to complain about the lack of qualifications of the students now entering the Faculty of Arts. Responding to the mood, the Faculty of Arts attempted in 1931 to reopen the issue of Latin as a pre-requisite for entry, on the grounds that 'Our numbers have enormously increased, and anyone who knows anything of Scottish education and Scottish conditions knows that with few exceptions all the promising pupils were recruited before the increase. The new entrants must of necessity be drawn from a lower stratum.'[36] However, lack of support from the other faculties limited the effectiveness of such protests.

Behind the arguments about the quality of new students there probably lurked issues related to social class and to the changing composition of the student body. From a careful analysis of the parental occupations of students contained in the matriculation records, a study published in 1938 established that the greatest growth of student numbers in the University between 1911 and 1931 came from among the working classes (the Registrar-General's classes 3, 4 and 5). This was largely, although not entirely, caused by the swelling numbers of students from working-class backgrounds reading Arts as a preparation for teaching. Indeed the study claimed that by 1931 Glasgow University was 'as much a working-class University as a resort of the petty bourgeoise . . . each claiming 36 per cent of the entrants' to degrees in Arts, Law, Medicine and Theology.[37] A distaste for the proletarianisation of the University, which gave rise to such phenomena as the 'Quad Boys', who hung around the quads at lunch-time and ate their 'pieces' in adjoining corridors because they could not afford the Union subscription,[38] may well have underlain objections to the University's 'wider access' policies and allegations of a decline in standards.

Complaints about lower standards of entrants to the Arts Faculty, especially those intending an Ordinary degree as preparation for a teaching career, as well as about the inadequacies of teaching by large lecture classes and the absence of tutorials, continued to rumble on through the pages of the student and public press during the early 1930s.[39] In 1933–4, the SRC presented a whole series of suggestions for reform in the Faculty of Arts, including the creation of a separate Faculty of Education for students intending a teaching career, a restructuring of the Ordinary degree to permit greater depth in study, limitations on the size of classes, and a restriction on the age of entry into Arts, none of which found favour with the Faculty of Arts or with the Senate.[40] By that year, however, some of the steam was already beginning to go out of the debate, for the onset of the international depression gradually brought relief to the hard-pressed departments in Arts and Science that offered classes for the MA degree – as declining personal incomes, greater financial hardship and reduced employment opportunities, particularly in the teaching profession, took their toll on student numbers, and graduations in Arts dropped off noticeably (see Figure 6.3).

Professor (later Sir) Robert Rait, who succeeded Sir Donald MacAlister in 1929, had the task of grappling with the inherited problem of large student numbers. As a Glasgow professor, he was certainly aware of the widespread complaints about teaching standards that washed around the University, and during his first year in office spoke publicly and eloquently about the need to 'adapt old machinery to new demands' and to tackle the overcrowding and understaffing which afflicted a large part of the University.[41] However, he appears to have had no clearly defined policy to enable him to find a way between the inertia of the Faculty of Arts on the one hand and the crushing millstone of financial constraint on the other. The drying-up of private bequests in support of teaching posts, the instability of UGC funding, which rose a little in his early years in office and then fell back again after 1934, and above all the absolutely low level of the UGC's recurrent grant per head gave him very little room for manoeuvre. His was the accumulated problem not just of the unforeseen consequences of his predecessor's policies but also the fact that during the 1920s and into the 1930s the University received the lowest UGC grant per head of student. It retained its lowly position at the bottom of the British universities' financial pecking order (Table 6.5). In money terms the picture was not static – the UGC grant per head of student rose from the miserly £11 of 1920–1 to £19 in 1924–5, before falling back to £15 in 1929–30 (as a result of the expansion of student numbers in the late twenties) and then improving again slightly in the early thirties. Comparatively, however, in respect of both the UGC grant and the total income available to it, the University's position did not change. It remained poorly funded in comparison

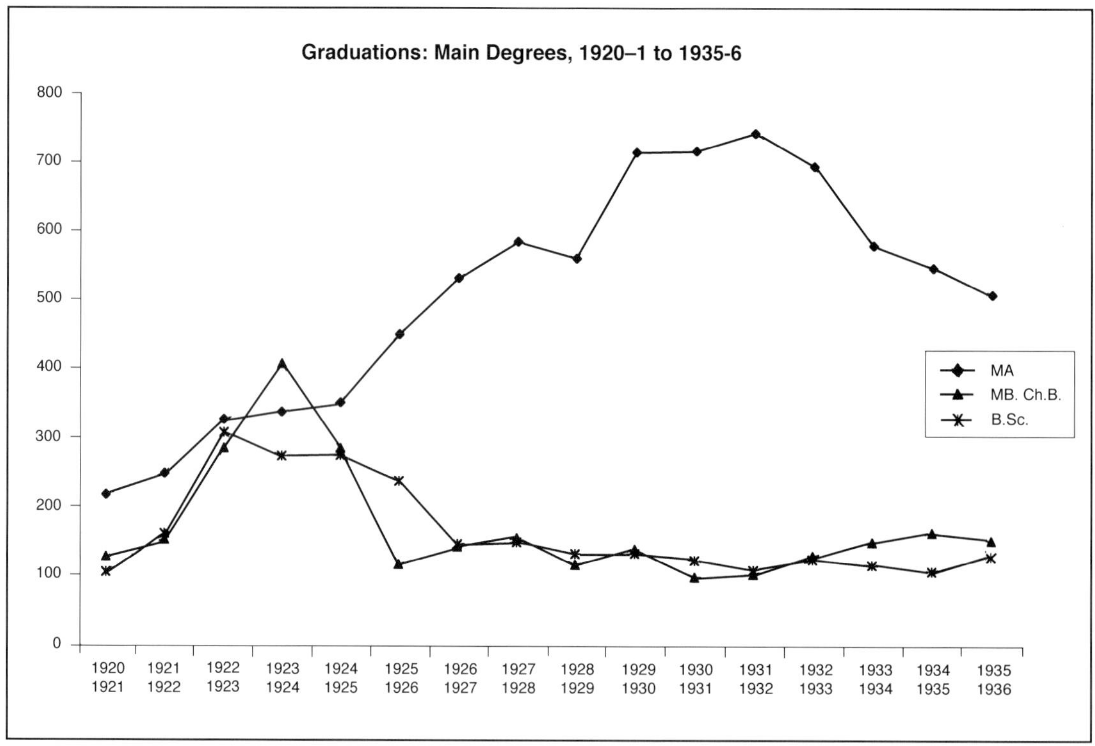

Figure 6.3

with the English civic universities, which enjoyed UGC grants and total incomes per student that were some two or three times greater than Glasgow's. Given economies of scale, a large university could be expected to have lower incomes per student than smaller ones, and levels of per capita funding could also be expected to vary with the mix of the student population, depending upon the relative numbers in classroom-based, laboratory-based and clinically-based subjects. The large numbers of Ordinary degree students in the Scottish universities would also have attracted less funding from the UGC than the mainly Honours students in the English universities. These factors, however, do not explain the enormous differences that existed between Glasgow on the one hand and the English civics on the other. Within Scotland, St Andrews remained significantly better funded than Glasgow, and even Aberdeen and Edinburgh managed to widen slightly the gap which existed between them and Glasgow. The University in 1935–6 was even more what it had been in 1920–1 – an institution that was less generously treated by the state than comparable universities within the British system, and which found it much more difficult than the others to raise the resources needed to meet the demands placed upon it. Whether through inadvertence or with foresight, it had opened its doors more widely than others to meet the needs

Table 6.5
University Funding: English Civic and Scottish Universities, selected dates

	1924–5		*1929–30*		*1935–6*	
	Treasury Grant per f/t student £	*Total Income per f/t student* £	*Treasury Grant per f/t student* £	*Total Income per f/t student* £	*Treasury Grant per f/t student* £	*Total Income per f/t student* £
Birmingham	53	120	51	135	51	147
Bristol	86	153	90	188	83	194
Leeds	54	159	51	165	47	159
Liverpool	51	128	53	133	43	118
Manchester	44	115	38	115	37	117
Sheffield	69	195	65	193	65	195
Aberdeen	35	80	37	86	46	101
Edinburgh	25	73	23	71	31	89
St Andrews	78	164	62	142	58	127
Glasgow	19	56	15	52	21	60

Source: UGC Returns for relevant dates

of the city, the region and the nation it served – more especially to meet the needs of the Scottish educational system – and in the process it had been poorly rewarded.

Seriously understaffed on the Arts side and under-equipped on the Science side, the University failed to make much headway in research and scholarship. In an institution which had always prided itself first and foremost on its teaching role, a research culture was not very highly developed. Inspired individual lecturing, which enthused the undergraduates, was not always accompanied by contributions to scholarly literature. But wherever an orientation towards research existed, it was subject to further squeeze from the resource constraints of the 1920s and early 1930s. The deficiencies were perhaps most obvious in Arts. Some of those who gave a lifetime of academic service without making any mark in scholarship, such as Dudley Medley of History, who retired in 1931 with only a student primer on constitutional history to his name, could at least claim to have been deeply involved in the corporate life of the city and University. Too many others had no such excuse and yet could be described on their retirement or death as having published little – including Gibson of Mathematics whose 'almost excessive devotion to teaching left him but little leisure for research', or Phillimore of Greek, who had many unpublished papers lying 'as they were left, the remains of great projects not abandoned indeed but subordinated to public duty', or Latta of Logic and Metaphysics, whose 'contributions to the literature of his subject were rare', or Bowman of Moral Philosophy, who had an enormous reputation as a lecturer but 'in his too brief life . . . was unfortunately prevented from publishing a volume of work in any way comparable with his ability', or Stevenson of Hebrew and Semitic Languages, who 'had not contributed in any large measure to Biblical writings.'[42] The situation, however, was scarcely any better on the Science side. In Natural Philosophy (Physics), where the spirit of Kelvin lingered on although the frontiers of knowledge in the subject were moving rapidly in new directions elsewhere, the creation of a second chair and of two separate departments proved to be a recipe for conflict not collaboration; in Chemistry, the influence of Ferguson lingered on in the Gardiner chair through Patterson's focus on the history of Chemistry while Henderson, in the Regius chair, had already done his best work at the Royal College before his appointment in 1919; and in Botany, J. M. F. Drummond, who held the chair from 1925 to 1930 'lacked a strong research background though he was a sound teacher.'[43] Some sound research and scholarship took place, it is true, and the picture was not uniformly bleak. The Earth Sciences, such as Geology under E. B. Bailey, were less hampered than the Physical Sciences by lack of investment in labs and equipment, and the Medical School, with its feet firmly planted in clinical practice, produced work of a standard that secured some of its members a continuing national reputation. In most of Arts, Science and Engineering, however, while individual members of staff undertook competent work this too frequently lay outside the developing thrust of mainstream research in their respective fields. Certainly, there was no example of the singular brilliance that won Frederick Soddy the Nobel Prize in 1921, for work done on radioactivity before he left the University for Aberdeen in 1914.

One possible measure of the University's difficulty in providing conditions conducive to research and scholarship in the post-war years was the problem which the Court experienced in filling some chairs – the chairs of Natural Philosophy in 1923–4 and again in 1925–6, Mathematics in 1927 and Logic in 1927, among others, were subject to lengthy searches for suitable candidates, with offers to likely individuals being politely spurned. Another is its mixed, and none too strong, performance in the development of post-graduate research degree work (Table 6.6). In 1919 the University committed itself to a new era in post-graduate research training by adopting, in common with the other British universities, the three-year period of supervised research for the degree of Ph.D., which had been pioneered in Germany. It did so partly in the expectation, which proved to be a forlorn hope, that American students who had previously gone to Germany for this purpose would turn to the British universities instead. The new degree did not prove attractive to the Medical Faculty (which awarded roughly half of all the doctoral degrees within the University) presumably because the older MD regulations were more suited to the clinical conditions in which most medical research was conducted at that time. However, in Arts, Science and Engineering (the latter became a separate faculty in 1921), the Ph.D. gradually replaced the older D.Litt. and D.Sc. degrees as a vehicle for higher degrees by research. In Engineering, where

Table 6.6
Doctoral Degrees, 1920–1 to 1935–6

	Arts		*Divinity*	*Medicine*		*Science*		*Engineering*		
	D.Litt	*Ph.D*	*Ph.D*	*MD*	*Ph.D*	*D.Sc*	*Ph.D*	*D.Sc*	*Ph.D*	*Total*
1920–1	3			12		10				25
1921–2	4			17		1				22
1922–3	1	7		15		4				27
1923–4	4	8		15		4				31
1924–5	2	20		17		2				41
1925–6	2	18		7		5				32
1926–7	3	13		14				2		32
1927–8	1	4		12			6		1	24
1928–9	3	3	3	17			10		3	39
1929–30	1	4	2	23		5	6		1	42
1930–1	1	5	1	28	1		4		3	43
1931–2	4	4		19		10	11		1	49
1932–3		1	3	26	1	5	10			46
1933–4		2	4	35		5	12		4	62
1934–5		5	1	26		5	13	1	2	53
1935–6		1		17		1	10		5	34

undergraduate numbers declined from the peak of the immediate post-war years and employment opportunities were slender, the number of those proceeding to the Ph.D. was understandably not very large. In Science, the numbers presenting for research degrees were larger than in Engineering, but less than might have been expected, given the relative size of the two faculties. The noticeable increase in Ph.D. submissions from the late 1920s was caused by two principal factors – the rationalisation of the British chemicals manufacturers into the giant Imperial Chemical Industries Ltd, which resulted in better employment prospects for research chemists, and the introduction by the Carnegie Trust in 1930 of Senior Scholarships to support three full years of postgraduate research.[44] It was in the Arts Faculty, however, that the impact on research of the large growth of undergraduate numbers could be seen most clearly. From a period of relatively high post-war activity, which resulted in twenty-two doctorates being awarded in 1924–5, the numbers declined perceptibly year by year until, at the very slough of despond in 1935, only one Ph.D. was awarded. For a couple of years in the thirties, in fact, the small Faculty of Divinity produced more Ph.Ds than the much larger Arts, which caused some resentment in Arts about the more leisured life-style of those in the ministry or engaged in the training of the ministry. More extraordinarily, the Faculty of Arts, apparently believing that its problems lay more in the nature of the Ph.D. than in its own research performance and its capacity to supervise research students, attempted to get the University to abandon the Ph.D. degree altogether.[45] It failed to achieve its goal, in the face of opposition from Science and Engineering, and by 1936 research for degree purposes as well as for the advancement of knowledge was almost moribund in the Arts Faculty. The undergraduate-friendly policies of the Court, the parsimony of the UGC and the predilections of the professors had combined to produce a regrettable narrowing of the Faculty's educational activities.

The pressure of student numbers and shortage of cash also resulted in the abandonment of the separate provision for women students which had been a feature of the University since the establishment of Queen Margaret College. Over the years, the numbers of female undergraduates outstripped the teaching space available in Queen Margaret College, with the result that by the later 1920s many classes that had previously been taught there, for females only, were converted into joint classes taught at Gilmorehill. Lectureships previously designated as being held at QMC were also converted, as they became vacant, into posts within the mainstream academic departments, helping to alleviate some of the pressures there. Consequently, by 1930 the College had become little more than an administrative shell, where women matriculated separately from the men and obtained academic guidance and pastoral care, and its continuing existence came into question. In an institution where gender difference had largely ceased to have any academic significance, although it still had a very strong social significance in the shape of separate unions, a women's college seemed to have outlived its purposes. There was therefore little internal dissent within the University when Principal Rait and the Court, desperately seeking cash for a new Chemistry building, proposed to integrate the College's remaining functions with the rest of the University administration and to sell the building. This was achieved in 1935, with the sale of the QMC building to the BBC for £25,000.[46]

If financial considerations helped to squeeze out of the University's constitution the only significant internal element of collegial organisation that it possessed, they also prevented the University from developing any external collegial dimensions through its relations with other institutions in the city. At no time did those concerned with the governance of this, the largest unitary university in the United Kingdom, consider the possibility of developing a more federal structure for higher educational provision, by drawing other institutions in Glasgow into a closer relationship which would transform them into colleges or proto-colleges of the University and enable them to undertake some of the teaching which the University itself was hard pushed to provide. The seeds of such a policy already existed, in the shape of formal associations with the Royal Technical College, the West of Scotland Agricultural College, and (from 1930) the Royal Scottish Academy of Music. There was also collaboration with the College of Commerce through the teaching of modern languages. However, the University treated these as a series of one-off relationships, carried out for limited purposes and usually under pressure from external sources like the business community or the Scottish Office, rather than as growth-points for academic development to be nurtured in harmony with the University's own interests.

The relationship with the RTC illustrates some of the complexities in this situation. The close association that had developed between the two institutions during the war and immediate post-war years did not survive for long. Its last significant manifestation was perhaps the establishment of a joint board for architecture in 1924, to oversee the teaching of a degree course for architecture that also involved the Glasgow School of Art.[47] However, in the meantime, the University, encouraged by the energy, enthusiasm and post-war fundraising skills of Professor John Cormack, had established its own Faculty of Engineering and the possibility that the RTC might become the University's College of Engineering and Applied Science, which was implicit in the agreement of 1913, was set aside. Rivalry and tensions began to creep into the relationship. During 1930–1, for example, there was a spat over whether, and under what conditions, holders of the Associateship of the Royal College might become eligible to be Ph.D. students.[48] Difficulties also arose over collaboration in Mining, in which there were separate departments and chairs in both the College and the University. The decline in the numbers of students entering the University for engineering degrees after 1922 was particularly marked in Mining (as well as in Naval Architecture), and eventually it was recognised that there was a need to rationalise efforts between the College and the University. In 1931, in an effort to save costs at a time of financial difficulty elsewhere in the University, the Court decided that the now-vacant University chair in Mining should be suppressed and all teaching and research in the field transferred to the RTC. But this decision was only taken, with the agreement of Senate, against the strong protests of Professor Cormack and the Faculty of Engineering, who objected on the grounds that the RTC was not a fit place for the chair because of the large amount of sub-degree or non-degree work done there.[49] Such dismissive attitudes towards neighbouring institutions of higher education also lay behind an unwillingness to collaborate too closely with the College of Commerce or to respond to student suggestions for a Faculty of Education, which might involve closer ties with Jordanhill College, and almost certainly contributed to the objections of the Science Faculty in 1933 to specific proposals for closer institutional links with the West of Scotland Agricultural College.[50] They cut across and constrained any leadership role to be played by the University within the city, and stood in the way of any wider 'federal' university structure being evolved. The University could therefore be said to have spurned the advantages that these other institutions enjoyed – and the University lacked – namely access to Scottish Office and local authority funding.

This in turn raises the question whether it benefited the Scottish universities in general, and Glasgow in particular, to have been brought under the umbrella of a British-wide UGC in 1919. Prior to the establishment of the UGC, the Scottish universities approached the Treasury for central government funds through the good offices of the Secretary for Scotland. Now there was no access to the Scottish Office in arranging funding for university education in Scotland. Becoming part of a British university system brought few if any noticeable benefits to the University – it was and remained seriously underfunded in a system dominated by the needs and interests of the English civic universities. Neither Court nor Senate appears to have been aware of this at the time, and the University was unwilling to question the fundamentals of the 'British' system of which it had become part. Curiously, therefore, when other Scottish universities began in the mid-1930s to express uneasiness about their place in the system, the University of Glasgow, which had done least well out of the post-war arrangements, proved to be among the most 'unionist' in sentiment.[51] On the other hand, the University was expected to relate to a Scottish secondary schools sector which was comparatively well funded in British terms – to open its doors to the products of that sector and to supply the teaching force necessary to its expansion and improvement – but to do so without any financial assistance from or constitutional relationship with the Scottish Office. It was the University's dilemma between the wars that it served the needs of a Scottish economy and society but received its state funding from a body which had no responsibility for or interest in that economy and society. In that mismatch lay the roots of most of its troubles.

In such a situation, where the external environment bore down heavily upon the University, the quality of leadership available to it mattered a great deal. The University, however, was not too well served by its Principals. With hindsight, it might have been better if Sir Donald MacAlister had retired rather earlier than he did – say by 1923, when the big drive to raise funds for student welfare was largely complete. During the mid-to-late 1920s Sir Donald was not a well man – he suffered from severe rheumatism and also, it seems, from stomach ulcers. Although in constant pain, he nevertheless continued to travel regularly to London to chair meetings of the General Medical Council and the CVCP and to conduct all the regular business of the University. By now, however, he appears to have been presiding over rather than leading the University. He had no further vision of its future, now that his hopes for better student facilities were being realised, and he appears to have had no solution to the problems which the relatively 'open door' entrance policy was building up for him and his successor. His main aim during these years of deteriorating staff/student ratios was to remain in office until the completion of the Memorial Chapel, to which he and his wife had contributed so much, both emotionally and financially.[52] His was a view of the University deeply rooted in the great sacrifice made by the young men and women of the University during the Great War, which he was determined to see suitably recognised. However, not only did he fail to plug the funding gap that opened up during his latter years in office but, having demitted his post in October 1929, he permitted the affection for him which had had built up among the graduates of the University to bring about his election to the vacant Chancellorship. He was the first former Principal of the University ever to fill that most distinguished office.

Had Sir Donald's successor come from outside the University, there would have been little danger of his being under Sir Donald's shadow. However, the Secretary of State for Scotland, acting for the Crown, made an internal appointment, translating Robert Sangster Rait from the Chair of Scottish History to the Principal's Lodging. Rait clearly felt the continuing presence of Sir Donald, deferring to him from time to time, particularly on medical matters, and penning an account of Sir Donald's role as Principal in the biography which Lady MacAlister published following Sir Donald's death in January 1934. Rait's main problem as Principal, however, was not so much an inability to be his own master. It was rather the major economic depression that closed in around him and the University from 1929 onwards, and which prevented him from securing the financial freedom to repair the deficiencies that he inherited. Rait showed signs of being an able administrator as well as scholar – he had served with some distinction in the Trade Intelligence Department during the war, had held several offices within professional historical circles, and continued to be the Historiographer Royal for Scotland. But surviving records give little hint that he had any clear vision as to where he wished to take the University, and he had almost no room for manoeuvre anyway.[53] His main achievements were in overseeing the new arrangements which had to be put in place in the Faculty of Divinity as a result of the Union of the Church of Scotland and the United Free Church in 1929, in selling Queen Margaret College to the BBC, and in persuading the Carnegie Trust and the Bellahouston Trust to put up money towards the future construction of a Chemistry building. He was also a man who was deeply affected by the great economic and social consequences of the depression in the West of Scotland, and was disheartened by its effects on the University. Whether because of this, or by failing to assert his new authority within the University, he became something of an aloof and distant figure who evoked little sympathy from the academic and administrative staff.[54] Eventually the strain told and in

6.5 *Sir Robert Sangster Rait, Principal 1929–36.*

the summer of 1935 Rait, then 62 years old, suffered a stroke. During the whole of the following academic session the University was without an effective head, as the Court awaited his recovery and eventually pressed for his retirement. His death in May 1936 came at the end of a period in the history of the University when the hopes of recovery and reinvigoration after the First World War had gradually given way to the realities of an institution under pressure from the twin forces of increased demand for its services and insufficient financial resources to meet these demands. Principal Hetherington would later sum the period up well: 'for a good many years . . . in spite of the generosity of a few individual benefactors, the rate of development in Glasgow was less than that of most other British Universities, and much less

6.6 *A Royal Visit, 1933. Sir Robert Rait, Principal, and Compton Mackenzie, Rector, accompany the Duke and Duchess of York.*

than it ought to have been in a place carrying the immense teaching load which in fact and inevitably falls on Glasgow. Just as the long depression left its mark on the social and industrial life of Glasgow, so did it, heavily, upon the University.'[55]

Notes and References

1. I. G. Hutchison, *The University and the State: The Case of Aberdeen* (Aberdeen, 1993), 43–4.
2. UGC Returns, 1920–21, 6.
3. *University of Glasgow Handbook* (Glasgow, 1919), 6.
4. UGC Report for 1929–30 to 1934–35 (1936), 28.

5. Such fears took different forms in the various universities; in Glasgow they emerged as a concern that an emphasis on 'pure and higher as opposed to vocational learning' that was detected in the UGC Report of 3 Feb. 1921 might lead to action adverse to the University's interests (Report of the Business and other Committees of the General Council, 26 Oct. 1921).
6. UGC Report, 1925, 10.
7. UGC Returns, 1927–28, 4, and UGC Report, 1930, 5–6.
8. Hutchison, *The University and the State*, 65–7; 'University Entrance', *Glasgow Herald*, 1 Sept. 1921.
9. G. E. Davie, *The Crisis of the Democratic Intellect: The Problem of Generalism and Specialisation in Twentieth-Century Scotland* (Edinburgh, 1986).
10. General Council, Report of the Business and other Committees, 16 March and 26 Oct. 1921, 26 April and 25 Oct. 1922, 25 April and 31 Oct. 1923.
11. Court Camera, 12 Jan. 1922; Senate, 1 March, 17 April, and 26 April 1923; 'University News: The Proposed Entrance Regulations', *Glasgow Herald*, 15 June 1923; General Council, 31 Oct. 1923.
12. General Council, Report of the Business and other Committees, 30 April 1924 and 28 Oct. 1925.
13. Draft Public Appeal for Joint Committee on Student Welfare (n.d.), Principal's Correspondence: Student Welfare, UG Archives, File 73392.
14. 'The GUM of the Early and Middle Twenties: 1920–21', by Ochre [C. A. Oakley], GUM, 45 No. 2, 1 Nov. 1933.
15. Senate, 23 June 1920.
16. General Council, Report of the Business and Finance Committees [hereafter General Council], 26 April 1922, 25 April 1923, 31 Oct. 1923, and 30 April 1924; Court Camera, 10 June 1920.
17. 'The GUM of the Early and Middle Twenties: 1923–24', by Ochre, GUM, 45, No. 7, 31 Jan. 1934.
18. C. A. Oakley, *Union Ygorra: The Story of the Glasgow University Student over the Last Sixty Years* (Glasgow, 1951), 45.
19. R. O. MacKenna, *Glasgow University Athletic Club: The Story of the First Hundred Years* (Glasgow, 1981), 46–51.
20. Court Camera, 13 Dec. 1923.
21. Report of the Sub-Committee on New University Union, 7 June 1927, UG Archives File 73392.
22. Court Camera, 28 Feb. and 2 July 1931.
23. Court Camera, 23 July 1925 and 10 Jan. 1929; correspondence on 'student levy' in UG Archives File 73392; MacKenna, *Glasgow University Athletic Club*, 51–53.
24. UGC Report for 1929–30 to 1934–35 (1936), 17.
25. GUM, 35, 9 (12 March 1924); UGC Report for 1929–30 to 1934–35, 14.
26. UGC Report for 1923–24 to 1928–29 (1930), 19.
27. The students disturbed a small dog (said to be Lady MacAlister's) whose barking gave the alarm and led to the arrival of a large police contingent. Most of the perpetrators escaped, the leader leaving the seat of his trousers on a spiked railing on University Avenue, but eventually 18 of them were identified by the

SRC and, offering an apology for their actions, were fined one pound each by the Senate. ('The GUM of the Early and Middle Twenties: 1921–22' by Ochre, GUM, 45, 3 (15 Nov. 1933), and Senate, 1 Dec. 1921.)

28. Court Camera, 12 Feb. 1920.
29. General Council, 24 April 1935.
30. UGC Report for 1923–4 to 1928–9 (1930), 6.
31. Court Camera, 9 June and 12 July 1921, 8 March, 19 April and 10 May 1923, 24 Jan. and 14 Feb. 1924; Senate, 24 Feb. 1924.
32. Court Camera, 22 April and 7 Oct. 1926, and 13 Jan. 1927.
33. Senate, 15 Dec. 1927; GUM 40, 10 (13 March 1929), and 40, 12 (15 May 1925).
34. GUM, 41, 8 (5 Feb. 1930).
35. *Glasgow Herald*, 5 Dec. 1928 and 27 Nov. 1929.
36. Senate, 30 April 1930.
37. A. Collier, 'Social origins of a sample of entrants to Glasgow University', *Sociological Review*, 30 (1938), 177.
38. Robert T. Hutcheson and Hugh Conway, *The University of Glasgow, 1920–1974: The Memoir of Robert T. Hutcheson* (Glasgow, 1997), 130.
39. See, for example, the editorial in GUM, 44, 3 (16 Nov. 1932), 83–4, 'Standard of University Students', *Glasgow Herald*, 23 April 1931, and 'University Problems', *Glasgow Herald*, 18 April 1936.
40. Senate, 15 March 1933–34.
41. In a speech to the Glasgow University London Club reported in *Glasgow Herald*, 31 May 1930.
42. Senate, 3 Oct. 1927 and 18 June 1936; General Council, 27 April 1927, 27 April 1932, and 28 April 1937.
43. R. Y. Thomson (ed.), *A Faculty for Science: A Unified Diversity* (Glasgow, 1993), 40–41, 81, 142–3.
44. General Council, 24 April 1929 and 30 April 1930.
45. Senate, 31 March 1931.
46. Court Camera, 12 Dec. 1929, 11 Jan., 8 Nov. and 13 Dec. 1934, and 9 May 1935.
47. Senate, 15 May and 2 Oct. 1924.
48. Senate, 6 Nov. 1930 and 19 Feb. 1931.
49. Court Camera, 3 Dec. 1930, and 12 Nov. and 13 Dec. 1931; Senate, 3 Dec. 1931.
50. Senate, 23 Feb. and 13 June 1933.
51. Thus, when the University of St Andrews suggested in 1934 that the Scottish universities should approach the Chancellor of the Exchequer separately from the Universities Bureau of the British Empire, on the grounds that it had become a mere lobby organisation for the English civic universities, the Court took the view that the UGC should not be by-passed in such a manner. Similarly, in 1936 it refused a request from the University of Aberdeen for a conference of the Scottish universities to consider withdrawal from the Universities Bureau. (Court Camera, 14 June 1934 and 16 April 1936.)
52. *Sir Donald MacAlister of Tarbert, by His Wife* (London 1935), 243, 259.
53. Unlike both his predecessor and his successor, Rait has not been the subject of

a full biographical account. However, biographical notices are to be found in the Senate Minutes (18 June 1936) and the General Council Report (28 Oct. 1936). A more detailed study of the man and his policies is perhaps necessary before we can accept his reputation within the University as a weak Principal wholly overshadowed by Sir Donald MacAlister and Sir Hector Hetherington.

54. Hutcheson and Conway, *The University of Glasgow, 1920–1974*, 65–6.
55. *Glasgow Herald*, 27 April 1944.

CHAPTER SEVEN

A New Broom and Another War, 1936–45

The University entered the academic session 1936–7 with a new Principal at the helm. Many hopes were pinned on Hector Hetherington's leadership qualities and on his capacity to revive an institution in distress. He in turn was admirably suited to the task, combining a close knowledge of the University, and a deep affection for it, with a wide experience of British higher education. A graduate of the University, with a degree in classics as well as in economics and philosophy, a representative of the humane scholarship in social sciences which had been the hallmark of Glasgow since the days of Adam Smith, and a passionate golfer, Hetherington began his academic career with periods on the staff at Glasgow, Sheffield and Cardiff, as well as wartime service in the Ministry of Labour. Then in the 1920s he became successively Principal and Professor of Philosophy at the College of the South-West of England at Exeter, Professor of Moral Philosophy in Glasgow and Vice-Chancellor of the University of Liverpool.[1] Having been a candidate for the post of Principal of the University when Rait was appointed in 1929, and been disappointed by rejection on grounds of youth and inexperience, he arrived on Gilmorehill in the autumn of 1936 determined to make his mark on his *alma mater*. He would lead the University for another twenty-five years, becoming one of its longest serving, most highly respected and most deeply loved Principals, as well as a major figure in the wider university scene. His immediate task, however, was to reinvigorate an institution that had been worn down by years of financial squeeze and neglect, which was drifting as a result of Rait's illness and the retirement of several senior professors, in which staff morale was at a low ebb because of staff/student ratios that would have been unacceptable in any secondary school, and in which the lights of research and scholarship flickered only dimly. It was a challenge that he relished and tackled with great energy.

Inevitably, the initial focus was on the University's precarious financial position. Drawing on his Liverpool experience, Hetherington quickly identified several areas of weakness. First, the municipal authorities made no direct contribution to the University's income. Second, student fees were too low – more especially in Arts and in Engineering where they were only about half the level charged by the University of Liverpool. And third, endowment income was badly skewed. Glasgow was the only university in Britain where benefactions for student scholarships exceeded benefactions for other purposes – in the six years to 1937 the University had received £130,000 for student support compared with £47,000 for land, buildings, equipment and endowed posts.[2] (Among the latter were bequests from the Gardiner brothers, which enabled a Medical Institute to be established at the Western Infirmary, 1937; and from Sir Daniel Macaulay Stevenson, who succeeded Sir Donald MacAlister as Chancellor of the University in 1934, which paid for a small extension to the Botany Building in 1938.) Solutions to these problems were not easily found. Although Hetherington favoured the raising of student fees, action on this front required a joint approach by all four Scottish universities, and the agreement of the others, especially Aberdeen, was not readily forthcoming. Changing the climate of public giving from one dominated by student welfare to one taking greater account of the University's development needs required delicate handing, so that potential donors for student purposes would not be turned away completely. Consequently, although Hetherington was of

7.1 *Arrival at Central Station, 1936. The Hetheringtons are welcomed back to Glasgow by student representatives.*

the view that over £60,000 of new capital investment was required, the Court decided against launching any general public appeal for funds for this purpose. Instead, it wrote privately to a number of 'friends of the University' to solicit contributions, by which means it obtained some £20,000 by the spring of 1939.[3]

Some compensation for the absence of a local government contribution came about through the introduction in 1937–8 of a grant to the Scottish universities from the Scottish Education Fund. In a changing political climate – the depression had boosted nationalist sentiment in Scotland and, among the growing litany of complaints about the relationship with England, allegations concerning the unfair treatment of the Scottish institutions by the UGC began to surface in the public arena, especially during the by-election for the Scottish Universities seat in 1935[4] – the Scottish universities pressed their case for improved funding on a reluctant UGC. Rejecting this, the UGC suggested that, in the absence of local authority support, the Scottish institutions might seek to tap the Scottish Education Fund administered by the Scottish Office, on which no Scottish university had hitherto made claims.[5] The Secretary of State referred their application to the Alness Committee, which rejected claims that the Scottish universities were unfairly treated by the UGC (on the grounds that Scotland received a bigger share of the Treasury grant than its population merited). Nevertheless, the Committee recommended that the Scottish universities should be permitted to draw up to £43,000 per annum from the Fund, which was the equivalent of 12.5 per cent of the UGC grant to Scotland. The Committee, noting Hetherington's opinion that Glasgow University 'has been systematically underfinanced for years', recommended that Glasgow's share of the windfall should be the largest: £12,000 immediately and £9,000 per annum from 1939 onwards.[6] At last the government recognised that the arrangements put in place at the time of the creation of the UGC in 1919 had been relatively disadvantageous to the Scottish universities.

Hetherington's principalship was therefore an early beneficiary (in 1937–8) of a new stream of recurrent income. It also benefited from the fact that the British economy was clambering back out of the depression, so that the Treasury grant to the UGC for the quinquennium starting in 1936–7 was increased by a quarter of a million pounds. Although the UGC continued to be less than generous to Glasgow in its allocation of these funds – the University's increase in grant of £3.56 per student between 1935–6 and 1938–9 was lower than for the other Scottish universities, and markedly lower than the figures of between £8.86 and £13.21 per student for Birmingham, Bristol, Manchester and Sheffield[7] – the extra money was still welcome. With these two increases in recurrent income, the University climbed out of the annual deficits which were the hallmark of Rait's last years and reached something approximating to financial equilibrium. The pressure to increase student fees eased somewhat, although it did not wholly disappear from mind.

The general improvement in the University's financial position enabled Hetherington and the Court to begin in 1938 the construction of some two-thirds of the new building for Chemistry that Rait had so badly wanted but could not afford. A non-recurrent grant of £16,800 from the UGC in 1938–9, the first significant contribution from that quarter since the early 1920s, also made it possible to start work on a new reading room for students on the north side of University Avenue. (Hetherington was acutely conscious of the essentially non-residential nature of the University and of the need to provide study facilities in the evenings and at the weekends.)[8] Another new source of funding for capital projects was the Physical Training Grants Committee, an agency set up by a government concerned by impending war and the need to improve the fitness levels of a new generation of youth. From that source the University obtained £10,000 towards a new gymnasium and swimming pool to be built in Oakfield Avenue.[9] Evidence of Hetherington's foresight in the area of capital development came in his creation of a committee on building policy, to plan and oversee the physical progress of the University estate. It

7.2 *The new buildings, 1939:*
(a) The Round Reading Room *(b) The Chemistry Building* (opposite)

was also to be found in his purchases of property in University Gardens and other locations to the north of University Avenue, whenever they became available, because it was becoming clear that if the University were to expand at any time in the future it would have to do so on the other side of the road.

But if Hetherington largely inherited the easier financial conditions of the late 1930s, and the greater freedom it gave him, his contribution to an improvement in the University's staffing situation was entirely his own. From the start of his principalship he devoted considerable time and energy to filling vacant senior positions, readerships and senior lectureships as well as chairs, by recruiting the most talented people he could find. He drew on his large network of contacts in England and Wales to identify likely candidates, he travelled the length and breadth of the country to meet and try to persuade such individuals to come to Glasgow to work, and he encouraged them to visit Glasgow informally to meet members of the Court and others over the tea cups. Not all of his efforts were successful. There was such a backlog of academic decline to overcome that it could be an uphill struggle to convince those accustomed to better conditions of the merits of Glasgow. One member of staff of the University of Manchester, having been invited to take an interest in the chair of French, visited Gilmorehill and on the basis of what he saw informed Hetherington that 'he could not possibly accept the chair if it were offered to him.'[10] Nevertheless, Hetherington proved adept at 'poaching' professors from other universities. These included Arthur Trueman of Bristol who took the chair of Geology in 1937, and George Barker of Edinburgh, who came to Glasgow on the strength of the new building for Chemistry but oversaw its construction for only one year before his untimely death. In 1936 Hetherington enticed J. W. McNee back to Glasgow from UCH London as Regius Professor of Medicine, the first of the professorial appointments he made in clinical departments to modernise their outlook and foster their commitment to scientific medicine and to research. From Edinburgh, to fill the chair of Surgery, came a young man named Charles Illingworth who had a strong background in research (and who, following a distinguished career in Glasgow, would become Hetherington's biographer). Not content with seeding the University with new expertise at senior levels, Hetherington also paid attention to the other end of the scale. He introduced a grading scheme for lecturing staff that, among other things, created the new post of 'Assistant Lecturer', which was temporary rather than probationary in character. The reform was presumably intended to secure a greater turnover among the younger staff, and to secure an inflow of fresh talent at that level, but it cut across the long established rights of the professors to appoint their own assistants and it was only against the protests of the Senate that the innovation was carried through.[11]

Hetherington's background in industrial relations came to the fore in his attempts to ensure that junior members of academic staff were also involved in the affairs of the University and their academic disciplines. Thus he instituted an annual meeting with the lecturers and assistants, in which he addressed the broad policy issues facing the University at that moment and encouraged questions and comment, and he set up a small fund from which they could secure financial support for attending meetings of learned societies. With students, conversely, he was inclined to be more of a disciplinarian. Although solicitous of their educational and welfare needs, and always willing to address their meetings, he was clearly impatient with certain facets of student culture on Gilmorehill. He tightened up the regulations surrounding the conduct of rectorial elections, particularly at the 'rectorial fight', and on at least one occasion he publicly rebuked a group of students for their over-boisterous behaviour at graduation ceremonies.[12] He and the deans also introduced a new system for monitoring student progress, designed to identify and exclude those 'perpetual students' who had become a feature of the University scene during the years of large student numbers.[13] His reforms, it is clear, were intended to reach into and reinvigorate every corner of the University.

His plans for the future included the absorption into the University of higher education activities conducted elsewhere in the city. This was first made explicit in his entering into discussions in 1937–8 with the Glasgow Veterinary College over forms of association that might be put in place between the two institutions. The College, which was in dire financial straits at the time, wanted an arrangement whereby the early years of the undergraduate course would be taught within the University and the later years at the College. The Science and Medical Faculties were warm in support of the Principal's initiative, but wished to see the College fully merged with the University. The stumbling block to either arrangement, however, was that the University would have to make an investment in new buildings for the teaching of anatomy, physiology and pathology to veterinary students, and a source for such funding could not be identified. Negotiations were therefore allowed to lapse.[14]

If relations with the Veterinary College were congenial (but meantime unconsummated) those with the two extra-mural medical colleges, St Mungo's and Anderson's, were extremely acrimonious. The historical anachronism whereby private centres for medical education and training continued to operate alongside the University's Medical Faculty, and to share teaching facilities in the Royal and Western infirmaries, caused little concern until the 1930s, when a series of events put pressure on the University's connection with the two extra-mural colleges. The dispute in turn caused Hetherington and others to question whether such private colleges should continue to exist as independent entities, and to look towards their eventual demise.[15] The origins of this little local difficulty lay on the other side of the Atlantic. In the USA the great flood of Jewish immigration from eastern Europe, and the subsequent surge of the children of the immigrants into the country's medical schools, had resulted in the introduction of an informal and little-acknowledged 'quota system' limiting Jewish entrance into medical education. By the late 1920s, those excluded from American medical schools in this way began to look to medical schools abroad, particularly those in Scotland.[16] The Medical Faculty of the University had long been accustomed to training students from overseas.[17] However, when faced in the early thirties by a growth of applications from American citizens for places within a total intake now fixed at 200 per annum, the Medical Faculty decided that priority should be given to local students and that there should be no more overseas admissions,[18] thereby deflecting the American tide to the extra-mural colleges, whose enrolments swelled dramatically. By 1937–8 there were about 200 American Jewish medical students in Anderson's and a further 100 in St Mungo's. There they studied for the Scottish Triple Qualification, which was offered through the Royal Medical Incorporations and was recognised for the practice of medicine in the USA. For the University's Medical Faculty, the influx of Americans into the colleges meant competition for teaching places in the city's hospitals, and a furious row broke out in 1937 over how many such places could be provided and how these might be distributed between the University and the colleges.

A sub-plot was a specific dispute over the Pathology Department in the Royal Infirmary to which both the University and St Mungo's College contributed financially. It would appear that some in the University, including Hetherington, thought that the extra-mural colleges were engaging in short-term profiteering from the fees of the American students at the expense of the longer-term viability of undergraduate medical education in the city. The argument rolled on through 1938 and into 1939, without any agreement being reached between the various parties, until the prospect of the outbreak of war brought a collapse in the American applications to the colleges.[19]

The dispute drew Hetherington into the affairs of the large and important corner of the University concerned with medical education, and into issues about its relationships with other institutions. He was obviously uneasy with a situation in which teaching for medical qualifications was divided between extra-mural colleges and the University, in which appointments were often shared between the hospitals and the University, with potentially conflicting demands on individuals, in which much of the teaching of undergraduates was

7.3 *Overseas Students Outing, late 1930s.*

undertaken by staff of either the hospitals or the colleges who drew no University emolument but were recognised as 'teachers of the University' for the delivery of certain courses, and in which, despite previous attempts to secure an 'inclusive fee' for medical education, students' fees were still paid on a class by class basis, to the personal benefit of the individual teacher. He harboured ambitions to bring greater order to what he saw as an unwieldy and inefficient system. Consequently, the row with the extra-mural colleges carried on through 1939 and into 1940, with Hetherington attempting to put the squeeze on the colleges by limiting their students' attendance at classes taught by the Professor of Pathology at the Royal Infirmary and by getting the Court to withdraw the recognition of extra-mural teachers. In neither case was he successful, however. The medical profession, including most members of the Medical Faculty, closed ranks against him, claiming that any attempt to delimit more sharply the respective spheres of the colleges and the University would undermine personal and professional relationships within the hospitals, as well as the relationship between the University and the Royal Faculty of Physicians and Surgeons, which had taken on a responsibility for overseeing the work of the colleges.[20] Hetherington secured a minor victory of sorts, in that the Court agreed that in future recognition would be granted only to teachers of medical courses which supplemented or extended ones taught by University staff, but he was forced in the meantime to walk away from his wider ambitions in the face of professional resistance and the countervailing demands of managing and leading a University caught up in another world war.[21]

That war had been threatening ever since he became Principal. As the University community responded to his reforms it also reacted nervously to the political forces and international tensions that had been unleashed by the depression of the thirties. Perhaps the earliest indication of what was to come was the influx into Britain in 1934–5 of refugee Jewish scholars from Germany, to some of whom the University offered temporary lecturing or research positions.[22] A further straw in the wind was the way that Sir Daniel Stevenson's introduction of student exchanges in German and Spanish, giving Glasgow students welcome opportunities to travel and study on the Continent, also had the effect of bringing to Glasgow German students with openly Nazi sympathies and styles of behaviour.[23] However, the probability that the rise of fascism in Germany, Italy and Spain had initiated a slide towards another round of global conflict was first signalled to the University in October 1936, when the War Office wrote to request information about the equipment and materials which the University could make available for experimental purposes in the case of emergency and the Medical Faculty was invited by the Scottish Office Air Raid Precautions Department to introduce training for senior medical students in 'preventive and curative aspects of gas warfare'.[24]

The drift of events naturally concerned the student body, which would be called upon to participate in any future war. Into its political debates and discussions, which had been enlivened during the early-to-mid thirties by the emergence of nationalist and social credit ideas, a new element of how to respond to the tide of European affairs began to intrude. Thus, in the spring of 1936 the University's Jewish Student Society joined sections of the press in condemning the Senate for sending a celebratory message to the University of Heidelberg on its centenary which could be construed as accepting Nazi policies in Germany. This was followed in the spring of 1937 by a row within the SRC over the support expressed by the editor of GUM for the Spanish government in the civil war.[25] The rectorial elections of 1937 and 1938, however, provided the main foci for the fears and anxieties. In October 1937, in a contest in which Winston Churchill carried the Unionist banner, Emeritus Professor W. Macneile Dixon represented the devolutionist aspirations of the Liberal and Scottish Nationalist students, and J. B. S. Haldane, Professor of Genetics at the University of London, represented socialist and 'popular front' opposition to fascism and the war in Spain, victory went by a comfortable margin to a fourth candidate. The Rev. Dick Sheppard, Canon of St Paul's Cathedral, who was widely known as 'the wireless parson' for his role in pioneering religious broadcasting, was sponsored by the recently-formed University branch of the Peace Pledge Union. His election marked the rise of a pacifist, anti-war tide of opinion within the student body, as the threats to peace in Europe had increased, and it was interpreted by his supporters as a statement of student acceptance of pacifism 'as a practical policy' and a rejection of war equivalent to the famous Oxford Union 'King and Country' debate of February 1933.[26] However, Sheppard died shortly afterwards, before assuming his duties as Rector, and at the election for his successor, in October 1938, Hitler's annexation of Austria and the Munich crisis of September 1938, together with the University's own preparations for war, appear to have produced a more sombre and less idealistic atmosphere. Student anger at Chamberlain's abandonment of Czechoslovakia was reflected in a vain last minute attempt to add the name of Dr Eduard Beneš, the recently-resigned President of Czechoslovakia, as a rectorial candidate, but this was disallowed under the rules for nomination. The ensuing election was won by the staunchly anti-Nazi but far from warlike figure of Sir Archibald Sinclair, the leader of the Liberal Party, who had offered to withdraw from the contest in favour of Beneš. The Peace Pledge Group's candidate came bottom of the poll, in a three-cornered contest, and the result was interpreted on all sides as evidence that 'collective security' rather than pacifism was the only way to halt Fascism.[27]

By the spring of 1939, the University seems to have become resigned to war. Refugees from Austria and Czechoslovakia were now seeking shelter on Gilmorehill; the scheme for air raid precautions introduced in 1938 was extended to include plans for storing the treasures of the Hunterian Museum in a safe place, for the establishment of first aid stations around the University, and for the fitting of dark blinds in halls of residence; and proposals for evacuating students from the University of London had identified Glasgow as the prospective host for some 150 pre-clinical medical students from Kings College.[28] Consequently, when Hitler's invasion of Poland brought Britain and France once again into military conflict with Germany in September 1939, there was on Gilmorehill little of the surprise that had surrounded the events of August 1914 or of the subsequent jingoism and war fever which had gripped students and staff alike. Instead, the prevailing mood appears to have been one of quiet determination to do what was necessary both to oppose German aggression and to continue the normal life of the University as far as it was possible. The most immediate casualties of the war were the new six-year medical degree, which the Faculty of Medicine had intended to introduce in 1939–40 but which was suspended in the face of the likely shortage of teaching staff, and the new Gymnasium near the Union, work on which had

7.4 *Sandbagging the Quadrangles, 1939.*

to be stopped because of a shortage of building materials and from which the government grant was then withdrawn.[29] Delays also occurred in the University taking possession of the Chemistry Building and plans for a special opening ceremony had to be abandoned. Meanwhile, although the Reading Room was formally opened in November 1939, it was now able to operate only during daylight hours and thereby lost one of its main functions, as a focus for student activity in the evenings. The most unfortunate individual on Gilmorehill was Professor Grillo of the Italian Department, whose status as an enemy national, once Italy entered the war in May 1940, meant that his appointment (one of the fixed-term ones created by the Stevenson bequest) was not renewed at the end of the 1939–40 session.[30] Contrasting with the harshness of such a decision, with its echoes of the Becker case in the First World War, was the welcome given not only to the medical students evacuated from Kings College, London, but also to a group of Polish student refugees for whom the Court agreed to accept responsibility.

In most respects, however, life and work in the University went on as usual through the 'phoney war' period from the autumn of 1939 through to the spring of 1940. Classes continued to meet, and student debates, dances and sporting activities went on much as before. Such was the air of 'business as usual', indeed, that the SRC agreed to hold a Charities Day in April 1940, which raised £8,000 for the voluntary hospitals.[31] Military conscription had been very slow in inception and when begun left large parts of the student body exempt from immediate service. Male students on course were not to be called up until after their twentieth birthday, but medical students were exempt under Reserved Occupation arrangements and students of engineering and science could apply to the recruitment boards for 'deferment' until the completion of their studies. The impact of military conscription therefore fell largely, and most immediately, on the older students in Arts, Law and Divinity, a few hundred of whom left their studies prematurely. In the interests of such Arts students, and also those in Science who did not seek deferment, the Senate agreed to an easing of class ticket regulations, so that degree exams could be taken on the basis of only two terms' attendance at classes, and then in July 1940 the Court, in concert with the other Scottish universities, passed an Emergency Ordinance for the introduction of a special War Degree. This could be conferred, both as an Ordinary Degree and a degree with Unclassified Honours, on individuals who had completed two full years of study in the University together with a recognised period of military service.[32]

By the early summer of 1940, however, the military situation had taken a turn for the worse – students sat their exams in the Bute Hall in June to the background noises of the evacuation of the troops of the BEF from the beaches and mole at Dunkirk. For the University and the nation the war began in earnest, and the entire conscription machinery was cranked up another gear.

7.5 *Charities Day, 1940 – The MacBrayne Hall Party.*

By July 1941, the age of call-up for males had been reduced to eighteen, with consequent effects on the numbers of the new intakes from schools and of the 'non-deferred' students within the University, and a decision to conscript women for some form of national service had also been taken in principle.

The general effects on the student population of the continuing transfer of manpower into military service were to accelerate the decline in male matriculations that was already underway on the eve of the war (partly as a result of the ending of the post-First World War 'baby boom') and to bring about a recovery in female matriculations until 1942–3, when arrangements for calling up women over the age of twenty came into play. The total student population fell from 4,696 in the last year of peace to 3,705 in the last year of war. This decline of about 20 per cent was markedly lower than the 33 per cent drop in the First World War. As in the First War, however, so too in the Second the burden fell mainly on the Arts students, whose total graduations fell by about 50 per cent between 1938–9 and 1944–5 while the number of total graduating students in Engineering and Medicine tended to rise over time and those in Science remained relatively stable (Figure 7.1). It was mainly as graduates, equipped with skills and knowledge crucial for ever more scientific and technical forms of total war, that the young men and women of the science-side faculties entered the fray.

Those called to the colours, whether as undergraduates or graduates, found themselves involved in a conflict that was more mobile than the trench warfare of the First World War, and was conducted over an even wider spread of

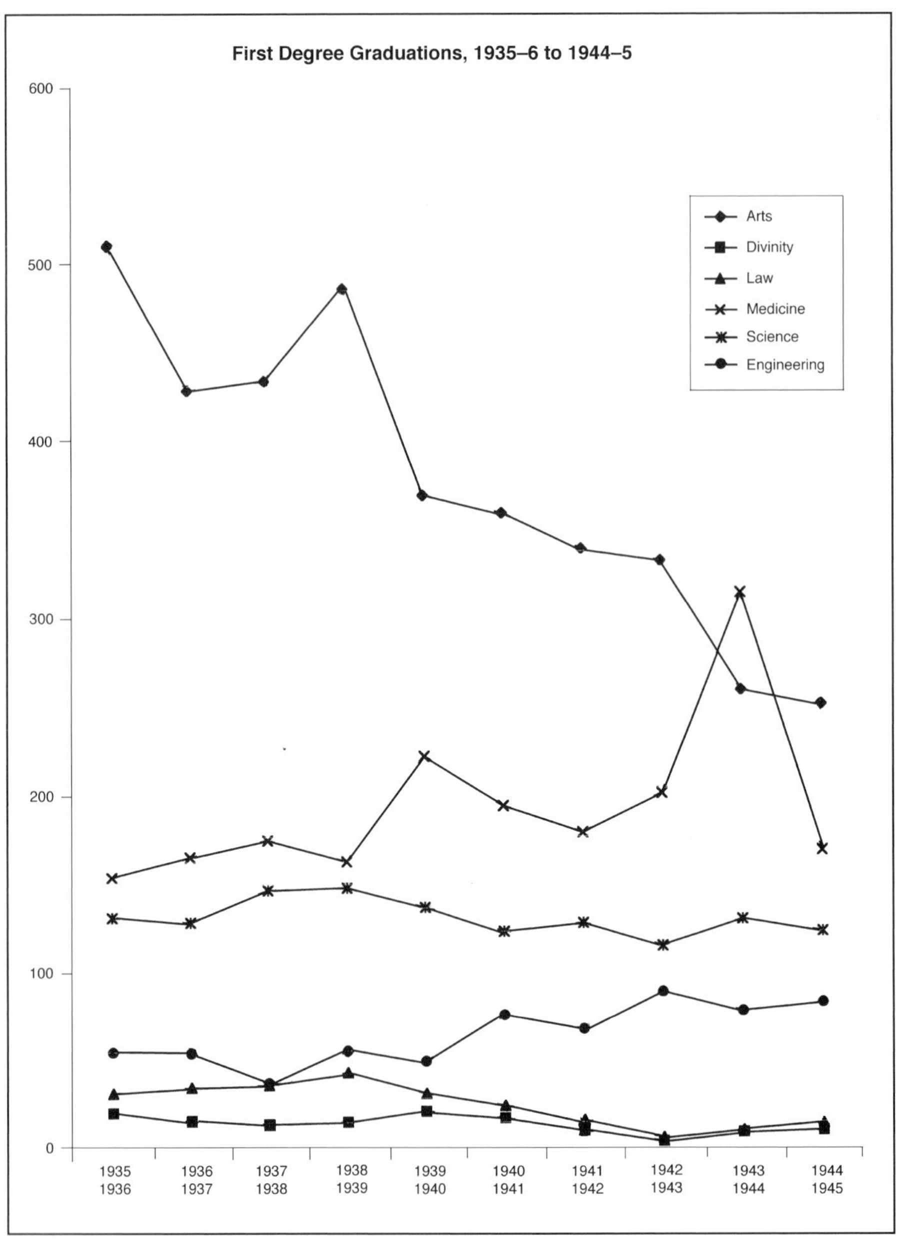

Figure 7.1

geographic locations. The diversity of military operations in which they engaged, and the global span of the theatres of war in which they served, is perhaps best illustrated by Hetherington's story, told at a graduation ceremony, of the Scottish saltire that went to war. This flag, which had been used in a nationalist prank on Coronation Day in 1937, was divided between five student friends before they left Gilmorehill for military service. 'To date', one of them wrote to Hetherington in 1944,

> three pieces certainly survive; and one has certainly been lost. One is carried in the mine sweeper; a second was borne with the Eighth Army from Alamein to Italy and is still there; a third is in Persia, having done, in the words of its wearer 'quite a few parachute descents'; the fourth was last heard of some time ago, in a tank, somewhere in the Eastern theatre; the fifth, in the keeping of a nurse, was lost in a torpedoed ship some 200 miles off the West African coast, though the nurse herself is safe.[33]

Members of the academic and non-academic staff also served in the Forces, either as conscripts or as volunteers. By 1 October 1943, some 55 of the 194 lecturers and assistants who were appointed one year at a time were recorded as being on national service. The most senior among the members of staff on service was probably Spencer Muirhead, the Secretary of Court and a part-time lecturer in Civil Law, who as Colonel Muirhead commanded the 74 AA Regiment TA in the North African campaign.[34] Few, however, served more colourfully than the University Chaplain, the Rev. J. Fraser McLuskey, who parachuted behind enemy lines in France in 1944, bringing to his SAS unit bibles not bullets. Several of the professorial staff obtained leave of absence to take up government duties, including William Atkinson of Spanish, who was attached to the Foreign Office, J. G. Riddell of Systematic Theology at the Ministry of Supply, and Arthur Trueman of Geology who was a member of the Commission on Higher Education in West Africa in 1943–4.

War intruded on Gilmorehill more closely than it had done during 1914–18. Most notably, late in March 1941, when the Luftwaffe was beginning to take an interest in the Clyde's shipbuilding capacities, a parachute mine landed in Kelvingrove Park and the explosion blew in windows along the south face of the main building, damaging the general administration office.[35] This mild brush with danger became a badge of honour for those who had remained behind on Gilmorehill. 'Freshers will see the marks of war on our premises', the Principal was able to boast to the new students arriving in October 1942, before going on to describe the sacrifices that were being demanded of them and of the University:

> the general conditions of University Life are not so comfortable as they normally are. The scarcity of coal may make us somewhat colder than we

> like to be; we have to contend with blackouts and difficulties of transport. We shall be short of materials of all kinds. Still, the things that really matter can all be done; and we shall hope to carry on, as even more hardly pressed Universities have managed to do.[36]

However, the main extra requirements on the student body were that all male students over eighteen years should undertake fire-watching and fire-fighting duties on behalf of the University (a scheme later extended to women students by giving them duties during the day-time) as well as compulsory training in the University's own military units.[37] This could be done in the Senior Training Corps (as the OTC was renamed in 1940) or in the University Air Squadron, established in February 1941 with headquarters in 4 University Gardens, and the University Naval Division, established in June 1942 with headquarters at 8 The Square. Entry to the new units, which had heavier attendance requirements, was restricted to 100 students each, by selection, and consequently the bulk of the male student population received training towards service in the Army.[38] Later, in 1943, Senate decided that students in the Faculties of Medicine, Science and Engineering, who could expect deferment until the end of their courses, should not only undertake the prescribed military training during their first year of study but thereafter also serve in the University Battalion of the Home Guard.[39]

The presence of three training units on Gilmorehill made it possible for the University to play host to officers or officer-cadets of the three services, through 'short courses' in which attendance at University classes was combined with intensive military instruction. This began in October 1940 with courses for the Royal Artillery, to which 'short courses' for a Royal Air Force badly in need of trained and qualified manpower were added in 1941–2. Then in 1943–4 attention switched to the needs of the 'Senior Service' with the introduction of courses for the Royal Navy. Towards the end of the war, the University's role as host to servicemen and women took a new direction with the opening, in the spring of 1945, of 6 University Gardens as a 'Services House' for the Canadian forces. For the Canadians visiting Glasgow on leave the Senate organised a series of lectures and the SRC a programme of dances.[40]

On the research side, the University provided laboratory facilities for the Admiralty, as it had done in the previous war. The naval researchers obtained access to the brand new facilities of the Chemistry Building, although it was a privilege for which they showed scant regard – their careless use of materials twice caused serious damage to the lab that they leased.[41] On the other hand, few direct demands would appear to have been made of the University's own research capacities in the pursuit of military success, one exception being the work done for the Admiralty on the design of mines by Professor Alty of Applied Physics. This relative lack of involvement may have reflected the deficiencies of most of the University's labs and equipment, and the backwardness of its pre-war scientific reputation, but is mainly to be explained by the fact that much of the nation's wartime research was conducted outside the universities, in institutes directly managed and funded by central government departments. The University's contribution to the war effort was therefore still confined mainly to its role as a teaching institution.

But if the great national struggle unleashed by Hitler's aggression absorbed and deflected much of the energy of the University community between 1939 and 1945, in other respects the war served as a backdrop to ongoing developments within the institution itself. The outbreak of war cut across ongoing business, more especially Hector Hetherington's drive to improve the organisation and revive the academic performance of the University. The war constrained and complicated the achievement of these objectives in a number of ways, while assisting them in others. Yet it never brought to a halt the application of Hetherington's vision and acuity to what he judged to be the longer term needs and interests of the University. Beneath the high drama of coping with the national emergency, the task of rescuing the institution from its past and preparing it for its future continued. The pace of that programme, it is true, slackened somewhat during 1940 to 1942, when the pressures of war on the University's resources were most intense and Hetherington himself was called upon by the government to undertake various tasks associated directly or indirectly with the war effort – as a member of the national tribunal to resolve industrial conflicts, as chairman of a committee on the general principles of post-war hospital policy in Scotland, and in a six-week tour of American universities in 1942 to explain how the British universities were coping with the war. As if anticipating these demands on his time, Hetherington had taken the precaution in April 1940 of proposing the constitutional innovation of a post of Vice-Principal, to represent the Principal in the event of the latter's absence or incapacity. Court and Senate agreed that the new office should be combined with the much older office of Dean of Faculties, which was in the gift of the Senate but which since 1893 had had only a ceremonial function. J. D. Mackie, of Scottish History and Literature, became the first Dean of Faculties to bear the new responsibilities.[42]

Despite the distraction of his other duties, Hetherington continued during those years to think ahead to the University's future needs. In another act of generosity the Chancellor, Sir Daniel Macaulay Stevenson, in celebration of his 91st birthday, gifted sums of £60,000 each to the University and to the Royal Scottish Academy of Music.[43] £50,000 of the University's share was set aside for the development of the Engineering Faculty on the return of peacetime conditions, but in the meanwhile there was a need to get the best possible return on the capital. This allowed Hetherington to persuade the Court to adopt a mechanism familiar to him from his Liverpool days – a specialist investment committee bringing members of the Finance Committee together with co-opted representatives of the local business community. However, it was typical of Hetherington's thinking that he saw the innovation as more than simply obtaining outside financial expertise at little or no cost. 'There is no doubt', he told the Court,

> that the University suffers as compared, for example, with the Technical College from the fact that we have not much room in our government for representatives of the business community. People are apt to be interested in an Institution which gives them a job to do: and I should expect that if we could pick half a dozen youngish men of business in Glasgow who would apply their minds to understanding the special problem of University investments, we should probably gain some benefits in our financial administration and quite certainly gain from the larger range of interest that would be attached to us.[44]

Hetherington returned from his visit to the USA apparently encouraged by what he had seen there, and in time to share the growing national mood of confidence that followed the victory at El Alamein in November 1942 and the news of the surrender of the German army at Stalingrad in January 1943. The year 1943 was consequently one of significant progress in his programme of reform. His actions were now buoyed up by a sense that the tide of war had turned. 'The end of the war is not yet in sight', he told the Freshers of 1943, 'we have still heavy blows to suffer, certainly overseas and possibly in our own cities. But it does begin to look as if we have crossed the halfway line and have the conditions of victory within our grasp.'[45] He therefore felt that he could put in place changes that had prospects of taking root in the longer term, and moved on three fronts.

First, he took additional steps to strengthen the role and significance of the physical sciences, convinced as he was that their research potential was central to the purposes of any modern university. The transformation was already underway in Chemistry, where James Cook, appointed to the Regius chair in 1940, was reorganising teaching and equipping the new laboratories. He was considerably aided in this task by the Court's decision to allocate the entire Carnegie Grant of £11,400 due in 1942–3 to that purpose. Cook repaid the investment by forging links with industrial concerns such as ICI and the Washington Chemicals Company which brought external funding and additional researchers to the department.[46] Now, in 1943 it was the turn of Natural Philosophy (Physics). The vacancy in the chair gave Hetherington the opportunity to discuss the department's present condition and future prospects with several possible candidates. One of these, Philip Dee of Cambridge, who was playing a leading role in radar development at the government's Telecommunications Research Establishment, drew up a shopping list of what was additionally required – three lectureships, three more junior and shorter-term posts, £5,000 for equipment, and in the slightly longer term a new physics building with better research accommodation. The Court agreed to provide the staff and the equipment immediately, and committed itself to finding £25,000 for a new research building as soon as possible. With these assurances, Dee accepted the chair.[47] Although he would not take up residence in Glasgow until the end of the war, his appointment brought the department into nuclear physics, one of the most active research frontiers in the discipline.

Second, Hetherington began to bring sharper definition to the respective roles and responsibilities of the University and the professions it served by abolishing the part-time professorships to be found in Engineering, Medicine and Law. In theory, such individuals combined teaching with professional practice in a way that invigorated and reinforced both activities. In reality, Hetherington believed, the demands of the external paymaster tended to lead to such individuals neglecting their University duties, and he was determined to move towards a full-time professoriate. Such an opportunity first presented itself as a result of the death in October 1942 of Percy Hillhouse, the holder of the John Elder Chair of Naval Architecture. When, following consultations with interested parties, it was decided that chairs in Naval Architecture should continue to be located in Glasgow and in Newcastle, the Glasgow one was advertised and filled on a full-time basis.[48] Similar considerations also came into play in Hetherington's relations with the Medical Faculty and the teaching hospitals, in the form of his proposals to transform the Muirhead Chair of Medicine and the Muirhead Chair in Obstetrics and Gynaecology into full-time chairs, and subsequently to concentrate the teaching of systematic medicine, surgery, and obstetrics under the charge of the full-time professors, while leaving clinical teaching dispersed around the various hospitals. The need to secure the agreement of the hospitals, especially the Royal Infirmary, to these changes, however, meant that the process was much longer drawn out than in the case of Naval Architecture.[49]

Finally, he returned once more to his policy of incorporation, to bring under the University's authority and into its classrooms educational activities already being undertaken by organisations and institutions elsewhere in the city. In January–February 1943 he secured the agreement of Court and Senate to a take-over of the Glasgow School of Social Study and Training, which was connected with the University Settlement in Anderston, and to transform it into a department of the University. Although its principal purpose was social work training, Hetherington foresaw an expansion of its activities into related areas as a result of the projected development of social services nationally, and saw potential for academic links between the University's social science departments and the practice of social administration.[50] Since the University already funded a large part of the School's activity, there was little additional cost to the merger.

On the Science side even greater prospects were opening up. Discussions began with the West of Scotland Agricultural College over establishing a Faculty of Agriculture to which the College's teaching and specialist advisory functions would be transferred. The Court and Senate gave agreement in principle to the scheme, but no decisions had been arrived at when, in January 1944, the Secretary of State for Scotland announced his intention to establish a committee to review the future of agricultural education in Scotland.[51] As that body (the Alness Committee) began its work, there appeared the second report of the committee on veterinary education in Britain (the Loveday Committee), which revived the concept of the University taking on responsibility for veterinary education in Glasgow through a merger with the Vet School. The Loveday Committee proposed the creation of a unit within the University capable of producing thirty graduates per annum, and costing £181,000 to establish. It also noted approvingly that 'there is a possibility of bringing agricultural and veterinary training into close relationship under the University. It would have the further advantage of enabling students of both subjects to live in close association during the later stages of their training.'[52] This referred to plans to relocate the Vet School at the Agricultural College's estate at Auchincruive in Ayrshire, to conduct more agricultural education activities there than before, and to encourage research and consultancy links between the two by having the Agricultural College specialise in dairying. These far-sighted proposals, however, were held up by the deliberations of the Alness Committee, and then thrown into confusion by the indeterminate outcome of its deliberations when it eventually reported in December 1945. The majority of the committee favoured the centralisation of agricultural education at degree and diploma level in a single Faculty of Agriculture at one of the Scottish universities (which almost certainly would have been Edinburgh) whereas a minority, which included the chairman, Lord Alness, saw no real advantage in such a concentration of effort and thought it unlikely that Glasgow and Aberdeen Universities would willingly abandon their stakes in agricultural education.[53] The nature and extent of the University's future involvement with veterinary and agricultural education were therefore still unclear at the end of 1945.

During the later years of the war, Hetherington's zeal for reform coincided with, and was informed and influenced by, a drive for change at the national level. The wartime coalition government was engaged in examining many aspects of social conditions within Britain and was intent upon delivering up a blueprint for post-war development. Welfare, health, social services and education were all under scrutiny from a slew of commissions and committees whose work impinged upon the University's future, and on which it was frequently consulted. Thus the Faculty of Medicine gave evidence to the Goodenough Committee which was charged with considering the future of medical education in Britain. The Senate responded to a range of ideas and arguments emanating from the Advisory Council on Education in Scotland, welcoming many of these while making it abundantly clear that the University had no intention of accepting any responsibility for the training of teachers after the war (and revealing once again a condescension towards the teaching profession and its educational needs). Of all the government departments and agencies looking forward to the post-war era, however, none was more important than the UGC, which in November 1943 invited the University to submit for consideration its plans for the post-war years. By contrast with the situation during the First World War, the University now had a national framework for preparing for the future as well as a Principal who was intellectually attuned to, and enthusiastic about the opportunities presented by, the planning of higher education.

Under Hetherington's guidance, in fact, the Faculties and Senate had already begun the task of considering their post-war needs, and between November 1943 and January 1944 each Faculty presented its 'wish-list' of desirable additional expenditures on buildings and staff.[54] Consequently, in responding to the UGC, the University was able to ask for an immediate increase in the recurrent grant of £100,000 per annum (in pre-war prices) on the grounds, first, that the pre-war University had been underfunded by about 30 per cent, taking account of its size and student profile, and that a figure of that level was required to place it on an equitable footing with the English civic universities, and, second, that the survey of faculty needs had identified that figure as the sum required to bring a university of over 4,000 students 'up to a reasonably high standard'. Beyond that the Court foresaw a future expansion of teaching and research activities which would require a total annual income of £450,000 to £600,000 per annum (in pre-war prices), although it was not expected that such a proposed doubling in the level of the University's income would come from the UGC. The programme for post-war capital development would include completion of the Chemistry building, an extension of the Engineering buildings (for which £50,000 was already in hand), a new Anatomy Department ('the present building is nearly a public scandal – though happily screened from the eyes of the curious'), further accommodation for Surgery and Obstetrics, extensions of the Medical Sciences, Arts, Mathematics and Natural Philosophy buildings, a restart on the gymnasium, a new student refectory, and more halls of residence. All of this added up to a large sum – '£1,000,000 will not do what ought to be done here' – and although some money would come in from private bequests and from the Carnegie Trust, it was envisaged that the greater part of the capital development programme would have to be funded by the public purse.[55]

The perception of the post-war University, which was also the first vision of the modern University, was therefore one which would be better housed, better equipped and better staffed than it had been in the dreary days between the wars. It would be better prepared to meet not only the higher educational needs of the West of Scotland but also the new national demands that would be made of it – for 'a considerable expansion of the national research organisation' and for taking 'educational responsibilities to the Colonial Empire more seriously in the future' than in the past.[56] However, despite these additional tasks, and despite the greater diversity of responsibilities that might come with the incorporation of the Vet School and the Agricultural College, it was to be a university in a steady state as far as student numbers were concerned. Once the expected post-war bulge of ex-servicemen and women had gone though the system, Hetherington argued and Court and Senate agreed, there should be no increase in student population above the immediate pre-war levels of somewhat over 4,000. The mistakes of the inter-war years of open access and declining per capita resources must be avoided. The emphasis was to be on quality rather than quantity, and to achieve this end admissions to all faculties would have to be controlled, in much the same way as admissions to Medicine were controlled.[57] In particular, the Faculty of Arts which, Hetherington claimed, had failed to keep pace with 'modern standards' and 'is now definitely below the standards in operation elsewhere', would have to introduce a system of selecting students based upon the Leaving Certificate, School Reports and a personal interview. With an intake restricted to 400 students per annum, the Arts Faculty would be able to rid itself of that large 'tail' of less able students whose presence before the war had been at the expense of the more able, and which 'could be denied entrance to the University with no harm to ourselves or to the national interest.'[58]

If the students of the post-war era were going to find it rather more difficult to gain access to the University, they were also going to have to pay more for the privilege. For in 1944, against a background of wartime inflation and falling incomes, the Scottish universities returned to the issue of student fees. The University of Glasgow's financial situation through the war years had been difficult, though not impossible. Some falling off in endowment income and in fee income, as student numbers declined, was offset by a rise in the 'additional income category' – mainly, it appears, from rents for the various University properties leased out for wartime purposes. Consequently, the University managed to break even financially through the most difficult years, and Hetherington even managed to find some elbow-room to pay for new lecturing staff in such departments as Chemistry and Physics through the voids created by delays in filling senior posts that fell vacant. Even so, it was clear that current levels of student fees, which in most cases had been unchanged since 1920 and which were also lower than in the English universities, would be unlikely to make any significant contribution to the very substantial post-war requirements. Consequently, in March 1944 a conference of the four Scottish universities agreed an increase in fees of approximately

25 per cent across the board (except for Medicine, which was under scrutiny from the Goodenough Committee).[59] These fees came into operation in the academic year 1944–5, and produced an immediate improvement in the University's finances. As might have been expected, the fee increases caused something of a fuss throughout Scotland, with protests from student organisations, from MPs, from secondary school pupils and headmasters, and from the Educational Institute of Scotland.[60] Much more than Hetherington's policy on admission to Arts (which was little known or understood outside Gilmorehill), the fee increases were seen as a barrier to working-class access to university education and a departure from the tradition of nourishing the 'lad o' pairts'. There was also, however, sympathy and support for the universities' decision. Even the Glasgow Corporation, which had to contribute to the increase through its student bursaries, accepted that the universities' needs justified the action.[61]

One year later, by the early summer of 1945, the controversy over student fees was a distant memory, lost in the excitement of the end of the war. The news of Victory in Europe on 7 May and the celebrations that surrounded it – riotously in the Men's Union by all accounts, but more sedately at the official University party – then gave way to a summer of awaiting the outcome in Asia. The dropping of the two atom bombs and the Japanese surrender on 2 September came in time for the Principal, the staff and the students of the University, including a number already returned from the European theatre of war, to start the new academic year with a considerable sense of relief, as well as great hopes and expectations for the future. 'Come back, then, sailor and soldier and airman,' the editor of GUM wrote immediately after VE-Day, 'We have tried to keep the spirit of our University alive for you. We have guarded our traditions and held fast to our way of life . . . We salute you, and we thank you, and we will be honoured to welcome you back.'[62]

However, amid the jubilation it was also a time to look back, and to count the cost. 429 members of the University community (staff, students and graduates) lost their lives in the conflict, together with another fifteen men of the RAF who had been 'short course cadets' in the University in 1941–2. Most of the casualties had been undergraduates in the years between Hetherington's arrival in 1936 and the outbreak of the war in 1939, and that generation of young men and women had paid a heavy price for the failures of international relations in the 1930s. For some – like William McKenna of Motherwell who graduated with an MA degree in 1939 and died as a private in the Black Watch in France in June 1940, or Roy Galbraith of Glasgow who graduated with an MA in the summer of 1941 and was lost only months later, in the sinking of the *Prince of Wales* in December 1941 – it proved to be a very short war. Others died in air operations over Germany, including Norman Gill of Wishaw, a Law graduate who went missing in an air raid over Bremen in September

1942 and Hugh Cowan of Dollar, an Arts graduate of 1937, who served in the RAF's Pathfinder Force. Some died a long way from home: such as James Devine of Greenock, a Lance Corporal in the Gordon Highlanders, who died in hospital in Changi, Singapore in June 1942, or William Aird of Glasgow, a Captain in the RAMC who died at Mandalay in May 1943. Yet others – like David Woods of Airdrie, also a Captain in the RAMC, who was killed by Allied bombing while a prisoner of war in Germany – met their end in the most tragic and poignant of circumstances.[63] Behind each death lay a story of service and sacrifice which their former classmates, the wider student body and the staff all wished to remember and honour. The names of the fallen duly joined those of the First World War on the walls of the Chapel.

The loss of life within the broad University community in 1939–45 was some 40 per cent lower than in 1914–18. But this was only one of the ways in which the experience of the Second War was different from the First. Partly because the conflict intruded more directly on to Gilmorehill and partly because of the significant developments which had occurred in the means of mass communication in the interval, there was a much greater sense of a University engagement in the war than there had been in 1914–18. The Second World War, it has often been said, was a 'People's War', marked by popular support for the war effort and popular expectations of the benefits to flow from its outcome. Although some historians have questioned whether the war was truly radical in its social and political consequences,[64] none have denied the great outburst of energy which popular participation unleashed. The University, a fragment of that society which had committed itself to total war in the knowledge of the horrors and burdens which were likely to result, shared the commitment. It also cooperated actively in the preparations for peace, and for the creation of a post-war society more at ease with itself than before, which were undertaken by the coalition government that conducted the war. The determination that was embedded in the submission to the UGC in February 1944, that the University after the war should be very much better placed to serve local and national needs for higher education and advanced research than it had been before the war, distinguishes the experience of the Second World War from that of the First. The conflict of 1914–18, regarded at the time merely as a grave and unfortunate interruption to normal life and purpose, had let loose forces that bore in heavily on the University in the 1920s and 1930s, transforming it into the most proletarian but also the most struggling of the universities of Britain. Now an opportunity had presented itself not merely of overcoming the difficulties of these decades but of putting the University on a footing to serve the needs and interests of the new Britain that was expected to emerge from the 'People's War'.

Notes and References

1. For Hetherington's early life and work, see Sir Charles Illingworth, *University Statesman: Sir Hector Hetherington* (Glasgow, 1971), 1–43.
2. Court Camera, 11 Nov. 1936 and 10 Nov. 1937; General Council, 28 April and 27 Oct. 1937; *Glasgow Herald*, 4 Dec. 1937.
3. *Glasgow Herald*, 28 April 1938; Court Camera, 18 April 1939; General Council, 25 Oct. 1939.
4. I. G. C. Hutchison, *The University and the State: The Case of Aberdeen* (Aberdeen, 1993), 63.
5. Court Camera, 11 Nov., 19 Nov. and 16 Dec. 1936, and 11 Feb. 1937; *Glasgow Herald*, 11 Feb. 1937.
6. Hutchison, *The University and the State*, 62; *Glasgow Herald*, 9 May 1938; *Report of the Special Committee appointed in April 1937 to enquire and advise regarding an Application by the University Courts of the Universities of Scotland for a Grant from the Education (Scotland) Fund*, Parliamentary Papers, Cmd. 5735 (1937–38).
7. Calculated from figures in the UGC returns for 1935–6 and 1938–9 respectively.
8. Court Camera, 2 June 1937.
9. Court Camera, 21 April 1938; General Council, 26 Oct. 1938.
10. Court Camera, 14 Jan. 1937.
11. Court Camera, 15 April and 13 May 1937, and 13 Jan. 1938.
12. *Glasgow Herald*, 17 May 1937 and 14 Nov. 1938.
13. Senate, 26 May, 23 June and 15 Dec. 1938.
14. Court Camera, 18 Nov. and 9 Dec. 1937, 10 Feb. and 13 April 1938.
15. Illingworth, *University Statesman*, 55–6.
16. For a detailed account of the American Jewish medical students in Scotland between 1925 and 1940, see Kenneth E. Collins, *Go and Learn: The International Story of Jews and Medicine in Scotland* (Aberdeen, 1988), 98–132.
17. Indeed, along with the Engineering Faculty, the Medical Faculty was the biggest attraction for an overseas student population (mainly from countries within the Empire) that peaked at 260 students in 1929–30 before declining to around 170 in the mid-1930s (figures which were less than half those of Edinburgh University).
18. Collins, *Go and Learn*, 113.
19. Court Camera, 24 June, 14 Oct. and 18 Nov. 1937, 13 Oct. 1938, 12 Jan., 9 March, 20 April and 31 May 1939; 'Medical Students in Glasgow', *Glasgow Herald*, 7 May 1938.
20. For Hetherington's relationship with the Royal College of Physicians and Surgeons, and its connections in turn to the extra-mural colleges, see Andrew Hull and Johanna Geyer-Kordesh, *The Shaping of the Medical Profession: A History of the Royal College of Physicians and Surgeons of Glasgow, 1858–1999* (London, 1999), Chapter Three.
21. Court Camera, 25 Jan. 13 June, 10 Oct., 11 Nov. and 16 Dec. 1940.
22. Senate, 25 Jan. 1934, 23 May 1935 and 6 Feb. 1936.

23. Robert T. Hutcheson and Hugh Conway, *The University of Glasgow, 1920–1974: The Memoir of Robert T. Hutcheson* (Glasgow, 1997), 131.
24. Court Camera, 8 Oct.1936; Senate, 22 Oct. 1936.
25. GUM, 47, 9 (4 March 1936) and 47, 11 (29 April 1936); *Glasgow Herald*, 10 March 1937.
26. *Glasgow Herald*, 25 and 26 Oct. 1937; *The Times*, 25 Oct. 1937.
27. *Glasgow Herald*, 17, 21 and 24 Oct. 1938.
28. Court Camera, 24 Jan., 9 Feb. and 11 May 1939.
29. General Council, 24 April 1940.
30. Court Camera, 29 July and 26 Sept. 1940.
31. GUM, 51, 4, 29 Nov. 1939, 51, 5, 13 Dec. 1939, and 51, 11, 15 May 1940.
32. *G.U. Student Handbook, 1941–2* (Glasgow, 1941).
33. Illingworth, *University Statesman*, 85.
34. Court Camera, 13 June 1940; Hutcheson and Conway, *The University of Glasgow, 1920–1974*, 7, 15.
35. Court Camera, 17 April 1941; Hutcheson and Conway, *The University of Glasgow*, 1920–1974, 83.
36. *G.U. Student Handbook, 1942–3* (Glasgow, 1942).
37. Court Camera, 24 March 1941.
38. *G.U. Students Handbooks, 1942–3* and *1944–5*.
39. Senate, 17 June 1943.
40. GUM, 55, 5, April 1945.
41. Court Camera, 25 Sept. 1941 and 6 Oct. 1943.
42. Court Camera, 18 April, 14 Nov., and 16 Dec.1940; *Glasgow Herald*, 4 Feb. 1941. The title of Dean of Faculties was later separated again from the office of Vice-Principal and reverted to being a title awarded to a distinguished retired professor.
43. *Glasgow Herald*, 8 Sept. 1942.
44. Court Camera, 30 Sept. 1942.
45. *GU Student Handbook,1943–4*.
46. Court Camera, 11 June and 24 Sept. 1942, 22 June 1943; R. Y. Thomson (ed.), *A Faculty for Science: A Unified Diversity* (Glasgow, 1993), 143.
47. Court Camera, 25 Feb. and 25 March 1943.
48. Court Camera, 28 Jan., 25 Feb., 24 June and 10 Nov. 1943.
49. Court Camera, 28 Jan., 2 June, and 6 Oct. 1943, 24 Feb. and 18 May 1944.
50. Court Camera, 28 Jan. and 25 Feb. 1943; Senate, 21 Jan. and 16 Dec. 1943.
51. Court Camera, 20 May and 24 June 1943, 27 Jan. 1944.
52. 'Second Report of the Committee on Veterinary Education in Great Britain', PP. Cmd. 651, 1943–4, 19.
53. 'Report of the Committee on Agricultural Education in Scotland', P.P., Cmd. 6704, 1945–6.
54. Senate, 11 Nov. and 16 Dec. 1943, and 20 Jan. 1944.
55. Finance Committee Minute, 16 Feb. 1944, Court Camera.
56. Hetherington's speech to the General Council, *Glasgow Herald*, 27 April 1944.
57. *Glasgow Herald*, 27 April 1944.
58. 'Memorandum on Admissions', Court Camera, 24 Feb. 1944.
59. Finance Committee Minute, 15 March 1944, Court Camera.

60. For examples of the protests in a West of Scotland context, see the pages of the *Glasgow Herald* for the early weeks of May 1944.
61. *Glasgow Herald*, 28 April 1944.
62. GUM, 55, 6, May 1945.
63. These, and other examples, of wartime casualties among the University's graduates are to be found in the Report of the General Council, 30 October 1946.
64. A. Calder, *The People's War: Britain, 1939–45* (London, 1969).

CHAPTER EIGHT

Renewal and Expansion, 1945–51

The University emerged from the Second World War into a political and economic environment very different from that which it had experienced after the First World War. There were, it is true, some similarities with the aftermath of the previous great conflict, most notably in the need to make arrangements for returning ex-servicemen and women whose studies had been interrupted or postponed by the war, or to repair whatever neglect in the physical or corporate fabric that had been engendered by war-time conditions. Because of what had occurred in 1918 and 1919, however, the University was now rather better prepared to cope with such immediate and temporary demands. The wider and more permanent implications of the post-Second World War era lay in the almost seismic changes that had occurred in the domestic and international political scene. Nationally, the war-time coalition government, which had included among its responsibilities the planning for peace as well as the prosecution of war, was replaced by an overtly reformist Labour government which was intent upon placing the British economy and social relations on a new footing – by completing the task of creating a Welfare State begun by the pre-1914 Liberal government, through interventions in health, housing, pensions, social services and education, and by transforming the prospects of a flagging British economy through the nationalisation of key industries and institutions, the use of economic planning, and the application of Keynesian techniques of demand management in pursuit of a policy of full employment. Internationally, Britain's role as a world power had been superseded by the rise of the USA and Russia as superpowers, and by the imminent independence and partition of India; but it still retained a large dependent colonial empire, in the Caribbean, Africa, Southeast Asia and the Pacific, to which the Labour government was intent on extending the policies and practices of economic planning and state welfare. This was a programme of renewal and reform in which the universities were expected to play a full part, as sources of the highly educated and trained manpower which would be needed in the new Britain, and as centres of creative thinking and experiment in the fields of science and technology which the government proposed to harness to its task.

One measure of the determination to make new demands on the universities was the large number of government committees which, between 1944 and 1947, recommended changes to or improvements in the way that the universities made provision for particular fields of study. The Goodenough Committee on Medical Schools, the Teviot Committee on Dentistry, the Barlow Committee on Scientific Manpower, the Clapham Committee on Social and Economic Research, the Loveday Committee on Agricultural Education in England and Wales, the Alness Committee on Agricultural Education in Scotland, the Loveday Committee on Veterinary Education, and the Scarborough Commission on Oriental, Slavonic, East European and African Studies all made recommendations for change in the universities, coupled with pleas for additional public spending to make this possible. A willingness on the part of government to find funds for these purposes, as well as for the more general expansion of the university system, was the second measure of the commitment to engage higher education in the task of national renewal. Treasury expenditure on the universities, which was around £2 million per annum before the war, was raised to over £5 million as soon as the war was over, and from that to £22 million by the academic year 1950–1.[1] These were heady years for all the universities of Britain. After decades of relative neglect and low esteem within the national policy framework, squeezed out of party and official priorities by the more pressing demands of war and depression, they were now invited to become partners with government in a programme of economic and social transformation which would move the country away from the relative stagnation and decline of the inter-war years. For the University of Glasgow in particular, it was a time of great opportunity. The poorest, the most proletarian, as well as one of the largest, of the British universities, it stood to gain most from the possibilities opened up by the new policies and the loosening of the public purse. The process of catching-up with the other major British universities, in which the University under Hector Hetherington had been engaged since 1936 and that the war had partially checked, was now resumed in much more propitious circumstances.

It was not immediately obvious within the University that the post-war era would be one of government-funded expansion in student numbers. The proposals Hetherington and the Court had brought forward in 1944 envisaged that, after a year or two of coping with returning servicemen and women, the University would settle down to a steady-state population of some 5,000 students. This would be achieved through strict entrance quotas that would enable the University to avoid the stresses of the inter-war years, when unrestricted entry resulted in great pressure on resources.[2] The fact that the other Scottish universities shared fears of unregulated post-war expansion seems to be indicated by the discussions within the Scottish Universities Entrance Board (SUEB) which resulted in 1946 in a raising of the standard level for entry. An attestation of fitness would now be issued only to those Scottish

8.1 *Celebrating the Peace. Sir Hector Hetherington with Mrs Churchill and Air Marshall Lord Tedder on Commemoration Day, 1946.*

students who passed four highers (including English) or three highers (including English) and two lowers in the Scottish Examination Board exams. Despite grumblings from some quarters that a pass in mathematics was not also required, it was widely accepted that the new arrangement represented a tightening-up on the conditions of entry which had prevailed before the war.[3]

On Gilmorehill, the brunt of the more restrictive policy was expected to fall on the Faculty of Arts, on which Senate in 1944 had imposed a post-war quota of 400 entrants. Although the Faculty found difficulty in implementing the new quota in the conditions prevailing in 1945,[4] it nevertheless came round fairly quickly to supporting the new policy – and indeed to taking advantage of it, by imposing additional requirements on potential entrants in the shape of a Higher pass in a language other than English and at least a Lower in Latin.[5] Those forces which had been on the losing side of the debate over wider access in the inter-war years now seized the opportunity to make amends. They were able to do so partly because they now enjoyed the support of the Principal and the Court, and partly because the teaching profession's attention was temporarily focused on a different matter – where, within the admissions quotas for all the faculties, the balance should be struck between places for those returning from the war and places for those proceeding to higher education from the secondary schools. Such bodies as the EIS and the Association of Headmasters of Senior Secondary Schools protested vigorously at the suggestion under consideration by the Scottish universities that, for entry in October 1946, some 90 per cent of the places might have to be reserved for ex-servicemen and women, leaving only ten per cent for school-leavers.[6] This issue, in fact, was something of a red herring, because estimates of the likely size of the ex-service intake rested on very large uncertainties about the numbers who would be deemed eligible under the new admissions requirements, and in 1946–7 and again in 1947–8 the University of Glasgow was able to admit roughly equal numbers of new entrants (excluding re-admissions) from service and school backgrounds. Nevertheless, the dispute served to divert attention from the fact that, partly under the guise of managing the post-war student bulge, the University had put in place a general system for selecting applicants on the basis of prior academic attainment which would continue to regulate the inflow from schools once the immediate needs were past.

As late as October 1947 Hetherington was still preaching the need for restrictions on student admissions and expressing the hope that the brunt of the government's plans to increase the numbers of university students would be borne by English universities.[7] By this time, it was clear that the tide of national policy – with the Barlow Report recommending a doubling of the number of British science and engineering graduates within ten years, and the Clapham Report also indicating a need for an increase in the numbers of social science graduates – was moving in a direction that would make it difficult, if not impossible, to hold to his objective of a student population of 5,000. Total numbers in fact quickly surpassed this target, rising to a peak of 7,414 in 1949–50 before beginning to fall a little again as the ex-servicemen left Gilmorehill. This brought the University to a 'normal' enrolment in the early 1950s of approximately 6,500 students, which was some 30 per cent greater than Hetherington's desired steady state.

Three factors undermined Hetherington's conservative admissions policy: first, the near impossibility of squeezing the 'bulge' of ex-servicemen into the new faculty entrance quotas; second, the influential voices calling for greater investment in the longer-term production of highly-educated and trained manpower, so as to help meet national targets in economic planning and social welfare; and third, the willingness of the Labour government to make resources for this purpose available through the UGC. The pressure of numbers on resources that had followed the First World War, it was clear by 1946–7, was not going to be repeated after the Second, and Hetherington, who had been chairman of the Committee of Vice-Chancellors and Principals since

1943, was very well informed about the government's intentions to allocate larger sums to the universities.[8] Behind his lingering public reluctance to commit the University to a policy of expansion, therefore, lay not so much a concern about the availability of funds as a desire to ensure that the University would grow in a controlled manner, and be transformed in character from the institution that it had become by the 1930s. If defeated – his own word – in terms of total numbers, he nevertheless enjoyed success in the way that his tighter controls on admissions made possible a redistribution of student numbers across the University, with the result that the University was a significantly different place by 1949–50 from what it had been in the 1930s (Table 8.1). The numbers of students on the Science side of the University – in the

Table 8.1
Distribution of Students by Faculty, 1934–5 and 1949–50

	1934–5				*1949–50*			
	Men	*Women*	*Total*	*% Univ. Total*	*Men*	*Women*	*Total*	*% Univ. Total*
Arts	1633	1375	3008	57.49	1358	840	2198	30.11
Divinity	105	1	106	2.03	127	1	128	1.75
Law	396	17	413	7.89	630	48	678	9.29
Medicine	687	135	822	15.71	1576	340	1916	26.25
Science	422	118	540	10.32	1154	224	1378	18.88
Engineering	342	1	343	6.56	1000	1	1001	13.71
Univ. Total	3585	1647	5232	100.00	5845	1454	7299	100.00

Faculties of Medicine, Science and Engineering – were some two or three times greater than in 1934–5. Conversely, the formerly over-stretched Faculty of Arts saw its student numbers down by a third, and its share of the total student population of the University reduced from 57 per cent to 30 per cent. (The shift away from Arts impacted mainly on women students, whose numbers fell both absolutely and relatively between 1934–5 and 1949–50.) Accompanying these figures were significant changes in the respective roles of the various Faculties, and the contributions they were expected to make in the way that the University engaged with the wider economy and society.

Reforms in medical education were underway even before the National Health Service Act of 1946 announced the new system of publicly-funded medicine to come into existence in 1948. The Goodenough Committee of 1944, one of the members of which was Professor James Hendry, the University's Regius Professor of Midwifery, brought forward recommendations on a range of issues that had concerned the Medical Faculty in the late 1930s and early 1940s. These included suggestions for curricular changes to give more attention to social medicine and public health, but were mainly concerned with new organisational arrangements to improve collaboration between university medical schools and the teaching hospitals. Special Treasury grants were made available, from which the University received £106,350 over the course of sessions 1945–6 and 1946–7, with a further £102,900 going to the teaching hospitals. Much of the work of the Medical Faculty and the Principal during these years was taken up by very close discussions with the hospitals over the changes to be put in place, with the aim of bringing greater definition to the respective roles of the University and the hospitals in the appointment and payment of staff, in the conduct of teaching, and in the provision of accommodation and equipment. A particular objective of the Goodenough Report was the placing of all clinical departments of a medical school in the charge of full-time professors appointed and paid by the university concerned, with sufficient remuneration that outside earnings need not be sought. This policy meshed with Hetherington's own thinking and began to be implemented in Glasgow with the translation of Professors McNee and Illingworth to full-time chairs of Medicine and Surgery respectively, followed shortly thereafter by the transformation of the chair of Medical Paediatrics into the full-time chair of Child Health. The University also took steps to increase the number of full-time lectureships attached to clinical departments, and it finally secured the agreement of the hospital-based teachers to the introduction of a composite fee for medical students.[9] Most of the necessary adjustment of relations between the University and the city's hospitals were therefore in place before the National Health Service formally came into existence in 1948. However, the creation of the NHS was also an act of great symbolic weight that encouraged the University and the UGC to invest in the further development of medical education, taking account of the need for a more community-oriented medicine and of the rise of new specialisms as a result of the growth of scientific knowledge. These new developments included chairs in Psychological Medicine and in Physiology in Relation to Social Medicine. The holder of the latter, Professor G. M. Wishart, also took on the new role of Director of Postgraduate Medical Education, which further strengthened the links between the Medical Faculty, the hospitals, the medical profession and the NHS.[10]

The Medical Faculty also grew as a result of its absorption of what remained of St Mungo's and Anderson's Colleges, the abolition of which was one of the most significant outcomes of the Goodenough Report. That document was scathingly critical of the way that Scotland's extra-mural medical colleges – St Mungo's and Anderson's in Glasgow and the School of Medicine of the Royal College of Edinburgh – had created difficulties for the universities in the 1930s, through their competing claims on the teaching capacities of the hospitals. Insisting that the 'training of medical students on modern lines can be conducted only under the aegis of a university and in institutions that conform to university standards', it recommended that the extra-mural colleges cease to train medical students.[11] Because their intake of overseas students had dried up during the war, and they had no access to the UGC funds which were now being used to bind the teaching hospitals more closely to the University, neither St Mungo's nor Anderson's College were in a position to challenge that recommendation, and they quietly wound up their affairs. The University duly transferred the remaining students into its undergraduate courses, while promising to give the staff consideration in future University appointments. It also acquired the Anderson's College building, conveniently located close to the Western Infirmary, while the St Mungo's building passed into the possession of the Royal Infirmary.[12]

Proposals regarding the absorption of the Dental School into the University were more closely connected to the introduction of the NHS. The Teviot Committee of 1946 foresaw a need for students of dentistry in Britain to treble in numbers (from 350 to 900) as a result of the dentistry profession's inclusion within the NHS scheme, and one of the measures it recommended to achieve this goal was that the dental schools based in the dental hospitals in Edinburgh and Glasgow should be incorporated into their respective universities. Negotiations between the University Court and the governors of the Dental Hospital proceeded rapidly and amicably, and ended with an agreement that the University would assume responsibility for the admission and teaching of students, and for the appointment and payment of the relevant staff, with pre-clinical teaching to be done at the University and the clinical teaching at the Dental Hospital. The Director of the Dental Hospital would also become the University's Director of Dental Education. Incorporation into the Faculty of Medicine on these terms took place formally on 1 October 1947, and the first students to be admitted under the new arrangements – some forty in all – entered the University at that time.[13] Although additional staffing proved necessary, both at the Dental Hospital and the University departments in the Royal Infirmary, and the curriculum for the B.D.S. required reform,[14] the assumption of responsibility for dental education caused the University few real problems because it was taking over a going concern in a good condition.

This was less true of the Glasgow Veterinary College, the building deficiencies of which had been identified during the late 1930s and a partial solution to which had been sought in the proposed merger of the University with the West of Scotland Agricultural College. These plans in turn had been put on hold by the divided and inconclusive Alness Report on the future of agricultural education of Scotland. In the event, early in 1946 the Secretary of State for Scotland rejected the majority opinion that called for the concentration of degree-level work in a single centre, leaving the way open for the University to negotiate a bilateral arrangement with the Agricultural College. However, these discussions in turn were complicated by the intervention of the UGC, which was concerned by what appeared to be an over-supply of places for agricultural degree work in Scotland, was critical of specific aspects of the University's provision of agricultural courses, and offered little or no support for the idea of a full merger of the Agricultural College with the University.[15] Although the University's relations with the College remained relatively amicable, the drive towards closer institutional relations appears to have faltered by 1948–9. These complications with the Agricultural College were in turn one of the main reasons why Hetherington and the Court were slow to respond to the second Loveday Report on Veterinary Education in Britain (1945), which called for the takeover of the Glasgow Veterinary College by the University (as part of a general pattern of inserting veterinary degree work into several British universities). The concept of locating all or part of a University Vet School alongside the Agricultural College at Auchincruive could not be pursued amidst the uncertainty about the University's relationship to the Agricultural College and the availability of the Auchincruive site. Although there were other delaying factors – notably a need for clarification of the role of the Royal College of Veterinary Surgeons in validating any University degree in veterinary science[16] – the need for a suitable site, where animals could be kept within access of the teaching facilities, was of prime importance. Consequently, the key to the Vet School project was the offer made in 1947 by Sir George Campbell, to donate his family home at Garscube to the University and to sell 125 acres of adjoining land on favourable terms.[17] The Garscube Estate, just a few miles from Gilmorehill, was much larger than was needed for the Vet School alone, and its acquisition constituted the creation of a landed reserve for a possible variety of future University initiatives. Its most immediate use, however, was as a site for a new animal hospital for the Vet School, financial support for which was promised by the UGC.[18] With that essential building-block in place, the incorporation of the Veterinary College into the Faculty of Medicine took place on 1 October 1949. William Weipers, chairman of the College's governing body, who had done much to persuade Hetherington of the merits of locating veterinary activities within Medicine rather than Science, became the University's first Director of Veterinary Education. This was the last act in a remarkable and rapid round of accretion of new responsibilities by the University.

In Science and Engineering growth came essentially from within, through an expansion and diversification of existing activities rather than by way of an addition of educational functions previously carried out elsewhere. Student numbers in the two faculties rose to a combined share of 32 per cent of the total, compared with a pre-war figure of 17 per cent, and a building programme designed both to cope with that growth and to provide laboratory facilities sufficient to the demands of new high-level research absorbed the greater part of the University's post-war estates development programme. Such expansion, however, would not have been possible without substantial investment from the public purse, in line with political and public perceptions about the increasing importance of science and technology for government and the economy. The main symbols of this new era in science and technology in the University were the electron synchrotrons – a 30 million volt one agreed in 1946 followed by a 300 million volt one agreed in 1948 – that Professor P. I. Dee persuaded government departments to fund for research in particle physics, together with a new building that the UGC agreed to finance to house the larger of these scarce and expensive pieces of equipment. Dee, fresh from a period of war-time scientific research spent mainly in the development of radar, was well placed to form a bridge between government research policy and the desire of Hetherington and other key individuals that the University should recover some of that scientific reputation which it had lost since the days of Kelvin. The larger synchrotron was in fact part of a wider programme of post-war national research in nuclear physics, in which Glasgow was one of five universities in Britain (the others being Cambridge, Oxford, Birmingham and Liverpool) that were selected by government to specialise in this major new, but extremely costly, research field.[19] Such was the significance attached to the project, indeed, that the new Natural Philosophy building to sit atop the synchrotron lab was given exemption from the controls over construction exercised by the Ministry of Works at a time of continuing post-war shortages of materials and skilled labour.[20] The experience of being so favourably treated by government was such a new one that it could only confirm the Court in the belief that the reviving Department of Natural Philosophy was one of the jewels in the University's crown. It therefore moved quickly to transform the vacant Cargill Chair into a new chair of Theoretical Physics, to which John C. Gunn, a Glasgow graduate, was appointed in 1948.[21]

The renewal of the University's national standing in Science was by no means limited to Physics. In Chemistry, the changes in personnel and research emphasis, including a close working relationship with the firm of ICI that began with J. W. Cook's appointment to the Regius chair in 1940, continued through into the post-war years. The Chemists were hampered, however, by lingering constraints on laboratory accommodation for teaching and research – for when the construction of the Chemistry Building started again after the war, its completion, already delayed by official building controls, was thrown into serious doubt by the discovery of late 18th century coal workings close to the surface of the land on which the extension was to take place. Expensive piling work meant that a project originally conceived in the mid-1930s was finally completed only in 1954. This in turn had a knock-on effect for plans for a new building, and related refurbishment of existing premises, for the Faculty of Engineering. Capital was available for these purposes through generous gifts amounting to £65,000 made to the University by Lord Weir in 1945 and a public appeal launched under the auspices of the Institution of Engineers and Shipbuilders.[22] However, until some movement of Chemists out of their existing labs took place, it was not possible to proceed very far with the scheme for Engineering. More fortunate were the departments of

Botany, for which new laboratory and classroom accommodation was made available through refurbishment of its existing building, and Zoology, which obtained a small extension to its premises and, through the generosity of Sir Iain Colquhoun and the Scottish Office, acquired a Freshwater Biology Station on Loch Lomond.[23] The new Genetics department, whose leading light was Guido Pontecorvo, the University's most distinguished Jewish refugee from pre-war fascism, moved into the refurbished Anderson's College building.

Much of the work of rejuvenating Science and Engineering in the University, it is clear, involved a transformation of the physical infrastructure, so as to raise levels of accommodation and equipment towards national standards. This was an expensive process, partly met by private benefactions but mainly through the new-found willingness of the state to invest in science and technology in the universities. The UGC, which between the wars had supplied the University with very little in the way of funding for capital purposes, now became a veritable cornucopia. Its non-recurrent grants to the University rose from £13,500 in 1945–6 to £418,003 in 1950–1, in the process raising Glasgow's share from 1.8 to 6.5 per cent of the UK total.[24] The large projects it supported in this way were all on the science side of the University – particle physics, inorganic chemistry, heat engines (Engineering), the animal hospital at Garscube, and a new building for the Department of Surgery. However, the development of Science and Engineering involved more than investment in bricks and mortar; it also required people. As student numbers rose, staff numbers followed, and the departments took the opportunity to recruit younger teachers and researchers to cover developing subject areas. Occasionally, too, a vacancy at a senior level permitted a strategic shift in a department's orientation – thus, just as the Cargill Chair in Natural Philosophy was transformed into a chair in Theoretical Physics, so too the Mechan Chair in Engineering was converted in 1949 into a chair in Aeronautics and Mechanical Fluids, to which W. J. Duncan was appointed from Cranfield College.[25] The UGC had a hand in that particular decision, reflecting the more interventionist role that that body was now prepared to adopt in the pursuit of what it perceived as national goals. Even more explicit examples of this were to be found in the way that the UGC interested the University in, and funded, a new lectureship in electrochemistry, as a joint venture between Chemistry and Engineering, and selected Glasgow as the Scottish university in which it wished to install a special postgraduate course in thermodynamics, as part of a nationwide scheme to develop the theoretical underpinnings of technological development.[26]

Science and Engineering, together with Medicine and its newly associated subject areas, strode forward into the post-war years with increasing vigour and confidence. Meanwhile, the Faculties of Law and Divinity continued to fulfil their traditional roles of preparing graduates for professional careers. In

Arts, on the other hand, which remained the largest faculty in terms of student numbers, uncertainty hung over the direction of educational diversification and over the part to be played by the Faculty in the revitalised University. Undercurrents of tension and debate about the future swirled around the meetings of the Faculty and the Senate. One reason for this was that limitation on undergraduate numbers – essential in Hetherington's view both for an improvement in the 'quality' of the student intake and to permit a greater attention to postgraduate training and research – had as its corollary an inability to rely on funding which followed student numbers as a resource for new departmental staffing strategies. Another was that while external funds were available for developmental purposes, these were mainly intended for the social sciences rather than the humanities and languages. By contrast with social sciences, an expansion of which was called for by the Clapham Committee and towards which the UGC earmarked £1.2 million in the quinquennium 1947–52, the traditional and predominant subject areas within the Arts Faculty had fewer claims to be able to make a direct contribution towards national economic recovery and improved social welfare. The Principal was fully in tune with the mood to advance social sciences within the University, and had indeed already signalled this in 1945 by securing a grant from the Rockefeller Foundation to finance the establishment of a social and economic research unit.[27] When funding for the social sciences became available from the UGC in 1947–8, he moved quickly to put in place several new appointments either under the umbrella of the research organisation or within existing departments – in the shape of lectureships in political institutions, modern economic history, international relations, sociology and social psychology. The Court also agreed to the creation of a chair in Applied Economics, the main purpose of which was to give leadership to the emergent research thrust within the social sciences, and in 1949 one of the University's own graduates, Alec Cairncross, was lured back to Glasgow from a distinguished career at Cambridge and in the civil service to take up this task.[28]

It is clear, however, that not everyone in Arts was satisfied with a developmental emphasis on social sciences within the Faculty. In February–March 1948 the Faculty formally complained to Senate and Court about the creation of the five new lectureships. Although ostensibly about an alleged lack of consultation, the real cause of complaint appears to have been a view that investment in social sciences did little to meet the Faculty's own priorities as outlined in a document presented to Court in November 1946. This had included a request for chairs in English Language, Ancient History and Psychology, and additional lectureships in Celtic Languages, Palaeography, Linguistics, and Fine Art.[29] The standard-bearer of the humanities and languages opposition to the advance of the social sciences was Christian J. Fordyce, the Professor of Humanity (Latin), who became Clerk of Senate in 1940 and Dean of Arts in 1948. Although he and his allies were unable fully to block decisions of the Principal and the Court which were backed by earmarked grants from the UGC, they were in a position to make life difficult for those involved in new social science initiatives within the Faculty.

The novel and suspect field of interdisciplinary 'areas studies' was a prime target. The Scarborough Report on Oriental, Slavonic, East European and African Studies of 1947 recommended an increased provision for teaching and research in these areas, no doubt mindful of Britain's continuing international and imperial commitments. A complex pattern of discussions involving the UGC and the four Scottish universities then resulted in the decision that Glasgow should be the recipient of funds for developments in two of these areas – Slavonic and East European Studies and African Studies. The first was a natural progression for a university which had taught Russian language since the First World War and during the Second World War had offered non-graduating classes in Polish, from a lecturer paid for by the Polish government-in-exile. Even so, the attempt to enlarge these operations in the aftermath of the Scarborough Report proved difficult. There was opposition within the Faculty to the idea that Polish and Czech languages were of sufficient merit to justify a place in the graduating curriculum and, more damagingly for the longer term, debate over the relative contribution of language and culture on the one hand and the social sciences on the other to the field of Slavonic and East European studies. This resulted in a departmental split, certain members of staff departing in 1949–50 to take shelter under the umbrella of the emergent social and economic research department.[30]

African Studies, which had no prior roots in the University, had an even rougher ride at the hands of the Faculty 'old guard'. Hetherington's willingness to host such an activity stemmed from his awareness of the government's post-war development schemes for colonial Africa, and the role which the universities were expected to play in them – an awareness no doubt sharpened by the experience of his friend Arthur Trueman's participation in the war-time commission on West African universities and his subsequent appointment as Deputy Chairman of the UGC. However, the Principal's sense of the appropriateness of what was being proposed was not shared by Professor Fordyce and other senior members of the Faculty. When informed that money would be made available for the purpose, they refused to accept it until a study had been made as to '(a) whether the setting up of a new centre for African Studies was necessary or desirable and (b) whether Glasgow was a suitable university in which to attempt to develop such studies *ab initio*.'[31] The outcome of such further consultations and deliberations was a grudging acceptance that African Studies was an appropriate field for postgraduate teaching and research, but that Glasgow's endeavours should be confined to preparing overseas students who intended to teach in African or other universities abroad. Glasgow graduates who showed any interest in the field would be advised to pursue it elsewhere. When, following these delays, two new members of staff were appointed to initiate developments in the field they found little support and a good deal of opposition. There was no intention, Fordyce informed the lecturer in African Studies, of setting up a diploma until teaching could be provided on a broad basis, while the lecturer in Social Anthropology, whose 'energy and goodwill should certainly be encouraged', was bluntly told that he would need to develop his teaching under the supervision of a professor who knew 'more clearly than a new-comer could the working of the academic machinery in the University.'[32] African Studies was something of a hothouse plant, not yet fully accepted by Western scholars as a legitimate field of intellectual endeavour, which nevertheless managed to put down roots in a number of British and American universities. In Glasgow it was planted in the open, to wither from the opposition of those objecting to an agenda of change for the Faculty of Arts which was driven by the interests of the Principal and the UGC.

Not every innovation in Arts during these years was led by government and UGC priority. As the University's financial position gradually improved it became easier for the Court to support developments that had internal or local sentiment behind them. Thus in 1948–9 it was able to respond to requests that the teaching of Fine Art be introduced into the Faculty, by creating a fixed-term post of curator of the University art collections and lecturer in Fine Art.[33] The Court was also able to meet demands that the teaching profession and the General Council had repeatedly pressed on it since the 1920s, by creating a chair of Education and appointing Stanley Nisbet of Queen's University, Belfast, to fill it in 1950.[34] This step was in line with thinking within the Scottish universities at the time, which rejected any role in initial teacher training, as happened in England, as well as the alternative suggestion that independent institutes of education, with degree-awarding powers, should be created around the training colleges in Scotland. The solution to such a threat was seen to be an advancement of the status of Education as a field of study within the universities, emphasising the scope for higher level work, and building closer links with the training colleges.[35]

Extending opportunities for full-time and part-time advanced study by members of the teaching profession, comparable to the new initiatives in post-graduate education for the medical profession, formed part of the University's local 'outreach' activity by which it contributed to the cultural and educational life of the city and the region. Such a role was played even more explicitly, and with broader effect, by the University's 'extra-mural' or 'extension' services, which reached out to the wider community from Gilmorehill and which post-war conditions now favoured. Since the early 1920s, a University 'extra-mural' committee had overseen a programme of lectures and classes delivered to the general public by members of the academic staff of the University, and from 1928–9 it became a 'joint committee' also embracing representatives of local authorities and the Workers' Educational Association (WEA). Several senior academics were enthusiastic supporters of this 'outreach' activity, not least Hector Hetherington, who had chaired the committee when he was a professor of philosophy and resumed the chair immediately on his return to Gilmorehill as Principal. The University's efforts in these directions were generally popular – reports from tutors in the 1930s frequently commented on the high numbers of unemployed men in the classes[36] – but the overall number of classes and students remained small because of the prevailing lack of cash for 'extra-mural' activities. This resulted both from the University's own financial predicaments and from the fact that, in contrast with their counterparts in England, the Scottish universities received no central government funding for 'extra-mural' purposes. Between the wars, therefore, most of the work rested upon unpaid voluntary activity by an academic staff growing increasingly hard-pressed in the performance of its other teaching duties. After the Second World War, as after the First, there was a renewed public appetite for higher education classes. On this occasion, however, the University was better able to respond. An agreement with Glasgow and other local authorities that gave the University access to the 'adult education' funds supplied to them by the Scottish Office, and the University's own gradually improving financial situation, which enabled it to increase the sums it devoted to these purposes, placed 'extra-mural' education on a new footing. A properly professional 'extra-mural' service, comparable to those that existed in the English civic universities, was put in place between 1947 and 1949, with the appointment of a full-time Director of Extra-Mural Studies, two full-time tutors for Glasgow, a full-time tutor for the more far-flung needs of rural Dumfries and Galloway, and the provision of appropriate accommodation on University premises.[37]

Broadening the undergraduate base and extending non-graduate provision were matched among Hetherington's priorities by the need to improve performance in the areas of research and higher degrees. His ambitions were focused mainly in Science and Engineering, into which so much post-war investment was placed, but they also extended to the 'professional' faculties and to Arts. The time was ripe for such a renewed emphasis. The Carnegie Trust, reacting to a situation in which Government funds now met most university capital requirements, shifted the bulk of its operations to supporting research and higher degree work through fellowships and scholarships. Other sources of funding were Government departments and large business organisations like ICI. Furthermore, thanks in part to the wartime advances in scientific knowledge and to the participation by individual members of staff in these developments, a research culture was now more widespread within the University. Interestingly, the most explicit statement of the new attitudes came from a Faculty of Medicine that was concerned that medical research might be siphoned off into special government-funded institutes. 'The Faculty believes', it stated bluntly, 'that the function of a University is to prosecute research as an end in itself as well as to teach. Moreover, however competent in didactic instruction, a university teacher, unless he is also engaged in research, can never have that vital inspiration so essential in undergraduate and postgraduate education . . . The Faculty would deplore any tendency to regard research as an academic sideline.'[38]

One measure of change is the number of graduations with doctoral degrees (Table 8.2). This shows a post-war expansion which, in terms of total numbers

Table 8.2
Doctoral Degrees, 1938–9 to 1951–2

	Arts		*Divin-ity*	*Law*	*Medicine*		*Science*		*Engineering*		*Total*
	D.Phil/D. Litt	*Ph.D*	*Ph.D*	*Ph.D*	*MD*	*Ph.D*	*D.Sc*	*Ph.D*	*D.Sc*	*Ph.D*	
1938–9					20			11	3	1	35
1939–40	1	3	1		17		3	17		3	45
1940–1	2	3			19			11	1	1	37
1941–2	2				15		2	8			27
1942–3		2			8			2			12
1943–4	1	2			21	1	4	4			33
1944–5	1	2	1		5		2	7			18
1945–6	1	1			9			5			16
1946–7	1	3		1	28		2	10			45
1947–8	1		1		24		6	7		1	40
1948–9		1			20	1	3	31		2	58
1949–50	2	2	2		19	1	2	33		1	62
1950–1	1	4	1		14	3		3		3	29
1951–2		1	1	1	19	1	1	40		4	68

of doctoral graduations, rose from between 35 and 45 per annum on the eve of the war to over 60 by 1950. The bulk of the increase came in the Faculty of Science, where the number of successful Ph.D. submissions rose from 5 in the first year of peace to 40 by 1951–2, but signs of research vigour can also be detected in Engineering and, to a lesser extent, in Medicine, where the Ph.D. finally became an alternative to the MD as a vehicle for advanced work. On the Arts side in general, and Arts in particular, there was no significant new postgraduate activity. Employment prospects may have played a part in this – the Ph.D. in Arts was above all a preparation for a university career, and fewer academic posts were opening up, in Glasgow at least, in the traditional Arts subjects than in Science or Engineering. But it would appear that low self-esteem was the crucial factor. Among the traditional Arts departments there was a view – which the newer social sciences did not share – that their role was predominantly one of teaching undergraduates, and that postgraduate training and research should be carried out elsewhere, namely in Oxford and Cambridge. Such a state of mind, born out of the fact that most of the senior Arts professors were products of the Oxbridge system, was reflected in the observation that Glasgow graduates interested in African Studies should take themselves off elsewhere for this purpose. It was expressed even more explicitly in the report of the Faculty of Arts of 1950 that recommended the introduction of a less rigorous research degree, the B.Litt., which was intended for overseas students and home students not intending to proceed to a Ph.D. – and commented that most Glasgow graduates would be encouraged to take research degrees outwith Glasgow.[39] Such limited ambition and lack of vision, perpetuating an arrangement whereby the Arts departments sent their best students off to the ancient English universities, and did little either to hold them or to attract other UK students into postgraduate work, was the hallmark of a group of subjects that remained out of step with the new vigour and self-confidence to be found elsewhere, in the Science-based faculties. Hetherington's hopes that restricting the entry of undergraduates into Arts would create head-room for postgraduate work foundered on the value system embedded there, which pre-war professors carried forward into the post-war era.

The new developments taking place across the University (although to a more limited extent in the established Arts departments) required a substantial increase in the numbers of academic staff. Total numbers grew from 211 in 1938–9 to 306 in 1946–7 and to 502 by 1951–2. Most of this growth took place at the more junior levels. While the ranks of the professors expanded – from 41 in 1946–7 to 54 in 1951–2 – the bulk of the increase occurred within the lecturing staff, more especially among the Assistant Lecturers whose numbers almost trebled from their pre-war level (from 39 to 105). This larger academic body was also a better-rewarded one; and other than in the most immediate post-war years, and in a few specialist areas, the University had little difficulty in recruiting the staff it needed. This happy circumstance was largely a by-product of the creation of the National Health Service. For in 1948 the Spens Report recommended salaries for consultants and specialists in the NHS which were well above those for clinical teachers in university medical schools; and in bringing the latter into line over time the universities could not afford to widen still further the gap which already existed between the clinical and the non-clinical academic staff. The upshot was the introduction in October 1949 of a new structure of national salary scales which roughly doubled salary levels over those of 1938–9 (the professorial average, for example, rose from £1,115 to £2,401, and the senior lecturers and lecturers from £477 to £995).[40] These changes, which were backed by Treasury funds, more than compensated for the increases in costs of living that had occurred in the meantime – except for Assistant Lecturers, who remained relatively underpaid.

Such changes were in turn made possible by a level of government funding which can only be described as generous. An almost four-fold increase in the UGC recurrent grant between 1945–6 and 1950–1 (Table 8.3) gave the University an inflow of funds on an historically unprecedented scale, and the difficulties in balancing the books which had been typical of the inter-war years quickly became a thing of the past. One significant consequence was that the University became more dependent on the public purse than ever before, as the proportion of the University's income derived from government grant rose from 35 per cent in 1938–9 to 67 per cent in 1950–1. Any stray thought that such dependence carried future dangers, if a different government were to take a less positive view of the role of universities in modern society, was overwhelmed by the prevailing mood of relief at having escaped from

Table 8.3
UGC Grants, 1945–6 to 1950–1

	Recurrent Grants		
	Glasgow £	*UK Total* £	*Glasgow* % *UK*
1945–6	239,791	4,767,350	5.03
1946–7	329,150	6,771,325	4.86
1947–8	450,600	9,320,455	4.83
1948–9	508,600	10,527,650	4.83
1949–50	712,700	13,605,595	5.24
1950–1	805,950	15,192,408	5.30

Source: UGC Returns for relevant dates

formerly dire financial straits. The new financial largesse in turn underwrote a rejuvenation of the academic life of the University, one that took place not only through the recruitment of new, and mainly younger, teachers and researchers but also through an expansion in the numbers and range of expertise in support staff, from lab technicians to departmental secretaries, librarians and administrators. In particular, it enabled the new Secretary of Court, Robert Hutcheson, to put in place the core of a more effective and professional central administration. Hutcheson, who had joined the slender and shaky administrative structure as a young man in 1920, had been dismayed by Rait's failure to follow the example of the other Scottish universities and establish a full-time Secretary's post to effect better coordination of administrative services. Hetherington's arrival, however, gave him his head, and by 1944 he had become both Registrar and Secretary of Court. This in turn provided a platform from which in the post-war era he was able to create an enlarged and more efficient administrative apparatus, better suited to the modern, dynamic and expanding institution that the University had become.[41]

Perhaps the most striking feature of these post-war years is that staff numbers grew more rapidly than student numbers. This resulted in the University's

8.2 *The Principal and SRC at Auchendennan Freshers' Camp, 1950/1. Those in the front row include Robert Hutcheson, the Secretary of Court, and, seated on Lady Hetherington's left, William Kerr Fraser, a future Principal and Chancellor.*

staff: student ratio, which was 1:22 in 1938–9, falling to a very much more comfortable 1:13 by 1951–2 – whereas the UK fall was from 1:10 to 1:8 over the same period. Consequently, educational developments for which student representatives had been campaigning for decades – notably the extension of small-group, tutorial-style teaching, more specialised work at the senior levels, and a wider range of combinations of honours subjects – began to assume the stature of attainable, if not yet universally adopted, goals. While there was some new investment in facilities for the post-war student population, notably the introduction of a student health service and the construction of a couple of temporary buildings to serve as refectories for those who did not wish to join the unions, the financial priorities of the Principal and the Court lay elsewhere. There was therefore no attempt to change the overwhelmingly local character of the student body by increasing the range of residential accommodation available. By 1951–2 only eighty-six places had been added to the stock of residential accommodation provided by the halls of residence in 1938–9.[42] When allied to a decline in the availability of private lodgings for students, this resulted in an even larger proportion of students, both men and women, living at home in 1950 than in 1940.[43] Nor did the University add to the range of social and sporting facilities which existed. Even the proposed new gymnasium and swimming-pool, whose construction had been blocked by the outbreak of war, was set aside in the immediate drive to improve the University's academic standing and performance.

That the University's stock was on the rise within British higher education cannot be doubted. Evidence is to be found at the personal level, as in Hector Hetherington's chairmanship of the CVCP, his participation in a range of national educational bodies, and his easy relationship with Sir Walter Moberly, the chairman of the UGC. This connection to national power and influence was strengthened by Arthur Trueman's appointment as Vice-Chairman of the UGC in 1948, prior to his succeeding Moberly in 1949. Evidence is also to be found in the rise of the University's share of the UGC's recurrent grant (Table 8.3) from a 'normal' level of about 4.8 (the figure for 1945–6 was unusual because of certain temporary post-Goodenough payments to medical schools) to 5.3 per cent in 1950–1. This in turn was linked to a fall in the University's SSR (staff : student ratio) that was more rapid than the national figure. The structural changes occurring in the University – the growth of Science and Engineering and the additions of Dentistry and Veterinary Medicine – meant replacing relatively inexpensive classroom- and library-based teaching and research with more expensive laboratory-based ones which employed larger numbers of staff, and in these circumstances the SSR was bound to improve. However, improvements in the SSR also seem to suggest that the University in its structure may have been growing closer to some national average, becoming more akin to the large English civic universities for which the UGC had shown a preference in the inter-war years, and that it was now being treated by the UGC in a more even-handed way. In Table 8.4 it is obvious that Glasgow University in 1950–1 was much closer in levels of grant and income per head to the group of universities with which it can most

Table 8.4
University Finances: English Civic and Scottish Universities, 1938–9 and 1950–1

	1938–9		*1950–1*	
	Grant per f/t student (£)	*Income per f/t student (£)*	*Grant per f/t student (£)*	*Income per f/t student (£)*
Birmingham	60.36	161.03	206.35	301.50
Bristol	95.84	236.98	238.14	371.11
Leeds	52.40	162.74	198.11	291.57
Liverpool	49.94	131.99	188.30	276.43
Manchester	47.60	138.13	203.64	275.62
Sheffield	76.35	220.75	202.89	300.11
Aberdeen	51.73	113.28	199.11	298.46
Edinburgh	34.94	98.42	132.58	203.35
St Andrews	64.12	146.81	197.76	271.63
Glasgow	24.19	69.67	144.28	214.29

Source: UGC Returns for 1938–9 and 1950–1

sensibly be compared than it was in 1938–9. In 1938–9, the ratio of the gap between Glasgow (the poorest) and Bristol (the richest) was 1:3.9 in Treasury grant per student and 1:3.4 in total income per student; by 1950–1 the ratios were 1:1.6 and 1.1.7 respectively. The gap had narrowed to one that could be plausibly explained by institutional differences in student numbers and subject mix. In this light, it may be argued that it was after the Second War rather than after the First that Glasgow University truly joined a 'national' UK system of university funding.

While one may debate the nature, extent and causes of the transformation of the University after 1945 – how much, for example, its improving fortunes owed to Hetherington's leadership and how much to more impersonal political and economic forces – it seems clear that the University was 'on a roll' as it approached its Quincentenary in January 1951. Both the University and its Principal had much to celebrate. And celebrate they did. The year of the Fifth Centenary began in January with a week of festivities organised by the student bodies. The highlights included a relay of runners bearing a flame from Bishop Turnbull's home in Bedrule in the Borders to Glasgow Cathedral, and then a mass torchlight procession from the Cathedral to Gilmorehill. This event was organised by the outgoing Rector, Walter Elliot, whose successor, John MacCormick, the former Scottish Nationalist leader, then faced one of the boisterous, not to say downright rowdy, rectorial installations for which Glasgow students were becoming notorious. MacCormick's installation was given an extra edge from the fact that only a couple of weeks before, at Christmas 1950, the Stone of Destiny had been removed from Westminster Abbey and a massive police hunt was now underway for this major symbol of Scottish sovereignty. Eventually, after the Stone's re-appearance at Arbroath Abbey early in April 1951, three of the University's student nationalists, Ian Hamilton, Gavin Vernon and Allan Stuart, admitted responsibility for the affair.

Hetherington's fears that the hostile press reaction to the rowdiness of the rectorial installation would overshadow and diminish the official University celebrations proved unfounded. Three days of dinners, receptions, and ceremonies were held in the middle of June. Attended by delegates from 220 universities and learned societies from around the world, they provided a vehicle for self-congratulation as well as a platform for the plaudits of the guests and an unprecedented amount of attention from the national press. Honorary degrees were conferred on no fewer than sixty-six men and women of distinction. Some distinguished guests did not manage to attend the festivities. The Royal Family withdrew because of King George's serious, and as it turned out, terminal illness (although rumour also suggested displeasure with the Stone of Destiny episode). Meanwhile, General Dwight Eisenhower, having been appointed Secretary-General of NATO since accepting an invitation, had more pressing matters to attend to in Washington. The delegate from the

8.3 *Fifth Centenary Celebrations, 1951:*
(a) bearing the Torch from Bedrule to Gilmorehill *(b) floodlights and searchlights*

8.4 *Fifth Centenary Celebrations. The Bedellus and the Chancellor (Lord Boyd Orr) lead a procession in the rain, 1951.*

Soviet Academy of Sciences, a victim of Cold War visa restrictions, arrived a week late for the party. These minor problems apart, the Quincentenary celebrations, which culminated in 800 people sailing 'doon the watter' on the steamer *Queen Mary II*, were a considerable success. They spoke volumes for the resurgent self-confidence of an institution that had been through some bad times in its recent past, and were presided over by a Principal who had done so much since his arrival in 1936 to turn its fortunes around. Hetherington and the University staff had much of which to be proud, and for once the back-slapping inherent in such institutional festivities was entirely justified.[44]

It was entirely appropriate that one of those honoured by the University on 21 June 1951 was the Prime Minister, Clement Attlee, whose government had done so much to create the conditions for a revival in the University's fortunes. Speaking on the theme of Government and the Universities, he drew attention to the way that public funds had been provided on a much greater scale than hitherto for reasons to do with changes in social policy. 'I have seen in my lifetime', he said, ' a wide extension of opportunity and a realisation by the State that economic conditions should not deprive the nation of utilising to the full the intellectual abilities of its citizens.' While accepting that much of the brunt of that change had been 'in the direction of levelling up the southern part of the island to the more enlightened practices of the north where the road to learning has always been broader', he nevertheless saw a demanding and challenging future for the University of Glasgow in meeting the future needs of the British economy and society, and identified his hopes for the way it would undertake that task. 'We need the discipline of the humanities and the teaching of social responsibility', he concluded, 'if we are to use rightly the immense material power which science has placed in our hands. I trust that while Glasgow University will continue to nurture the finest minds and to give opportunities for research, she will also do her utmost to see that every student who goes out from her into the world will have graduated in a school

8.5 *The Prime Minister, Clement Attlee, speaks on behalf of the Honorary Graduates in St Andrew's Hall, 1951.*

of citizenship.'[45] With this restatement of its civic role and responsibilities ringing in its ears, the University entered the second half of the twentieth century and the sixth century of its existence.

Notes and References

1. UGC, *Report on University Development, 1947–1952*, P.P. Cmd. 8875, 1952–53; *UGC Returns*, 1945–6 to 1950–1.
2. Speech by Hetherington to the General Council, *Glasgow Herald*, 27 April 1944.
3. *Glasgow Herald*, 8 and 25 April 1946; General Council, 30 Oct. 1946.
4. Senate, 13 Sept. 1945; Court, 2 Oct. 1945.
5. Senate, 13 Dec. 1945.
6. Senate, 13 June 1946; *Glasgow Herald*, 17 and 18 June 1946.
7. General Council, 29 Oct. 1947.
8. See, for example, Court, 6 March 1946.
9. Court, 20 Sept 1945, and 9 Jan. and 16 May 1946.
10. Court, 17 April 1947.
11. *Glasgow Herald*, 20 July 1940.
12. Senate, 16 Jan. 1947; Court, 15 May and 19 June 1947.
13. Court, 21 Feb. and 21 March 1946; Hetherington, *Letter to Graduates*, 12 Aug. 1947; Senate, 16 Oct. 1947.
14. Senate, 18 Nov. 1948.
15. Court, 18 April and 16 May 1946, 23 Jan. and 5 March 1947, 28 April, 8 July and 23 Sept. 1948.
16. Court, 20 Sept. 1945, 24 Jan. 1946.
17. Hetherington, *Letter to Graduates*, 12 Aug. 1947; *Glasgow Herald*, 30 Oct. 1947.
18. Court, 23 Sept. 1948.
19. UGC, *Report on University Development , 1947–1952*, 44.
20. Court, 18 March 1948.
21. Court, 8 July and 25 Nov. 1948.
22. Court, 15 Nov. 1945.
23. Court, 20 March 1947.
24. *UGC Returns*, 1945–6 to 1950–1.
25. Court, 10 July 1947, and 8 Aug. 1949.
26. Court, 28 Jan. 1948 and 27 Sept. 1949; UGC, *Report on University Development, 1947–52*, 59, 88.
27. Court, 22 March 1945; Hetherington, *Letter to Graduates*, 12 Aug. 1947.
28. Court, 7 and 22 Jan. 1948, 28 Nov. 1948, and 27 Sept. 1949.
29. Senate, 12 Feb. and 11 March, 1948; Court, 21 Nov. 1946.
30. J. M. Kirkwood, 'Russia and Eastern Europe', unpublished paper presented to the Seminar on The University and the Wider World, 1870–2001.
31. Senate, 21 Oct. 1948.
32. Senate, 17 Feb. 1949, 10 May and 13 Dec. 1951.
33. Senate, 18 Nov. 1948.
34. Court, 23 Feb. 1950.

35. Senate, 15 June 1950.
36. Extra Mural Education Committee Annual Reports, 1928–9 to 1939–40.
37. Court, 4 June 1947 and 9 Feb. 1949.
38. Senate, 18 Jan. 1951.
39. Senate, 11 May 1950.
40. UGC, *Report on University Development, 1947–52*, 37–8 and Appendix VIII.
41. Robert T. Hutcheson and Hugh Conway, *The University of Glasgow, 1920–1974* (Glasgow, 1997), 14–18.
42. UGC, *Report on University Development, 1947–52*, Appendix VII.
43. J. Wakeling, 'University Women: Origins, Experiences and Destinations at Glasgow University, 1939–1987' (Ph.D. thesis, Glasgow, 1998), 112, Figure 3.1.
44. For the details of the Fifth Centenary arrangements and the way in which the University was projected through them, see *The Book of the Fifth Centenary* (Glasgow, 1952), *Fifth Centenary of Glasgow University*, a special supplement of *The Glasgow Herald*, 6 Jan. 1951, Hetherington, *Letter to Graduates*, 21 March and 24 Sept. 1951, and *The Curious Diversity: Glasgow University on Gilmorehill: The First Hundred Years* (Glasgow, 1970), 104–108.
45. *The Book of the Fifth Centenary*, 97–101.

PART III

1951–2001

CHAPTER NINE

The Real Meaning of a University, 1951–61

With the triumph of the fifth centenary celebrations over, the University looked forward to the new quinquennium full of doubts and uncertainties. Clement Attlee, whose speech at the honorary graduation had been so encouraging, was no longer Prime Minister. In the wake of a serious balance of payments crisis in the summer of 1951, the Labour government had been swept from office and replaced by a Conservative administration under Winston Churchill, which was committed to cutting public expenditure. Such policies would inevitably affect higher education. Moreover the post-war programme for educating servicemen, with all its innovations and excitement, was complete and plans had to be made for a return to normal peacetime conditions, where the bulk of students had of financial necessity to be drawn from the immediate locality. The difficulty was to guess what should be planned for against an economic background which looked all too familiar to those whose memories stretched back to the 1920s when seven years after the previous war the local West of Scotland economy had been in the grip of serious recession. The spectre of another depression troubled Sir Hector Hetherington as he gazed from the Lodging windows towards the City's busy shipyards – 'I suppose there must always be some anxiety about the economic future of the Clyde Valley, so deeply dependent on the heavy industries and therefore sensitive to a fluctuating world demand for capital goods. It has to save its life and make its way in a highly competitive world.'[1] This was no abstract musing. Sir Hector was well aware that the University was tied to the performance of the local economy. Students were increasingly reliant on local authority grants and most came from the region and could continue to live at home. In the current climate of curbs on public spending many authorities were only willing to fund students attending their local university, largely because more awards could be made in this way. If there was to be any real expansion in the undergraduate population it would have to come from students whose parents could meet the costs of university education only if Clyde industry continued to prosper. Disturbingly there was already evidence that with the unprecedented prevailing rates of personal taxation to pay for the welfare state, some middle-class parents were thinking twice about university education for their children.

There were those in the University, encouraged by Government predictions of a fall in numbers in the short term and calls for economic retrenchment, who argued for a halt to any further development. Such views were not simply elitist but rooted in a genuine concern about the function of universities in democratic societies. There was a fear that the assimilation of all professional and technical training within universities would so weaken them that they would be unable to provide the intellectual basis to defend a liberal democracy. Academics were still haunted by the fear of what had happened in the 1930s to the German universities, which for almost a century had been the model for the development of higher education throughout the world. Sir Hector had some sympathy with this position, but he doubted if the steady state was practical. Against a background of consolidation the University Grants Committee was continuing to press for the development of new subject areas, particularly in science, technology, and social sciences. Moreover the incorporation of all undergraduate dental, medical and veterinary teaching within the University from 1949 necessitated the creation of new posts.

In framing the University's estimates during 1952 for the UGC's forthcoming quinquennium, Sir Hector and the Court and Senate steered a careful course, seeking to maintain student numbers at about 5,500 while continuing to improve facilities and staff/student ratios in certain subject areas. Apart from the Senate, which had 77 members, the only forum for discussion of development was the Standing Committee on Senate Business (later the Senate Business Committee), which had been established by Hetherington in 1947 to mitigate Fordyce's domination of the Senate. It comprised the members of the Principal and Deans Committee and five other members nominated by the Senate from amongst its members. Although the UGC had followed a pattern of quinquennial estimates and visitations, modelled on the Carnegie Trust, since its inception in 1919, the Committee intervened little in the affairs of individual institutions once a budget had been agreed. With the formation after 1945 of specialist sub-committees in arts, science, medicine, agriculture, technology and social science, there were clear indications that this was set to change, particularly as non-recurrent and 'earmarked' recurrent grants for specific projects were now being made on a regular basis. All building projects and plans for expansion included in the estimates had to be supported by the relevant sub-committee, before allocations could be made. Consequently universities had much less discretion over their expenditure than in the inter-war years and policy became a matter of complex and time-consuming negotiation between the institutions, the UGC, and its committees.

At Glasgow the greatest obstacle to increasing the number of staff and adding new facilities remained the shortage of space on the Gilmorehill site. This problem had been immediately addressed by Hetherington on his return to Glasgow in 1936, when he had established a New Buildings Committee which had commissioned the architects Hughes and Waugh to provide a long-term scheme for development to the north of University Avenue, on the site of Hillhead House, between Hillhead Street and Southpark Avenue. Their plan was for new offices for the administration and the SRC, an art gallery and recreational facilities around a quadrangle with at its centre the Round Reading Room – the only part of the scheme to be constructed because the war intervened. Although the University, with a view to further expansion, began to buy property in Hillhead as it came on the market, the Corporation was reluctant to re-designate domestic property in Hillhead for University use because of Glasgow's chronic housing shortage. With new facilities urgently needed for many departments, Sir Frank Mears, the distinguished Scottish architect, was commissioned in 1949 to reconsider the development of the Hillhead area.

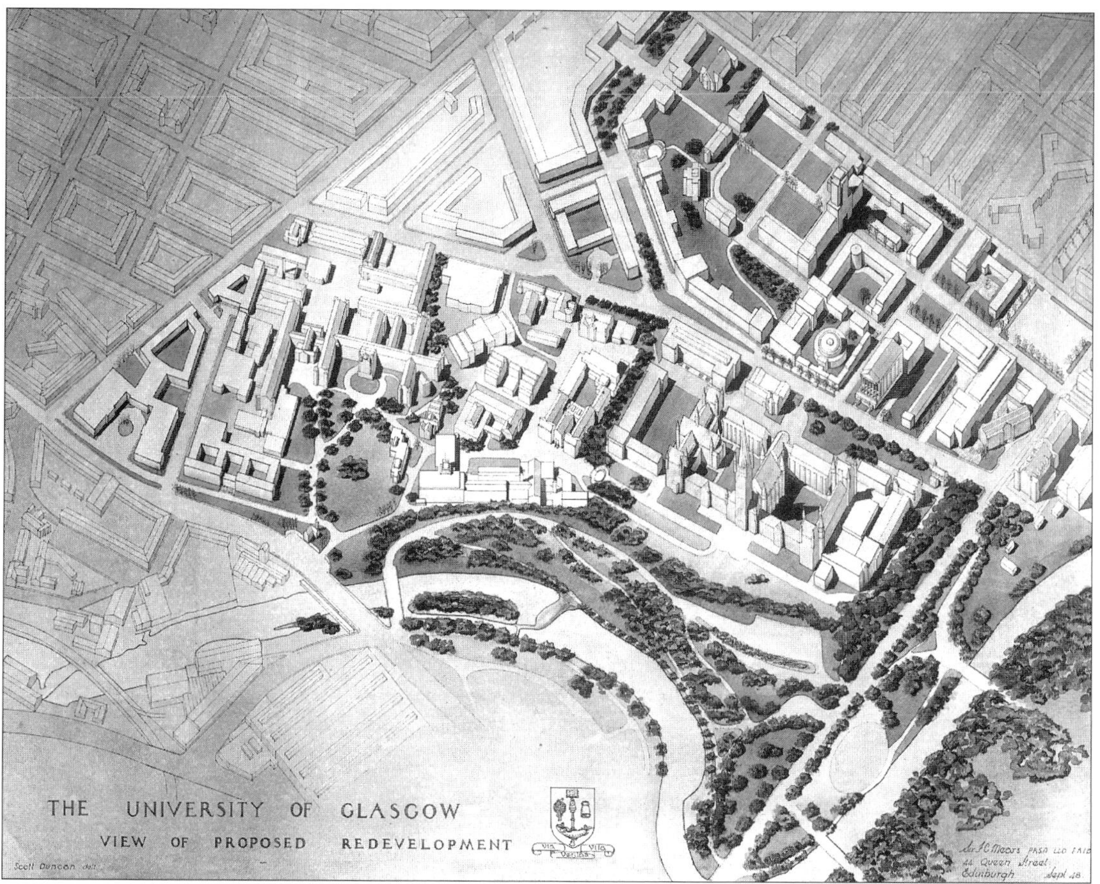

9.1 *Sir Frank Mears' first plan for the development of Hillhead, with only Wellington Church and the old Belmont Church in Great George Street left standing. The plan also proposed the demolition of Professors' Square.*

Submitted in 1951, the Mears plan was intended to provide the framework for new building over the next thirty years. He proposed a much wider scheme to include all the properties in Hillhead in the rectangle bounded by University Avenue, University Gardens, Great George Street and Bank Street with the exception of Wellington Church. The whole area was to be flattened to make way for new buildings for Arts departments and student and staff facilities. Some new buildings were to be incorporated into Gilmorehill, including extensions to the West Medical Building, the conversion of the Principal's Lodging into the College Club, the demolition of the Botany building to make way for a new Mathematics building and an extension on the north front of the Gilbert Scott building to house Geology. To facilitate student access to the library, which until then had been restricted to honours students, a new library was to be built on the north side of the Square, replacing Nos 1–4. In the immediate future the Court decided to continue to purchase houses and tenements in Hillhead between University Avenue and Great George Street as they became available, with a view to eventual demolition. With the completion in 1952 of the current building programme (Chemistry, Natural Philosophy, Surgery and Veterinary Studies) – the largest of any university other than London and Cambridge – it was hoped to construct a physical welfare building, an engineering extension, a women's hall of residence, a biochemistry and physiology extension, an Arts building, and teaching and research blocks at the Royal and Western Infirmaries.[2] This was an ambitious programme largely dependent on government grants which were made a year at a time by the UGC. Very high personal and corporate taxation both of income and capital, which for the wealthy could be over 90 per cent, made it almost impossible to raise benefactions from either individuals or businesses.

Under the UGC's earmarked recurrent grants scheme, which was introduced largely to implement the Goodenough, Teviot and Loveday reports on medical, dental and veterinary education, the main thrust of expansion was, not surprisingly, in the Medical, Dental and Veterinary Schools where staffing levels were 'considerably below optimum point'. The Dental School urgently required to appoint six new lecturers and on completion of the Animal Hospital at Garscube twelve academic staff were to be recruited, along with 'a considerable establishment of technicians and attendants.'[3] Although the number of medical students had been reduced to balance supply and demand, to meet its new responsibilities the Medical Faculty needed to increase the staff in infectious diseases, psychological medicine, child health and obstetrics, pathology, bacteriology and biochemistry. Hetherington had to sacrifice his long-cherished plans to expand the social sciences to give these proposals a fair chance of success. In humanities and science, where earmarked grants were not available, it was intended to strengthen departments by creating new chairs and senior lectureships from the University's own resources.

In responding to the quinquennial bids the UGC and the Treasury had a difficult balancing act, of appearing not to hinder expansion but at the same time to be following the Conservative government's policy of restraining expenditure. The recurrent grants were not announced until late November 1952. In common with other universities, Glasgow received about half the additional revenue requested, with all significant expansion postponed until 1955 to 1957, by which time it was anticipated the economy would have recovered. The earmarked grant scheme was abandoned as impractical in the economic circumstances; universities were given greater flexibility in how they used their recurrent income, but with a general exhortation to 'scientific and technological progress'.[4] Applications for non-recurrent grants for building work in the immediate future were treated harshly. In July 1952 the University submitted bids for an extension to the Engineering Department (£650,000) and for a new Arts building (£116,000). Both were rejected because the building ration allocated to the UGC was so small that only minor works could be approved. Disappointed, but determined that new buildings were an essential condition for expansion, the University pressed ahead with detailed consideration of the Mears development plan. The Buildings Sites Committee of Senate endorsed the plan with some minor objections and a general concern about the lack of an adequate gymnasium and a swimming pool. By 1953 the actual location of three major projects still needed to be resolved: the Library proposed to be built on the north side of Professors' Square, the Picture Gallery, and the Gymnasium. These did not affect the Engineering Extension on the east side of the main building and it was decided to begin work using the University's own resources. The site was cleared of the Chemistry huts and the 'Glastonbury Kitchen' – the original chemistry laboratory – was demolished. It was not until the abolition of building control regulations during 1954 that the UGC was able to release more funds for buildings, and then only on condition that the universities contributed not less than ten per cent of the costs from their own resources. Although Glasgow had no difficulty in making this commitment for the Arts Building in University Gardens to begin in 1956, other Scottish universities were less fortunate and it was agreed that as far as possible universities should not compete with each other for private funds. There were also doubts as to whether commercial sponsors could be found for major infrastructural projects such as libraries and halls of residence. This still left unresolved the financing of the Engineering Extension, now estimated to cost over £745,000. It was not until the foundations had been laid and the steel framework more or less completed in July 1956 that the UGC agreed to meet two-thirds of the cost. By 1960 the University had spent £4.3 million since 1951 on building, of which it had to find £1.4 million – over 32 per cent.

The urgent need for a large addition to the Engineering Department in the early 1950s was to meet the government's continuing call for the development of technological education to improve British competitiveness. Glasgow's

9.2 *The extension for the Engineering Department on the east side of the Scott Building in 1956.*

response was inextricably linked to the future of relations with the Royal Technical College, funded by the UGC since its inception in 1919. With its distinctive range of subjects and its less restrictive entry requirements, the RTC was naturally regarded by the Scottish Education Department (SED) as the main vehicle for expanding applied technological training and research in the west of Scotland. The RTC had well developed plans to expand into new disciplines – textile technology, applied microbiology, food sciences and industrial administration. However the University departments of Chemistry, Engineering and Natural Philosophy did not want to lose out to an institution which was regarded as a poor relation and whose teaching they examined under the terms of the Affiliation Ordinance of 1913 which demanded broadly similar curricula in both institutions, particularly in engineering (see p. 117). The Engineers had already brought forward plans to reform the curricula by giving the Honours degree, taught solely in the University, a very distinct syllabus from that of the Ordinary degree taught in both institutions.

The whole question of re-defining the relationship with the RTC was first raised in 1951 following similar reviews elsewhere and centred ostensibly on proposals for a new degree course in textile technology. There were two choices: either closer cooperation or greater autonomy. Sir Hector Hetherington's natural reaction was to favour the latter, but later under pressure from his colleagues he became more ambivalent. At first he proposed the institution of a new degree, B.Tech., to be awarded to students taking 'the whole or the greater part of their courses at the College'.[5] This would necessitate the creation of a Board of Studies of Technology incorporating all the heads of department at the RTC, operating as a sub-faculty of Science. There were some obvious difficulties with this plan, which would require some RTC staff, including the Director, to become members of the Faculty of Science and the University Senate. The RTC for its part refused even to discuss the plan until the government had announced its intentions for the 'establishment of technological institutions of University rank'[6] following proposals from the Advisory Council on Education in Scotland floated in 1950. It had hopes, encouraged by Churchill's wartime scientific adviser, Lord Cherwell, and the Lord President of the Council, Lord Woolton, of becoming the Imperial College of Scotland. The Conservative government had a different view. On 8 July 1953 R. A. Butler, the Chancellor of the Exchequer, wrote to Sir Hector informing him that the government wished to see the two institutions resolve their difficulties within the framework of the 'policy to develop higher technological education' – 'How the University and the College can best develop their technological work, so as to allow each an adequate degree of freedom and yet to provide for proper coordination, is primarily a matter for the University and the College themselves and HM Government do not wish to make any prior conditions about the methods to be adopted, provided they are effective and agreed'.[7] He made it clear that it would be possible for the RTC to have degree-awarding powers if desired, and ended by threatening the University with a Royal Commission if a settlement could not be achieved. A Joint Advisory Committee was hurriedly convened.

The meetings were tense and confrontational with neither side in a mood to compromise. The University found itself in a difficult position, as Hetherington willingly admitted to Sir Arthur Trueman, Chairman of the UGC:

> The situation is sticky. We do not want an inquiry, which would be a bore and almost certainly unsatisfactory in its outcome. On the other hand, I do not want to concede under the threat of an inquiry, something that seems to me to be intrinsically undesirable . . . Tactically the RTC is in a strong position. It has a lot of political backing, most of it pretty ignorant and quite unaware of the damage that all this can do to the University fabric of this country.[8]

There was much at stake: access to the large funds being made available for higher technology education and research, notably in nuclear sciences, and future relations with Scottish industry and commerce. The RTC, taking the Chancellor at his word, wished degree-giving powers, supervised by a Council on Academic Policy with representatives of all four Scottish universities, along with a Standing Joint Committee with the University of Glasgow to coordinate technological work. This proposal appealed neither to the University nor to the government, which was determined that there should not be two universities in one city. After a visit to Glasgow in June 1954, the UGC unequivocally backed Sir Hector's original scheme for a 'new faculty of Applied Science (or Technology)', with the RTC's degrees being approved by the Glasgow Senate. However, suspecting that the University's attitude to the College was coloured by elitism, the UGC and SED insisted that honours degrees, particularly in engineering, should be taught in both institutions and supervised by the same joint boards of study – 'any distinction between the titles of degrees should be related to the content of the course and not to the institution at which it is studied'.[9] In conveying their views the UGC and SED maintained the pressure by letting it be known that the Chancellor and the Secretary of State for Scotland were being kept informed.

Tired of being forced back on the defensive, the University was adamant that 'there was no good reason for limiting the freedom of either party by compelling both to operate as a single unit'.[10] After stating where compromise would be possible, the University proposed the radical alternative of outright merger with the RTC as the best way forward, but this was 'wholly unacceptable to the College'. Most of the science and engineering professors at Glasgow could see little future in the current negotiations. Professor James Small of Mechanical Engineering, who had taught in both institutions, went so far as to suggest that 'the present Affiliation Ordinance has for forty years been the greatest possible hindrance to the full development of the teaching of applied science in Glasgow'.[11] Despite the government's attitude, the RTC remained committed to independence and was not afraid to seek Cherwell's support in Parliament. After a further year of protracted and fruitless discussion, Sir Hector persuaded Sir Andrew McCance, chairman of the Board of Governors of the RTC, to admit that 'the prime desire of the College was to receive degree-granting powers in Technology'.[12] When it became clear that there would be no change in government policy and the UGC expected a solution, discussions resumed in the summer of 1955. In November the University agreed that a new Faculty of Technology should be formed with powers to award degrees and that membership of the Senate be open to those holding chairs at the RTC on condition that in future they be appointed and paid by the University Court. The RTC was prepared to allow there to be two separate faculties of engineering but wished the new faculty to be of 'Applied Science'. However the Governors were unhappy about the terms for appointments to chairs and refused to ratify the scheme. Their preferred option was now to amend the

Affiliation Ordinance. The University Court was split between those willing to pursue this alternative and those who clung to the idea of a new faculty.

Sir Hector recognised that changing the ordinance, which would only provide a short-term easing of relations, was better than nothing. So as to give each subject greater recognition, he advocated minor modifications and the replacement of the single Joint Board of Studies with two or three Boards – for engineering, other subjects, and architecture. The only drawback to this revised plan was that it did not answer the UGC's objection that there should be no duplication between two degree-awarding institutions in the same city. The University had no doubt that such problems could be solved by joint negotiations. The Senate endorsed the draft amendments, which were approved by the three other Scottish universities before being submitted to the General Council in January 1957. Influenced by Dr Hugh Buchanan, its Court Assessor, the General Council rejected the new ordinance unanimously on the rather specious grounds that it gave the RTC too much freedom. Sir Hector was not going to be brow-beaten at the eleventh hour and recommended the Court to reject the General Council's view. The amended ordinance was approved in September by which time the RTC had, also, changed its name to the Royal College of Science and Technology of Glasgow (RCST).

Always in the background to negotiations with the RCST was the allocation of funds made available by government for the sciences. In 1952 Professor Philip Dee had won a very large grant of £72,500 from the Department of Scientific and Industrial Research (DSIR) to service the 330e MeV electron synchrotron and the Cockroft-Walton high tension accelerator (HT set) being installed in the newly completed extension to the department of Natural Philosophy. The grant provided for five academic and sixteen technical staff to carry out a programme of nuclear research, further strengthening the powerful research team Dee had already built up. When this equipment was commissioned in 1954 Glasgow could once more claim international standing in the physical sciences. In January of that year general bids for technological education and research were invited by the UGC. In framing its proposals the Science Faculty was careful not to trespass on the RTC's territory with the one exception of metallurgy which had been ceded to the College in the 1920s (see p. 179). Emphasis was placed on the biological sciences where important advances were being made at Glasgow in mycology under Sir James William Howie (Bacteriology from 1951), genetics under Guido Pontecorvo (Genetics from 1955), and pharmacology under Norman Davidson (Biochemistry from 1947). All three areas needed modern equipment to compete with other institutions and more space for undergraduate and postgraduate work. Imaginatively Dee proposed the creation of a biological and chemical physics unit within his department to exploit the potential of innovative nuclear

9.3 *The extension to the Department of Natural Philosophy to house the synchrotron under construction in 1949.*

techniques, including X-ray crystallography and the use of radioactive tracers and their derivatives. These units would also service the important research initiatives of Ralph Alexander Raphael (Chemistry from 1957) and Sir Maurice Yonge (Zoology from 1944). Most of the science and engineering departments wanted ready access to a large computer 'such as has been developed in various centres in England' but not in Scotland.[13]

A large section of Glasgow's submission was taken up by a request to support industrial management training, building on a part-time evening course for those in business launched in 1952 by Professor Alec Cairncross of the Department of Social and Economic Research and Professor Robert Browning of Accountancy. They had decided to provide post-experience training in skills like cost accounting and methods of market analysis, and in theoretical subjects such as industrial psychology and sociology. When 170 applications were received from a hundred firms for thirty places, it was decided to run two twenty-week courses supplemented by weekend schools. Although the course was originally intended to be for a year, it was immediately extended at the request of the students to three. By 1954 there were a hundred management students. Cairncross and Browning did not wish to set up a School of Management on the model of other universities – and the RTC – but they sought funds to support 'an element of technical stiffening' through the creation of a chair of production engineering.[14] While making it clear that it had no intention of trespassing on the RTC's territory, the University was sufficiently enthusiastic to underwrite the chair for the remainder of the quinqennium on condition that the UGC met the cost from 1957.

A UGC decision was delayed for a year, largely because of the slow progress of negotiations with the RTC. All the Glasgow bids were accepted apart from mechanical engineering, metallurgy, the biological and chemical physics unit and industrial management. The UGC considered that further progress in nuclear physics was more a matter for DSIR than its higher technology programme. The reservation about a chair in production engineering stemmed from the reported difficulty other universities had encountered in filling such posts rather than any doubts about the utility of the University's initiative. Not to be thwarted, in 1958 a full-time one-session Certificate in Industrial Administration was introduced aimed at both recent graduates and managers in post. Although the course was designed to allow managers to develop their careers, the response from industry was not encouraging and there was an impression that recent graduates simply enrolled having failed to find a job.

Glasgow's bid for a regional computing centre to be used by other institutions and local industry was supported in principle by the UGC and referred to DSIR. Delighted, John Gunn, Cargill Professor of Theoretical Physics, and Robert Rankin, Professor of Mathematics, recently recruited from the chair at Birmingham, quickly set about fleshing out a proposal. Within weeks they visited Manchester University to inspect the Manchester Electronic Computer (Mark 1), designed by Professor F. C. Williams and Dr Alan Turing and built by Ferranti; and Cambridge to see the EDZAC computer – the first in Britain – built by Dr Wilkes. Both these machines were already being used by Glasgow chemists and physicists. Like many others they were impressed with what they saw. They had, however, no illusion about the difficulties of setting up a centre in Glasgow. The computer was very large; it had ideally to be housed in an airconditioned environment to prevent overheating; it required constant supervision as well as maintenance. Electronic engineers and mathematicians were needed both to write programmes and update libraries of 'routines'; qualified staff, particularly at senior level, were understandably in short supply. The estimated cost of a new Ferranti Mark II computer was £55,000 and the annual running costs over £20,000. Encouraged by the funds Manchester was able to attract from local industry, Glasgow believed that there would be little difficulty in raising £10,000 towards the capital cost. Professor Williams offered Rankin and Gunn first refusal for their Mark I machine when the new Mark II was installed early in 1956. In the autumn of 1955, following a report by Sir David Brunt, the UGC assumed responsibility for financing computer centres on the understanding that a proportion of the costs would be met from outside users. In the following spring the UGC confirmed the offer to Glasgow of the now obsolete Manchester Mark I machine. This was refused, mainly because the University was unable to identify a building big enough to house it.

It was decided instead to buy a Ferranti Mark II (Mercury) computer, now estimated to cost £90,000, to be housed within the Chemistry department. The UGC indicated that matching funds would be provided as it was anticipated half the running time would be available for commercial work. By the late 1950s Clydeside industry was finding it increasingly difficult to compete with the resurgent economies in Europe and the University found fundraising on this scale hard. There was no doubt that numerical processing was vital for a modern successful shipbuilding and engineering industry, but Clydeside firms had become wary of any new investment in plant. As a result the appeal only secured promises of about £17,000 from ten companies – and one later withdrew. Characteristically the largest contributions came from G. & J. Weir and Barr & Stroud, both of which were heavily dependent on defence contracts. Worse still for the University, the cost of the installation had risen to £120,000 within a year. To the disappointment of many of the scientists who had hoped Glasgow would have facilities comparable with Cambridge and Manchester, there was no alternative but to opt for a smaller less powerful machine. An English Electric DEUCE – Digital Electronic Universal Computing Engine – computer (costing £65,000) was chosen in preference to a Ferranti Pegasus. Meanwhile the post of director of the Computer Laboratory had been advertised and Dr Denis Gilles appointed. When the decision had been taken, the RCST (too late in the day) asked to the University's surprise on what terms access would be provided since they had just appointed a computational mathematician. The Computer Laboratory became operational on 4 November 1958 and was officially opened on 2 February 1959 by Lord Halsbury, the chairman of the National Research Development Corporation. It was only the third computer in Scotland and the first in a University.

However from its inception the DEUCE lacked the power to be a useful research tool and within a year an application was being prepared for a replacement English Electric KDF9 machine, costing over £250,000. No sooner had the bid been submitted in the autumn of 1960 than Edinburgh responded with a proposal that a high-speed time-sharing Ferranti Atlas computer (costing £½ million) should be purchased jointly by all the Scottish universities. The Atlas was to be located on a suitable site with line communications to each university's computing laboratory. This proposal found no

9.4 *The console of the newly installed DEUCE computer, 1958.*

favour. However it did result in the establishment of a Joint Technical Study Group by the Conference of University Courts which concluded that 'any large scale computing facilities should be made equally available to all the Scottish Universities'.[15] The UGC awarded a grant of £225,000 towards the cost of the KDF9, on the understanding it would be available to St Andrews and the RCST, and offered Edinburgh a second-hand Pegasus. The KDF9, with a lower specification than planned because of the reduced budget, was finally installed early in 1964.

The long and heated debate about relations with the RCST was not simply concerned with technological training and scientific research. It was rooted in what was meant by a university education. Time and again the University returned to the problem of validating degrees of students who had never studied at Gilmorehill, and to concern at the concept of non-university degree-granting institutions. The criticism by Professor Small of the Affiliation Ordinance (see p. 249) centred on a widespread belief that it encouraged the cramming of RCST students for degree exams 'fatally narrowing to the undergraduate's reading in his subject'.[16] Sir Hector went further in a personal letter to Sir Keith Murray, the chairman of the UGC, when discussing the RCST ambition to become a degree-awarding institution:

> We have a notion that graduates of a University ought to spend some time in the place, and have some chance to learn what it is and is trying to do . . . This infidelity to the real meaning of a University degree is by far the worst element in the present situation: and we do not feel any happier about it because it has come about by our own act of forty years ago . . . But of course we do not really believe in this variant of a technological University [a reference to the RCST], either on national or on local grounds . . . And inevitably, this would be the beginning of a radical change in the British University system. Maybe the change is coming anyhow. I sometimes wonder if in these necessitarium days, the whole notion of a 'University', a *studium generale*, is not falling into decay. But I hope it will last my time.[17]

This view of what an undergraduate experience should be was heavily coloured, as it had been in the past, by the problems the Appointments Committee had encountered in finding jobs for graduates because of their lack of all-round education. For this reason Sir Hector remained deeply opposed to the admission to the Committee of Vice Chancellors and Principals of 'Non-U' institutions of higher education funded by the UGC, such as the RCST. Writing towards the end of his career to his close friend Harold Dodds, President of Princeton, he singled out engineers and medicals as lacking a broad liberal education in their curriculum, even when taught in British universities. 'But outside the Faculty of Arts (and not always there), there is little in this country to encourage the notion that liberal studies are central to a genuine University experience'.[18] He knew from the Appointments Committee that this gave Oxbridge graduates with their collegiate system an enormous advantage in the jobs market.

Knowing the consequences, in his annual addresses to first year students Sir Hector repeatedly spelled out this creed, telling them that they were students not pupils and that it was:

> nobody's business to stand over you to make you work . . . Read for yourself and read big important books: not digests or snippets . . . Read round your subject and outside it altogether. Don't keep your eyes fixed only on the next exam . . . Examiners are much better pleased to see some evidence of independent reading and thinking than to see their own lecture notes.[19]

Unfortunately in many departments (with the notable exception of social sciences) the teaching, itself, rarely lived up to this ideal. Hetherington was also at pains to emphasise that being an undergraduate demanded social contact outside the classroom – in the unions, in clubs and in societies. These addresses were permeated with the philosophy of a liberal university education and echoed the views of the UGC:

> Many university students will come to hold senior positions of responsibility in the various walks of life which they will enter. If they are to acquit themselves well in these positions they will need more than the specialised knowledge provided by their undergraduate course. They will need to become educated men and women.[20]

This was by now the accepted view of the function of a university, rooted in 'idealism' and the views expressed by Cardinal Newman and Wilhelm von Humboldt. Such an outlook had significant implications at Glasgow for the provision of library space and the encouragement of corporate life through communal areas, student unions and sports halls. It also raised questions about standards of entry and demanded a style of teaching that would encourage independent reading and thinking – tutorial groups, reading parties and subject based student clubs.

The greatest obstacle in translating Sir Hector's vision of what a university education should be into a reality at Glasgow was the continuing high percentage of undergraduates living at home – the so-called 'brown-baggers' who attended from 9 to 5, if that. Students who were involved in the Students' Representative Council, the Unions and the Athletic Club – an estimated 12 per cent – were aware of the problem. All the University's student facilities were inadequate. Students repeatedly drew the UGC's attention to the need to extend or rebuild both unions, to construct a new library with more seating capacity, provide far more playing fields and to build modern halls of residence. From the students' perspective better facilities could only be used effectively if grants were sufficient to meet more than basic expenses: 'it is cheaper to go home and eat there. Corporate life of any kind seems to be expensive'.[21] For most students University was simply an extension of school, dull and monotonous and still firmly centred on their home, family and childhood friends. The pattern of life was lectures in the morning in uncomfortable nineteenth-century lecture halls, lunch in one of the unions, if they could afford it, followed by laboratories or study in the Reading Room and return home for supper. Although segregation in classes and the Reading Room had been abolished in 1951, men and women still kept themselves apart. Few minded, as for most a university education in the long term was a well-trodden path to social advancement and an escape route out of the west of Scotland.

9.5 *The Freshers' Camp at Auchendennan, 1950/1, with Sir Hector and Lady Hetherington.*

In 1953 the Scottish Union of Students scored a notable victory in persuading SED to raise grants by 60 per cent on the grounds that 'the traditional Scottish lad o' pairts independence is in this modern world a convenient myth'.[22] However this still left the level of maintenance grants in Scotland far behind that in England. Moreover it was determined on an entirely different basis. In England the Ministry of Education fixed the whole grant; whereas in Scotland SED only fixed the cost of accommodation and a clothing allowance, leaving local authorities individually to determine the cost of travel, books and equipment, and subscriptions to unions and clubs and societies. Unlike England there was also no allowance for study in the vacation. Because of this, capitation fees to fund student organisations at Glasgow were about half those at English universities, making it difficult to generate income to pay for improved facilities. It was recognised that higher grants and better funding were not of themselves enough: 'Apathy has other causes than the No 14 Tram. University life, work and society has to be more attractive than the pictures [cinema] or his youth club to the student who lives at home, and has, therefore, just added another facet to his life, instead of having his total existence revolutionised . . .'.[23] There was a genuine sense that the corporate life of the University had been steadily eroded since the beginning of the century and was badly in need of a revival if Glasgow students were going to be equipped to compete for jobs elsewhere in the United Kingdom. The response of the SRC to this issue was to engage in a debate about the governance of the University, which was in the hands of the lay members of Court and its professorial senate assessors, with only the Rector representing student opinion. Many members of the SRC believed that formal representation of students on the Court and Senate was desirable and would help to enrich the undergraduate experience, preventing the University 'becoming a technological desert'.[24] A change came when elected non-professorial staff joined the Court, in 1966 and made common cause with more progressive professors and General Council assessors such as Sydney Checkland (Economic History from 1957) and the Reverend Johnston McKay to raise contentious issues. In any case by this time many of the old guard of professors were nearing the end of their careers.

Despite Sir Hector's challenge to students not simply to regurgitate lecture notes, the curriculum continued to be dominated by lectures. A student commented in GUM in 1956:

> Come with me to the back of one of the lecture-rooms in the Scott buildings, and sit through the discourse of Mr X, lecturer in Y. He is rather a tired man. His lectures have changed little over a decade; his voice can scarcely be heard by the foot-stampers in the back row. He drones on at nearly dictation speed. His material is almost completely factual, there is no suspicion of inspiration in his delivery or his subject matter. Mr X is, in fact, a complete damper of any enthusiasm his students may have in their hearts at the outset of his course.

The author claimed that most lectures were of a poor standard and that 'degree examinations require verbatim reproduction of what is delivered, with all the special points of the lecturer'.[25] It was proposed that lectures should be replaced by tutorials and seminars where there would be closer staff/student contact. For most students such tutorials as there were, were either in large groups or perfunctorily brief. Another proposal was to revive the 'regenting' system whereby a member of staff acted as 'guide, philosopher and friend' to a group of undergraduates. Sir Keith Murray, the Chairman of the UGC, drew attention during the 1956 visitation to the need for more support for first and second year students, because drop-out rates were unacceptably high (over 15 per cent).[26] The University did not need to be reminded of the gap between the ideal and the reality. In 1959 the Glasgow Association of Lecturers and Assistants was so concerned about the problem that they presented a memorandum to the Principal and Senate calling for attention to the large first year classes 'where too many students seem to have no desire to gain anything from the University other than the right to say they have a university degree'.[27] The Association wanted more tutorial work where 'contacts between staff and students come most naturally', and easier social access to staff, with no segregation in refectory areas.[28] Apart from regenting, which had been tried recently and failed, the Senate, consisting largely of professors who had never experienced tutorial teaching, had no simple answers. Although staff/student ratios were improving, it was unlikely there would ever be sufficient staff or space to maintain a tutorial system in anything other than the Honours classes. In any case staff were increasingly expected to devote time to their research, which in turn would feed into Honours teaching and attract postgraduate students. Efforts were made through advisers in studies to help first and second year students who were experiencing difficulties; but the overall impression of many senior staff was that a large proportion of Ordinary degree students lacked both the ability and aptitude for serious university study. Enterprisingly the Medical Faculty introduced a system of moral tutors whereby each member of staff was assigned six students.

An attractive response for members of the Senate to high drop-out rates and criticism of teaching, especially in the large Ordinary class lectures, was to restrict entry and encourage more students to take Honours. The prudence of such an approach seemed to be confirmed by the results of an investigation into the school qualifications of undergraduates suspended for lack of progress, which showed that the majority had only scraped through their Highers. Consequently a certificate of fitness to enter university from the Scottish Universities Entrance Board continued not to be an automatic qualification for admission to Glasgow. The Science Faculty demanded a high standard in Mathematics, and Arts required a 'reasonable competence' in a language other than English. During the early 1950s, although the number of suitably qualified applicants to Science was consistently ten per cent below the spaces available, standards of entry improved; those in Arts declined, due largely according to the Faculty to inadequate language teaching in schools. This claim, which became a mantra, overlooked the fact that nearly all secondary school teachers in the west of Scotland had been taught at Glasgow. If blame was to be apportioned, the University's language departments deserve their fair share for placing undue weight on literature rather than language. Glasgow's entry requirements were criticised in the national press in the autumn of 1955 when the parents of two Airdrie boys complained that their sons had been turned down despite having sufficient Highers. The grounds for rejection were their lack of competence in French, but this did not prevent Edinburgh admitting both students immediately afterwards. To Glasgow's annoyance the matter was referred to the Secretary of State by the MP for Airdrie and Coatbridge, Mrs Jean Mann. The Secretary of State was unequivocal in declaring in Parliament that admissions policy was a matter for a university and not subject in individual cases to external scrutiny. Public criticism of the University's entry requirements in Arts, which extended to the need to pass 'Lower' Latin even to read for an Ordinary degree, was only fuelled by this response. Undaunted, the Arts Faculty refused to relax its requirements. (At this time an Ordinary MA degree required at least an Ordinary pass in a language class and the Arts Faculty used this to insist on Latin and a modern language pass at Higher school standard.) Nevertheless it found it impossible to peg its first year entry at 400, being forced to take about 10 per cent more suitably qualified students. Even in Science admissions increased from 286 in 1955 to 392 by 1959. A further review at the end of the 1950s reinforced the belief that those who did poorly in Highers did badly at university. This showed that of the 1951 intake 18.6 per cent had not graduated by 1958 and that of all students suspended because of lack of progress less than 16 per cent ever graduated. This analysis was not universally shared. Barbara Napier, the Adviser to Women Students, in an independent review of all female students, questioned whether the existing entry criteria could be used to predict performance in finals.[29] Throughout these years the ratio of men to women at the University remained almost unchanged at about 80 to 20, slightly adverse to the national average. This can be largely explained by the greater opportunities for good school education for men in the west of Scotland at the time. By the end of the decade school education for women and Roman Catholics was improving but this would not be reflected in admissions until the 1960s.

Restricted entry did not lead as anticipated to an increase in the number of students in Arts taking Honours degrees. As before the war it remained at below 25 per cent. Even more unexpected was a sharp fall in the number of Honours students taking first class degrees from 25 to 11 per cent in the mid-1950s, prompting the University to commission an enquiry. A comparative analysis revealed that Glasgow alone of all the Scottish universities had pruned entry to Arts. In the other universities an increase in numbers had been matched by a growth in Honours degrees and an improvement in quality. Before the 1939 war Glasgow had twice as many firsts as Edinburgh, now it had less than half. There seemed to be many possible explanations, including poor university teaching. More compelling was the retention by Glasgow of the two-subject requirement for Honours, which had been replaced elsewhere by single Honours, arguably making a Glasgow Honours degree more difficult. It was, also, all too readily believed that the standard of teaching in schools in the west of Scotland, a consequence of wartime disruption, was to blame – a theme Sir Hector returned to regularly throughout the 1950s. Although lack of funding was partly responsible, there was also a shortage of qualified graduate staff capable of teaching to Higher level, especially in English and Mathematics as many graduates left the west of Scotland after their experience in the armed services. This in turn led to discussion, with prompting from SED, of the universities' role in teacher training and their relationships with the colleges. Edinburgh wanted closer relations while Glasgow preferred to leave things as they were. Little was done. There remained an unanswered question over the Ordinary degree – still the principal route into the teaching profession in secondary schools in the west. If Glasgow restricted admissions in the Arts Faculty, how could the demand for graduate teachers in the west of Scotland be met and standards raised at a time when it was widely recognised there was a general shortage of graduates? Disturbingly, some of the students excluded by the entry qualifications were in receipt of grants under the Special Recruitment Scheme for Teachers administered by the National Committee for the Training of Teachers.

Until the end of the decade there was no serious consideration within the Faculties or the Senate about the possibility of a large expansion in student places in Scotland on similar lines to proposals south of the Border. It was argued even by SED that the problem was much less pressing in Scotland. The birth-rate had not accelerated as rapidly as in England during and after the war and the proportion of pupils leaving school at fifteen to work was higher than in England. Moreover participation rates in higher education in Scotland, as Attlee had pointed out at the time of the Fifth Centenary, had always been greater than in the rest of the United Kingdom. Nonetheless, heroic efforts were being made to encourage Scottish pupils to remain at school – additional bursaries in 1953, family allowance up to eighteen for school pupils in 1955, a well-directed promotional campaign and a review of the curriculum. As a result the percentage of students completing a five-year course at school in Scotland (at least a year less than in England) rose from 26 per cent (6,000) in 1952 to almost 35.5 per cent (8,661) in 1960. Typically the University's response was to suspect a decline in standards and to stand out against reform in entrance qualifications agreed by the other Scottish universities in 1958 following a review of the curriculum in secondary schools. Glasgow's main objection was to the Entrance Board's replacement of Higher with Lower or Ordinary English, providing the candidate had a Higher pass in a foreign language, and the acceptance of three Highers for a certificate of fitness. The University, the Educational Institute of Scotland and the Association of University Teachers appealed to the Privy Council. In presenting Glasgow's case Hetherington deplored the decline in the standard of students' English: 'There is hardly anything of which more complaint is made by teachers of all faculties than the untidiness in the speaking and writing of English'.[30] The Committee of the Privy Council, chaired by Lord Reid and meeting in the National Library of Scotland, rejected the appeal on the grounds that the other three universities had accepted the change, leaving Glasgow as in the past to set its own entry criteria. Although Hetherington's attitude to reforming entry requirements was consistent, it did not chime with the mood of the times nor did it take account of potential students, particularly Roman Catholics and women, who through no fault of their own lacked an adequate school education. He was aware of this, and Barbara Napier's review raised doubts in his mind about the wisdom of Glasgow's admissions policy, but he was nearing retirement and did not relish a confrontation with Fordyce and his barons in the Faculty of Arts.

It was simpler to attribute Glasgow's lack of enthusiasm for increasing numbers to the apparent lack of space for further development. In 1957 the Senate under pressure from the Faculty of Arts resolved that there should be no further expansion, to preserve 'what remains of open spaces and other amenities on the Gilmorehill site'.[31] The Engineers and Scientists, who favoured expansion, still wanted better accommodation if they were to admit more students. As Sir Hector was first to admit, the building programme 'advanced somewhat creakily' in the 1950s due largely to the shortage of funds.[32] The demand from the UGC that Glasgow find part of the cost for a computer was only an expression of a policy shift in the mid-1950s away from total reliance on the Treasury towards greater dependence on other sources of funding. As the fundraising for the computer demonstrated it was difficult to find suitable benefactors in the west of Scotland. The other source of income was student fees, which the Chancellor of the Exchequer demanded should be increased to bring their contribution to university finances up from twelve per cent in 1953 to the pre-war level of twenty-four per cent . Any increase in fees automatically impinged on student grants and the willingness of parents to pay. More parents paid for their children's education in Scotland than in England. The Scottish universities were required to act together in setting fees. When the question was discussed at the meeting of Courts in December 1954 Aberdeen refused to give in to government demands. After a year of discussion fees were raised across the board by six per cent; but at the same time the level and extent of existing grant provision by local authorities in Scotland were questioned.

There was disquiet at the method used by the SED in calculating the level of Educational Authority Awards which failed to take into account the 'real cost' of a university course. In England a student living at home received a grant of £156 a year compared to an average of £93 in Scotland and a parent earning £1,600 after allowances made a contribution of £172 in England compared to £326 in Scotland. All the Scottish universities wanted the system of local authority awards replaced by state scholarships from SED. In the mistaken belief that the Goschen formula (on which the Scottish Office budget was calculated) was responsible for the unfavourable situation in Scotland no formal complaint was made until 1957, when a committee chaired by Professor Edward Wright of Aberdeen was formed to take up the matter. Pushing at an open door the Wright Committee negotiated improvements in the level of grants, the introduction of a vacation allowance, and a substantial revision in the level of parental contributions and the means-test scale. In June 1958 the government appointed a Committee on Grants to Students chaired by Sir Colin Anderson. Wright was appointed as Scottish representative with A. Dingwall-Smith as SED observer. The Committee reported in 1960 and its recommendation of a system of universal means-tested student grants, administered in Scotland by SED, was introduced in 1961. Under the new system there was no difference in grants between

Scotland and England and students were free to study in either country. These two reforms had a dramatic effect on the number of students in Scotland in receipt of state support, rising from just under 62 per cent to over 83 per cent. Despite their significance they attracted no comment from the Glasgow student press. As there was now no barrier to students attending universities away from home, it became more imperative than ever for Glasgow to build new residences and provide better communal facilities. Moreover since any student with a Scottish Universities' Entrance Board certificate of fitness was entitled to a grant, it would be much more difficult for a university to justify restricted entry. The University feared that in these circumstances better students would be encouraged by their teachers 'to take advantage of the chance to have their University experience elsewhere than in their home environment'.[33] Nevertheless it was another twelve years, and only after Strathclyde had shown the way, before the Senate agreed to introduce 'an annual conference for schools . . . with the aim of informing school pupils about the nature and content of University courses in Arts, particularly (but not exclusively) in those subjects not commonly taught in schools.'[34] Following the success of this initiative, the first 'Open Day' for schools covering all faculties was held in 1976.

When the UGC visited the University in 1956 the lack of adequate provision for student life was emphasised – 'We have no proper student residences at all . . . we now feel severely the want of this accommodation. Everything else – Unions, playing fields, gymnasium, refectory – was designed for a much smaller University. They are now quite inadequate . . .'[35] Shortly afterwards the UGC announced a grant of £102,000 towards the estimated cost of £232,000 of a Physical Education building. Unable to find £130,000 from the University's own resources, Sir Hector approached the remaining trustees of the estate of Sir Daniel Macaulay Stevenson, of whom he himself was one. After much bargaining he was able to persuade them to make over the residue of the estate, more than covering the difference. In the quinquennial estimates for 1957–62 two halls of residence – one for women and one for men – extensions to the unions, a refectory and other student facilities accounted for almost half of the building budget of £2 million. The only other major projects were a new building for physiology and biochemistry and a further extension to natural philosophy to be funded on a Technological grant. Although a new library and veterinary school at Garscube were recognised as essential they were left over to the next quinquennium but with agreement that planning work could begin. On the understanding that there would be 6,000 students by 1966, the UGC, its budget frozen by another period of restraint, could only allocate £1.5 million to the building programme to which the University had to contribute at least £100,000. The approved programme, delayed until the beginning of the 1960s, included a refectory, an extension to the Men's Union, a new Women's Union, and a women's hall of residence, along with new

9.6 *The swimming pool in the newly opened Stevenson building, 1961.*

buildings for biochemistry, mathematics and fine art. Some projects, which had already been approved as part of the Technology Programme – for example experimental high speed wind tunnels – were postponed indefinitely. It was estimated that the approved works would cost £2 million excluding professional fees and equipment, leaving a shortfall of £600,000 to be found by the University. When the final budgets were discussed early in 1961 the UGC raised its allocation to £1.75 million, which because of increases in building costs left the University with an even larger shortfall. Glasgow was 'not merely disappointed but outraged' with this outcome, believing with the other Scottish universities that funds were being diverted to expanding the system in England.[36] The large contribution made to building projects in the 1950s left the University very short of capital. Moreover the bulk of its free capital was invested in medium-term government stocks which had recently fallen heavily in value due to uncertainties about the government's ability to control inflation. If losses on realisation were to be avoided, the only ways forward were either to borrow from the banks at high rates of interest – something

Sir Hector had always refused to do – or choose projects where it might be possible to raise outside funds. On this basis the Fine Art building was abandoned and an experimental test tank for Naval Architecture supported. As with the computer, it proved very difficult and time-consuming to raise the hoped-for £30,000 from the Clyde shipbuilding industry.

Planning for this delayed building programme began in 1957. The new women's hall of residence to replace Queen Margaret Hall in Lilybank House was to be situated a mile from the University in Kirklee on the site of the Bellshaugh Bleachfield, with accommodation for 150 students in the first instance and the potential for doubling its size. Because the site was surrounded by some of the finest nineteenth-century housing in Glasgow, the Corporation suggested that the building should be faced with stone, adding an extra £30,000 to the estimated cost. The UGC refused to sanction this proposal and as a compromise the ground floor was of stone and the upper storeys of brick and concrete. Even then local residents and the feu superior complained about the intrusive design of the building in a residential neighbourhood. Since all the ground had been artificially made up, the foundations had to be piled adding another £25,000 to the cost. In the event the UGC was only willing to give £270,000 out of a total estimate of almost £300,000, which when tenders were finally received in 1961 had risen to £433,000 – later reduced to £357,000. Such planning problems and related increases in costs bedevilled University development in the 1960s.

Directly it became clear that only the women's residence would be funded, Sir Hector approached the Wolfson Foundation for a grant to build a men's residence at Garscube. Isaac Wolfson had started his retail career in Glasgow and retained an affinity with the city. After lengthy negotiations, the Foundation made a grant of £300,000 in February 1959. Determined that this new hall should be an architectural showpiece, the University decided to hold a closed competition on the model of the plans for Churchill College, Cambridge. Nine architectural practices – three from Glasgow, three from Edinburgh, and one each from Liverpool, Newcastle and Preston – were invited to submit schemes for a fee of £300. The competition was adjudicated by Professor Robert H. Matthew of the Edinburgh School of Architecture. He chose a design submitted by Grenfell Baines and Hargreaves of Preston, which he described as 'compact and interesting in its variety of shape'. Private funding had its price. From the design stage the Principal had to keep the Wolfson Foundation informed and re-assured not just about the scheme but about all the affairs of the University.

The prospect of better student facilities made it possible to contemplate a faster rate of expansion in the 1960s when the post-war bulge reached school-leaving age. The findings of the Anderson Committee negated all the old arguments about lower birth-rates in the west of Scotland, and Glasgow could now draw undergraduates from the whole of Scotland, indeed from the

9.7 *Laying of the foundation stone of Wolfson Hall, 1962. In the front row is Sir Hector Hetherington. On the far left, Professor Christian Fordyce, Clerk of Senate.*

whole of the United Kingdom. Moreover, with the success of the campaign to persuade pupils to stay longer at school, SED in 1959 revised its estimates of the university population in the 1960s upwards from some 20,000 to over 25,000. The UGC wished to know urgently how universities would cope with demand. Glasgow was split over the question of whether demand in the 1960s would represent a bulge or lead to sustained growth. The Arts Faculty, wishing to believe the problem would be temporary, continued to favour the *status quo* of limiting entry to 400 a year. A whole battery of arguments was advanced in defence of this entrenched attitude: shortage of suitably qualified teachers, lack of space, the poor performance of many students, lack of suitable students and so on. A sharp rise in the Scottish birth-rate in the late 1950s, above most other western European countries, suggested the Arts Faculty was mistaken. Although all were agreed that expansion on the restricted Gilmorehill site was undesirable, those who believed numbers would rise steadily to 9,000 by 1970 advocated radical solutions. There were four proposals: the establishment of a first or first and second year mainly residential college in Ayrshire or Stirling; the provision of junior or sixth form colleges and the reduction of the degree course to three years; the division of the Universities of Glasgow and Edinburgh into two or more constituent colleges; and the establishment of a new university in Scotland on the model of those being set up in England, as well as giving the RCST and Heriot Watt university status. Each idea had its supporters both within and outside the University. The progressive Glasgow Association of Lecturers and Assistants favoured a new university, while the majority of those committed to expansion preferred the construction on another site of a first and second year college, which might eventually achieve degree-awarding status. Sir Hector privately sympathised with this latter point of view. Neither of these plans found favour with the Court or Senate, which wanted modest expansion to say 6,500 by the mid-1960s on condition that the Mears plan for developing Hillhead as part of the campus was approved and funds for further new buildings, particularly the Library and a Social Science building, were forthcoming. The students endorsed this policy with the added proviso that more halls of residence were constructed. Before any conclusion could be reached, the question of university expansion was thrown open to scrutiny by the government's appointment early in 1961 of the Committee on Higher Education under the chairmanship of Lord Robbins, Director of the London School of Economics, to investigate the whole system and make recommendations about long-term expansion. The Scottish representatives were Sir David Anderson, who had recently retired as Director of the RCST, Professor James Drever, professor of Psychology at the University of Edinburgh and H. H. Donnelly of SED. By the autumn of 1961 the Committee had engendered widespread public interest, taking the issue entirely out of the control of the universities into the unfamiliar territory of the press and the media.

In common with the other Scottish universities, Glasgow attracted most publicity, usually unfavourable, at times of Rectorial elections with their traditional 'fight' between the supporters of the candidates for possession of the east door at the front of the main building and high-spirited behaviour at installations. There were three Rectors between 1951 and 1962: Dr Tom Honeyman, the recently retired Director of Glasgow Museums (1953), R. A. Butler the Home Secretary (1956), and Lord Hailsham (1959). Elections took place by tradition at the beginning of a session on a Saturday in October or November. After a car was wrecked and two students injured in the 1953 fight, the students agreed in exchange for moving the rectorial election to a weekday to abandon the fight and hold a secret ballot. This reform resulted in higher turnouts with 57 per cent of students voting in the Butler election, compared with less than 35 per cent in Honeyman's. Despite the efforts of members of the SRC and warnings from the University authorities, installations in the downtown St

9.8 *The last Rectorial fight for possession of the door to the east quadrangle, 1953.*

Andrew's Hall were boisterous. At Honeyman's, 'the arrival of the dignitaries was greeted with howls, fireworks, bugles and balloon bombs'.[37] The speech was punctuated by heckling and the premature playing of the National Anthem. Three years later Butler and the platform party were shied with fruit, eggs and bags of flour and soot. Undaunted and wreathed in toilet paper the new Rector spoke on over the hub-bub of bugles and even an impromptu jazz band. The world press was full of pictures of a flour- and soot-spattered Butler in his Rector's gown. Sir Hector, angrily and uncharacteristically, rebuked newspaper reporters for encouraging the riot. This prompted a vicious response. The editorial in *The Times*, under the headline 'Teddy Boys in Cap and Gown', declared 'If Scottish undergraduates are such exhibitionists that they throw decency to the winds when they know that their behaviour will be reported, then the sooner higher education stays south of the Tweed the better'.[38] The University was inundated with letters of protest to Sir Hector's obvious distress. He commented bitterly on 'the fruits of a good many years work undone by such senseless and unmannerly behaviour'.[39] Although Professor Fordyce, the Clerk of Senate, suspected a conspiracy led by

James S. Gordon (the President of the University Union) the Disciplinary Committee could find no evidence to support such a contention and imposed fines rather than rustication. Despite his irritation, Hetherington was unwilling to support Fordyce's draconian proposal to close the Men's Union at 6 o'clock for the remainder of the term. A consequence of the fracas was the refusal of the Corporation to allow the St Andrew's Hall to be used again. Hailsham's installation was a well-policed ticket-only ceremony in the Bute Hall, marking the end of the old-style Rectorials. Sir Hector made no bones about his dislike of the power of the Rectors. Heading off the possible candidacy in 1959 of Billy Butlin, the holiday camp pioneer, he commented to General Sir Harold Redman – 'The Rector is by statute the Chairman of the University Court which is the governing body of the University so the system has all the merits of a situation in which the shipyard apprentices elect the Chairman of the Board of the Shipyard'.[40] Although Hetherington dealt with such entrepreneurs regularly in his work for the Thuron awards and the Nuffield Trust, and in advising them on the education of their sons and daughters, he did not want them chairing the Court.

Student behaviour at Rectorials was in marked contrast to the tenor of day-to-day student activity in the SRC, the Unions, and clubs and societies. Throughout the 1950s the students who participated in the life of the University took their duties seriously, perhaps at times too seriously. In 1961 they solemnly overturned a decision to buy two copies of D. H. Lawrence's *Lady Chatterley's Lover* – then the subject of a pornography trial – for the Union Library. There were regular discussions about the need to improve standards of debate and there was admiration for undergraduates such as Donald Dewar, James Gordon, Andrew Kennedy, Donald and Neil MacCormick, Menzies Campbell, Dickson Mabon and John Smith whose skills repeatedly won for Glasgow the Observer Mace for inter-university debating. The appearance and content of the *Glasgow University Magazine* remained the same with the re-use of tired vignettes drawn years before. A new tabloid newspaper, the *Glasgow University Guardian*, was launched in 1959. Although the content was more topical, concerned with elections to the SRC and Union Boards and sport, its editorial policy was unadventurous. Much of the comment in both publications supported the University's own very cautious approach to change, for example in defending the notion of a 'liberal' university through restricting numbers. The SRC evidence at UGC visitations had a similar tone, seeking to enlarge but not disturb the close Gilmorehill community.

This innate conservatism was nowhere more clearly demonstrated than over the proposed new Queen Margaret Union and the extension to the men's Union. The latter set up a Committee on Extensions in March 1954 to discuss the possibility of enlarging the existing premises by building on adjacent ground belonging to the University on the corner of University Avenue and Gibson Street, but because of the building quotas no work could begin before

9.9 *R. A. Butler, escorted on the left by Jimmy Gordon, leaving the University to deliver his ill-fated Rectorial Address, 1956.*

1957 even if funds were available. Encouraged by the Principal's challenge to 'take any risk to break up that gigantic mass movement'[41] represented by the Union, the Senate's response was to suggest the construction of several smaller unions and make membership of a union compulsory. The members rejected any such proposals, confirming as was customary at their annual meeting that the Union should remain all-male and voluntary. Nevertheless in the summer of 1955 the University agreed to the use of a site for the extension. Although a fund-raising campaign was launched, the Union recognised that a UGC grant was essential. To qualify the Union would need to be seen to provide a service for all male students and possibly all students irrespective of their sex. The situation was complicated by the University's wish to build a student refectory, arguably robbing the two Unions, which provided most student lunches, of their main source of income. The Union opposed the new refectory, while the SRC and the QM Union endorsed the Court and Senate decision to go ahead, to build a new QM Union, to make extra provision for male students, and to require Union membership. After clarification of the University's requirements about the management of the new building, the constitution of the QM Union was revised to allow for mandatory membership for all women students. Despite a plea from the newly elected Rector Lord Hailsham, the Union in December 1959 unanimously rejected compulsory membership, a condition of the UGC grant in the 1957 quinquennium. Concerned that as a result no extension would be built until the late 1960s after student numbers had peaked, the Court gave the Union a last chance to reconsider. When no progress was made, the Court resolved to proceed with an amenity building open to all male students on the site of the proposed extension, at the same time as the new QM Union at the west end of University Gardens. In these prolonged negotiations, Sir Hector, who suffered a mild heart attack in November 1958, was not at his best, often displaying his irritation at the lack of progress. As he himself confessed to a friend, student relations were not his forte – 'I do not go to a great many student functions, and when I do, I don't stay long'.[42] Not until he was recuperating from his illness in 1959 did he attend a University rugby match and he only spoke twice in the Union. For all that, he was idolised by the students, largely because he was essentially a modest man who believed that the University existed to serve their needs. At a personal level he devoted time and a great deal of attention to students in financial or personal difficulties – supporting them out of his discretionary funds, writing letters on their behalf to the Carnegie Trust, and carefully following their progress.

Sir Hector in the 1950s persisted in his efforts to foster good relations with graduates, seeking to create 'a body of opinion which could be rallied if ever the University got into a public difficulty'.[43] In the front of his mind was the danger of government using its financial power to interfere directly in university affairs as had happened in Germany in the 1930s. Following the example of American alumni, he championed the newly formed Graduates Association largely through its journal *The College Courant*. This publication was a blend of nostalgia and current news about the University and its departments. By the early 1950s the Association had over 4,000 members and an active social programme. Building on existing graduate clubs founded before the First World War (see pp. 100–1, 113), branches were established in a number of British towns and abroad. On foreign visits Sir Hector made a point of contacting local graduates and encouraging participation in the Association. The annual letters he had started penning to students and graduates during the

9.10 *Sir Hector Hetherington visiting the annual camp of the University Air Squadron.*

war became longer, containing a mixture of news about the University, graduates, and his own activities and concerns. For all the reports of new building and more students, the letters portrayed a life on Gilmorehill familiar to even the oldest graduate. Sir Hector wrote with pride of the achievements of student sportsmen – 'Wet-Bobs', the Sailing Club and the Boat Club, and 'Dry-Bobs'. He told of the success in 1952 of D. K. Gracie, a vet student, in winning a place in the British Olympic Team and reported regularly the contribution of Glasgow rugby players to the Scottish team. He was delighted to announce Dr Evelyn Camrass's ascent of an unnamed 22,000 ft peak in the Himalayas shortly after her finals. The staff he mentioned all shared his passions for golf, fishing and holidaying in the Highlands. He conjured a sense of tradition handed down the generations, even in his own family:

> As usual, much of this patchwork was written on Speyside. The fortnight there was cloudy and cold with none of the brilliance of 1955, or for that matter of the earlier summer of the present year when even our rainy West felt some anxiety about its water supply. Still, that noble countryside was green and lovely. We had some profit from that well-established doctrine

> it never rains on a golf-course: and in the less propitious hours, I read some books, besides advancing the education of my grandchildren in the classics of the Scottish Students' Song-book, so that if later on they contrive to satisfy the requirements of the Scottish Universities' Entrance Board, they may do something to improve the musical taste of their contemporaries.[44]

These annual reports and the stimulus they gave to the Graduates Association throughout the world succeeded in generating goodwill and certainly softened reaction to the hostile press at the Butler Rectorial. However Sir Hector never thought that, as in America, alumni had sufficient resources to make any meaningful contribution to University funds, and spoke against changes in fiscal policy to stimulate such giving for fear it would lead to a reduction in government grants.

Likewise the initiative taken in 1947 to endow the staff with a sense of corporate identity through the publication of the *University Gazette* was maintained. The publication contained news of new appointments and departures. The articles were similar to those in the *Courant*, never controversial and never rising to the standard of those in the *Cambridge Reporter* or *Oxford Magazine*. Under pressure from the UGC and the Glasgow Association of Lecturers and Assistants (ALA) some progress was grudgingly made in involving the non-professorial members of staff in the government of the University. In 1958 the Principal agreed to meet members of the ALA twice a year and in 1960 the Deans began circulating edited minutes and discussing matters of interest. All lecturers were still not represented on Boards of Studies nor adequately on faculties, notably in that bastion of conservatism the Arts Faculty. The ALA pressed for reform and wider participation of lecturers in the work of both Senate and Court to reflect their numbers and responsibilities. Since the war the number of lecturers had doubled from 208 to 428 in 1959, while the number of professors had only increased from 54 to 75. With student numbers only struggling back to the 6,000 first reached in the post-war boom, this made for a considerable improvement in the staff/student ratio. There were 134 assistants in 1959 (compared with 94 in 1947), who continued, unlike their English counterparts, to be on short non-renewable contracts 'with no material hope of promotion'.[45] Sir Hector maintained his close control of appointments: 'I will not have anyone appointed to the permanent staff whom I have not seen myself and approved: and I do myself practically all the correspondence over the appointment of professors and other heads of departments'.[46] This work dominated his desk in the 1950s. He wrote to his wide circle of contacts soliciting names of suitable candidates and did the same for them. He tried hard to recruit talented scholars from Oxford and Cambridge to chairs. He had some successes such as Sydney Checkland from Cambridge to the chair of Economic History and Tom Wilson from Oxford to the chair of Political Economy; but there were many failures. By the end of the decade he conceded that it was now impossible to attract such talent unless for personal reasons someone wished to live in the west of Scotland. His biggest problem was to fill medical and science posts. The number of applicants was usually very small, sometimes just a single candidate. The national salary scales introduced by the National Health Service made it hard to persuade those with chairs in smaller less prestigious medical schools to apply. Some did come, such as Edward Wayne from Sheffield to the Regius chair of Medicine and Ian Donald to the Regius chair of Midwifery, but then only after considerable wrangling, usually over the administrative load and poor accommodation. The attraction of Glasgow for clinicians of this calibre was undoubtedly the presence of Sir Charles Illingworth (Surgery, 1939) who almost single-handed had revived Glasgow's reputation for surgical training and pioneered new procedures for the treatment of peptic ulcers. Perhaps Sir Hector's greatest achievement was the appointment of Professor D. H. R. Barton from Birkbeck College to the Regius chair of Chemistry in 1954, after he had failed to get the Oxford chair, to succeed J. W. Cook, who had recently been appointed Vice-Chancellor of the University of Exeter. Although he only stayed for three years he brought with him a team of senior colleagues, some of whom remained. Nearly all science and non-clinical medical lecturers had to be appointed well up the scale, putting further strain on the University's scant resources.

Sir Hector's retirement at the age of seventy-one in September 1961 marked the end of an era. From the time of his appointment to Liverpool thirty-five years earlier, he saw his role 'as the chap who really shapes the policy and action of the University'. He believed a Principal's 'first concern, beyond question, is academic leadership. He must know what he wants his place to be, and day in day out, in spite of all the difficulties, exert himself to keep it moving in that direction. He must, that is to say, have an educational philosophy and, as well as he can, get it into the heads of colleagues who most of them look at general issues through the spectacles of their department'.[47] Living up to this ideal he more than anyone else had shaped and revitalised Glasgow. It was no accident that David Donaldson's official portrait showed him as large and domineering, looking in Sir Hector's own words like a 'well-pickled Scottish judge'.[48] Nevertheless he had always to have an eye to the art of the possible, particularly in his dealings with the Arts Faculty. The post-war years had been frustrating. Glasgow and the Clyde no longer had a vibrant economy that could be turned to in emergencies for funds. The restricted Gilmorehill site made expansion difficult. After the first flush of funding following the war, UGC finance had been tight, preventing many developments. The negotiations with the RCST had been largely fruitless and time consuming. Nevertheless there had been achievements, new chairs and departments, new buildings, a computer and the definite prospect of better student facilities. He stayed too

9.11 *David Donaldson's official portrait of Sir Hector Hetherington.*

long, and after his heart attack he lacked the strength to address the issue of further expansion with determination, allowing Fordyce to impose his views on restricted entry on the Senate which ultimately had damaging consequences for the University's finances. As he left Glasgow the university system in which he had played so large a part was subject to external scrutiny by the Robbins Committee and other committees for the first time in Scotland since the 1920s.

Only after Hetherington had gone did the University Court discover that for years they had paid the most experienced university vice-chancellor in Britain much less than all the other Scottish principals.

Notes and References

1. GUA, Letter to Graduates, 21 March 1951.
2. GUA, No. 55283 Mears Plan.
3. *Report of the University Court*, 1951.
4. Minutes of the University Court 1952–3, 15 December 1952, p. 95. Cf. M. Shattock, *The UGC and the Management of British Universities* (Buckingham, 1994).
5. Ibid. 1951–2, 17 December 1951, p. 101.
6. Ibid. 1952–3, 4 September 1952, p. 321.
7. Ibid. 17 September 1952, p. 303.
8. GUA, DC8/1046 letter to Sir Arthur Trueman, 15 May 1954.
9. Minutes of the University Court 1954–5, 16 September 1954, p. 341.
10. Ibid. 29 October 1954, pp. 44–6.
11. GUA, DC8/364.
12. Minutes of the University Court 1955–6, 29 September 1955, pp. 352–4 and accompanying papers.
13. Ibid. 1954–5, 28 April 1955 accompanying papers.
14. Ibid. and 2001 seminar paper by Sir Alec Cairncross deposited in GUABRC.
15. Minutes of the University Court 1960–1, 13 July 1961, p. 425.
16. GUA, DC8/364.
17. DC8/1046 letter to Sir Keith Murray, 24 May 1954.
18. DC8/1098 letter to Dr Harold Dodds, 15 July 1959, p. 1.
19. DC8/34 Sir Hector Hetherington notes for address to first year students, 1953.
20. *Report of the Committee on University Teaching*, London, 1964, p. 9.
21. SRC evidence to the UGC visit May 1956 in papers of Minutes of University Court 1955–6, 21 June 1956. For an in-depth investigation of student life at Glasgow, with an analysis of the roles of men and women, see J. Wakeling, 'University Women: Origins, Experiences and Destinations at Glasgow University, 1939–1987' (Glagow University Ph.D. thesis, 1998).
22. GUA, DC157/17/2/1 Minutes and memoranda of the Scottish Union of Students, 1953–58 and DC8/1106 papers of SUS, 1952–7.
23. DC8/39 Sir Hector Hetherington, notes for address to first year students, 1958.
24. Minutes of the University Court 1960–1, 23 March 1961 item 474 and papers for the UGC visitation.
25. *Glasgow University Magazine*, December 1955 vol. 67, p. 125.
26. GUA 51403, 23 February 1959.
27. Minutes of the University Court 1958–9, 19 March 1959 item 452 and accompanying papers.
28. Ibid.
29. Minutes of Senate 1958–9, 4 June 1959 accompanying statistical report on admissions.
30. Minutes of University Court 1958–9, 23 October 1958, pp. 30–1, 20 November 1958, p. 100, 15 December 1958, p. 123, 22 January 1959, p. 176, and 18 June 1959, p. 365 and accompanying papers.
31. Minutes of University Court 1956–7, 23 May 1957 item 472 and accompanying papers.

32. GUA, Submission to the Committee on Higher Education by Sir Hector Hetherington, May 1962, pp. 1–2, Principal's papers Robbins Committee file.
33. Minutes of University Court 1961–2, 25 January 1962 item 277 and accompanying papers.
34. Minutes of Senate, 1 February 1973, no. 191.
35. Minutes of the University Court 1955–6, 29 September 1955, pp. 352–4 and accompanying papers.
36. GUA, DC8/3/70 Address to the General Council 1961.
37. *Glasgow University Magazine*, 1954, p. 79.
38. GUA, DC8/718, *The Times*, Saturday 22 February 1958.
39. DC8/1085 letter to Sir Ernest Field, 26 February 1957–8.
40. DC8/1098 letter to Sir Harold Redman, 5 October 1959.
41. Minutes of Senate 17 November 1955 and accompanying papers.
42. GUA, DC8/1098 letter to Dr Harold Dodds, 15 July 1959, p. 3.
43. DC8/3/70 Address to the General Council 1961.
44. DC183/3 letter to graduates, 24 June–2 September 1956.
45. Submission to the Committee on Higher Education by Sir Hector Hetherington, May 1962, pp. 1–2, Principal's papers, Robbins Committee file.
46. DC8/1098 letter to Dr Harold Dodds, 15 July 1959, p. 1.
47. Ibid.
48. DC8/582 correspondence and speeches relating to his portrait.

CHAPTER TEN

Economising Resources, 1961–84

Just as Sir Donald MacAlister had marked him down as his successor, so Sir Hector Hetherington had long before chosen Dr Charles Wilson, whom he had got to know as a member of the Committee of Vice-Chancellors and Principals, to follow him. Graduating from Glasgow in 1928, he had gone on to the London School of Economics before succeeding Denis Brogan as tutor in modern history at Corpus Christi College in Oxford. After a successful career there teaching mostly politics, Wilson had been appointed Principal of University College, Leicester, in 1952 and its first Vice-Chancellor in 1957 when it became a fully-fledged university with degree-awarding status. There he had developed a relaxed relationship with the students and was widely regarded as a model of a progressive university administrator. In addition to his duties at Leicester, Wilson had helped to establish the University of Sussex and the University of East Anglia, where he chaired the committee. He was reluctant to leave Leicester but was finally persuaded to return home. The Clerk of Senate, Professor Fordyce, was less than enamoured of this choice and warned the new Principal that he could not expect to enjoy a similar relationship with the students at Glasgow. He vetoed Charles Wilson's wish to move the Principal's office from the old Scott building to the much more accessible McIntyre building. Nevertheless on his arrival Charles Wilson attempted to stamp his mark on the student body but did not share his predecessor's concerns about the so-called 'brown-baggers' who did not join in. As he knew well, any attempt to enforce corporate activity was out of keeping with the new mood of the 1960s. He told the *Glasgow University Guardian*, 'Students have different reasons for being at a University and the lone wolf who prefers not to take part in social life should not be condemned.'[1] He was determined, however, to build more halls of residence and thus make the University less reliant on the West of Scotland. This ambition was destined to be frustrated by the UGC, which favoured funding such investment in the new universities, which were predominantly in England.

There can have been no greater contrast to Leicester than Glasgow, an old institution resistant to change with an outmoded curriculum still controlled by the cumbersome mechanism of consultation between the other institutions

10.1 *Sir Hector Hetherington (right) on his way to introduce Dr Charles Wilson (left) to the Senate, 1961.*

under the terms of the 1889 Act. The Senate remained deeply divided between the younger progressive professors and those against both further expansion and the granting of degree-awarding powers to the Royal College of Science and Technology (RCST). Although the Robbins Committee had been established earlier in the year, there had as yet been no meaningful discussion of its remit at Glasgow, largely because Christian Fordyce had no sympathy with the concept of an inclusive system of higher education. He reminded Charles Wilson that the University was opposed to expansion – 'I should not wish to be committed to the view that everybody who can obtain a minimum qualification for a University should be in one.'[2] Following the appointment of the distinguished nuclear physicist, Dr Samuel Curran, as Director in 1959, the battle with the Royal College was as good as lost. With his predecessor, Sir David Anderson, on the Robbins Committee, he was pushing at an open door when he launched a vigorous campaign in May 1961 for the granting of university status to the RCST and laid the blame for the breakdown of the 1913 concordat firmly at Glasgow's door. By the end of May 1962 the University

Grants Committee (UGC) had let it be known that a recommendation to this effect had been made to the Treasury. Charles Wilson lent his personal support and as a member of the Academic Advisory Committee (appointed in the summer of 1963) to the neighbouring institution contributed his wealth of experience in similar ventures south of the Border. This gesture of goodwill did nothing to endear him to some of his professorial colleagues, particularly James Small (Mechanical Engineering) and William Marshall (Civil Engineering) who remained deeply opposed. They rehearsed old arguments about the need to provide a liberal education for scientists, which failed to recognise that the newer universities (influenced by men of the stature of A. D. Lindsay who had preceded Hetherington in the chair of Moral Philosophy) were striving to do just that but with a radical approach to the curriculum. Others, notably Walker Chambers (Dean of Arts and professor of German) and John Gunn (Natural Philosophy) keenly recognised the need for change and better relations with the RCST, soon to be the University of Strathclyde. They supported the gift of an olive branch to their new sister institution in the shape of a mace to be used on ceremonial occasions.

The removal of this longstanding source of friction did little to improve strained relations within the Senate. As a result the University's response to Robbins was unimaginative and grudging, focusing largely on the shortcomings of the 1889 Act, a vestige of plans for a national university on the Irish model. However, unlike the RCST, the University singularly failed to make any suggestion as to an appropriate form of governance if the Act was repealed – 'How this is to be done we do not venture at this stage to suggest. The problem will require expert study.'[3] The response was largely the handiwork of Fordyce, composed without consulting Charles Wilson who in the first months of his appointment divided his time with Leicester, which was without a vice-chancellor. It was left to the General Council and to Sir Hector Hetherington to provide a more cogent response, explaining the historical reasons which lay behind many of Glasgow's problems. Reacting to the concept of dual funding for both teaching and research, Hetherington made it clear that:

> The aim and hope in Glasgow was to give to established members of staff a 50:50 distribution of their time between teaching and research. This was not achieved, was not even attempted in every particular case: nor outside the Social Sciences in the Faculty of Arts.

He concluded with a warning:

> But recognising that research is a primary function of the University both in its relationship to society and for the vigour of its own life, I should like to make clear my own view that without a quite radical alteration of the whole system and given the present length of school life, with the

> present possibilities of staffing the schools (which are likely to endure for a long time), the most important function of the Universities is undergraduate education. The difficulty of that function varies with different types of courses, and with different stages in each course. But over all it is demanding and laborious work, and, on the whole, it is too little regarded.[4]

The General Council went further by offering an explanation for Hetherington's point of view by drawing attention to the enormous disparity in the unit of resource between Scottish universities and their English redbrick counterparts. In 1959/60 at Birmingham the total expenditure per student per year was £628 whereas at Glasgow it was £455.[5] Unless this inequality was redressed, it would be impossible for the University to achieve anything approaching a 50:50 balance between teaching and research.

The Robbins report, published on 23 October 1963, as expected firmly endorsed expansion. Projecting that student numbers at Scottish universities would rise from some 19,550 in 1961 to 61,610 in 1985, Robbins estimated that on the basis of a staff/student ratio of 7:52 the number of staff would need to rise from 2,979 to 8,193. There was disagreement from the outset about these projections. The Scottish Education Department estimated a more realistic increase to 44,000 students with a total staff of 5,585.[6] Nevertheless whichever figure was used the estimated staffing levels posed a huge challenge, demanding greatly enlarged postgraduate programmes as the Robbins report recognised. Referring to the problems in 1929–32, Charles Wilson responded:

> From the standpoint of the quality of the University it was not an example to be copied. Students were instructed in crowds and individually neglected. We are not going back to that. It is no good bringing more students into the university in order to teach them less. If it sought to do this expansion on the cheap the nation would destroy the potential for teaching and research which it seeks to develop.[7]

In 1964 he was elected chairman of the Committee of Vice Chancellors and Principals and was responsible for orchestrating the complex negotiations with the incoming Labour government about the implementation of the Robbins proposals.

The debate about expansion was now resolved, and the day after the report was published Charles Wilson asked the Senate to consider the problem of accommodating an additional 4,000 students and the development of postgraduate work. He avoided further obstruction from Fordyce and his supporters by referring the matter to the Deans and the faculties where there was broad endorsement for the Robbins proposals on the clear understanding that the unit of resource would be increased and additional capital be available for new buildings. Walker Chambers in Arts with the backing of his more farsighted and recently appointed colleagues, such as Sydney Checkland (Economic History, 1957), Tom Wilson (Political Economy, 1958) and Archie Duncan (Scottish History, 1962), agreed to take 20 per cent more students in the coming year and 40 per cent in 1965. Already the faculty had taken steps to improve relations with local schools and appointed six teacher fellows. These commitments, which signalled an end to the damaging policy of exclusion, were a gamble in the expectation that the UGC would urgently address Glasgow's staff/student ratio which the report had shown was the worst in the United Kingdom. It paid off with an increase in the recurrent grant in 1964 largely devoted to recruiting new staff across the Arts faculty. Further increases in the following two years were also to be devoted to improving the faculty's position, giving many staff for the first time the opportunity to conduct research. The UGC gave permission in 1963 for the construction of a new library designed by William Whitfield, and an additional grant was made available early in 1964 for the Adam Smith (Social Sciences) Building which was urgently needed to accommodate new staff. Assistant lecturers recruited to the Arts faculty at this time recall having to share cramped offices and to lecture in overflowing halls in the Scott building. The Adam Smith Building was completed in 1967 and Phase 1 of the University Library in 1968.

With the Labour government (elected in October 1964) as committed to the expansion of higher education as their predecessors, new recruitment continued for the next ten years. By 1966 the number of full-time academic staff had risen to 1,110 from 723 in 1963 including thirty new professors bringing the total to 102. New chairs and departments had been established in every faculty, including chairs in economics, neurology, fine art, biochemistry, statistics, and town and regional planning. Thereafter the rate of growth slowed. In 1974 there were 1,520 academic staff, including 141 professors and contract researchers, and 2,310 non-academic staff. Further new chairs had been founded, particularly in medicine and dentistry but also belatedly in management studies and in archaeology and drama. Additional departmental buildings were squeezed on to the campus – for example the Mathematics building and the Rankine Engineering building, both completed in 1969. The marked improvement in the staff/student ratio made it possible for teaching to become more personal, with individual tutorials on written work and later the widespread adoption of seminars even for the large first and second year classes in Arts. Only gradually did the relationship between staff and students become less formal.

The university had shown considerable foresight at Charles Wilson's prompting in being willing to have 10,000 students by the early 1970s. This target was, however, pruned back to 9,250 by the UGC and the Scottish Office, because of the foundation of the new university at Stirling and encouragement for the creation of arts and social science faculties at Strathclyde and Heriot

10.2 *The foundations of the new Library under construction, 1963. On the left the Adam Smith Building for the Social Sciences is nearing completion.*

Watt. As a result it was not until 1975 that Glasgow had more than 10,000 students for the first time. By then the gender balance at Glasgow had changed markedly with a steady growth over the previous decade in the number of women students, who now accounted for more than 40 per cent of the student body. Although much more difficult to determine, there had also been a marked growth in the proportion of Roman Catholic students, reflecting improvements in the Roman Catholic schools and the introduction of grants. Originally it had been intended that the number of students in arts and science, including engineering, would increase at the same rate. As in the past this proved impossible as there were insufficient qualified students with science passes at Higher in the immediate catchment area to fill the places. There was a reluctance to take those with only minimal qualifications without a basic science building in which to teach such first year students until the Boyd Orr Building was opened in 1972. Moreover with the Clyde shipbuilding and heavy industries in rapid decline, engineering lacked appeal. Consequently the Arts faculty almost doubled in size between 1964 and 1975 to reach just under 4,000 students with more women than men. Science on the other hand only grew from 1,800 to 2,500 and engineering from just under 700 to 850 students. There was little growth in the number of students in medicine, dentistry and veterinary medicine, which were fixed by the UGC to allow new medical and veterinary schools to develop elsewhere. At the same time the ratio of men to women in these faculties, which had been held for some time at 7:3, was abandoned to attract more women to these professions. The medical curriculum was shortened in 1962 from six to five years and the Faculty proposed that no students should be admitted for a year to keep within the quota. The Dean of Arts, Walker Chambers, protested that this was unfair on would-be students and the proposal was overturned.

The well-publicised collapse of the local economy and the accompanying social problems made it almost impossible during this period for Glasgow to attract able students from other parts of the United Kingdom where there was anyway increasing opportunity to take courses in both new and old institutions much nearer to home. The proportion of undergraduates living within a thirty mile radius of Glasgow actually increased from 74 per cent to 78 per cent, and those from Scotland as a whole from 92 per cent to over 95 per cent, while those coming from other parts of the United Kingdom remained almost level at 3.5 per cent. Although with the completion of Dalrymple Hall, Queen Margaret Hall and Wolfson Hall Glasgow now had a greater proportion of students living in residences (11 per cent as compared with 6 per cent in 1963), provision still lagged a long way behind other universities. Almost 66 per cent of students continued to live at home, just 4 per cent less than a decade earlier.

For the four ancient Scottish universities, perhaps the most important recommendation of the Robbins report was that the provisions of the 1889 Act should be repealed as soon as practicable. Discussions began in the summer of 1964 and the new Act was on the statute book by the spring of 1966. The four universities could now govern their own affairs by resolution of their courts. The Science faculty immediately took advantage of this new freedom to liberalise the curriculum by allowing students to include any arts subject, rather than those prescribed by regulation, and in 1971 completely overhauled the syllabus. As was only to be expected the Arts faculty refused to make any alterations until the 1970s, even though the newer universities had adopted innovative approaches to their curricula in arts and social sciences. This refusal caused enormous resentment amongst Glasgow's social scientists who believed they were being denied good students because of the faculty's language requirements. Matters came to a head in 1969 when, after a heated debate, the sub-faculty of social science was formed and the MA regulations altered to allow students in social sciences to take an Ordinary degree who had passed in higher (i.e. second level) mathematics or statistics instead of a foreign language. A pass at higher in Latin was still required for admission to many higher and Honours classes in Arts itself, and this rule only began to be relaxed in 1970 as the end of Fordyce's hegemony loomed. With the absence of adequate Latin teaching in many state schools, this requirement resulted in able students, many from poorer backgrounds, being denied entry to Glasgow and instead going to Strathclyde. The greater obstacle to Honours teaching was the requirement (not always strictly enforced) under the 1908 regulations that candidates had to take at least two subjects. After single Honours courses in French and German were approved in 1973, the whole structure and content of the Honours degree were overhauled. It was no coincidence that Fordyce had retired in 1971 after thirty-seven years as professor of Humanity and thirty-one as Clerk of Senate. He was succeeded as professor of Humanity by the liberal-minded Patrick (Peter) Walsh. The Senate vowed that never again would the Clerk of Senate be a perpetual appointment, and in future would be elected for five-year terms and would be able to serve for no more than a further two years. Robert Rankin, who had been professor of Mathematics since 1954 and was committed to reform, became the new Clerk. With no longer any opposition to the Principal delegating authority, Charles Wilson appointed Walker Chambers and John Gunn as vice-principals for three years. They were both deeply committed to the future well-being of the University. With the Senate now consisting of 109 members, there was an urgent need for a new committee to consider in detail future development. Accordingly Rankin immediately formed the Academic Development Committee, consisting of himself and the seven deans.

In these circumstances it is not surprising that Honours teaching hardly progressed at all in Arts, with the proportion taking Honours remaining almost unchanged at 30 per cent between 1964 and 1974. By that time at Edinburgh the proportion taking Honours across all subjects had risen to 55 per cent. The percentage of firsts at Glasgow, which had concerned Hetherington, actually fell. In the sciences and engineering there was a marked advance, with the proportion taking Honours rising from 40 to over 60 per cent. Whatever the intellectual merits of the Scottish Ordinary degree, continuing to encourage so many Arts students to take it did not serve them well at a time when many professions (including teaching) increasingly required Honours if not for entry then certainly for promotion. Moreover the grind of Ordinary class teaching contributed to dissatisfaction in the Arts and Social Sciences where new staff (particularly those recruited from England) expected to be able to draw on their own research and specialist interests in Honours classes. In some departments there were attempts to instil a research culture. In Economic History Sydney Checkland and Roy Campbell secured agreement for the inclusion of a large store in the new Adam Smith Building to house the archives of the fast disappearing Clyde shipyards and heavy engineering workshops. Records flowed in to provide the raw materials for research into what had been one of the most vibrant regional economies in the world in the late nineteenth century. Alec Nove, the Bonar Professor of Economics from 1963, William Mackenzie, Bryce Professor of Politics from 1966, William Brock, Professor of Modern History from 1967 and Donald Robertson, who succeeded Alec Cairncross as Professor of Applied Economics in 1961, were international authorities; but they were beacons of hope in an otherwise largely barren landscape.

Although the undergraduate population in the medical sciences only rose slightly during the decade after Robbins, medicine, dentistry and veterinary medicine benefited from the improvement in funding. In medicine and dentistry new buildings for teaching and research were the subject of complex and time-consuming negotiation between the Western Regional Hospital Board, the Scottish Home and Health Department and the UGC. Urgently needed new buildings for both the Royal and Western Infirmaries were proposed shortly after the war but it took almost twenty years of frustrating discussion for approval to be given for the first phase of both projects. The academic staff in the medical faculty, who had put up with very cramped offices for years, were frustrated by the slow progress and resentful when Norman Davidson (Biochemistry) calculated that the cost of teaching medical students in Scotland was much cheaper than in English provincial hospitals and much lower than the major London hospitals. This underfunding combined with the pooling of all hospital endowments, unlike in the English teaching hospitals, hampered research and compounded the difficulty experienced by Hetherington in attracting staff. Both the Royal and the Western projects were further delayed by the economic crisis in the mid-1970s and were not completed until the end of the decade. Midwifery was more fortunate after Ian Donald was appointed to the Regius chair in 1954. Hetherington had used Donald's reputation as an outstanding research worker to cajole the Western Regional Hospital Board into providing him with new facilities. The new Queen Mother Hospital adjoining the Royal Hospital for Sick Children at Yorkhill opened in 1964, and it was there that Donald conducted his path-breaking work on the diagnostic use of ultrasound. A new sick children's hospital was completed six years later after the old hospital was discovered to be structurally dangerous. Progress in research into the aetiology and prevention of periodontal disease, dental caries and salivary gland disease was frustrated by delays in work on the new dental school, which was not completed until 1970. Nevertheless there were successes. In Surgery Sir Andrew (Drew) Kay maintained Glasgow's reputation as a centre for surgical excellence and G. M. Wilson (Practice of Medicine, 1967) built on the foundations laid by McNee and Wayne until his early death.

From the time of his inspired appointment as professor of Veterinary Surgery in 1951, William Weipers was determined to make the school one of the leading centres for research in the United Kingdom. This required patience both in establishing new chairs which only came slowly – animal husbandry

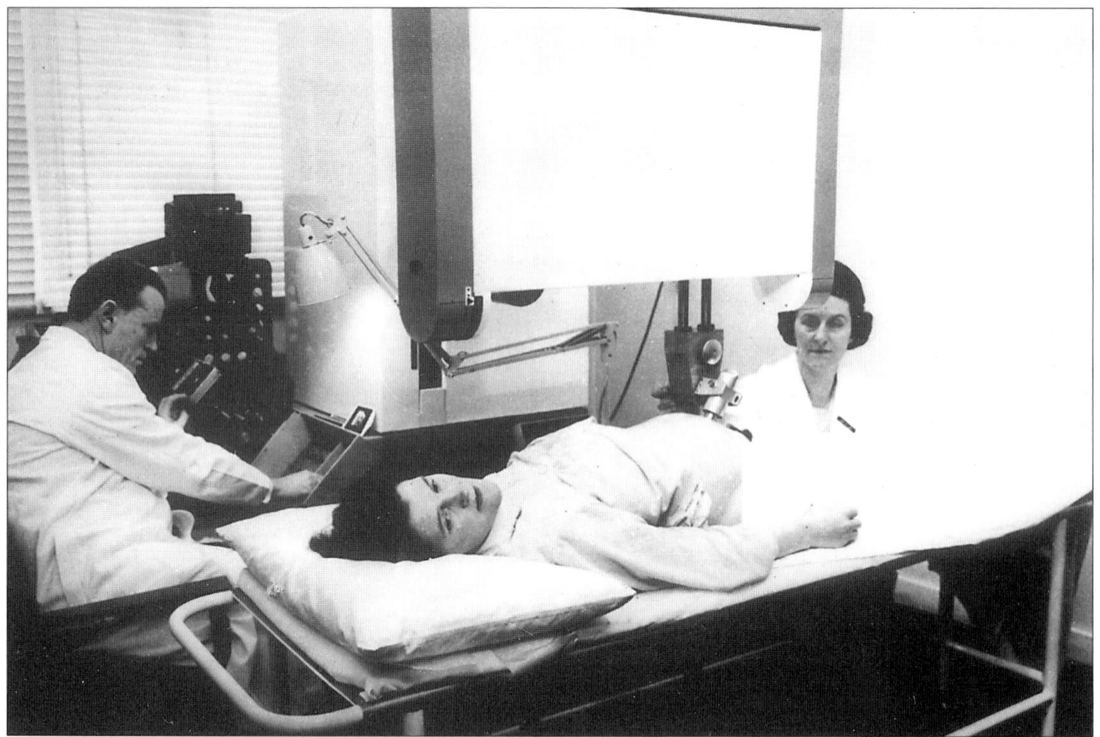

10.3 *Professor Ian Donald experimenting with ultrasound in the examination of a developing human foetus.*

(1956), medicine (1960) and physiology (1962) – and in seeking funds for the new veterinary hospital and school at Garscube, which was authorised in 1963 but not finally completed until 1970. Despite the rundown facilities in the old school in Buccleuch Street, Weipers was able to claim in 1968, the year the veterinary faculty was created, that all departments 'were engaged in research'.[8] He had attracted James Black, the future Nobel Laureate, to work in the department and other clinical researchers, who were later to hold distinguished chairs. Projects included investigation of death in newborn calves and parasitic worms in domestic animals. The recruitment of William Jarrett to the chair of Veterinary Pathology in 1968 brought to the school a researcher with an international reputation for his work on feline leukaemia. Just as in dentistry, the opening of the new hospital bolstered research with the number of research students climbing from seventeen in 1968 to twenty-six in 1975. However, by 1979 the laboratories and working conditions at Garscube for clinical teaching and research were considered inadequate by the Royal College of Veterinary Surgeons – a surprising and preposterous judgement on what were relatively new buildings.

The growth of Honours in Science certainly contributed to the sense of excitement in the Faculty and a feeling that they 'had ceased to be intellectually the poor relations of the great American laboratories.'[9] There were active research programmes in every department well supported by the Department of Scientific and Industrial Research (DSIR) and later by the new research councils called into being by Robbins. Natural Philosophy in 1964 was the first physics department in the United Kingdom to be funded by DSIR to move into the second generation of powerful measuring and computing facilities with substantial support for operating staff. These resources attracted a galaxy of able students, including several of the department's own graduates. Some went on to become distinguished physicists, notably James Drever at Caltech. David Newth, who was appointed to the Regius chair of Zoology in 1965, transformed both research and teaching by forming research groups to investigate such diverse topics as the nervous system of insects and aphid biology. Chemistry under the leadership of John Monteath Robertson and Ralph Alexander Raphael developed an international reputation for crystallography and organic synthesis and attracted research students from all over the world. Norman Davidson, who had already done much to develop Biochemistry since his appointment in 1945, and Martin Smellie (Cathcart chair 1966) created one of the most vibrant and best equipped departments in the country. At the Royal Infirmary Gemmell Morgan (1965) was building one of the largest and most successful pathological biochemistry teams in Europe. Despite these achievements the number of research students in science increased only gradually, with the award of 62 Ph.D.s in 1963 and 63 in 1974. However the number of postgraduates in the medical faculty studying for Ph.D.s expanded markedly. In Arts the rise was more impressive but from a tiny base of just two Ph.D.s in 1963 to fifteen in 1974. The tradition of persuading able Arts students to undertake their research at Oxford or Cambridge died hard. Encouragingly almost 40 per cent of the 750 postgraduate students matriculated in 1974 came from other parts of the United Kingdom or overseas.

It was perhaps this failure to develop research teaching in much of the University that led several of Glasgow's outstanding scientists to leave just as they had done in the past. Percy Brian resigned the Regius chair of Botany after only five years to go to Cambridge and two years later his successor went to Oxford. In 1970 (Sir) Thomas Symington left Pathology to be professor of Pathology in the British Postgraduate Medical Federation in London, and in 1972 Ralph Raphael departed for Cambridge. At the reader and senior lecturer level many were tempted away including the leaders of the two research groups in Zoology. Several went to the United States where there was a shortage of qualified staff and much more attractive facilities than in the United Kingdom. For junior staff there were other frustrations. Remarkably, in many departments there were no staff meetings where common concerns could be discussed. Such meetings were not required by the University, which still regarded the professor and the faculty as the main channels for communication.

The only official fora for debate were the boards of studies which were also dominated by the professors. Irritated by what seemed astonishing obscurantist authoritarianism, able junior staff, mostly in the arts, left. There were plenty of posts to choose from in the more progressive Scottish universities, the new universities and abroad. Glasgow's staff turnover at over 12 per cent was the highest in the country,[10] but nothing was done to stem the flow. The promotion procedures were cumbersome and often failed to recognise talent. As the west of Scotland economy collapsed and the University became well-known for its conservatism, it became more and more difficult to recruit replacements except for those who wished to work in the west of Scotland for family reasons.[11] As a result Glasgow's reputation as a centre for research, which Hetherington had done much to foster through his appointments, ebbed away.

In other universities in Europe and North America during the 1960s, junior staff made common cause with students to press for change in a sequence of protests known as *les événements*. This did not happen at Glasgow despite a rather half-hearted attack on the College Club (the rather stuffy staff club) in 1967. *Glasgow University Magazine* remained set in the time-warp of the generation of James Bridie and the more recent *Glasgow University Guardian* maintained its domestic focus. Although the *Guardian* carried reports on an inside page of the student riots throughout Europe in April 1968, the front page headline REVOLUTION? NO—BUT REFORM IS ON THE WAY AT LAST referred to proposed changes in the constitution of the University Union.[12] The following year, affirming their distance from these events, the male students elected a Conservative as president of their union and, out of keeping with the spirit of the times, petitioned the Lord Lyon for a coat of arms. With so many drawn from the locality and living at home, Glasgow students, like Glasgow itself, were isolated from the wider world. An even smaller proportion than in the previous generation played any part in student clubs and societies. The International Club had the largest constituency, with 540 members, who demonstrated their concern over apartheid by organising the successful Rectorial election campaign of Chief Albert Luthuli in 1962. Although seven years later there were demonstrations against Enoch Powell's infamous 'rivers of blood' speech, 500 students supported his views with 1,000 against.[13] The burning issue of America's involvement in Vietnam scarcely rated a mention. After the great demonstration outside the American Embassy in 1968 the *Guardian*'s leader declared: 'The demonstration some weeks ago in London when Communists and their sympathisers battled with police outside the US Embassy did the student image a great deal of harm; unjustified in our opinion as they were not students. Don't let people think we're all red hooligans.'[14] Such attitudes were consistent with the election as Rector in 1965 of the reactionary, Lord Reith. Although few students were members of political clubs, with the Conservatives having almost twice as many members (500) as other parties, turnout at Rectorials since the change in the timing in 1956 was now usually in the order of at least 40 per cent, and can be taken as an accurate reflection of student opinion. In 1968 in a high poll George MacLeod of Fuinary defeated Danny Cohn-Bendit, the apostle of the European student movement, who was driven into third place by that strangely Scottish hero Lt-Colonel 'Mad' Mike Mitchell, who campaigned successfully to save the Argyll and Sutherland Highlanders. Lord MacLeod was certainly a radical, but in a particularly Scottish tradition overlaid with a pacifism bred of his experiences in the trenches on the Western Front.

The election in 1971 of Jimmy Reid, the leader of the shop stewards in the work-in at Upper Clyde Shipbuilders, appeared to chime with wider concerns. However the issue was local and Jimmy Reid, like many trade union leaders, was understandably more concerned at that time about the future of the workforce than wider political issues. There were some pockets of radicalism, such as the group of students who gathered round Father Gerry Hughes, the Catholic Chaplain, to challenge the Church's rigid attitude to ecumenism and morality; but even that was quenched when he left. George Brechin, a recent graduate and still a student, was chosen from amongst this group by Jimmy Reid to serve as his assessor on the University Court. Even when Glasgow's students elected a student Rector in 1977, the successful candidate was John Bell, a theology student with strong links to MacLeod's Iona Community. He was later to become a well-respected minister and the author of immensely popular hymns. Testimony to the mood of the student body were the overwhelming votes during that year to keep the Union and the QM Unions segregated, an issue which was to dominate the next three years. Shortly afterwards a general meeting at QM Union agreed to admit men. This change in the constitution could only take effect if it was ratified by the Senate. The Court had no alternative now but to review the future of both unions if it was not to be in breach of the Sex Discrimination Act. Two years of bitter wrangling with the University Union then ensued until with ill grace in February 1980 the members agreed to admit women.

In 1965 the Senate and the Court engaged in a spectacular confrontation with the Students' Representative Council in what became known as the Marr case. During the spring Mrs Whiteford, clerk to the SRC, complained to the police that she had received obscene telephone calls from officers and members from 15 February to 8 March. During April the police informed the Principal that the appropriate response was to invoke the University's disciplinary procedures. The Principal and Deans Committee, acting with vacation powers, appointed a committee of enquiry to hear evidence and as a result some twenty members of the Council were summarily disciplined including the President (Michael J. McManus, suspended for life) and the Secretary (Thomas Marr, suspended for a year). The committee's procedure was ill-advised and flawed. The students concerned were interviewed and questioned without being told the nature of their offence. These sentences (later confirmed

10.4 *Jimmy Reid, the UCS shop steward, being installed as Rector of the University, 1971.*

by the Senate) were condemned by the friends and families of the accused. There were ten appeals, including one from Marr. The President declined to appeal: already a graduate, he departed protesting his innocence of any wrongdoing, and scorning further process. Marr's defence was energetically taken up by a friend of the family, the Reverend Andrew Herron, clerk to the Presbytery of Glasgow.[15]

The role of the University Court as appellant authority in disciplinary matters was obscure (it was later to be confirmed in the 1966 Act), and precedents were non-existent. Lacking a stated case from the Senate, the Court decided to re-hear all the evidence relating to the appellants afresh, a task which kept its *ad hoc* appeals committee, chaired by Sir William Robieson, in intermittent session for four months until Christmas. With one exception, the

Appeals committee endorsed the findings of the Senate, though moderating some of the penalties. In the case of Marr, the committee unanimously recommended acquittal, a recommendation rejected by the Court which in January 1966 substituted a reprimand for the original suspension. Tom Honeyman, a lay member of Court, opposed this substitution.

Andrew Herron wondered aloud, in an article in the *Glasgow Herald* in January 1965, how the Court could overturn the patient deliberation of its own committee without hearing new evidence or indeed troubling to re-read the evidence before it. The Court's response was silence. There was a public outcry. Tam Dalyell, MP for West Lothian, declared – 'If a Government department or a politician behaved like this Court they would be hounded and murdered by the organs of public opinion and rightly so.'[16] He was much later to apologise to Charles Wilson for this outburst. The Court maintained its silence. The outcry redoubled, spreading to the national press, and only subsided when the Court, apprehensive of possible action in the Court of Session, set aside Marr's reprimand on a technicality. The whole affair seriously damaged the University's standing in the local community and was deeply felt by Charles Wilson. Three years later the Senate reviewed its disciplinary procedures and agreed that in future students should be involved. This was the prelude to discussions about wider student participation in the work of the University, which started in 1968 and resulted in the establishment in 1969 of a joint council of Senate, Court and the SRC. During the following year students were admitted to boards of studies in pure science, an innovation strongly resisted in Arts.

The University by now was too large to be managed effectively by the Principal with the support of the Clerk of Senate and the Secretary of Court. For some time Charles Wilson had wanted to appoint a deputy, not least to cover for him when he was absent from the University. Fordyce resisted such a move as he feared he would lose out. Eventually at the same time as students were given a role in governance, Professor Donald J. Robertson, a brilliant applied economist, was appointed Principal's assessor on the Court – in effect Vice-Principal. Unfortunately he died prematurely within a year.

One of the consequences of an even larger proportion of students living at home was that team sports declined as more and more chose to 'turn out for their old boys' clubs', which themselves were becoming more competitive. Rugby, which had prospered in the 1950s with the fullback N. W. Cameron being capped for Scotland, fell by the wayside. When the national league was formed in 1975 the team was placed in division three; by 1980 it had fallen to division seven. Over the same period, men's hockey, which produced a series of internationalists in the early 1960s, dropped from division three in the national league to division five. Individual sports, which made use of the new Stevenson building, attracted most interest. The University excelled in badminton, boxing, fencing and swimming.

Athletics never lost its appeal, largely because the University's facilities were better than those at local clubs. The men's golf team was strong, with regular wins in both the Scottish and British championships. Nevertheless sports of all kinds remained a minority interest and, despite the new gymnasium, facilities for both indoor and outdoor activities fell far short of those at other universities. Catering facilities were improved with the opening of the staff/student refectory opposite the new Library in 1966.

By 1972 there were indications that relative freedom from government interference and the generous funding which had characterised the rapid

10.5 *Students protesting at the rise in overseas student fees, 1980.*

10.6 *Simon Boothroyd, Murdo McDonald and Charles Kennedy campaigning for the election of the TV personality Reginald Bosanquet as Rector, 1980.*

expansion of higher education was coming to an end. In August Margaret Thatcher, Minister of Education and Science in the Conservative government, elected in 1970, had insisted that the University purchase a British-made ICL computer instead of the preferred IBM 370/165. This was the final straw in a long saga stretching back four years to a visit by the UGC Computer Board to Glasgow to discuss a replacement of the KDF9 machine by an ICL 1906A. After a review of available machines a request was submitted for an IBM 360/75 with superior functionality to the ICL model. As in 1964 the UGC favoured a regional solution catering for the needs of Edinburgh, Glasgow and Strathclyde and building on the existing Edinburgh Regional Computing Centre (ERCC). After lengthy negotiations it was agreed that Glasgow would acquire the new IBM 370/165 machine, which 'was more than twice as powerful as any computer available from ICL.' Edinburgh was to develop expertise in ICL computers in the expectation that a 'New Range ICL' computer would be installed as soon as available. The UGC supported this submission, and there was no reason to believe that it would be unacceptable to government as similar solutions had been agreed for Cambridge, London and Manchester. Mrs Thatcher's rejection of the plan on the grounds that 'support for our own computer industry must be the overriding consideration' came as a shock. Charles Wilson protested at this fickle decision in a strongly worded letter, which was made public:

> The unnecessary damage inflicted on our Universities by this cycle of delay is clear, but the damage does not stop there. We shall have to live with the technically unsatisfactory solution forced on us. The 1906S and 1904S computers at Glasgow and Strathclyde will together provide no more than half the power of the IBM system we hoped for, at about the same capital cost.[17]

Mrs Thatcher's brief reply was non-committal and simply stated without any supporting evidence that 'the decision was not an easy one'. This was just a foretaste of what was to follow.

The Conservative government did, however, support further growth of the university sector, albeit at a slower pace. Glasgow's undergraduate population was projected to rise from almost 9,000 in 1971–2 to 11,500 in 1976–7; but the government had costed the additional recurrent grant required during the next quinquennium at 1971 prices despite rising inflation. With considerable foresight Sir Charles Wilson commented: 'It is hard to see how any Government can promise to redeem all the cost of inflation without thereby building into the economy the very forces it is trying to control'.[18] When the new quinquennial grants were announced in January 1973 for the period 1972 to 1977 universities were left in no doubt that they were 'to gear down their costs while gearing up their operations with a view to an economy over the whole of their expenditure of two per cent.'[19] To help accommodate this reduction a steering committee was constituted at Glasgow to consider improvements in university structure and administration. It immediately established a number of topic committees to examine, not before time, such issues as the role of departments and non-professorial representation on faculties. Nevertheless, confident that the recurrent grant would be index-linked, the University made new appointments to cater for the increased number of students.

Wilson told the General Council in December 1973 that the 'the University was in good heart, better than at any time in the last five or six years . . .'[20] By the end of the month the rapid deterioration in the economy during 1973 had forced the government to make severe cuts, including a moratorium on all new building projects and more damagingly the withdrawal of the 'guarantee' to make good the effects of inflation by withholding what was known as the 'Tress-Brown' supplementation. The quinquennial system was abandoned and replaced by grants to be announced annually like any other government department. Estimates of student numbers were revised downwards by the Department of Education to give credibility to government policy.[21] At Glasgow this announcement could not have come at a worse time with six chairs falling vacant at the end of the session including Biblical Criticism on the retirement of the legendary William Barclay. An economy committee was formed to review all appointments. Anxious not to over-react at a time of self-evident national crisis, the six chairs were advertised and the commitment to develop management teaching was honoured with the establishment of new chairs in business policy, organisational behaviour and accountancy. There was hope that the Labour government, elected in February 1974, might reverse the policy of economies but this was soon dashed. Moreover the new government failed to provide any guidelines as to how universities still committed to costly programmes of expansion as a consequence of the Robbins report were to scale down their operations without incurring any additional expenditure. Sir Charles Wilson for the first time since his appointment wrote to all the staff to tell them 'We are at a kind of pause in our affairs'.[22] With inflation running at 20 per cent the outlook was grim. One immediate effect of the crisis was to improve internal communications with regular encyclicals from the Principal informing staff of the progress of events. The recently formed Academic Development Committee, instead of being the vehicle for monitoring expansion, became an uneasy forum for managing contraction with since 1973 the Principal rather than the Clerk of Senate in the Chair.

It soon became clear that the 'pause' was in fact an abrupt halt. The deficit for 1975 was a little over £325,000 and the recurrent grant for 1975–6 'allowed no room for development nor even for easement of the present economy measures.'[23] Posts were frozen and draconian cuts made in non-pay items. The planned new arts (Hetherington) building, phase 2 of the University Library and a new Geology building were postponed indefinitely. The Wolfson foundation, however, made funds available for the construction at Garscube of the Wolfson Laboratory of Molecular Pathology for the Beatson Institute for Cancer Research. Meanwhile the University found other funds to complete the Hunterian Art Gallery and the reconstruction of the home of Charles Rennie Mackintosh alongside the Library. Trinity College, the old Free Church training college on Park Hill, was closed with the agreement of the Church of Scotland and its large library gifted to the University. Writing in his farewell encyclical in 1976 Sir Charles Wilson declared, 'It is in my view vital to economise the resources of the University as cleverly in these next few years as can possibly be done for the national expenditure plans for these years contain no promise of relief for any part of the education sector.' He explained that expansion could only take place where there was outside – private – funding. Forgetting his plea of 1964, Sir Charles, whose own education had taken place during the difficult times of the 1920s, reminded his colleagues that it was perfectly possible to provide a good education with much less favourable staff/student ratios than those proposed by Robbins.[24] The Glasgow branch of the Association of University Teachers did not agree and, echoing feelings throughout the country, protested: 'for academic staff, this means fewer jobs and a more furious competition for them, heavier workloads, no security of employment and an erosion of working conditions at every level.'[25] What particularly annoyed university staff was that whereas the miners had received pay awards above the cost of living after the 1974 election, they had not. While sensitive to these concerns, the new Principal, Alwyn Williams, was only too aware of the urgent need for 'manoeuvrability in planning a response to suddenly imposed cuts'.[26] He had worked at Glasgow as a lecturer before becoming professor of Geology at Belfast where he had been secretary to the Academic Council and Pro-Vice Chancellor at the height of the troubles. In 1974 he had moved to the prestigious chair of Geology at Birmingham. Familiar with Belfast, which was experiencing a similar decline in its industrial base to Glasgow, he was well qualified to tackle the University's mounting problems. He was the last principal to be appointed by the Scottish Office (albeit strongly advised by the UGC) and the first non-Scot to hold the office.

One of Alwyn Williams' first actions on accepting the appointment to Glasgow in 1976 was to invite the president of the SRC (John Deykin) and the vice-president (Aylene Gardiner) to dinner in Birmingham to discuss the problems confronting the University. They identified three areas of grievance: the unnecessarily secretive conduct of business and the absence of all but the most perfunctory means of communication throughout the campus; the lack of student representation within decision-making bodies; and the still nominal nature of halls of residence. On his arrival in Glasgow Alwyn Williams immediately addressed these issues. Despite some opposition from senior staff, he co-opted the president of the SRC onto the Court until such time as Privy Council approval for formal representation could be obtained. He appointed Rodney Hirst (Logic) as Vice-Principal with an initial brief to launch a twice termly *Newsletter* to report on all aspects of the University's affairs. This innovation was to be of vital importance when the cuts began to bite after 1979. Furious at the apathy towards the provision of further halls of residence, within weeks he personally intervened to rescue a private benefaction for the refurbishment and extension of Dalrymple Hall. Such decisive action in the face of crisis was to be the hallmark of his principalship.

This disquiet amongst staff added to the importance of the deliberations of the steering committee on improvements in university structure and administration and its topic committees. The more progressive members of staff, such as Sydney Checkland, Gordon Cameron (Town and Regional Planning), John Lamb (Electronics and Electrical Engineering) and John Gillespie (Pharmacology) saw this as an opportunity at long last to reform the University's antiquated and unnecessarily secretive system of governance. The topic committee on the role of departments reported after more than two years of deliberation in October 1975 and unusually made both its report and all the evidence it had received available to all members of staff. The steering committee, concerned that the topic committee had, as the authors readily admitted, 'trespassed extensively into questions of structure and organisation' in proposing that departments should be formally constituted, appointed a further topic committee to recommend good working practice for departmental administration. However the steering committee accepted the revolutionary proposal for Glasgow that the professor should no longer automatically be head of department and members of department be free to elect whomever they wished in a secret ballot, subject to ratification by the Court. Opinion was divided over this question with the Science faculty holding out for nomination rather than election. Discussions dragged on with little sense of urgency throughout 1976 and into 1977 while opinion in each faculty on every recommendation was canvassed. These were to be discussed at a special meeting of Senate on 30 May which had to be adjourned because so many wished to participate. Archie Duncan (Scottish History and shortly to become Clerk of Senate) commented on the lengthy debate: '. . . as the talk flew faster (and there are some notable talkers in Senate, a few you would never want to have on your side) the boredom and frustration of the outsiders seemed obvious. Is there any way to silence these chaps?'[27] (At the time there were very few women members of Senate.) It was not until February 1978 that the scheme for departmental organisation and practices was finally accepted by the Court. The scheme eventually adopted provided for departmental opinion about headships to be canvassed by a court committee, which could be informed by an advisory ballot. In practice many chairholders demitted office and were succeeded either by 'titular professors' (personal chairs), readers, or senior lecturers. What is remarkable about these constitutional changes is that they came so late, almost a decade after *les événements* of the 1960s had changed the administrative structure of most universities in Europe.

During the course of these protracted and at times acrimonious discussions the conflict between the Arts faculty and the sub-faculty of Social Sciences reached breaking point with a plea from the leading departments in the social sciences for an immediate divorce. During the winter of 1975 it was agreed that Social Sciences should become a faculty in its own right from the beginning of the next session, with its own Ordinary degree which placed a stronger emphasis on social science subjects than was possible under Arts regulations. The first group of 139 undergraduates was admitted in 1977. A separate identity helped attract more research grants from the Social Science Research Council and a greater number of postgraduates, with seventy-nine new entrants in 1977. As part of the terms of the divorce it was agreed that it would be re-examined in five years' time, but this never happened.

By prudent management and tight control of expenditure, coupled with some good fortune, the University succeeded in recording a surplus between

1975 and 1978 and at the same time the number of staff increased from 1,468 to 1,560. The number of professors rose from 140 in 1974 to 158, and readers and senior lecturers from 283 to 357 – largely through promotions to reward able staff for the recent lack of movement between universities in the United Kingdom and prevent them being tempted away to Australia where the university system was expanding Robbins-like. More significantly, there had also been success in obtaining funds for new chairs from other sources, such as the General Accident Insurance Company for the Norrie-Miller chair in General Practice in 1974, and the Cancer Research Campaign for a chair in oncology in 1975. However Glasgow's income from non-governmental grants and other sources remained tiny by comparison with other universities, reflecting the deepening crisis in the local economy. With one or two notable exceptions, such as Robertson and Baxter, the whisky distillers, and Barr and Stroud, the optical instrument makers, no west of Scotland companies had the resources to lend support. Thus the University had to pay a price – a rapid deterioration in the fabric and in support services – for the surge in promotions.

During 1978, with inflation subsiding, the government indicated that expansion would resume to accommodate another bulge in student numbers in 1986 but within tighter budgetary targets than those envisaged by Robbins. Inevitably this would involve a deterioration in staff/student ratios with a consequent decline in standards whatever solution was chosen. The immediate upshot of revised forecasts in demand was a realisation that the age profile of staff was increasingly skewed towards the upper end of working lives. In an effort to correct this imbalance a premature retirement scheme was introduced – the first time academics had ever been asked to leave tenured posts early. In planning for future expansion in the new funding environment five models were proposed:

1. a system which would expand and contract in response to demand, leaving staff exposed to redundancies during downturns;
2. a system that restricted entry to protect staff from such uncertainty;
   an 'expansion on the cheap' system where no new staff were appointed to cope with an increase in numbers leading to a staff/student ratio of 1:10;
3. a shortening of the undergraduate degree course to two years, placing equivalent strain on staff and resources;
4. a system, because of changes in the demography of birth-rates and educational policy, where more and more students were qualified to enter higher education thus avoiding the need for contraction after the bulge had passed.[28]

All these models, or permutations of them, were to be actively explored over the next decade; but in the meantime Scottish universities were reluctant to recommit themselves to expansion since the demographic trends north of the

Border were very different, as the government recognised. Although presentations at Higher had risen by 20 per cent between the raising of the school-leaving age in 1970 and 1974, numbers had now levelled off. The west of Scotland with a declining population and high emigration of graduates and skilled workers was particularly adversely affected by these trends, which made predicting the future undergraduate population at Glasgow even more difficult. Nevertheless the University was on the horns of a dilemma: if they did not respond positively to calls to take more students there was no prospect of any additional resource. By November 1978 Glasgow had agreed to increase undergraduate numbers by nine per cent over the next three years, which would result in substantial deficits in the first two years, but the additional funds promised in the third year would bring the accounts back into balance. An additional problem for Glasgow was the large number of self-financing postgraduate students, who had been forced to convert to part-time because of the steep rise in tuition fees imposed by the government which they could no longer afford to pay. Although the Labour government had capped the number of overseas postgraduates, they paid fees at the same rate as domestic students. Against this background and with proposals for the radical reorganization of the school curricula, the Senate established the Educational Policy Committee charged with the 'intelligent anticipation of changes and proposals for change' and to 'monitor, report and initiate discussion in Senate and Faculties'.[29] This committee with the ADC and the Senate Business Committee, rather than the increasingly unwieldy Senate, were to be used by Alwyn Williams as his main sounding boards in framing policy when grappling with further cuts.

This discussion about the future took place at a time when the government was proposing that the country should have some measure of regional autonomy. From the mid-1970s the remaining Scottish Central Institutions saw devolution as an opportunity to end the autonomy of the universities through the creation of a Council for Higher Education in Scotland, responsible for managing the whole higher education system in Scotland. There was a logic to this argument; Scottish institutions of higher education enjoyed distinctive regional patterns of recruitment from schools and were, even after Robbins, much more part of an integrated education system than their counterparts in England and Wales. The Scottish universities were not enthusiastic about this proposal; but were unable to agree amongst themselves as to the future shape of higher education under a devolved government. Staff were very anxious to remain firmly integrated with the rest of the United Kingdom system, not least because of the implications of separation for the resourcing of research.[30] The devolution proposals failed to win the necessary support in a referendum in March 1979; but the idea of Scottish control of the whole system of higher education remained alive.

Such considerations, along with the premises on which the projected expansion of student numbers had been based in the previous autumn, were swept away by the election of Margaret Thatcher's Conservative government in May 1979. Whereas the cuts imposed by the previous Conservative and Labour governments had been pragmatic responses to economic difficulties, the Thatcher government came to office with a doctrinaire commitment to dismantle the corporatist state and to improve efficiency in all areas of public spending. For universities a 'value for money' philosophy could only mean deteriorating staff/student ratios to reduce costs and paradoxically more rather than less government interference.[31] The new government instantly made its new approach to higher education felt by imposing strict cash limits on universities and refusing to give any guarantees about future resourcing. Alwyn Williams, whose political sympathies were on the left, was convinced that the Conservatives were in earnest and immediately planned for an eight per cent cut over two years. Commenting on the savageness of this new round of cuts he wrote: 'I cannot see how we can sustain these economies for very long without seriously impairing the teaching and research activity of the University'.[32] Projecting a deficit of £1.7 million for the coming financial year, he persuaded the Court to accept a package of economies which included the loss of 110 academic posts. Since other universities did not seem to be taking the government's threats so seriously, there was unease and Allen Potter (Politics), newly appointed Vice-Principal, reported falling confidence in the Principal by the end of the year.

With commendable courage it was decided to proceed with the opening of the new Hunterian Art Gallery in June 1980 even though there was a projected deficit on the project of £320,000. The University had already found £570,000 from its own resources, despite the initial understanding that its contribution would be nominal. It was now declared publicly that the deficit would be covered by the sale of eleven oil paintings by James McNeill Whistler gifted to the University by Miss Birnie Philip. In the circumstances there was no other alternative if work on the gallery was not to be suspended as part of the economy measures. The eleven Whistlers were exhibited at the Bond Street galleries of Agnews in March 1980. The press condemned the University's action even though it was expressly permitted in the terms of Miss Philip's will in the event of just such an emergency. On 15 March the *Sunday Times* carried the headline – 'University shocks by sale of art treasures', and other London newspapers followed suit. The reaction in the Scottish press was more muted and there was little opposition within the University, which was coming to appreciate that the Principal's prediction about the sheer scale of the cuts was possibly an underestimate. Alwyn Williams was able to turn the outcry in the press to the University's advantage by launching an appeal to both graduates and members of the public with the help of the Chancellor, Alec Cairncross. With the deadline for the decision to go ahead with the sale set for 31 July – the end of the university's financial year – the response was magnificent and allowed a grant from the National Heritage Memorial Fund to be matched.[33] The opening by Sir Hugh Casson on 17 June, the day before Commemoration Day, was a great occasion. As a result of the cuts this was the last time the civilised world witnessed the remarkable sight of a Glasgow professor in white tie and tails and doctoral robes dancing eightsome reels at a *conversazione*, a kind of social event inaugurated by Dudley Medley at the beginning of the century (see p. 101) and now discontinued as an economy.

Despite the grim financial situation the second phase of the Art Gallery, including the reconstruction of Charles Rennie Mackintosh's house, opened in 1981 and the modified second phase of the Library in 1982. Four years earlier Alwyn Williams had wrung the funds for this last project out of the UGC with a characteristically forthright declaration that if 'the Hollywood set posing as our Library had been located in London, it would have been completed a decade ago.' Almost by return the UGC sent up architects to confirm the truth of this allegation and work started almost immediately.

In October 1980 the government announced the withdrawal over three years of that part of the UGC grant which supported the training of overseas students, who would now be required to pay full economic tuition fees. This cut was almost eight per cent, the figure Alwyn Williams had predicted the year before. Every university in Scotland was now in trouble. There was even talk of some smaller universities, such as Aberdeen, St Andrews and Stirling, being forced to close or amalgamate. Within a year the Chairman of the University Grants Committee was demanding more cooperation in teaching between institutions and had laid an axe at 'the golden ideal of a UGC floor for research which would enable *anyone*, *anywhere* to do *anything* . . .' He also made it clear that he would not let 'a mulish opposition to any form of change based upon sterile application of a concept of academic freedom' stand in his way.[34] This was the real flaw in the Conservatives' logic, the conflict between a greater emphasis on a mix of public and private funding with the greater measure of autonomy that it would give to university administration, and the ambition of the government to manage the system in the interest of narrowly conceived objectives such as to train more engineers. Only when the government announced its forecasts for university expenditure in March 1981 did the real extent of the cuts become apparent, which confirmed the reduction of eight per cent in real terms below budgets for the current year by 1984.[35] There could now be no doubt that the whole system was in crisis and that Robbins was dead and well buried. When the cuts were finally apportioned by the UGC in July, Glasgow and Edinburgh, the two largest universities in Scotland, escaped relatively lightly with a cumulative reduction of 10 per cent in budgets over the next three years, while at the other extreme Aberdeen's grant was slashed by over 22 per cent and Stirling's by 26.5 per cent.[36]

To protect the unit of resource (the funds made available for each student) the UGC imposed limits on future intake despite the fact that for the next five

10.7 *A meeting of the University Court, 1980, with student representatives present when the cuts were discussed.*

years there was expected to be an unprecedented increase in the number of applicants for entry into the university system. Universities that exceeded their targets were to be penalised, a decision condemned by Alwyn Williams as 'easily the nastiest piece of bureaucratic fatuity to emanate from the UGC.'[37] As a result the number of places at Glasgow were to be reduced by 435 or 4.7 per cent, with the Arts faculty on instruction from the UGC bearing the brunt. The University was also informed that there would be 'an above average reduction in the level of funding in clinical medicine' at the very time the new facilities at the Royal and Western Infirmaries were being commissioned. Convinced that the UGC's policy would inevitably allow other higher education providers, the central institutions in Scotland, to expand, Alwyn Williams refused to be browbeaten by these threats. Telling his colleagues that they would need to teach more students and put up with an inevitable reduction in the staff/student ratio, he publicly encouraged the faculties to accept all the qualified students who applied. The *Times Educational Supplement* endorsed this stand: 'There is great attraction in Dr Williams's view. He is arguing that universities should stop bemoaning their fate. They are powerful organizations which should do what they regard as right and face retribution if it comes'.[38] Unnerved by his robust opposition, the UGC relented and Glasgow was not penalised.

Whatever the level of cut, all the Scottish universities had to take emergency action to bring expenditure into line with projected income by freezing all expenditure and by accelerating schemes for early retirement of academics. At Glasgow it was estimated that 430 jobs would have to go, including 150 teaching posts, in addition to the 110 staff who had already volunteered to retire. Even then the projected deficit was in the order of £1 million a year by 1985. An inventory was urgently drawn up of 'all possessions which could be sold without affecting our academic capability'.[39] Houses in the west end with an estimated value of £350,000 were put on the market and, despite the reaction to the proposed sale of the Whistlers, it was decided to sell duplicate prints, pewter and jade from the Hunterian Museum, and the remarkable collection of Hill Adamson calotypes and Gould's *Birds of Australia* from the Library. Not surprisingly there was another angry outburst and the sales were again abandoned, but it was essential for the whole of the University to be

10.8 *Sir Alwyn Williams leading the procession of Honorary Graduates on Commemoration Day, 1981.*

seen to be making sacrifices. One outcome was the formation of the Friends of Glasgow University Library who would act as a vehicle for raising funds to enhance research collections. Every faculty agreed to raise new income (mostly from fees from overseas students) to prevent further staff losses, and to allow an urgently needed programme of refurbishment to begin in 1983–4 as well as the much-delayed construction of the Hetherington Building for instruction in language and literature.

As part of its economy drive the government sought to encourage greater cooperation between neighbouring institutions. Given the past history of relations with the University of Strathclyde, this was not universally welcome at Glasgow. Although talks were initiated, there was little real commitment and entrenched opposition in some quarters. A topic committee on the University and the Community in the 1980s had already been appointed under the chairmanship of Sydney Checkland. In May 1980 its draft report made a number of imaginative proposals for much needed improvement in the University's relations with the city, particularly the deprived areas from which, given the decline in the birth-rate, more students needed to be drawn. It also called for far greater collaboration with the University of Strathclyde, particularly the merging of departments and the rationalising of teaching and research. The first draft was embargoed by the Senate as few departments had taken the trouble to respond to the committee's enquiries about their individual relations with the community. It was subsequently circulated to faculties and departments for consideration. The central recommendation was the appointment of an additional vice-principal for community relations, supported by a standing committee of Court and Senate.

Before Senate had an opportunity to discuss the revised report an article by Allen Potter, still a vice-principal, appeared on the front page of the *Newsletter* under the single word NO![40] Potter condemned the whole initiative as misguided and encouraged Senate to throw it out. The press got hold of the story and an even more extreme article appeared in the Glasgow *Evening Times*. Alwyn Williams was furious and called for an explanation. Although Potter, who had worked at Strathclyde, claimed he had been misrepresented, he had 'no regrets about writing "No"'.[41] Sensing a good scrap, the Senate obligingly threw the proposals out. Concerned about the damage to relations with Strathclyde, which the government regarded as fundamental to the rationalisation of the system, Alwyn Williams persuaded a disgruntled committee to consult further. In February 1981 a very watered down series of proposals, which made no reference to an additional vice-principal or a standing committee, was accepted by Court and Senate. These still called for a better working relationship with Strathclyde, particularly the possibility of developing a science park, but did not recommend greater collaboration in teaching and research. The imaginative proposals for improving the University's standing in the community were shelved and instead the report proposed discussions

10.9 *A cartoon illustrating the consequences Professor Allen Potter feared would follow from the report on the University in the Community, 1980.*

with trade unions 'in the face of impending economic and social change', the widening of the social basis of the student intake, greater opportunity for graduate recruitment by the local authorities, extra-mural courses tailored to the needs of the community, and oddly a review of the role of the chaplaincies within the University.[42] Only the Social Sciences faculty clung steadfastly to the need for the University to review its 'contribution to ameliorating the social problems of the community, its present effectiveness and possible future improvement.'[43] Although several of these ideas were to be adopted in the coming decade, in the short term the report's findings were overwhelmed by the sheer scale of the cuts. This episode was characteristic and typified the short-sighted conservatism which persisted in many parts of the institution. This was a missed opportunity as closer ties with Strathclyde and the community would have almost certainly met with approval from both the UGC and the government. However in 1983 the Strathclyde Regional Council, which had been set up at the time of local government reform in 1974, put pressure on both universities to widen access for students from under-privileged backgrounds.

During 1982 inflation fell sharply and the government could begin to take a longer-term view. Writing to the chairman of the UGC in July 1982, the

Secretary of State for Education Sir Keith Joseph confirmed that no further cuts in expenditure were planned after 1983–4 providing the economy did not deteriorate; but by then he expected universities to have reconstructed themselves in such a way as to give greater emphasis to science and technology 'to enhance the contribution which the universities make to commerce and industry and the production of wealth.' In their forward planning he called for 'substantive consideration to questions like: the length and intensity of courses; the balance between undergraduate, taught postgraduate and research provision, and between initial and post-experience provision; subject balance; institutional relationships; the role of non-UGC funding, both government and private; and the overall scale of provision.'[44] The universities were left in no doubt that replies to all these questions were expected. Already efforts had been made at Glasgow to make cuts within the context of a redevelopment plan designed to encourage growth and income generation in priority areas such as the application of new technology in both teaching and research. Towards the end of the year the government relaxed its policy by making some new money available on a competitive basis to fund new lectureships for young researchers – so-called 'new blood posts' – and posts in new technologies. The invitations to bid were framed almost deliberately to cut across established lines of development within departments and faculties. This was just the tonic the more innovative staff at Glasgow needed, allowing them to put together imaginative bids to harness the new technologies to their disciplines. As a result the university did well out of the competition, being placed in the top quartile of universities with twenty-four new posts.

This success was heralded by the more optimistic as a return to a stable if less generous and more onerous funding environment within the context of a fall in student numbers by the end of the decade. They were mistaken. The government was no less committed than before to its value for money philosophy and to cutting public expenditure, forcing universities to seek an even greater proportion of funds from the private sector. This was bad news for Glasgow, which for historic and geographic reasons was more dependent on government funds (65.7 per cent) than other Scottish universities (62.9 per cent) and English universities (58.4 per cent). Although Glasgow did a little better than other Scottish universities in attracting research grants, it had less other income and fewer overseas fees. Of particular concern was the low proportion of postgraduate students at Glasgow compared to other universities of comparable size. Recognising 'somewhat reluctantly that the government would in due course require notice of university policies on research support when setting university grants', a survey was made of all research activity within the university.[45] This only served to emphasise the low priority given to research in many parts of the institution; ten departments submitted nil returns and forty-one neglected to reply.

Alwyn Williams, who had always maintained his research interests even as

Principal, was appalled, but determined that Glasgow's weakness should not become a matter of public comment at a time when several of the small band of the university's distinguished scholars had retired. Most were over 65 but had tenure until 70 under the old dispensation. They included Robert Rankin (Mathematics), Sydney Checkland (Economic History), Tom Wilson (Economics), John Gunn (Natural Philosophy), Alec Nove (International Economic Studies), Ian Sneddon (Mathematics), Peter Butter (English) and Norman Grist (Infectious Diseases). Wherever possible, and sometimes at considerable personal risk, Williams diverted resources and gave promotion to promising researchers. Like Hetherington before him he went to great trouble to attract young scholars to chairs in an effort to reinvigorate departments and faculties. His appointments included William George (Surgery), David Vines (Political Economy), Raymond Ogden (Mathematics), Miles Houslay (Biochemistry) and David Sherratt (Genetics). His greatest gamble was to throw his weight behind computing science. He brought Malcolm Atkinson from Edinburgh in June 1983 to a new second chair in the subject with the promise of further appointments and a completely refurbished building in Lilybank Gardens; Atkinson was soon joined by Keith van Rijsbergen. Quicker than most of his contemporaries, Alwyn Williams grasped the fundamental importance of this new technology to the future prosperity of the United Kingdom, and it was an issue to which he would constantly refer over his final six years in office. This adventurous move, which exactly mirrored government policy, more than matched expectations; not only did the department flourish but Atkinson and van Rijsbergen acted as a catalyst for a whole variety of new technology initiatives across the campus. In response to a request from the UGC during 1983 for information on research expenditure in thirty-seven 'departmental cost centres', a research committee was set up in 1983 under the vigorous convenorship of Professor John Gillespie with the remit of building up an inventory of all research projects and the extent and nature of their support in terms of staff and external funding.

After the landslide victory of Mrs Thatcher's government at the polls in May 1983, the Secretary of State for Education, Sir Keith Joseph, broadened the debate about the future shape of the whole of higher education. In an environment where the government had abandoned direct economic management he believed education was an area where it could 'properly' intervene without betraying its principles. Both the UGC and the National Advisory Body (NAB) for Local Authority Higher Education (which despite its title only covered England – Wales had a separate board, WAB) were invited to submit evidence. In the autumn the Secretary of State went further, instructing the UGC 'to discuss with NAB basic policies of rationalisation and co-operation within the field of higher education'. Universities were invited to take more students with no equivalent increase in funds. It was now evident that the government was intent on attacking the universities' unit of resource that, in its view, compared very favourably with that of the polytechnics which were expanding rapidly as a result of the UGC quotas. As a result, staff/student ratios in universities could be expected to deteriorate and possibly the amount of time available for research be reduced.[46] Dr John Burnett, the Principal of Edinburgh, condemned this proposal as 'a drive to get youngsters into higher education on the cheap' and refused to admit more. Alwyn (now Sir Alwyn) Williams did not disagree, but deduced 'Despite our over crowded classes and impoverished resources we are concerned about the social problems if many qualified school leavers were to be denied a place and left bitterly disappointed'.[47]

For the Scottish universities Sir Keith Joseph's action posed special problems. The Scottish Central Institutions were not to be party to the discussions between the UGC and NAB, and it was unlikely that the UGC would have time to consider the distinctive features of the Scottish system, notably the more broadly based school curriculum and the four-year Honours degree. Responding tardily to the calls in 1979 to establish a Council for Higher Education in Scotland, the Secretary of State for Scotland had announced in July 1983 the establishment of the Scottish Tertiary Education Advisory Council (STEAC); but no members had been appointed by the spring of the following year. The Scottish universities were arguably on the horns of a more serious dilemma than they had been during the devolution debate four years earlier. While few Scottish university principals shared the monetarist outlook of the government, most were sympathetic to even wider access in a country where provision had always been more generous than in England and Wales. However, as in 1979, they did not wish their institutions to be cut adrift from the rest of the United Kingdom university system. For their part the English provincial universities did not want to lose the Scottish connection, as it helped to counterbalance the weight of Oxford, Cambridge and London. Frustrated by the lack of progress with STEAC the Scottish principals led by Sir Alwyn Williams called on the UGC in March to establish a Scottish Committee to liaise with STEAC when that body began its deliberations. Sir Peter Swinnerton-Dyer, the new chairman of the UGC, was sympathetic and asked for a reasoned case, which was submitted in May. Before the UGC could respond the Secretary of State appointed the members of STEAC, which included only one representative of the Scottish universities, Sir Alwyn Williams. He now believed that the end of the binary divide between universities and polytechnics/central institutions was inevitable – a view not shared by other principals or the chairman of the UGC. Immediately the chairman of STEAC, Donald McCallum, a businessman, requested information on the relationship between the universities and other higher education institutions in Scotland.[48] In a country where, even amongst Conservatives, Mrs Thatcher had little standing, the committee was not simply going to rubber-stamp government policy. In the wake of these developments the UGC rejected the proposal for a Scottish sub-committee because of 'a reluctance to take an irrevocable step at a time when the situation is so fluid and unclear . . .'[49]

By the time STEAC began its deliberations in earnest both the UGC and NAB had issued their reports on the future of higher education in the next decade and beyond. The UGC's response was largely defensive, seeking to protect the *status quo*, particularly the unit of resource, without offering any proposals for better monitoring of the return on government investment in both teaching and research.[50] The NAB recommendations were more imaginative, calling for a common unit of resource across higher education, a more flexible approach to course structure and content, and favouring more competition between institutions. The government responded by appointing a committee to investigate the role and function of the UGC under Lord Croham. At the same time the UGC set up three working parties to advise on research selectivity within the sciences and technology, the clinical subjects, and the humanities and social sciences. It was widely rumoured that the government planned to withdraw some £50 million from the UGC recurrent grant to give additional support to areas of research excellence.

Sir Alwyn Williams had his doubts about this further round of soul-searching, particularly as it was clear that the UGC lacked the funds to contribute much to restructuring the sector. His main quarrel was with the capriciousness of government policy which, contrary to public perception, was not driven by any coherent policy for redeveloping the sector within the framework of a reduced budget. There were no consistent plans, except in the crudest terms, as to how Britain was to match the participation rates in higher education of its major competitors, such as the United States and Japan, or how the graduate needs of the fast-emerging electronics industries were to be met. When the UGC visited Glasgow on 25 November 1983 it was emphasised that 'universities, even of our size and antiquity, should no longer try to cover the whole range of knowledge. If we wish to cultivate new subjects in response to changing demand, we should be prepared to fund them by abandoning less productive fields of scholarship even if they are part of the historical perspective of the University.'[51] Although this was the premise on which the redevelopment plans had been based, this was easier said than done when there was so little room for manoeuvre in the budget.

Since Robbins, the University had experienced the classic economic cycle of boom and bust. Although much of the ground work of the development of the University had been laid by Sir Hector Hetherington in the immediate post-war years, his vision had been realised under Sir Charles Wilson, who had overseen the largest expansion the University had ever witnessed. For a variety of reasons including the regional economic decline, Glasgow failed to take full advantage of this growth to become a powerful voice in the world of higher education. It was increasingly on the periphery of the select band of leading-edge research institutions, with staff and able graduate students easily attracted away by brighter prospects elsewhere. As Sir Charles Wilson had so rightly guessed, the generous funding of the 1960s was inevitably curtailed by economic circumstances. He, and later Sir Alwyn Williams, had to grapple with cuts on an ever increasing scale which threatened the very fabric of the institution. In some ways the seriousness of the situation helped Sir Alwyn Williams and his more progressive colleagues to modernise the University and to change attitudes to both teaching and research.

Notes and References

1. *Glasgow University Guardian*, 12 June 1962.
2. GUA, Principal's papers, Robbins Committee file, handwritten note by Professor C. J. Fordyce.
3. Principal's papers, Robbins Committee, University of Glasgow's evidence to Robbins.
4. Submission to the Committee on Higher Education by Sir Hector Hetherington, May 1962, pp. 1–2, Principal's papers Robbins Committee file.
5. Submission to the Committee on Higher Education by the General Council, p. 11.
6. Robbins Report, 1963, and Scottish Education Department circular, 1963.
7. 'Educational Change and the University' speech by Dr Charles Wilson to Educational Institute of Scotland Congress, 27 December 1963, pp. 6–7.
8. *Report of the University Court 1967–8.*
9. R. Y. Thomson (ed.), *A Faculty for Science: A Unified Diversity* (Glasgow, 1993), p. 17.
10. Information supplied by Sir Alwyn Williams.
11. Deduced from the UGC annual statistics for the 1960s.
12. *Glasgow University Guardian*, 22 April 1968, p. 1.
13. *Glasgow University Guardian*, 13 May 1968, p. 1.
14. *Glasgow University Guardian*, February 1968, p. 1.
15. See Andrew Herron, *A Record Apart*, (Glasgow, 1985), p. 65.
16. Reported in *Glasgow University Guardian*, 1965, p. 1.
17. *Report of the University Court 1972–3*, pp. 6–7, letter to Mrs Thatcher, 31 October 1972.
18. *Report of the University Court 1971–2*, pp. 2–3.
19. *Report of the University Court 1972–3*, p.1
20. Report of General Council Meeting, December 1977.
21. GUA, Letter from Fred Dainton, Chairman UGC, to all Universities 18 January 1974 ref 22/24/02674; I. G. Hutchison, *The University and the State* (Aberdeen, 1993), John Hargreaves with Angela Forbes (eds), *Aberdeen University 1945–81: Regional Roles and National Needs* (Aberdeen, 1989), pp. 113–15.
22. GUA, Letters of Dr Charles Wilson to all staff February and June 1974, Staff file.

23. Minutes of Senate 1974–75, p. 309 item 419.
24. GUA, Letter of Dr Charles Wilson to all staff, March 1976.
25. Ibid. 'The UGC and the Principal's letter', an open letter to all staff from the unions, 1974.
26. *Report of the University Court 1974–5*, p. 2.
27. *Newsletter University of Glasgow*, No 4, 16 June 1977, pp. 1 and 9–14.
28. Ibid. No. 11, 20 April 1978, pp. 1–4.
29. Minutes of Senate 1977–8, item no. 160.
30. *Newsletter University of Glasgow*, No. 8,19 June 1978, pp. 1–2 and 6.
31. Hutchison, *University and the State*, pp. 117–18.
32. *Newsletter University of Glasgow*, No. 26, 6 December 1979, pp. 1–2.
33. 'Oh Whistle and I'll come to you my lad', speech of Sir Alwyn Williams to the Adam Smith Club, 25 October 1989.
34. Sir Edward Parkes' speech at the meeting of the Committee of Vice Chancellors and Principals, 24 October 1980, text in GUA; *Newsletter University of Glasgow*, No. 35, 11 December 1980, pp. 3–6.
35. *Newsletter University of Glasgow*, No. 39, 16 April 1980, pp 1–2.
36. Ibid. No. 42, 6 July 1981, p. 5.
37. Ibid. No. 44, 8 October 1981, pp. 5–6.
38. *The Times Educational Supplement Scotland*, 24 December 1982, leading article.
39. Minutes of University Court, 20 February 1982, p. 142 item 163.
40. *Newsletter University of Glasgow*, No. 34, 6 November 1980, p. 1.
41. GUA, Letter to Alwyn Williams, 13 November 1980.
42. Minutes of University Court, 18 February 1981, pp. 179–80, item 264.
43. Ibid. paragraph 4.
44. Minutes of University Court 1981–2 Vol. 2, annex to minute of meeting of Academic Development Committee, 20 September 1982, letter of Secretary of State to Chairman of the UGC, 14 July 1982.
45. Minutes of University Court 1983–4 Vol. 2, minute of Academic Development Committee, 21 May 1984 item AD. 50.
46. *Newsletter University of Glasgow*, No. 62, 6 October 1983, pp. 1–2.
47. *Glasgow Herald*, 26 October 1983.
48. *Newsletter University of Glasgow*, No. 71, 11 October 1984, pp. 2–3.
49. GUA, Letter from Sir Peter Swinnerton-Dyer to Sir Alwyn Williams, 18 June 1984 STEAC file.
50. *A Strategy for Higher Education into the 1990s*, UGC circular letter 12/5, September 1984.
51. *Report of the University Court 1983–4*, p. 6.

CHAPTER ELEVEN

NEVER THE SAME AGAIN, 1984–2001

During the early 1980s the economy of the west of Scotland began to make a slow recovery after the traumatic failure of its traditional industries in the previous decade. The torchbearer of this renaissance in the fortunes of Glasgow was Dr Michael Kelly, Lord Provost of the city from 1980 to 1984, who launched a promotional campaign with the beguiling slogan 'Glasgow's Miles Better' with as a mascot one of Roger Hargreaves' Mr Man characters. It quickly caught the public imagination, instilling a new mood of confidence that Glasgow's enormous social problems would be solved, and led directly to Michael Kelly's election as Rector of the University in 1984. This improvement in the mood of the city reinforced the efforts Alwyn Williams had made to garner the resources to improve facilities on Gilmorehill. Writing at the end of the year, he was unusually optimistic that not only had the University survived the cuts but was entering 'the early phase of an exciting re-invigoration of [its] academic life'.[1] He had good grounds for such cheerfulness. The chairman of the UGC at the end of the visitation on 25 November 1983 encouraged the Court by saying it had in its charge 'a great and successful University'.[2] There was, however, no time for complacency with Lord Croham's committee investigating the future of the UGC and the mounting criticism by the Secretary of State for Education, Sir Keith Joseph, of the management of universities, which he underlined during 1984 by imposing an efficiency saving of one per cent in the coming financial year and two per cent in the next. The Committee of Vice Chancellors and Principals (CVCP) responded to this threat by appointing a committee, chaired by Sir Alexander Jarratt, to look into the 'efficiency' of six universities including Edinburgh and University College London.

The University's response to the UGC's circular, submitted in March 1984, challenged the assumption by the Department of Education and Science that demand for higher education was likely to fall over the next decade and therefore funding could be pegged at the 1983/4 level, and called for a Royal Commission to review the future of the whole of higher education, something the Senate would never have supported a generation earlier.[3] There was particular concern that the dual support system for teaching and research, as envisaged by Robbins, was no longer working as the University was finding it increasingly difficult to supply properly staffed well-found laboratories. There was worry that proposals for the selective funding of research would rob staff working in unsupported areas of the opportunity to conduct research in their chosen field. In September, when all the returns had been analysed, the UGC published advice to the Secretary of State in a widely-circulated document *A Strategy for Higher Education into the 1990s*.[4] The University welcomed most of the twenty recommendations, particularly the plea for level funding to the end of the decade, an increase in the equipment grant to meet the exceptional costs of Information Technology, and acceptance that demand for university places would remain buoyant. The chairman of the UGC, Sir Peter Swinnerton-Dyer, in a series of well-publicised speeches, made it clear that he did not believe this advice would be accepted and that more cuts were almost inevitable. He recommended that universities should make no plans until the government's intentions were made clear in the promised Green Paper – *The Development of Higher Education into the 1990s*.[5]

Glasgow took these warnings seriously and by February 1985 the Court and Senate had accepted a further package of economy measures based on the accurate assumption, as it turned out, of a fall in income of three per cent per annum over the next three years. Since this would involve the loss of a further seventy-five posts, an immediate freeze was imposed on all recruitment with the exception of engineering and mathematical sciences. By the end of the year the cuts imposed since 1980 had resulted in the withdrawal of forty-three courses, the closure of ten departments including Linguistics, Norwegian, History of Scots Law, International Economic Studies and Infectious Diseases, and the merging of Humanity with Greek and of Logic with Moral Philosophy. For Sir Alwyn Williams this new crisis was a bitter personal disappointment at a time when he hoped the University might share in the renaissance of the city. Whatever his regrets, he turned a virtue out of a necessity by emphasising that the central purpose of the university was to provide a wide spectrum of choice of disciplines to students from the west of Scotland, who more than ever before lacked the funds to go elsewhere.

Following a back-bench revolt in the House of Commons over proposals to increase parental contributions to student fees, publication of the Green Paper was postponed. In the meantime in March the CVCP published the so-called *Jarratt Report*[6] which flatly contradicted Sir Keith Joseph's allegations that 'universities were inefficiently managed at the tax-payers' expense'. Its principal recommendations were that laymen (in other words non-executive directors) should play a greater role in the governance of universities, that the planning process involving both Court and Senate should be streamlined, that universities should adopt a more managerial style, and that management training should be introduced. The tenor of the report reflected Jarratt's background in the civil service, which was already introducing such changes, rather than his more recent experience in the private sector. The Scottish universities regarded it as 'too dogmatic' in their particular circumstances where lay members had played a central role in governance since 1858. They recognised, however, that it behoved them to show 'they were efficient and gave value for money.'[7] Unfortunately Sir Keith Joseph, who admired dogma, believed ardently that Jarratt's recommendations were prescriptive, which had never been the intention. At Glasgow a committee was set up under the chairmanship of Sir Robert Smith, the Chancellor's Assessor on the University Court, 'to advise on any management changes that should be introduced'.[8] Reporting in the autumn of 1986, he concluded that most of the changes had already been anticipated at Glasgow when the academic plan had first been compiled in 1983. However two new committees were established. The more important one was the Planning and Resources Committee (later renamed the Management Group), consisting of the Principal, Vice-Principals, Clerk of Senate, Secretary of Court, Finance Officer, and two Senate Assessors on Court. It was to be responsible for the coordination of strategic planning (in consultation with the existing Academic Development Committee) and the presentation of policy proposals to Court and Senate. The growth in the volume of business and the doubling in the size of the Court to 33 members since 1962 made the need for such a grouping inevitable. The overall effectiveness of the corporate plan was to be assessed regularly by the second new group, a Review Committee, consisting of up to seven lay members of Court. An inevitable consequence of Jarratt and the cuts was that the role of the finance officers became more important in the management structure of all universities.

The Green Paper did not finally appear until May 1985.[9] The main recommendations were for wider access, more accountability and the removal of polytechnics in England and Wales from local control. The intention to transfer resources to science and technology was confirmed, along with the decision to shut down institutions as numbers declined. Alwyn Williams condemned it as 'a grave disappointment not only because it says nothing new but does so in such a banal and dispiriting fashion'.[10] Immediately Swinnerton-Dyer wrote to all universities with the bad news that the recurrent grant for the next three years was to be reduced by a further 1.5 per cent below the government's estimates for inflation, which were to be consistently overshot. With the cuts imposed at the time the Jarratt committee was set up, this made for a total cut of at least five per cent per annum in real terms. Although Swinnerton-Dyer paid lip service to Sir Keith Joseph's concern that 'universities must continue to take excellence as their prime objective in teaching and research', he recognised that such draconian cuts made this impractical. He reassured academics that the UGC would resist pressure to use research selectivity to implement government policy of supporting science and technology, but he made it clear that redistribution between institutions and within institutions was both necessary and inevitable. All universities were asked to submit plans by 30 November showing how they intended to accommodate the cuts and selectively support research across thirty-seven cognate groups, which had been identified by the UGC as cost centres. A detailed research statement and a forecast of student numbers had also to be submitted. On the basis of these submissions the UGC would then assess the research activity of the whole sector in a system of peer review.[11] There was no doubt that this was the most challenging and potentially divisive task the universities had yet been asked to undertake.

At Glasgow Sir Alwyn Williams was determined to make the process as transparent as possible within the very tight timetable imposed by the UGC. Decisions about research selectivity were to be made by the Academic Development Committee on the recommendation of the Research Committee, which in turn was to be advised by the faculties. Throughout the summer a bewildering mass of statistics was assembled and drafts and plans were discussed with faculties, departments and the trade unions. All members of staff were given an opportunity to comment on sections of the submission which might affect their work. There were two major difficulties. The first was to try to guess which areas of research activity across the whole University were likely to be well regarded in what, as the UGC readily admitted, was only a first stab at such an exercise. The second was to agree cuts in cost centres which were not expected to do well, but without damaging them irrevocably if the results of the review turned out differently. To complicate matters further the UGC let it be known that it would be more likely to favour subject areas, and by implication institutions, which had a track record of raising funds for research from outside sources. Such a policy would inevitably damage Glasgow, which, partly because of the parlous state of its local economy, had not been successful in attracting large grants even from the UGC itself. The only major award reported to the Research Committee in 1985 was a grant from the Computer Board to establish an innovative centre for the use of computers in the teaching of history, secured by the departments of Modern, Economic and Scottish History and the University Archives. By September research priorities had been agreed, with molecular pharmacology heading the list followed by other areas of investigation in medicine, science, engineering and computing. At the end came research in law, the humanities and social sciences. When finally completed the University's submission contained almost 30 pages of argument and evidence.

The results of the research selectivity exercise were announced by the UGC in May 1986. Altogether Glasgow had nine cost centres which were judged to be better than average and three considered to be outstanding: veterinary parasitology and pathology, electrical engineering, and history. There was a certain irony in the award of a 'star' rating to two departments in the Veterinary school, as a year earlier the UGC had threatened its closure, a threat which had only been prevented by proposals to integrate undergraduate

11.1 *Rector Michael Kelly (left) at the opening of the Design and Implementation of Software in History computing laboratory in 1986.*

teaching with Edinburgh. Three departments were assessed as below average: nursing studies, civil engineering and geography. Immediately the press seized on the ratings to produce league tables comparing all universities, which not surprisingly ranked Cambridge, Oxford, Imperial College and University College London, at the top. Overall the Scottish universities fared worse than those elsewhere in the United Kingdom. Only Edinburgh and Glasgow scored above the average, and even then they were well down the scale. Sir Alwyn commented, 'Many such rankings have been presented by the media and, flawed though they may be, they have shattered the illusion of a university monolith of excellence in research'.[12] Although the results were a disappointment to Glasgow, in that so few research areas had been considered outstanding, the Research Committee on the whole had judged accurately in selecting those areas to support. Sir Alwyn Williams, in reviewing the whole exercise, for which he had never disguised his dislike, observed: 'the British higher educational system will never be the same again even though these research assessments will affect less than one-third of the recurrent grant.'[13]

He rightly predicted that research selectivity, which was to take place in four-year cycles, would inevitably set one institution against another and lead to fragmentation.

More serious for the whole sector in the short term was the inclusion in the UGC letter announcing the results of the research selectivity exercise of details of the recurrent grant for 1986–7. Ostensibly Glasgow did well, with an increase of 1.9 per cent, placing it in eighth position out of thirty-three institutions with improved grants. However when estimated inflation of 5.25 per cent was discounted, the spending power of the University was set to fall by at least three per cent, and when salary increases were taken into account the shortfall was predicted to be more than double the two per cent on which the submission to the UGC had been based. With a projected deficit of £1.5 million, the Court announced a state of emergency on 1 August. Any post falling vacant would only be filled 'if it would be in the managerial interest to do so', and the Principal wrote to all staff inviting them to take early retirement or voluntary redundancy.[14] Worse was to follow when the recurrent grant for 1987–8 was announced in February 1987, which showed a further reduction of £230,000 due to Glasgow's less than average income from the research councils and charities over the previous decade. It was hoped that efforts made to remedy this situation would lead to the restoration of this additional cut. There was no way that the University could conceivably meet the costs of redundancy and restructuring on this scale and retain any semblance of solvency. The reserves, such as they were, had already been spent simply on keeping the fabric as wind and watertight as possible.

In the meantime the UGC had arranged for a two-man team from the Treasury and the Department of Education and Science to review the financial plight of the sector by analysing the Academic Plans of six universities including Glasgow. In considerable secrecy the team visited the University in May 1986. When their report was completed in September the Principal, Secretary of Court and Finance Officer were given an opportunity to comment in confidence on the annex relating to Glasgow. They were appalled by its superficiality and its ignorance of the assumptions on pay and inflation which universities had been instructed by the UGC to adopt in framing their academic plans. Towards the end of October the *Independent* newspaper published an article based on the whole report, which Glasgow had been assured would be highly confidential and restricted to only a few senior civil servants and ministers. The article was critical of staffing levels at Glasgow and referred to problems of tenure which could only have come from an exchange of correspondence between the Principal, the Treasury and the DES. Outraged, Sir Alwyn at once went public and protested to the Chancellor of the Exchequer and the Secretary of State that 'remarks about weak management of universities that continue to circulate in Whitehall sit ill with this particular incident.' The response from Kenneth Baker, who was now Secretary of State, was bland.[15] One outcome of this review, however, was an announcement the following month from the DES that the recurrent grant would be increased in the coming year once universities had shown that progress was being made in selectivity, rationalisation, financial management and standards of teaching.

In December 1986 the UGC advised its weary and demoralised constituents that the additional funding for 'Rationalisation and Change' announced by the DES would be dependent on the preparation of yet another academic plan to be submitted by 11 February. In an atmosphere and with language redolent of a war footing, University staff toiled over the Christmas and New Year period to meet the deadline. The objective was to keep Glasgow in the first rank of British universities. The most imaginative reconstruction proposal, responding to the government's emphasis on science, was for the formation of a School of Biological Sciences, initially comprising Botany, Cell Biology, Genetics, Microbiology and Zoology. This would require major alterations to the Chemistry building at an estimated cost of some £10 million, of which the University would have to contribute about a quarter. Medical Sciences was to be reorganised into four integrated centres, three on Gilmorehill and one at Garscube. The review did contain good news: the funding in the last two

11.2 *Sir Alwyn Williams hosting a press conference to announce the state of emergency, 1986.*

years of twelve posts entirely from endowments, including the Arthur Young professorship in accounting, the Britoil professorship in Geophysics, and two Burton chairs in Neurology and Medical Genetics.[16] The credit for this success belonged largely to Sir Alwyn and his wife, Joan, who had worked tirelessly to rebuild the University's relationship with the wider community in the city and the region. Despite the exhausting rounds of meetings, they entertained regularly in their home not just to raise endowments but also to sustain the fragile morale of those on whose commitment the University depended. In the future much of this fundraising effort was to be shouldered by the newly formed University of Glasgow Trust, directed by Professor Hugh Sutherland. Unlike those of most universities, Glasgow's academic plan was submitted on time and by 1 May was one of only two which had been accepted. This did not bring the promised largesse, just an offer to fund 50 per cent of the costs of early retirement and voluntary severance for one year only. This still left a shortfall of some £3 million. On 19 May the UGC added insult to injury, no doubt at the behest of the Treasury, by requesting financial forecasts to 1991 within a fortnight. Sir Alwyn, who despite his forthright views on government policy, had always persuaded or cajoled his colleagues into meeting impossible deadlines, had had enough. He refused, condemning it as 'crackpot harassment'.[17]

In the midst of this maelstrom the Scottish Tertiary Education Advisory Council (STEAC) had reported in December 1985, arguing that the falling population of school-leavers in the 1990s should be seen as an opportunity to provide wider access to higher education in Scotland. Impressed by the quality of tertiary education, STEAC saw no reason for any fundamental change in either structure or strategy. However the Council, determined to protect Scotland's broadly based educational system and its distinctive four-year Honours degree, was convinced that there was an urgent need for more coherent strategic planning across higher education. Various models were explored and it was recommended that a joint funding and planning body – the Scottish Higher Education Planning and Funding Council – be set up, responsible for both the universities and the central institutions. Sensitive to the reservations of the universities and their staff, STEAC believed that this radical step should not be taken until a satisfactory UK-based peer review system for teaching and research had been developed, adequate safeguards had been secured for access by the Scottish universities to research council funding, and agreement had been reached for the transfer of funds to the Scottish Office. In effect STEAC was proposing the blurring, if not the ending, of the binary divide which had become less and less meaningful. Not for the first time, Sir Alwyn Williams found himself in conflict with most of his colleagues on Gilmorehill, who along with the staff of the majority of Scottish universities rejected the recommendations as cutting them adrift from the whole university system.[18] Sir Alwyn, rightly as it turned out, had correctly read the political runes in seeing a separate funding council both as inevitable and as a useful mechanism for protecting the unique features of Scottish higher education.

In the meantime in the autumn of 1986 the Croham Committee had also reported, recommending the replacement of the UGC by the Universities Grants (Funding) Council, directly sponsored by the Secretary of State for Education. Performance indicators for research and teaching were vigorously endorsed and a triennial system of funding proposed. Croham's attitude to the STEAC report was neutral; if a Scottish Higher Education Council was set up then there should be reciprocity between the two bodies and if not then the UGC should form a separate Scottish Committee on the lines envisaged in 1979. The Scottish universities were dismayed that Croham did not seem to have explored alternative funding methodologies, but welcomed endorsement for a separate Scottish committee and for the emerging system of peer review.[19]

The Conservative government responded with a glossy White Paper entitled *Higher Education – Meeting the Challenge*,[20] published perhaps appropriately on 1 April 1987. Most of its conclusions were already well known – expansion was to be resumed at at least the rate proposed by Robbins; the emphasis was to continue to shift towards science and technology; there was room for greater efficiency throughout the system which would make for greater participation at no extra cost; and yet more resources were to be found from the private sector. The White Paper proposed the concentration of control of higher education in the hands of the Secretary of State through the establishment of a Polytechnic and Colleges Funding Council (PCFC) and a Universities Funding Council (UFC). However, it rejected STEAC's Scottish Higher Education Planning and Funding Council in favour of a Scottish Committee of the new UFC. On many issues the White Paper revealed a lack of understanding by government. There was no mention of the high cost of information technology now employed extensively in all disciplines, or issues of accountability where discussions were still progressing after more than two years of debate. Although the binary divide had been preserved, there was no explanation as to how the constituent parts were to work together. As Sir Alwyn was quick to point out, the new funding regime, which was to be based on a system of contracting, bore no resemblance to its predecessor. He called for the plan to be abandoned; otherwise, he prophesied, 'our entire higher educational system will quickly be given over to pointless paperwork, disorder and a migrant workforce of deteriorating quality.'[21] Discussion of the White Paper was muted in the hope that the Conservative government would be defeated at the forthcoming general election in June.

Following another landslide victory, the Secretary of State for Education, Kenneth Baker, pressed ahead with the implementation of the White Paper in an Education Reform Bill, which became law early in 1988. Sir Alwyn was scathing in his criticism:

> Will the Education Reform Bill give us the kind of planning and funding system which will serve the country well into the 90s and into the 21st century? I think not. It will assemble machinery to pump about £3.7 bn (currently) being spent on higher education into three independent channels: one leading to universities; another to polytechnics in England and Wales; and a third to the central institutions and colleges in Scotland. There will be few interconnecting spillways between the distributaries for the transfer of funds let alone ideas. This kind of rigid separation has all the faults of any kind of segregation. We have all experienced the bickering, inertia and even administrative sabotage which can attend shotgun meetings between representatives of independent systems which have to bid against one another for funds and smiles from the top. The world of education is not any different in this respect and the proposed structure is a recipe for half-baked political expediencies thinly crusted as policies.[22]

He no longer needed to hide his feelings, because at the end of the session he retired as Principal to return to academic life as a geologist, long after lesser men have turned to bowls. If Sir Charles Wilson at the end of his career had to sustain repeated assaults on the system of higher education he had helped to shape after the War, Sir Alwyn Williams for most of his time in office fought a campaign with the Conservative government whose repeated attacks on the universities were both inconsistent and unpredictable. Like a good general he had done his best to protect his troops from the worst of the action, but they had not always responded loyally to his calls for reinforcement when the battle was at its height. Although at times disheartened and cross, he was never bitter. As he happily admitted in his farewell address, he had enjoyed being Principal and found it as 'exciting an intellectual challenge as any sustained research programme'.[23] The University recognised the contribution of Sir Alwyn and Lady Williams by conferring honorary degrees on them both on the day of their retirement in September 1988.

The new Principal, the first to be appointed by the University rather than the Crown, was Sir William Kerr Fraser, whose background and style of management were very different. Sir William, who had recently retired as Permanent Secretary at the Scottish Office, was a distinguished graduate of the University who had been Secretary of the SRC at the time the Stone of Destiny was stolen from Westminster Abbey. His wife Marion, distinguished in her own right for her leadership in the charitable world, was also a Glasgow graduate and had been President of QM Union. This was not the first time a Principal had been appointed from outside the academic world in difficult times. Thomas Barclay had come from the parochial ministry in 1853 and masterminded the move to Gilmorehill (see p. 27). In a sense Kerr Fraser saw himself in such a pastoral tradition, guiding and caring deeply for the University community. He was later to reflect on his long association with the University since his matriculation in 1946:

> While I have since passed through the gates thousands of times I don't think the feeling of excitement has ever left me whether as a student in a noisy mass spilling out of lecture room or examination hall or, in more recent times, walking round the deserted quad late in the evening with the moon shining through the lattice work of the tower. This is to me, as to thousands of my fellow graduates, a very special place.[24]

No less irritated than his predecessor by Conservative government policy, he preferred argument and debate to the combative style which had characterised Sir Alwyn's recent confrontations with the government and the UGC. So as to emphasise this change in approach, he converted the Planning and Resources Committee into the Management Group with weekly meetings to provide the focus for a more 'cabinet' style of governance.

At the same time the University's public face was overhauled. A start had already been made in 1988 with the publication of *Avenue*, a new magazine for graduates and sponsors in imitation of such publications being produced by many other universities. Following an initial survey of academic and administrative staff attitudes to the University and its relations with the outside world, the *Annual Report* was revamped in 1989 as a vehicle for publicising the activities of the University with greater emphasis on students and external relations. An important objective was to build on the foundations laid by Sir Alwyn and Lady Joan Williams in strengthening the links with the city which had resulted in the appointment of Professor Laurie Hunter as the first Vice-Principal for External Relations. This found expression during 1988 in the contribution made by the University to the very successful Glasgow Garden Festival held on the banks of the Clyde – notably to the Crystal Pavilion, the Tropicarium, the Wildlife Garden, and the Britoil Timetreck. During 1989 MORI was commissioned to carry out a market survey which concluded that Glasgow University had a strong image in Scotland but was almost unknown in the south of England. Nowhere was Glasgow perceived as 'a powerful postgraduate institution, drawing students from all over the world.'[25] It was hoped that playing to research strengths in the *Annual Report* and press releases might help to correct this impression. As part of this process during 1990 a Visitor Centre was opened in the north front of the Scott building to provide a showcase for the University. Successive Rectors, the television personalities Johnny Ball (1993–6) and Richard Wilson (1996–9), gave their enthusiastic support to improving Glasgow's image in the wider world.

Nowhere was the support of the city to be more important than in the

11.3 *The High Street with a stylised representation of the University tower at the Glasgow Garden Festival, 1988.*

campaign during Kerr Fraser's first year to save the Vet School. Following the proposals made in 1985 to integrate veterinary undergraduate teaching with Edinburgh, a UGC Working Party on Veterinary Education was formed under the chairmanship of Sir Ralph Riley. They visited Glasgow's Vet School for a day and a half in May 1988 and held discussions with students and staff and toured some but not all departments. Although the committee praised the quality of the research, there was criticism of the UGC-funded staffing levels, especially in the clinics. Subsequently there were requests for further information, particularly a profile of clinical expertise within the Faculty. The Riley committee reported in January 1989 and proposed the concentration of veterinary education in four centres instead of the existing six. There was to be only one Scottish School of Veterinary Studies, based in Edinburgh, created by merging parts of the veterinary activities there and in Glasgow. The implication was that in effect the Glasgow school would have to close, despite the acknowledgement in the report of the outstanding world-class quality of its research. One of the grounds for this proposal was the lack of room for expansion compared to Edinburgh's Bush estate, which was manifestly untrue.

There was an immediate and widespread outcry against the proposal. The Glasgow *Evening Times* mounted a vigorous campaign and organised a petition, which collected over 70,000 signatures. The Principal wrote to all the Scottish MPs and MEPs and to members of the House of Lords who were either vets or Glasgow graduates. The Dean of Veterinary Medicine, Professor James Armour, and Sir William Weipers contacted every graduate of the school seeking their support. The response was considerable, reflecting and contributing to the start of a revival in the strength of the University's ties to its various communities. There was extensive coverage in the national press and surprisingly support from the Prime Minister herself. Under the gale of criticism the new Universities Funding Council, which took over from the UGC in March, retreated and announced in April that a decision on the future of veterinary education would be postponed until a review of veterinary manpower requirements had been completed. It was not until February 1990 that the UFC confirmed that the school would remain open and at the same time recognised the Marine Biological Station at Millport as a national facility for shore-side biology teaching.

While the Vet School campaign was being waged, the University was engaged in another massive exercise to prepare the return for the second research selectivity exercise which was to be delivered at the end of March 1989. (This came to be known as the research assessment exercise and is hereafter referred to as the RAE.) It was to be more considered than the first, with panels appointed to peer review each area and award a score from 1 (bottom) to 5 (top), which would be used as a multiplier in calculating the research element in the recurrent grant. The results when they were announced in August were mixed, not just for Glasgow but for the majority of the Scottish universities. This almost certainly reflected the distinctive tradition in Scotland with a particular emphasis on undergraduate teaching especially the large first and second year classes. Glasgow scored 5 ratings in just three subject areas – Para-Clinical Veterinary Science, Statistics and Electronics and Electrical Engineering. There were eight 4s, largely in areas which had been supported by the ADC, such as Clinical Medicine, Biological Sciences, Physics, Environmental Sciences, and Computing Science. The Science Faculty emerged on this assessment as amongst the leaders in the UK. It was anticipated that these successes would provide a good platform for the future. In Arts and parts of Medicine there was real disappointment. Anatomy, Nursing, Civil Engineering, Arabic, German and Italian scored 1s and there were nine 2s. History, which had been rated as outstanding in the previous exercise, was awarded only a 3. Moreover there was criticism that the University had dragged its feet in the implementation of selective funding of research. In fact a system of formula-based budgets (reflecting research ratings and external income) for running costs and equipment had been introduced the previous year. By this time it should have been clear that to improve performance,

11.4 *A T-shirt produced as part of the campaign to save the Vet School, 1989.*

rationalisation of subject areas was essential, but the faculties were reluctant to reduce further the spread of subjects on offer to students, particularly in minority areas where there was no alternative provision in the west of Scotland. It was agreed that there needed to be a tighter monitoring of research, but before this decision could be implemented the UFC required that such a mechanism should be incorporated within an institutional plan which would provide the framework for bidding for student numbers under the terms of the Education Reform Act.

Integral to this latest planning exercise was the implementation of the Jarratt report with a clear commitment to the devolution of responsibility and accountability in affirmation of the selective support for research. Throughout the private sector and within the civil service, this had either already happened or was taking place and there were pressures from both faculties and departments, particularly those with above average research ratings, for greater autonomy, especially devolved budgets. Shortly after his arrival Kerr Fraser had concluded that too much detail crossed his desk and there was a need to recast the management structure of the University to devolve some of the decision making. This process had been interrupted by the threatened closure of the Vet School and work on the RAE, so it was not until June 1989 that the Management Group decided that the structure and operations of the University management and administration should be reviewed. Acting on this recommendation the Court commissioned a report from the consultants Coopers & Lybrand.[26] Although they had experience of university finances, this was one of the first reports they had been commissioned to undertake into a university as a whole. Since Coopers & Lybrand were selective in gathering information, their report (presented in February 1990) betrayed a lack of understanding of the nuances of the checks and balances between Court and Senate, which remained unaltered since the 1889 Act, and the role of the Principal as *primus inter pares*. It assumed too readily that the Principal had more executive power to direct the University than in fact was the case, something which Hetherington with his experience in English universities had always known instinctively. This was a fundamental error as the report did not satisfactorily address the relationship between the two bodies, preferring to give priority to the powers of the Management Group. Equally the consultants failed to understand the nature of scholarly activity, in that academics are often engaged in research which transcends institutional boundaries and loyalties. None of this boded well for the report's recommendations.

The report proposed the establishment of planning units, either individual departments or groups of cognate departments if they were not large enough, which would be responsible for managing the devolved budgets, resource allocation and forward planning. It proposed two models for the future management of the University. In the first model the Deans would take direct responsibility for planning and resource control as well as for chairing the faculty and representing the faculty on University-level bodies. In the second model the Vice-Principals would undertake line management responsibility for planning and resource control for a group of planning units; the Deans' primary role would be to chair faculties and represent faculty interests to University-level authorities. The preference of the consultants for the second model was odd, as throughout the private sector companies were moving away from divisional structures because they led to conflict at executive level. Instead the private sector had adopted functional divisions with executive directors responsible for different functions, finance, human resources and so on. The report was at its weakest in discussing such support services. The whole enquiry, because it was conducted in apparent secrecy, caused considerable unease throughout the University at a time when staff morale was low due to poor research ratings and low pay.

Directly it was available the report was circulated widely to all heads of departments and academic sections and a summary sent to every member of staff. A tight timetable of two months was set for discussion and implementation to meet the deadline for the submission of the institutional plan on 22

June. This was unfortunate, as it did not allow time for adequate reflection on such important changes at what was a very busy period of the year with examining in full swing. The reaction across the University to Model Two was hostile, particularly to the downgrading of the faculties and the conversion of unelected Vice-Principals into super-Deans. If there was to be change, which many did not want, the Senate's preference was for Model One. The Principal refused to consider this option – 'I find it difficult to believe that the Faculties, even with minor adjustments in the *number* of Faculties (either up or down), would throw up a regular supply of people who have the necessary interest in administration and are prepared to give the time to it: it would be very different from the present post.'[27]

The Principal believed there were three options open to the Court. The first was to reject the report completely and give more executive power to the Deans, which would leave the Management Group with little effective power to change the direction of the University. The second was to accept Model Two but recognise that the creation of Planning Units would be an evolving process with the Deans still having considerable influence in formulating policy in consultation with heads of planning units, who in most cases would be heads of department. He knew this proposal would be unacceptable to a substantial minority of the Senate, but he was uncertain how the third model advocated by a majority in Senate (and in fact adopted successfully by the University of Edinburgh) would work in practice. This would involve the Vice-Principals having 'a clearly defined portfolio of policy and resource responsibilities across the University, rather than a sectoral responsibility in terms of subject area'.[28] Instead an uneasy compromise was agreed whereby the position of the Deans and Faculties would be protected, with the right of appeal over the head of the Vice-Principal to the Management Group. The Vice-Principals instead of having executive authority would only be engaged in 'advisory and monitoring functions in the context of the formulation of Faculty plans and in the area of income generation.'[29] Although such a plan was fraught with potential difficulty and overburdened the Vice-Principal responsible for planning and external relations, the Senate agreed as it represented for the first time a genuine attempt to devolve financial and therefore managerial responsibility. The new structure was to be put in place from 1 January 1991.

The haste of this reformation was driven by the (as it turned out unreal) agenda of the bidding process introduced under the Education Reform Act, which Kerr Fraser had already condemned uncharacteristically in public as 'disgraceful'.[30] Throughout the year a great deal of time and effort had gone into developing the institutional plan. Much of the content was familiar, with an emphasis on the quality of both teaching and research, on service to Scottish education and on the maintenance and further development of the University's international reputation and clientele. Although the Sciences had done notably better than the Arts and Social Sciences in the 1989 research selectivity exercise, nothing was to be done to disturb the balance of (43:57) undergraduate admissions between the two. In the belief that 'no department can teach adequately to Honours level without being involved in research', research funding was to continue to be made available to all departments but within the priorities set by faculties.[31] Overall the plan gave the impression of being cobbled together with little indication that the University had any real priorities for either teaching or research. This was not entirely true, and simply reflected the exhaustion and cynicism of the majority of staff with the seemingly never-ending planning process. In the event it did not matter, as in the accompanying tender document every university in the United Kingdom bid at the guide price (in other words precisely the same price) for the majority of their places. As a result at the beginning of November the UFC summarily abandoned the whole exercise, leaving the universities to wait until the spring of 1990 before their recurrent grant was announced and with no indication of what assumptions it would be calculated on.

In the meantime the Management Group had been pressing ahead with the introduction of the new administrative structure, particularly the formation of the Planning Units. Although it was agreed that faculties could by a majority vote become planning units, this would not prevent individual departments or groups of departments forming their own planning units. At the same time the University's committee structure was reviewed in the hope of reducing the number of committees. With a few exceptions, this initiative was a failure, but it did have the effect of downgrading the role of the Academic Development Committee which took over the function of the Senate Business Committee in reviewing the business of the Senate; policy and resource issues were now a matter for the much smaller Management Group, while wider educational issues now rested with the Educational Policy Committee. As might have been expected from the nature of the compromise arrangement, the process of forming the planning units was tense and protracted. The Faculties of Arts, Divinity, Social Sciences, Law and Financial Studies and Veterinary Medicine became planning units in their own right, but the other Faculties of Engineering, Medicine and Science dissolved into a number of units. Science was most fragmented with no fewer than nine planning units. These units operated in shadow from 1991–2 and were fully activated from 1992–3. Having agreed that there would be twenty-two units, a model for resource distribution (RDM) had to be devised. This was equally fraught as the Management Group wished to establish a model that would keep the University in balance but allow resources to flow to areas of excellence; whereas the Senate wanted to stick with the income-driven methodology used in the now discarded tender, which had accompanied the institutional plan. The Senate accused the Management Group of 'abdicating responsibility for deciding on the shape of the University'.[32] Departments which had scored

5s in the research selectivity exercise complained that the model would give them very little additional resource per year. When the model was adjusted to take account of these concerns, the Arts Faculty, which with its low research rating was likely to be in deficit, was vociferous in its complaint that it set in concrete Arts' historic cross-subsidy of the Science Faculty. Nevertheless there was little evidence that the Arts Faculty had taken any significant steps to improve its research performance. Bowing to pressure, the Court recognised that there would inevitably be inequalities, and conceded the need for a revised RDM in future years. In the meantime the Vice-Principals were to use their considerable discretionary powers to support areas of excellence within their own bailiwicks.

Mrs Thatcher was ousted as leader of the Conservative Party in October 1990 and succeeded as Prime Minister by John Major, whose task was to restore the government's standing in the opinion polls by pursuing more 'friendly' policies. In higher education policy had already begun to move in the direction of wider access, and there had been some relaxation in funding to allow for the recruitment of young lecturers so as to correct the age imbalance. In the Spring of 1991 a White Paper *Higher Education – A New Framework*[33] was published, that committed the government to encouraging more young people into higher education with a projected rise in student numbers of 16 per cent over the next five years. It proposed, as Sir Alwyn Williams had foretold, the abolition of the binary divide and the creation of separate funding councils in the four constituents of the United Kingdom. As a result the Council for National Academic Awards (CNAA), which was responsible for validating qualifications in the polytechnics, would be wound up and each polytechnic (now dignified with the title of university) would take over this function. The system of dual support for research was preserved and the government recognised that the allocation of resources should not be just a function of the number of students but include measures of quality. The White Paper dwelt at length on the quality of teaching and proposed that a quality audit unit should be established covering the whole of the United Kingdom. There was relief at Glasgow that the research councils would continue to serve the whole of the United Kingdom, but concern that the termination of the binary divide might result in the dilution of resources available for research. The Scottish Higher Education Funding Council (SHEFC) took over the functions of the UFC in Scotland in October 1992 and the two polytechnics in the West of Scotland, Glasgow and Paisley, achieved university status as Glasgow Caledonian University and the University of Paisley respectively.

One recommendation of the White Paper, which had been widely canvassed beforehand, was that closer links should be established between universities (both new and old), and with teacher training colleges. In the expectation that the CNAA would be wound up, the University opened discussions with

Paisley College of Technology and Jordanhill College during 1989 with a view to improving opportunities for students, promoting collaboration in teaching and research and permitting joint academic planning. The Management Group set up working groups to consider a range of options. The Paisley working group reported in October and recommended the appointment of a joint academic council whose main function would be to validate degree programmes in cognate disciplines in both institutions. The Faculty of Science, which was most affected by the proposal, was 'strongly opposed to the establishment of any formal links'[34] and was deeply troubled by the idea that the University rather than CNAA would validate Paisley degrees. The arguments were reminiscent of those advanced during the discussions with the RCST thirty years earlier. At the time it was generally believed that with the new dispensations the funding councils would designate universities as research (R), teaching (T), and hybrids (X) with different funding streams. In retrospect such a decision was wishful thinking on the part of the older universities as it was the antithesis of the spirit of the reforms. Yet, despite its poor showings in the RAEs of 1986 and 1989, Glasgow desperately wished to be 'R' rated. It was this as much as concern about the quality of courses that killed further discussions.

Negotiations with Jordanhill progressed in parallel. In the past, although the University provided academic courses for students at Jordanhill College and validated and awarded degrees, the relationship had been at arm's length. With the decline in demand for teachers in recent years the College had extended its vocational training into other areas and now offered courses jointly with the University in nursing and with engineering in the training of teachers of technology. These developments led naturally to discussions about more formal links, but stopping short of integration. Just like Paisley, the working group proposed in May 1991 to set up a joint planning council, but by now (unknown to the University) Jordanhill, which had a large projected deficit, wished for full integration with a university as soon as practicable. The Management Group and the Senate were reluctant to be hurried into a decision for the same reasons that had led to the rejection of links with Paisley. Concerned that the University might be missing an opportunity, the Management Group consulted the Scottish Office Education Department but the response was equivocal. Annoyed by this seeming vacillation, the Principal of the College, Dr Tom Bone, approached the out-going Principal of Strathclyde, Sir Graham Hills. He was enthusiastic and at once recommended the proposed merger to his successor Professor John Arbuthnott. To Glasgow's chagrin, a joint working party was set up in October and by March 1992 had framed a proposal for amalgamation, which was accepted by the UFC's Scottish Committee. The Scottish Office gave its approval on 1 September and Glasgow lost a connection which stretched back for almost a century to the establishment of the lectureship in Education in 1894. Although it was recognised that the merger would have major implications for courses in Education, Engineering and probably Nursing Studies, in the interests of the students the Court had no alternative but to agree to the orderly transfer of responsibilities.[35] These unhappy episodes suggested that members of the Senate had learned nothing from the sorry tale of the negotiations with the Royal College of Science and Technology, Strathclyde's predecessor, in the 1950s.

There was no time for recriminations as submissions for the third research assessment exercises were due in June 1992. This time far more information was required about the research intentions and endeavours of every department and every member of staff. Altogether Glasgow's submission amounted to 186,000 sheets of paper covering 56 out of the UFC's now 72 categories – more than for any other university in the United Kingdom. On this occasion seven units of assessment achieved a 5 rating: Biochemistry, Veterinary Science, Statistics, Computing Science, Social and Economic Research (Urban and Housing Studies), Politics and Theatre, Film and TV Studies. Although an improvement, it was less than Strathclyde. No department scored a 1, but the overall outcome was disappointing and there was now real concern about the lack of progress in Arts, Law and Financial Studies, and Medicine. The problem was that, even if there was improvement, other universities had also improved, thereby reducing the amount of resource to be distributed. There was also evidence that the RAE was becoming a self-fulfilling prophecy with able research-active staff unwilling to work in any department that was not rated 4 or above. As before, Glasgow remained reluctant to concentrate research on a few areas for fear it would damage its overall capability.

While these events had been unfolding the student population at Glasgow had been growing rapidly from about 11,000 in 1988 to over 13,500 by 1992. Although the majority of students still came from Scotland, they now only accounted for 70 per cent, proportionately fewer than in the 1980s. With the population in the west of Scotland falling, the decline in numbers would have been greater had not the University in partnership with the Strathclyde Regional Council put in place schemes to widen access to those from less privileged backgrounds. The numbers coming from other parts of the United Kingdom had risen markedly to almost 15 per cent by 1993, reflecting in part the Troubles in the North of Ireland. Glasgow was exerting its historic role of providing education, and by implication an escape route, for members of the Protestant community. More encouraging from the perspective of the hard-pressed University finances was the growing number of students who were coming from overseas, mostly to take postgraduate courses – almost 10 per cent by 1992. At last the University was able to address the long-standing problem of accommodation by building the Murano Student Village with space for 1,200 students on the site of a derelict glassworks at Ruchill. Innovatively this bold £18.5 million project was financed by means of a bank loan of £17.25 million to be repaid from revenue. At the same time a further 650 places were provided at Cairncross House in Kelvinhaugh funded by the University Trust, the Glasgow Development Agency and Scottish Homes.

The other barrier to expansion was inadequate lecture theatres and seminar rooms, particularly in the older buildings, many of which remained little changed since the early part of the century. Successful fundraising from both the public and private sector allowed for the refurbishment and restoration of many of the buildings on the campus during the remainder of the decade. The intention was to make the historic buildings on the campus relatively 'maintenance free' by renewing roofs and stonework, because of the declining skilled workforce in the Works Department. By 1994 the University's building programme totalled almost £100 million, including the new student accommodation, the refurbishment of Chemistry and Physics and Astronomy, the Robertson Building for Dermatology and Genetics, all of which had been completed.[36] At the reopening of the Chemistry Building, in January 1994, Professor Geoff Webb, the head of department, declared: 'we have increased the accommodation for undergraduate teaching as much as 50 per cent to meet the increasing demand for student places'.[37] In addition this allowed for the relocation of five Biology Departments within the building. The projects in hand were the redevelopment of the Anderson's College of Medicine, the Clinical Research Initiative into heart disease to link the West Medical Building and the Biochemistry building, a lecture theatre complex on the

11.5 *Sir James Black, the Nobel prize-winner and a graduate of the University, discussing his research with Dr Gareth Griffiths at the opening of the Robertson Building, 1992.*

11.6 *Gavin Hastings, former captain of the Scottish rugby team, opening the refurbished Stevenson building, 1995.*

Western Infirmary site, and the Weipers Equine Centre at Garscube. A grant from SHEFC made possible a radical extension to the Library with the construction of an extra storey to house Special Collections and the conversion of the whole of the ground floor and basement as undergraduate study space. Much of the Scott Building, including the Hunterian Museum, and the whole of University Gardens, which housed Arts departments, was subsequently refurbished. The Gilmorehill Halls (a former church) at the foot of University Avenue were converted into a Centre for Theatre, Film, and Television Studies. The Sports and Recreation Service's Stevenson Building was completely refitted to provide state of the art facilities. The old sportsfield at Garscadden was sold and new grounds, some with all weather surfaces, were laid out on the Garscube estate. This upgrading of the University's estate was the most extensive since the late 1950s and early 1960s and was one of Kerr Fraser's lasting legacies to the University.

Any expectation that the formation of a separate funding council for Scotland and the end of the binary divide would herald a period of stability was to be quickly disappointed. As was only to be expected the Scottish Higher Education

Funding Council quickly developed its own distinctive methodologies for funding and the assessment of the quality of teaching. However these had to be set in the context of policy set by the Westminster government, which during 1994 abandoned further growth (achieved by the abolition of the binary divide). At much the same time the per capita allocations by the Funding Council for courses in Arts, Law, Divinity and Social Sciences were slashed by 30 per cent, supposedly to encourage students to embark on Science and Technology courses. The only explanation for such a massive reduction can be penny-pinching of the most unpleasant kind as it failed to take into account the cost of the provision of libraries, the laboratories as it were of the humanities. This was a bitter blow to these faculties at Glasgow, which had successfully made the case for better treatment in a revised RDM. The grant from SHEFC, which allowed for an additional 600 funded places for 1994–5, was only increased by 5.3 per cent compared with a national average of 6.1 per cent. Professor James Armour, the Vice-Principal for Planning and Resources, was relieved – 'This is a better award than many feared at a difficult financial time'.[38] The settlement incorporated a new funding formula for the research component, which further disadvantaged the University by including an unrealistic estimate of the income which could be expected to be derived in overheads from research council grants. In addition the proportion of the grant for four subjects in which Glasgow had done relatively well in the RAE was reduced because Scotland as a whole excelled in these areas.

Further reductions in the unit of resource, together with a growing emphasis on inter-disciplinarity and the failure of the large science departments to gain 5s in the RAE, made rationalisation of the planning units inevitable. Servicing over twenty planning units was an administrative nightmare and prohibitively expensive. The Management Group proposed in June 1993 that the number should be halved. Over the next six months there were lengthy consultations with the departments most likely to be affected. Despite reservations focusing on fears about the possible loss of departmental identity, in some cases stretching back a hundred years or more, the Senate agreed amicably in February 1994 that the eleven science planning units would be reduced to three, and Engineering's three planning units to one. In Science Charles Fewson, the hardworking and outspoken professor of Biochemistry, took the initiative in welding together the Institute of Biomedical and Life Sciences (IBLS) out of the departments of Anatomy, Botany, Biochemistry, Cell Biology, Genetics, Microbiology, Pharmacology, Physical Education and Sports Sciences, Physiology, Virology and Zoology. He wanted to reduce unnecessary duplication of administrative effort, giving staff more time 'on work directly related to their teaching and research'. The pooling of resources would also 'enable large items of equipment to be purchased and research and teaching initiatives to be more readily funded'.[39] A Physical Sciences Planning Unit was crafted out of the departments of Physics, Astronomy,

Chemistry, Applied Geology and Geography and Topographical Science, and another from Computing Science, Mathematics and Statistics. Psychology joined Social Sciences and after much debate the Faculty of Divinity, one of the original faculties of the University, merged for resource purposes with the Faculty of Arts. There were to be two new planning units: Central Administration, and Academic Services (embracing the Library, Media Services, Computing Services, Archives, and the Hunterian Museum and Art Gallery). This further reform made it possible to provide all planning units with the administrative support necessary to discharge their devolved responsibilities and capitalise on their increasingly coherent identities. The protracted but fundamental structural reformation of the University was a major achievement for Kerr Fraser, as significant as his contribution to transforming its physical estate.

Meanwhile SHEFC was pressing the Scottish universities to make radical changes to the curriculum by splitting courses into modules, which would be transferable with other institutions, and the replacement of the three-term year with two semesters. As in Germany, the transfer of courses, validated by class tickets, had been a feature of the British system of higher education for over two hundred years and had only disappeared with the advent of structured degree courses during the later nineteenth century. A Senate Working Party

Dr Noreen Burrows

Dr Dorothy Geddes

Dr Sheila Maclean

Dr Lorraine Smith

11.7 *1989–90 saw four more women as Professors, three of them representing 'firsts': Dr Noreen Burrows, appointed to the Chair in European Law, became the first woman to hold a permanent Chair in Law in Scotland; the late Dr Dorothy Geddes, as Titular Professor in Oral Biology, became the UK's first female dental professor; Dr Sheila Maclean of Forensic Medicine & Science was appointed the first incumbent of the new IBA Chair in Law & Ethics in Medicine; and Dr Lorraine Smith was appointed to the Chair in Nursing.*

endorsed these proposals and suggested semesters should be introduced from the academic year 1997/8. Although the University in effect had had a two-term year until 1910, opinion was divided on this apparently radical step. The Arts Faculty favoured semesters so that the year would be clearly divided between teaching and examining and research. The Science Faculty was opposed. The Senate eventually rejected semesters, but accepted modularisation within the three-term structure. There was, however, disagreement about the length of modules. Arts opted for 'short fat' modules delivered over a term, whereas Science went for 'long thin' modules delivered over the whole teaching year. There were good pedagogical arguments on both sides, but the net effect was to confirm the 'cafeteria' style of many courses and to increase pressure on students.

The Medical Faculty used these discussions to review its courses in response to a discussion document *Tomorrow's Doctors*, published by the General Medical Council, which with the move away from hospital care argued for the need to train doctors with a more rounded view, particularly of ethical questions. At the beginning of 1995 the Faculty announced that in 1996 a new innovative curriculum (at least in the United Kingdom) would be introduced focused on 'problem-based learning' of the type already widely practised in North America, Europe and Australasia. The emphasis would be away from the traditional set-piece lecture, which had characterised teaching at Glasgow since the sixteenth century, towards small-group teaching with a facilitator. The development of the new curriculum was watched with interest by other medical schools, which were also under pressure to change as evidence mounted that they were failing to train doctors with the necessary skills to work in a changing environment.[40]

Just as SHEFC was seeking to re-establish greater flexibility in the curriculum, Mrs Gillian Shephard, the new Secretary of State, announced in 1995 yet another review of the universities (to be completed in three months) at first in England and then later extended to the whole of the country. She posed three fundamental questions – 'what is the purpose of higher education, what are the implications for the future shape of higher education, and what are the implications for the future size of higher education?' Like Sir Alwyn Williams seven years before, Sir William Kerr Fraser, who was to retire at the end of the session, had had enough of this perpetual revolution, reminiscent of a Maoist regime. He attacked the short timescale of the review, which he dubbed 'Mrs Shephard's examination paper' and was forthright in his advice:

> The truth is this. The Government can decree that the country's universities will provide mass higher education, or it can decree that there shall be no fall in the quality of higher education. What it cannot have is both quality and mass higher education without a greater flow of funds, not necessarily from the taxpayer, into the universities.[41]

Despite this solemn admonition, there was some cause for celebration. During 1994 a Teaching and Learning Service had been established to disseminate 'good' practice and to prepare the University's submissions for the newly introduced assessment of teaching. In October Glasgow received five 'excellents' for the quality of its teaching in chemistry, computing science, geography, geology and physics in the quality assessment exercise undertaken by the Scottish Higher Education Funding Council. This success, which confirmed Glasgow's long commitment to teaching and mitigated the disappointment of successive RAEs, brought welcome additional resource in the shape of extra funded student places. In December the University received a coveted Queen's Anniversary Trust Award in recognition of its distinguished service to the community through a diversity of activities ranging from the educational programmes of the Hunterian Museum and Art Gallery, the extensive activities of the Department of Adult and Continuing Education, the work of the Student Volunteer Service and a wealth of concerts, lectures and other events. The Visitor Centre was recognised as a pioneering example of excellence. Kerr Fraser could take much credit for this distinction which flowed in large measure from the MORI survey in 1989. The University bade him and Lady Fraser farewell at a ceremony in the Bute Hall in June 1995, when he was presented with his portrait. Unlike Hetherington, he was well pleased with his likeness.

At the same time Sir Alec Cairncross announced he would stand down as Chancellor in December 1995. A graduate of the University and a distinguished economist, he had taken his duties seriously from the time of his election in 1972. This had come as a surprise. When Sydney Checkland nominated him, Cairncross replied that he thought it must be a joke. He chaired meetings of the General Council and would spend his time during his visits to Gilmorehill with his wife Mary exploring in his unassuming way every nook and cranny and making friends with all he met. More importantly he acted as a 'father confessor' to successive Principals, dispensing his advice with a twinkle in his eye. He and Charles Wilson were longstanding friends and shared a love of the Solway. Alwyn Williams regularly turned to him for advice and help, particularly in appointments in the humanities and social sciences. Kerr Fraser drew inspiration from his well-studied knowledge of the strengths and weaknesses of his *alma mater*. He was the first Chancellor to retire. All his predecessors had either died or been expelled. In the subsequent two-cornered election Kerr Fraser was elected, becoming the second Principal to succeed to the office.

The new Principal, Professor Graeme Davies, had been an academic engineer, first at Cambridge and then at Sheffield. Then like Hetherington he had been Vice-Chancellor of the University of Liverpool from 1986 to 1991. He was then appointed chief executive of both the Universities Funding Council (UFC)

11.8 *Sir William Kerr Fraser admiring his portrait, painted by the young Aberdeen artist Alexander Fraser to mark his retirement, 1995.*

and the Polytechnics and Colleges Funding Council; subsequently he headed their successor the Higher Education Funding Council for England (HEFCE). On his arrival at Glasgow in October 1995 he at once set out his stall with a shift in emphasis away from building (very necessary under Kerr Fraser) towards investing in people. He believed that there would be little further expansion in the undergraduate population but he looked for a growth in postgraduate numbers, which were still lower than those at universities of equivalent size in the rest of the United Kingdom. He immediately recast the Management Group by adding the Director of Estates and Buildings and the Director of Personnel Services and giving the Vice-Principals functional responsibilities for Staffing, Estates and Buildings, Research and Academic Support Services (this function was later divided with the appointment of a separate Vice-Principal for Research), and External Relations and Marketing. He created a Resources Strategy Group bringing together the Management Group and the heads of Planning Units to broaden the decision-making base, 'so that those involved in the management of the University at levels below the central administrative group are further involved in initiating strategy and policy'.[42] These measures were early steps in a concerted campaign to modernise the University's management and administration. With the next RAE a year away, he laid particular store by research and improving the University's mechanisms for submitting proposals. He introduced twice-yearly 'state of the union' addresses, repeated at various locations throughout the University to improve communications with individual members of staff who had been alienated by the seemingly interminable cuts and changes in policy direction. He was enthusiastic in support of the University's manifold contributions to the wider community in Glasgow and beyond. Moreover as an expert on the UK higher education system, he was determined that Glasgow should position itself among its preeminent institutions in the challenging times that lay ahead. Such success he believed would be fostered by a coherent, confident institution – a goal pursued by an open door policy and a vigorous programme of hospitality, mounted with his wife Florence, a fellow academic.

During 1996 the Principal, who was knighted in the New Year honours, encouraged the development and strengthening of the University's links with other institutions in the west of Scotland. In January the University secured funding from SHEFC under its regional strategic initiative (RSI) for twenty-nine projects including the creation of a travelling astronomy facility to promote public awareness of science, the setting up of a centre for research in theatre and performance along with Glasgow School of Art and the Royal Scottish Academy of Music and Drama (RSAMD). In May the University responded to an invitation from Dumfries and Galloway Council about the establishment of a University College on the site of the Crichton Hospital so as to provide access to higher education in that region. The original intention of the benefactor, Elizabeth Crichton, was to establish a university, but this was over-ruled by the government of the day and the benefaction was used for a very large mental hospital, now closed. Plans for the College were announced in July and an accord was signed in February 1997 between the University and the three other local partners in the enterprise. While some members of staff at Gilmorehill worried about a diversion of resources, there was enthusiasm for the project in south-west Scotland. At the ceremony the Convenor of Dumfries and Galloway Council, Allan Baldwick, declared that the signing was 'one of the most important events in the history of the Council'.[43] Following an approach formulated by Jan McDonald, professor of Drama, the plan was to operate the College in the style of an American liberal arts college, with the possibility of Honours-level study at Glasgow to follow. The hope was that educational innovations introduced at Crichton would eventually impact on Gilmorehill. Rex Taylor, professor of Social Policy and Social Work, was appointed first Director. Aided by grants from SHEFC and infrastructural

11.9 *Sir Graeme Davies delivering his 'state of the union' address at the Vet School, March 2000.*

collaboration at Dumfries with the University of Paisley, teaching began in 1999 with the admission of some sixty students.

Discussions about Crichton were followed by proposals in the spring of 1997 for a closer relationship with the Catholic St Andrew's College of Education in Bearsden, which had had its funding cut by almost five per cent the previous year. SHEFC supported the integration with universities of all Scotland's teacher training colleges and the University was eager to strengthen its ties to the school sector and the teaching profession. Even in a more secular age, such a connection posed unique problems for Glasgow with its long established association (despite its Papal origins) with the Church of Scotland and the Protestant faith. In Divinity the Church of Scotland still retained the right to approve appointments that concerned matters of faith. Although the University had been admitting Catholic students in larger and larger numbers since the 1930s and had a vigorous and respected Catholic chaplaincy, there were genuine fears that the amalgamation might fuel sectarianism on the campus. There were long and heated debates in Senate, redolent of the arguments at the time of the Disruption in 1843 rather than the late twentieth century. There were misunderstandings on both sides. Many senators failed to understand how much Roman Catholicism had changed since the Second Vatican

Council, whilst some Catholics were slow to grasp concerns about separate school education and the seeming authoritarianism of some of the pronouncements of members of the Catholic hierarchy, particularly on questions of morality. As in the past there was the same tiresome concern about amalgamation with an institution which was not research-led, despite the fact that merger with Jordanhill did not seem to have damaged Strathclyde's reputation. It was not until March 1998 that the University and the College were able to agree on merger proposals to be submitted to the Secretary of State. After approval, the College together with the University Departments of Education and of Adult and Continuing Education formed a new Faculty of Education with the Principal of the College, Professor Bart McGettrick, as its first Dean. When this was announced McGettrick chose his words carefully: 'This positive move by St Andrew's College allows us to take a wider role in serving education in Scotland and we hope to take real strides towards an appropriate and harmonious place for Catholic education in contemporary Scottish society'.[44] The process took much longer than anyone could have anticipated and the merger was not finalised until 1999.

While these alliances were being negotiated, the University was facing a further funding crisis. The Conservative government, taking up Kerr Fraser's challenge, brought expansion to a halt in April 1996 and at the same time adopted a very tight fiscal stance. This resulted in massive cuts in allocations to English universities and slightly smaller reductions in Scotland, but severe enough. Glasgow's share fell by three per cent and the funds to be made available under the regional strategic initiative were severely pruned. With an election only a year away which the Labour party was almost certain to win, there was widespread agitation against these cuts at a time when it was widely recognised that the sector was seriously underfunded. Bowing to pressure the government set up an inquiry into the funding of higher education chaired by Sir Ron Dearing (with a parallel inquiry in Scotland chaired by Sir Ron Garrick), which was not expected to report until after the election. Both the Labour and Conservative parties agreed to implement their findings. For Glasgow worse was to follow.

At the end of April 1996 the University's submission for the Research Assessment Exercise was completed, 56 submissions for 51 units of assessment. When the results were announced at the turn of the year, they showed the hoped-for improvement with two-thirds of research-active staff in subject areas awarded grades of 4 or 5. There were seven departments with 5s: Biochemistry, Computing Science, Electronics and Electrical Engineering, Molecular Genetics, Politics, Russian and Eastern European Studies and Urban Studies. Both Computing Science and Urban Studies had coveted 5* ratings. There had been real improvements across the board in Engineering, Law, Social Sciences and in several Arts departments such as Classics and French. Sir Graeme Davies commented: 'The improvement in our average

11.10 *Ian Carter of the research office holding the discs which contained the University's RAE submission, 1996.*

was greater than that for Scotland as a whole, which in turn was greater than that for the UK, so we have much to be proud of, especially since, with entries in 56 subject areas, we had the most comprehensive submission to the RAE of any university in Britain'.[45] Nevertheless there was still disappointment. Although research-inactive staff had been excluded from the returns, in Arts there was frustration in History and English, and in Medicine none of the clinical departments had excelled. Despite the large investment in Chemistry, it had only achieved a 3.

The real pride in the improved overall ratings was quickly overshadowed by the announcement of the University's grant from SHEFC for 1997/8. Because most universities had improved their ratings, the proportion of grant allocated in the higher grades was reduced. However because the multiplier for 5 and 5* departments was increased, those with 4s, which represented the majority of research-active staff at Glasgow, were further disadvantaged. Since Glasgow had only 76 per cent of research-active staff (Edinburgh had 94 per cent) and only seven 5s, the RAE element of Glasgow's grant was slashed by a massive 8.5 per cent. Fortunately the grant for teaching rose by 3.7 per cent to reflect the University's continuing success in the assessment of the quality of its teaching. Overall the cut was just under 1 per cent compared with a rise of 2 per cent for the sector as a whole. This was the worst position of any of the older Scottish universities. Sir Graeme Davies at once went on the offensive to reassure his colleagues who had put so much effort into improving Glasgow's standing:

> The important thing we must do is to recognise that we have made significant progress down a very difficult road and the most important thing for the future is that we must not in any way waver in our resolve. Redeveloping the research base is not a short term activity . . .[46]

He was well aware that the explanation for Glasgow's relative failure had a long history with little encouragement or opportunity in some areas for staff to maintain their research interests once their postgraduate work was completed. He was adamant that there would be no witch hunt, rather confidential enquiry and encouragement. This approach formed part of a new strategy for a research-led university which incorporated an effort to produce 'well-supported academics' whose teaching and research reinforced each other and who interacted effectively with administrators, technicians, secretaries and manual staff. A new Vice-Principal post for Research was created with responsibility for improving the grades in the next RAE, increasing research income and encouraging a growth in postgraduate numbers. The biggest challenge was to increase the number of research-active staff to bring the proportion up to the level of Edinburgh.

In their evidence to the Dearing and Garrick inquiries, the Scottish universities endorsed the principles of the Robbins report and drew attention to the role of higher education in wealth creation (now a favourite theme of both main political parties) while at the same time defending the traditional values of intellectual endeavour for its own sake. They saw little room for central direction except to set the parameters of the sector, preferring that collaboration, cooperation and rationalisation should be left to individual institutions. They drew attention to the damage that successive cuts had done to the sector, driving many institutions into serious funding difficulties. They appreciated there were two distinct but related funding problems, the additional funding needs of the institutions and the problem of student support. They endorsed the CVCP's proposal that if no 'new' funds were available then student maintenance grants should be replaced by loans, 'and create in that way additional funding provision available to the system'.[47]

As widely expected the Labour Party won a landslide victory in the general election in May 1997. The academic community was very hopeful that the new government would respond positively to the plight of the sector. They were quickly to be disillusioned as the new Chancellor of the Exchequer,

Gordon Brown, was committed to the same tough fiscal stance as his predecessor. Dearing and Garrick reported in July, recommending the introduction of a flat rate tuition fee of £1,000 a year. Scottish students with their unique four-year degree would only have to pay a total of £3,000. This additional funding would be available to the sector as a whole, which would also benefit by the reduction in the cuts over the next two years of nearly 9 per cent imposed by the previous government to just 2 per cent. The report proposed that the research councils should pay full overheads on all grants, and that an Arts and Humanities Research Council be established. The Scottish Garrick committee called for greater collaboration in research between institutions and with industry. The government's response was as unexpected as it was uncharacteristic of a party that had consistently opposed means-testing of benefits. Student fees were to be introduced as Dearing proposed, but means-tested maintenance grants were to be abolished and replaced entirely by loans set at a level which more or less obliged students to work if they wished to study away from home. There was to be no Arts and Humanities Research Council, and overheads paid by the other councils were to be met by reducing the RAE element in the recurrent grant. This new funding regime was intended to permit further expansion of higher and further education as part of the government's commitment to lifelong learning.

The immediate implication for Glasgow of this failure of the Labour government to live up to the promises made before the election was 'a very significant' projected deficit, which could only be addressed by saving some £6 million a year largely in staff costs. It was estimated that there was a need to shed between six and nine per cent of staff, but the Principal pledged that there would be no compulsory redundancy.[48] There was no comfort from the annual grant which was increased by less than one per cent, confirming that higher education was as low on Labour's agenda as on that of the Conservatives. The financial crisis, which rocked the Far East during the spring, added to the uncertainty as many students from that part of the world studying at Glasgow found it difficult to pay their fees. By the autumn 331 staff had agreed to take advantage of the early retirement and voluntary severance scheme, making restructuring possible. Of necessity this fresh financial crisis resulted in a shift of financial influence to the Management Group from the planning units.

Despite the deepening gloom, the Principal remained as confident as his predecessors had been in similar circumstances that the future could be assured. He could draw comfort from much good news, notably a very significant increase in funding for research grants and contracts from around £40 million in 1995–6 to over £70 million in 1998–9. In May Glasgow had become a founder member of Universitas 21, a group of major universities in the United Kingdom, Australia, New Zealand, China, Canada, Singapore and the United States, opening up opportunities for increased student mobility, exchange fellowships, and collaboration in major research initiatives. The award of two more 'excellents' for teaching in July placed Glasgow in pole position amongst the Scottish universities and augured well for the future. To ensure that this lead was maintained a Vice-Principal (Learning and Teaching) was appointed to be responsible for developing a new learning and teaching strategy with greater emphasis on a student-centred approach. On 30 September a research partnership was signed with Strathclyde, helping to lay to rest the distrust that had characterised the relationship between the two institutions since the signing of the concordat in 1913. Both universities were convinced the understanding would bring 'excellence to the science base, benefit the community, boost the economy and ensure that Glasgow is seen across Europe as a major research city'.[49] A year earlier the two universities had collaborated to establish the multi-million-pound Yoshitomi Research Institute into Neuroscience in Glasgow (YRING) funded by Yoshitomi Pharmaceutical Industries to develop drugs for the treatment of schizophrenia. In December

11.11 *Launching the 'Synergy for the Scottish Parliament' initiative between the Universities of Glasgow and Strathclyde, 1999. From left to right: Sir William Kerr Fraser (Chancellor of the University of Glasgow), Sir Graeme Davies (Principal), Muir Russell (Permanent Secretary, Scottish Executive), Sir John Arbuthnott (Principal of the University of Strathclyde), and Lord Hope (Chancellor). This was a facet of the strategic alliance between the two institutions.*

1998 the 5* Computing Science department was awarded a Queen's Anniversary Prize for the outstanding quality of its teaching and research, 'with a policy of outreach addressing the practical problems of industry and the community.'

One of the Labour government's principal policy commitments was devolution for both Wales and Scotland. In a referendum in the autumn of 1997 the people of Scotland voted overwhelmingly in favour of devolution. The first elections under a system of proportional representation to the new parliament took place in May 1999, with the Conservative, Liberal Democrat and Scottish Nationalist parties committed to the abolition of student fees with little concern for the future funding of higher education. As there was no clear victor, Labour had to broker a coalition with the Liberal Democrats on the condition that the whole question of student fees would be investigated. To buy time the new government appointed a committee of inquiry chaired by the businessman Andrew Cubie. Reporting late in the year, Cubie proposed that rather than being abolished the payment of fees should be 'deferred' until a graduate was in remunerative employment. The system of student loans was also to be reviewed to provide greater support for students from disadvantaged backgrounds. This compromise was accepted by the Liberal Democrats and it remained to be seen what effect it would have on universities' hard-pressed finances. Meanwhile, in collaboration with Strathclyde, the University mounted a campaign to call to the attention of the new Scottish governing structure the wealth of relevant expertise available in the two institutions.

There can be no doubt that since 1979 students have borne the brunt of the cuts. However, unlike the 1920s and 1930s, there has been little real student poverty. At a time of relatively full employment, students have been able to get part-time jobs during term time. As a result as the financial pressures have grown, they have become more and more tired and less and less can be fairly expected of them. The ideal of a university propounded by Hetherington's generation has become almost untenable in universities, such as Glasgow, where a large proportion of students come from less well off backgrounds. It is hardly surprising that corporate life has suffered and that students have become more serious with the pressing need to get a full-time job as soon after graduation as possible. In these circumstances continuous assessment has won out and replaced the time-consuming and cumbersome system of class exams. As a result the proportion of firsts has increased and the level of achievement across the board has gone up. By 1999, apart from student loans, the average indebtedness of students at Glasgow was about £2,400. Testimony to the increasing preoccupation of students with their affairs was the demise of Charities Day in 1985.

Given the battering they have received since 1984, the wonder is that universities have survived at all and gone on attracting able and dedicated staff. Amongst the older universities in the United Kingdom, Glasgow clearly suffered worse than most, due in large measure to a long legacy of underfunding and its firm commitment to provide a wide range of opportunities for students in the west of Scotland, many of whom came from under-privileged backgrounds. The decline and uncertain recovery of the local economy hampered development, as did repeated and often misleadingly poor performance in published league tables. Adversity in a sense has brought out the best in staff who have been determined to demonstrate to the city and the wider world the University's capabilities. Great strides have been made in updating internal structures and in restoring good relations with the local community: the University's role in the regeneration of the region is now recognised as one of the largest employers in the city. Since the University arrived on Gilmorehill to occupy a half-completed building, funding has been uncertain and although this may have hindered development, it has not prevented academic enquiry even in the leanest times of the inter-war depression. The highly rated departments for teaching and research stand in a proud tradition stretching back to Kelvin and Macquorn Rankine on Gilmorehill and to Joseph Black, William Cullen and Adam Smith at the College in the High Street.

Notes and References

1. *Report of the University Court 1983–4*, p. 5.
2. Ibid.
3. Minutes of University Court 1983–4, Vol. 2, minute of meeting of Academic Development Committee, 1 March 1984, Annex A.
4. *A Strategy for Higher Education into the 1990s*, UGC, 1984.
5. *Report of the University Court 1984–5*, p. 6.
6. *Report of the Steering Committee for Efficiency Studies in Universities*, Committee of Vice Chancellors and Principals, March 1985.
7. Minutes of University Court 1984–5, Vol. 2, Report of the Annual Conference of the Standing Committee of the Scottish Universities, 7 June 1985, p. 4.
8. Minutes of University Court 1984–5, Vol. 2, Minute of Academic Development Committee, 23 September 1985, item AD. 59.
9. *The Development of Higher Education into the 1990s*, 1985.
10. *Report of the University Court 1984–5*, p. 2.
11. Minutes of University Court 1984–5, Vol. 2, Minute of Academic Development Committee, 15 April 1984, paper A.
12. *Report of the University Court 1986–7*, p. 3.
13. *Report of the University Court 1985–6*, p. 2.
14. Ibid. p. 1.
15. *Report of the University Court 1986–7*, p. 3.
16. Ibid. pp. 5, 9–10, 20, and 22.
17. Ibid. p. 4.
18. Ibid. p. 2.
19. Minutes of University Court 1986–7, Vol. 2, Report of the meeting of the

Standing Committee of the Scottish Universities held on Friday 20 March 1987, pp. 2–3.

20. *Higher Education – Meeting the Challenge*, April 1987.
21. *Report of the University Court 1986–7*, p. 1.
22. *Report of the University Court 1987–8*, p. 3.
23. Ibid. p. 6.
24. *Newsletter University of Glasgow*, No. 182, 29 July 1986, p. 2.
25. Minutes of the University Court, 1989–90, meeting of 25 October, MORI survey attached.
26. Ibid. meeting of 21 February 1990, Coopers & Lybrand Deloitte report attached.
27. Ibid. meeting of 24 May 1990, p. 335 item 245 and memorandum by Principal attached.
28. Ibid.
29. Ibid.
30. *Report of the University Court 1989–90*, p. 1.
31. Minutes of University Court 1989–90, p. 372 item 264 and institutional plan attached p. 15.
32. Minutes of University Court 1990–91, pp. 382–3 item 256.
33. *Higher Education – A New Framework*, 1991.
34. GUA, Paisley file No. 365/3/28.
35. Minutes of the University Court 1990–91, p. 321 item 231; 1991–2, p. 26 item 18, and John Butt, *John Anderson's Legacy : The University of Strathclyde and its antecedents 1796–1996* (East Linton, 1996), pp. 240–1.
36. *Newsletter University of Glasgow*, No. 157, 21 February 1994, pp. 10–11.
37. Ibid. No. 156, 24 January 1994, p. 3.
38. Ibid. No. 159, 18 April 1994, p. 1.
39. Ibid. No. 161, 13 June 1994, p. 2.
40. Ibid. No. 167, 8 February 1995, pp. 1–2.
41. *Report of the University Court 1994–5*.
42. *Newsletter University of Glasgow*, No. 174, 1995, pp. 10–12.
43. Ibid. No. 186, 22 January 1997, p. 3.
44. Ibid. No. 198, 4 March 1998, p. 1.
45. Ibid. No. 186, 22 January 1997, p.1.
46. Ibid. No. 189, 16 April 1997, p. 10.
47. Ibid. No. 184, 20 November 1996, pp. 1–2.
48. Ibid. No. 197, 4 February 1998, p. 6.
49. Ibid. No. 203, 7 October 1998, p. 3.

Statistical Appendix

Sources: Matriculation and Graduation Albums (GUA), University Calendars (GUL), Reports of the University Court (GUL), Returns to the University Grants Committee (GUA), Glasgow University Statistics (GUA).

Notes:

All figures: Years on figures are the calendar years in which the academic sessions finished.

Abbreviations used for faculties:

Soc Sci = Social Science
Edu = Education
Eng = Engineering
Med = Medicine
Vets = Veterinary Medicine
Dent = Dentristry
Div = Divinity

Figure 1	Includes Associated Institutions: Glasgow School of Art, Royal Scottish Academy of Music and Drama and Jordanhill College.
Figure 4(a) and (b)	Logarithmic scale. All degrees, whether undergraduate or postgraduate; in medicine, the award in a single year of both a medical and surgical degree is counted only as one degree.
Figure 6	Home residence is the family residence rather than the term-time residence. 'Scotland' category replaced by 'Radius of 30 miles' (of Glasgow) and 'Other UK' includes Scots living more than 30 miles from Glasgow from 1925 to 1975.
Figure 7	Assistants are included in 'Assistant Lecturers'. 'Assistant Lecturers' were subsumed into 'Lecturers' from 1970/1. From 1989/90 'Lecturers' include all non-professorial academic staff. 'Professors' do not include Clinical Professors.

Figure 1

Student Matriculations by Gender 1858/59 – 1993/94

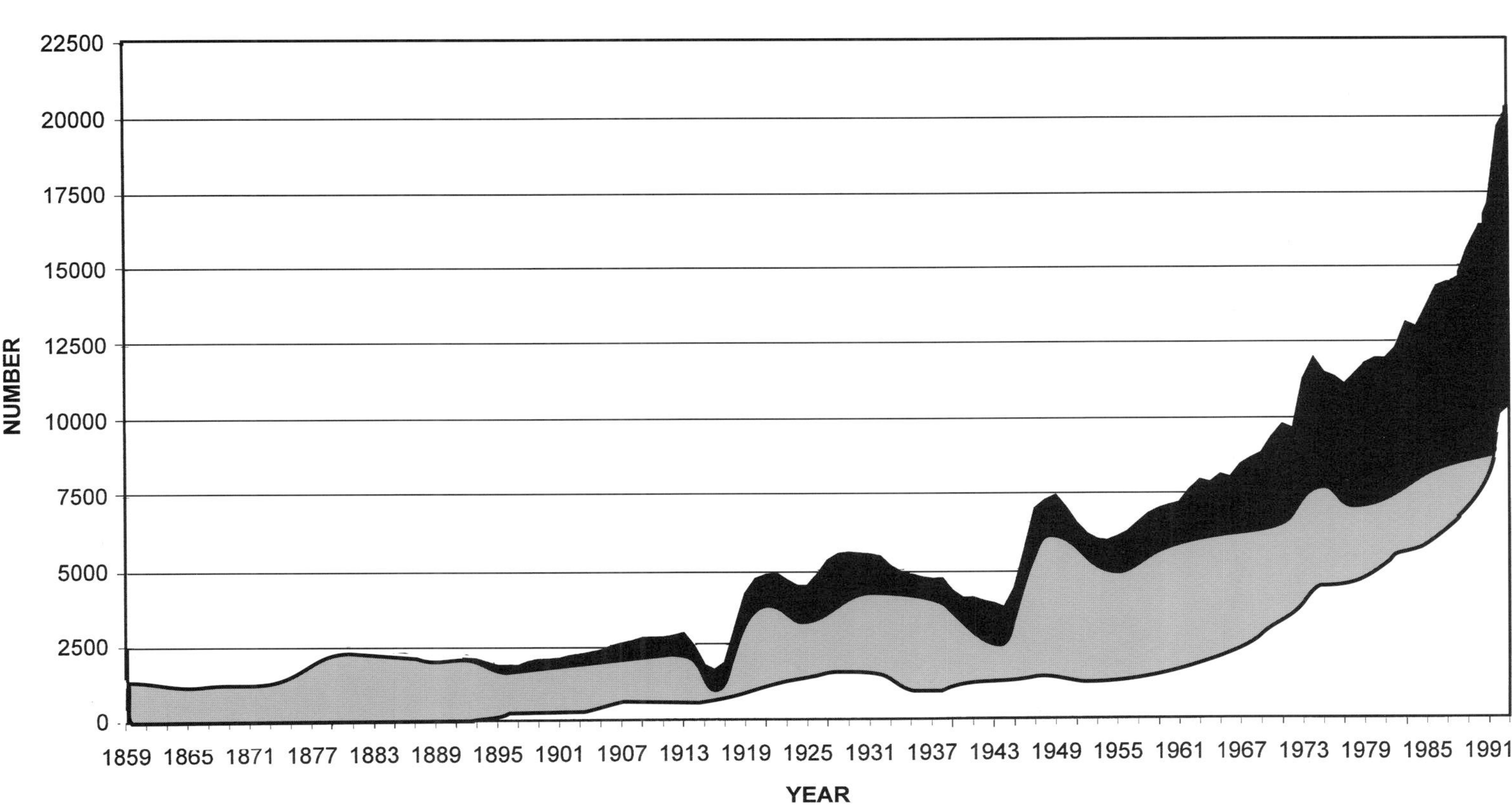

Figure 2

Matriculations by Faculty 1854/55 – 1993/94

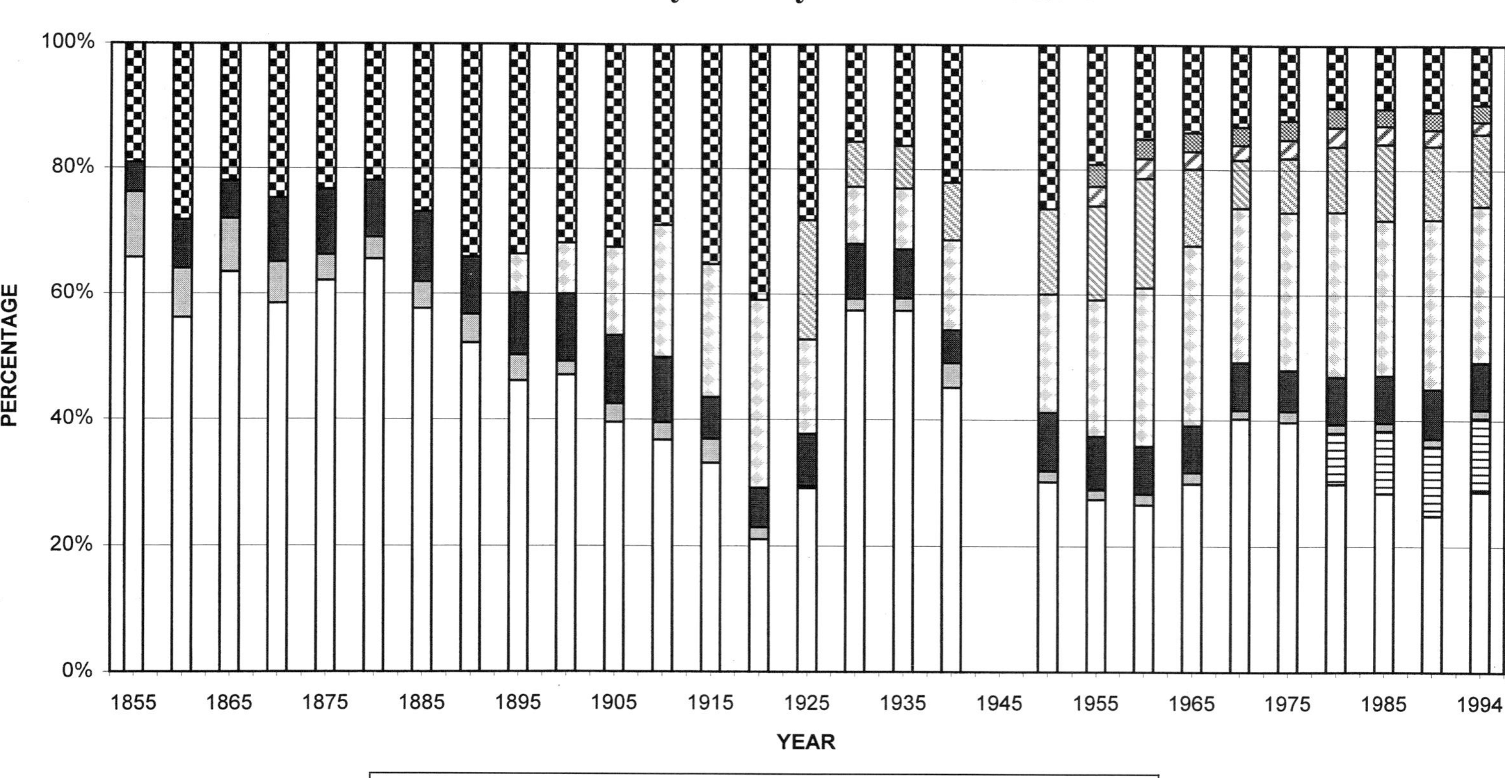

Figure 3 (a)

Male Matriculations as a Percentage of Total – Arts, Social Science, Divinity, Law 1894/95 – 1993/94

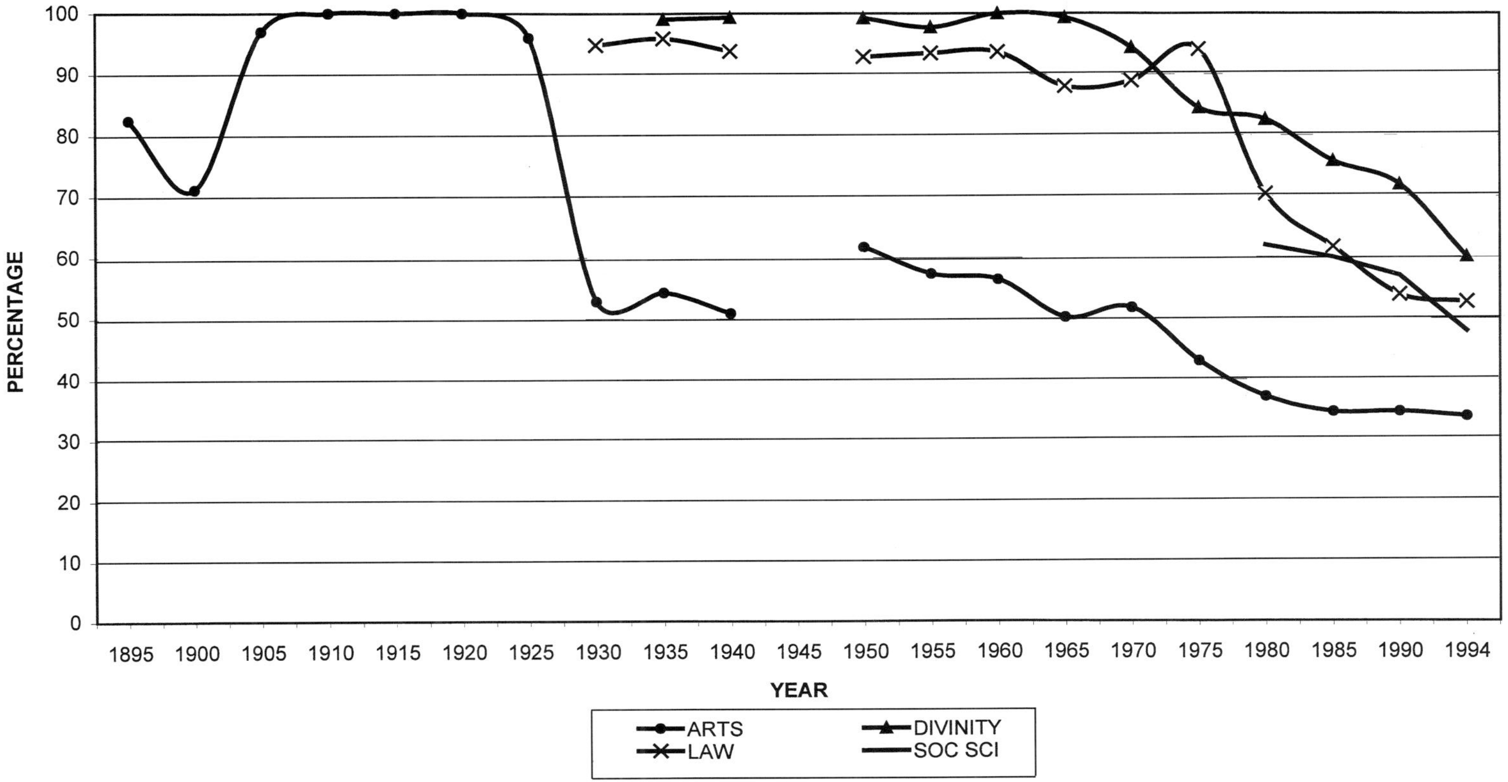

Figure 3 (b)

Male Matriculations as a Percentage of Total – Medicine, Dentistry and Veterinary Medicine 1894/95 – 1993/94

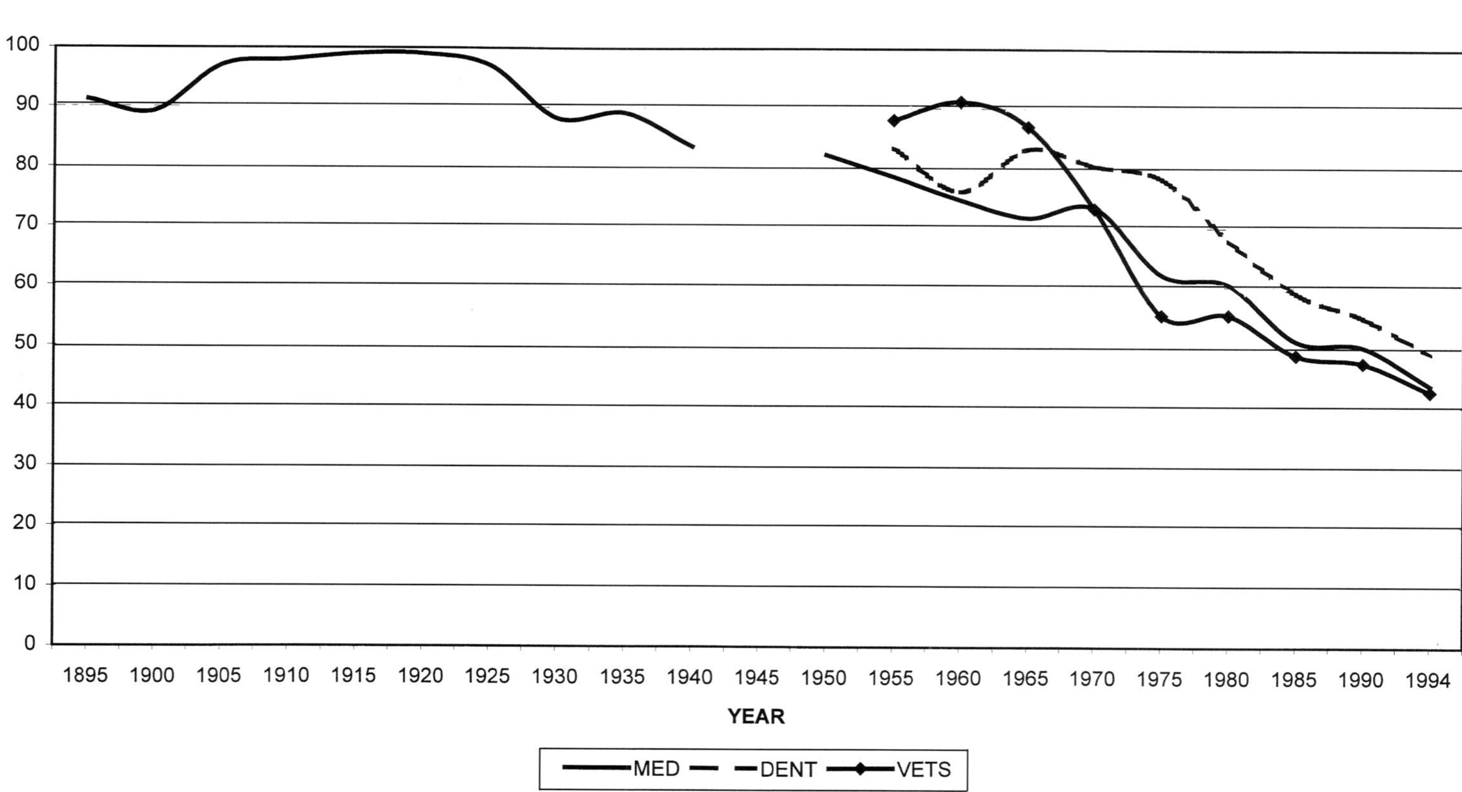

Figure 3 (c)

Male Matriculations as a Percentage of Total – Science and Engineering 1894/95 – 1993/94

Figure 4 (a)

Degrees Awarded by Faculty 1873/74 – 1965/66

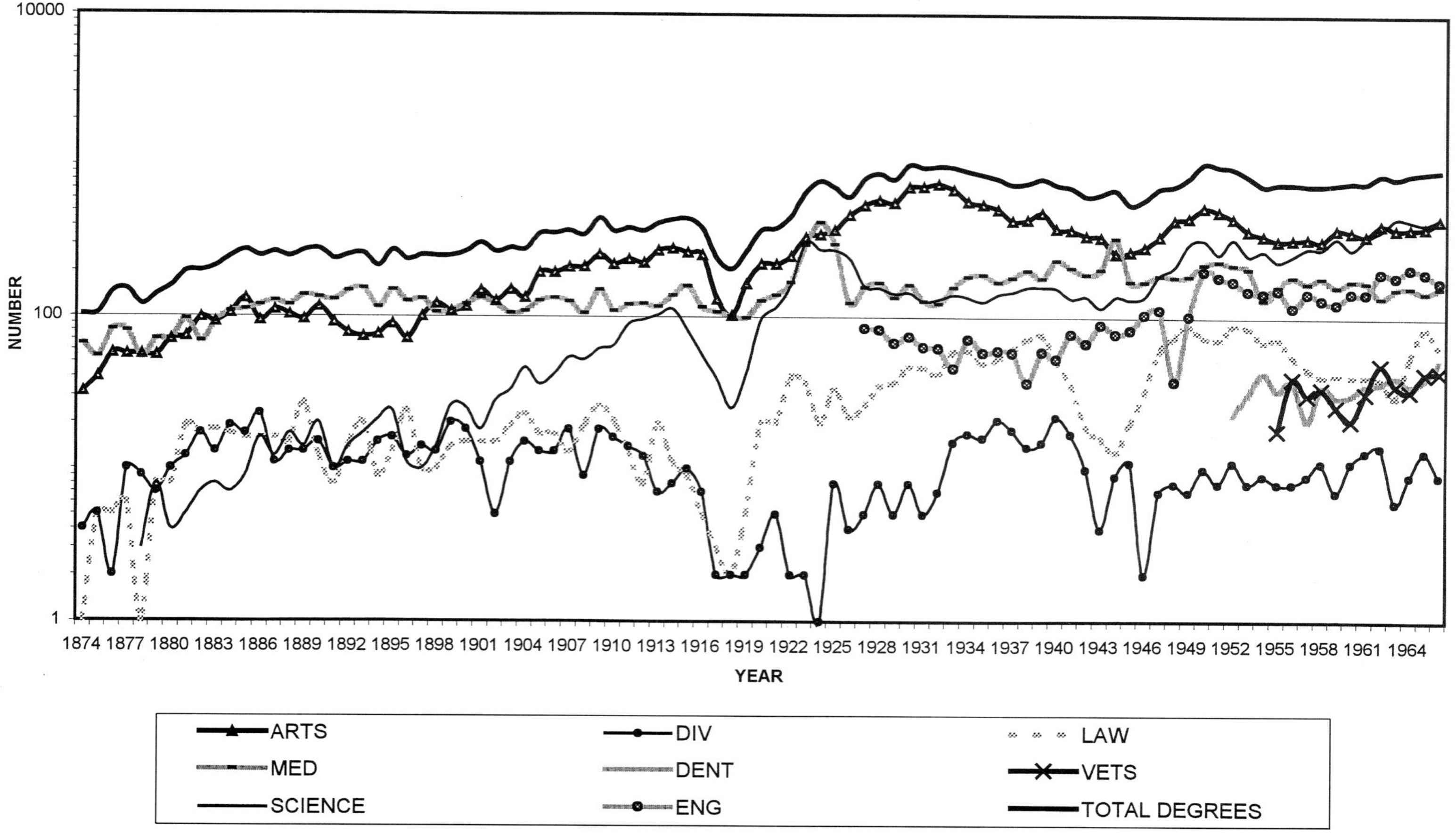

Figure 4 (b)

Degrees Awarded by Faculty 1975/6 – 1988/9

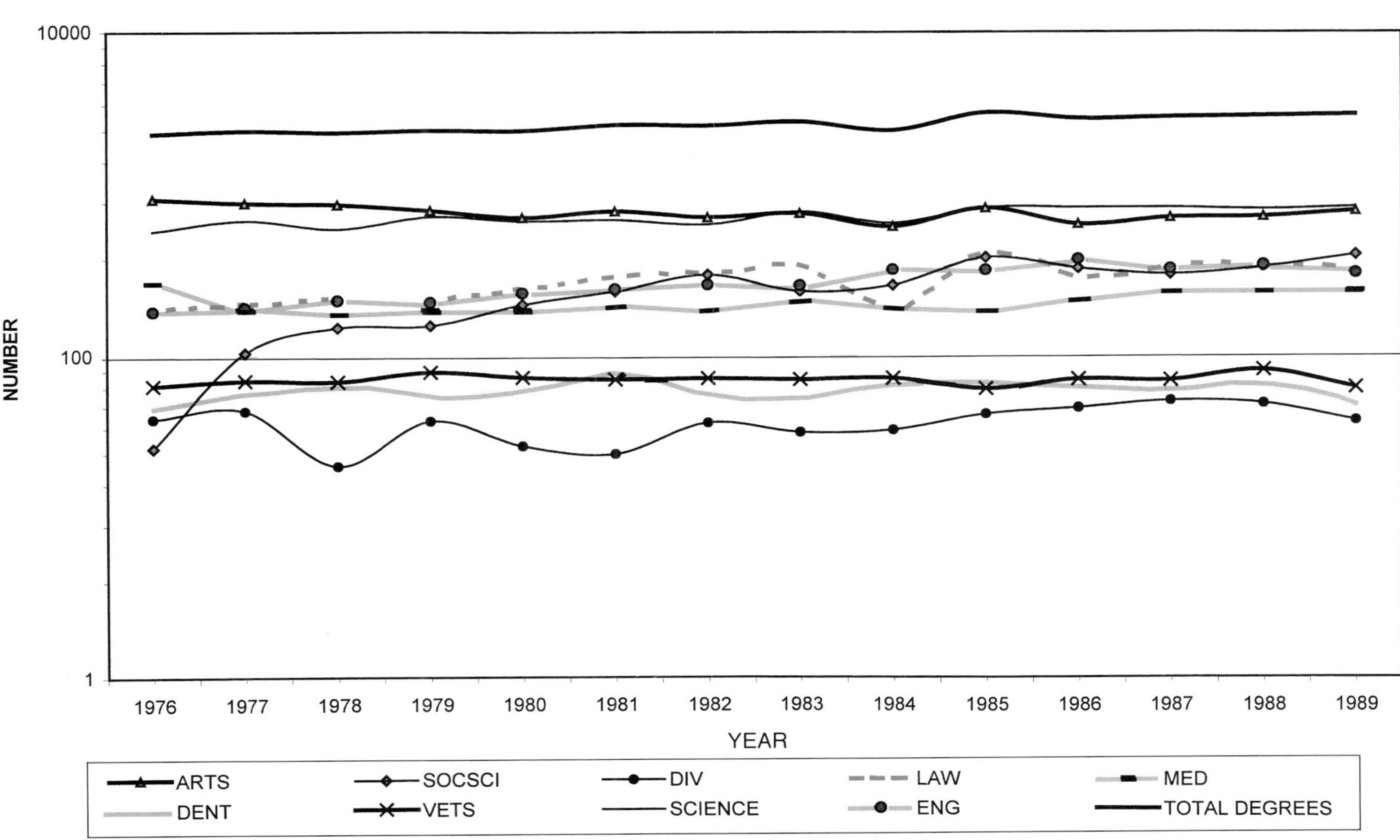

Figure 5 (a)

Percentage of Ordinary and Honours BSc Degrees 1922/23 – 1985/86

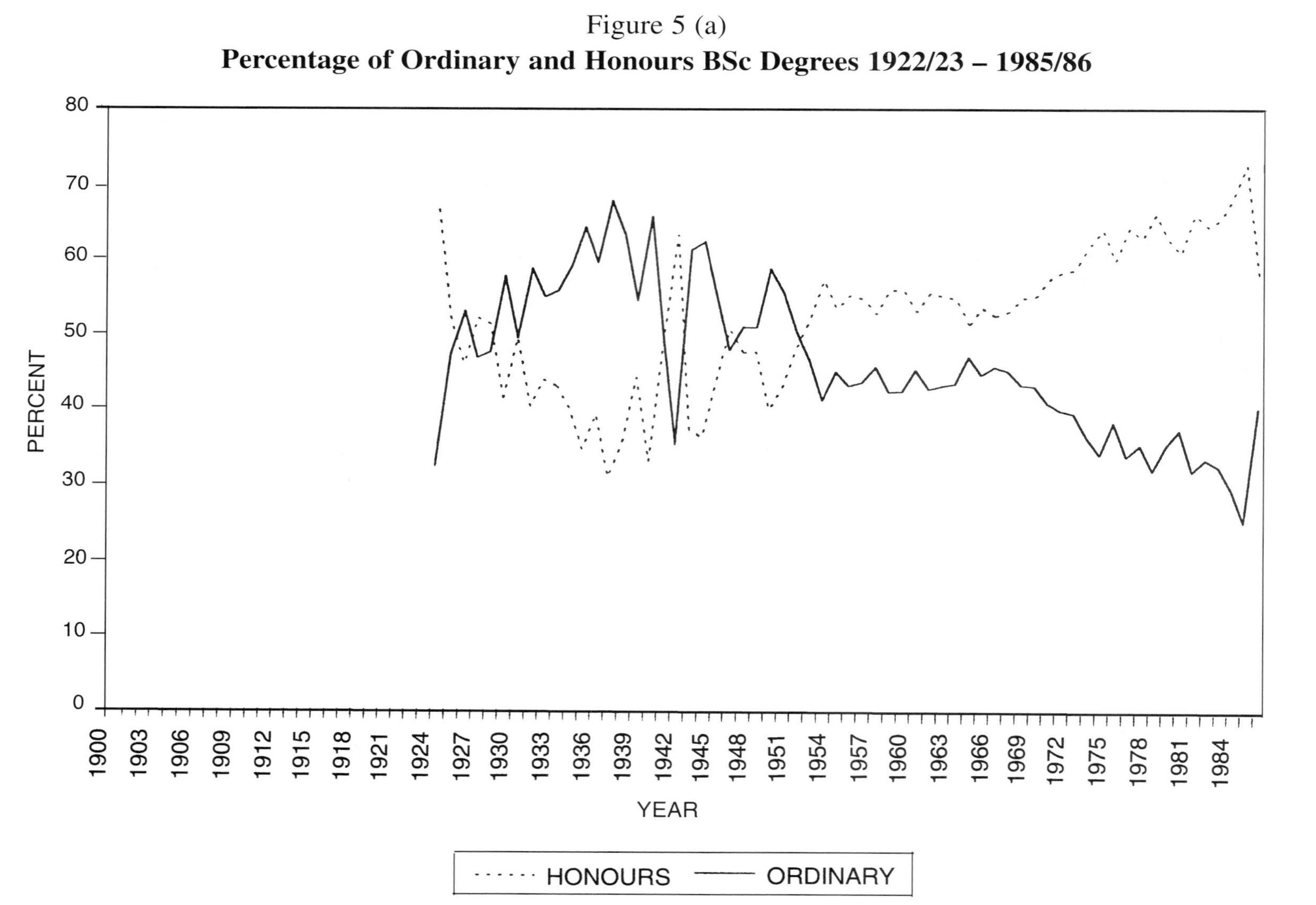

Figure 5 (b)

Percentage of Ordinary and Honours Arts Degrees 1899/1900 – 1985/86

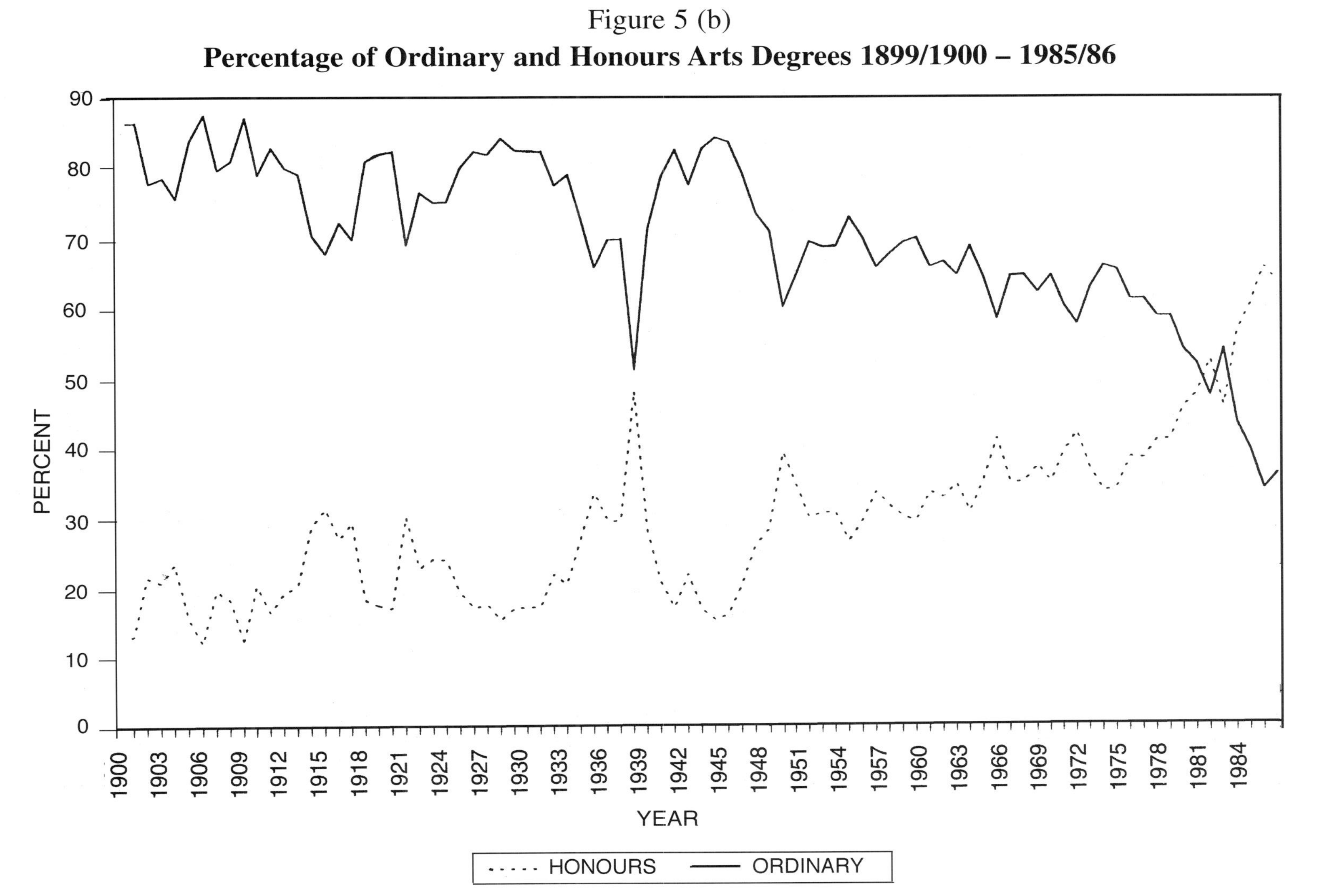

Figure 5 (c)

Percentage of Arts Honours Class Results 1899/1900 – 1985/86

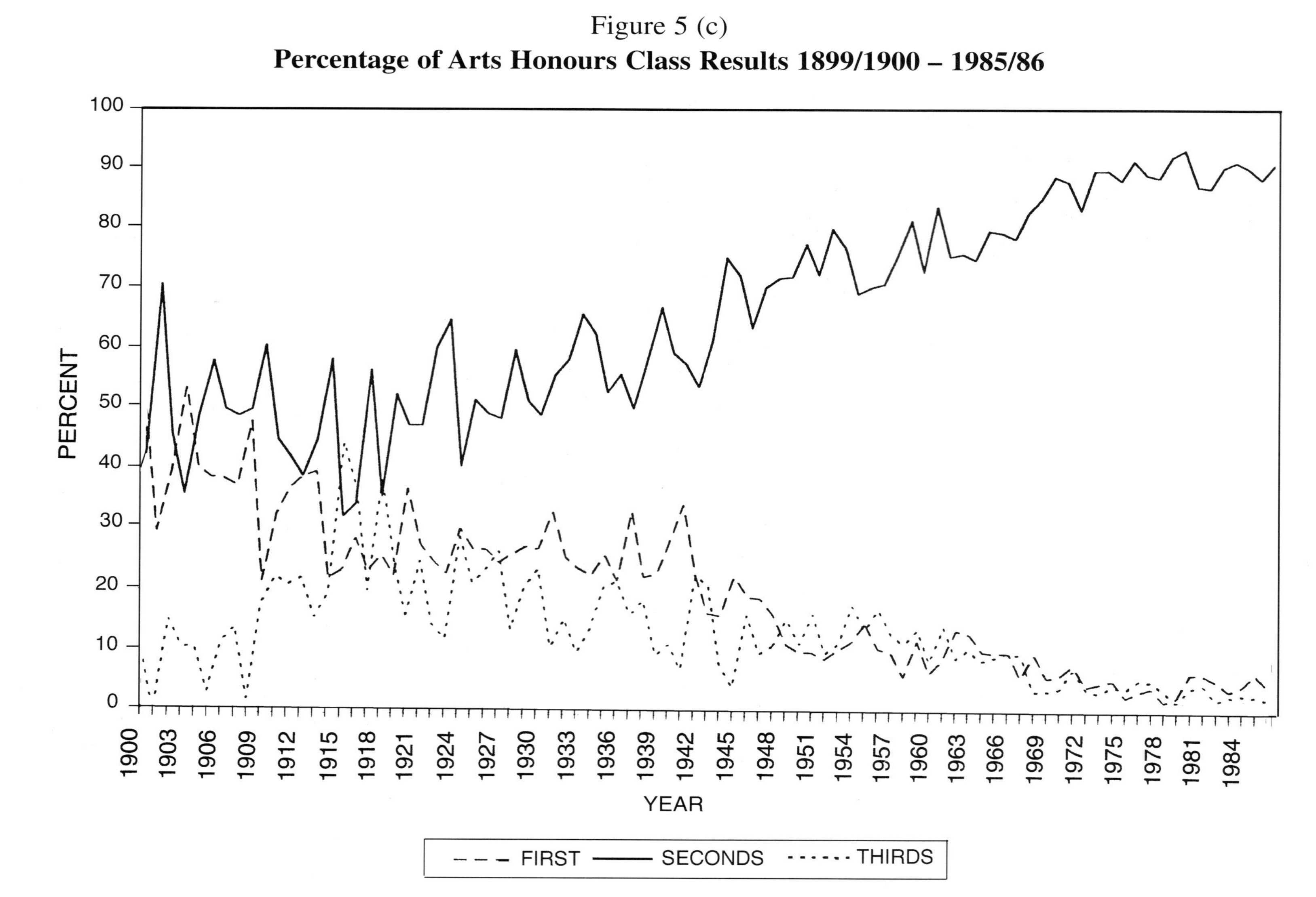

Figure 6

Home Residence of Full Time Students 1894/95 – 1993/94

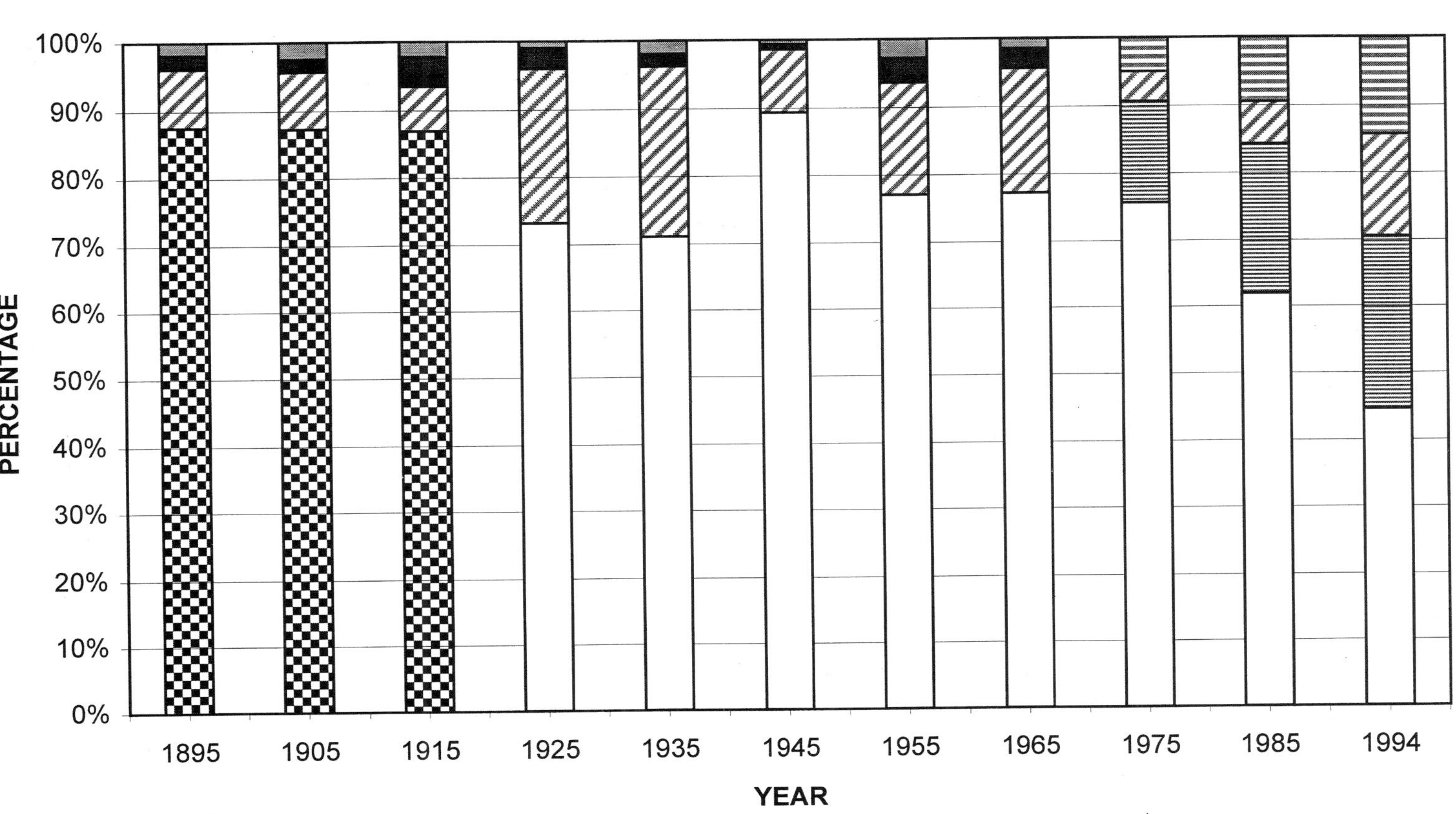

Figure 7

Academic Staff by Category 1863/64 – 1993/94

Figures for Total Staff and Lecturers 1987/88 – 1988/89 are two period moving averages

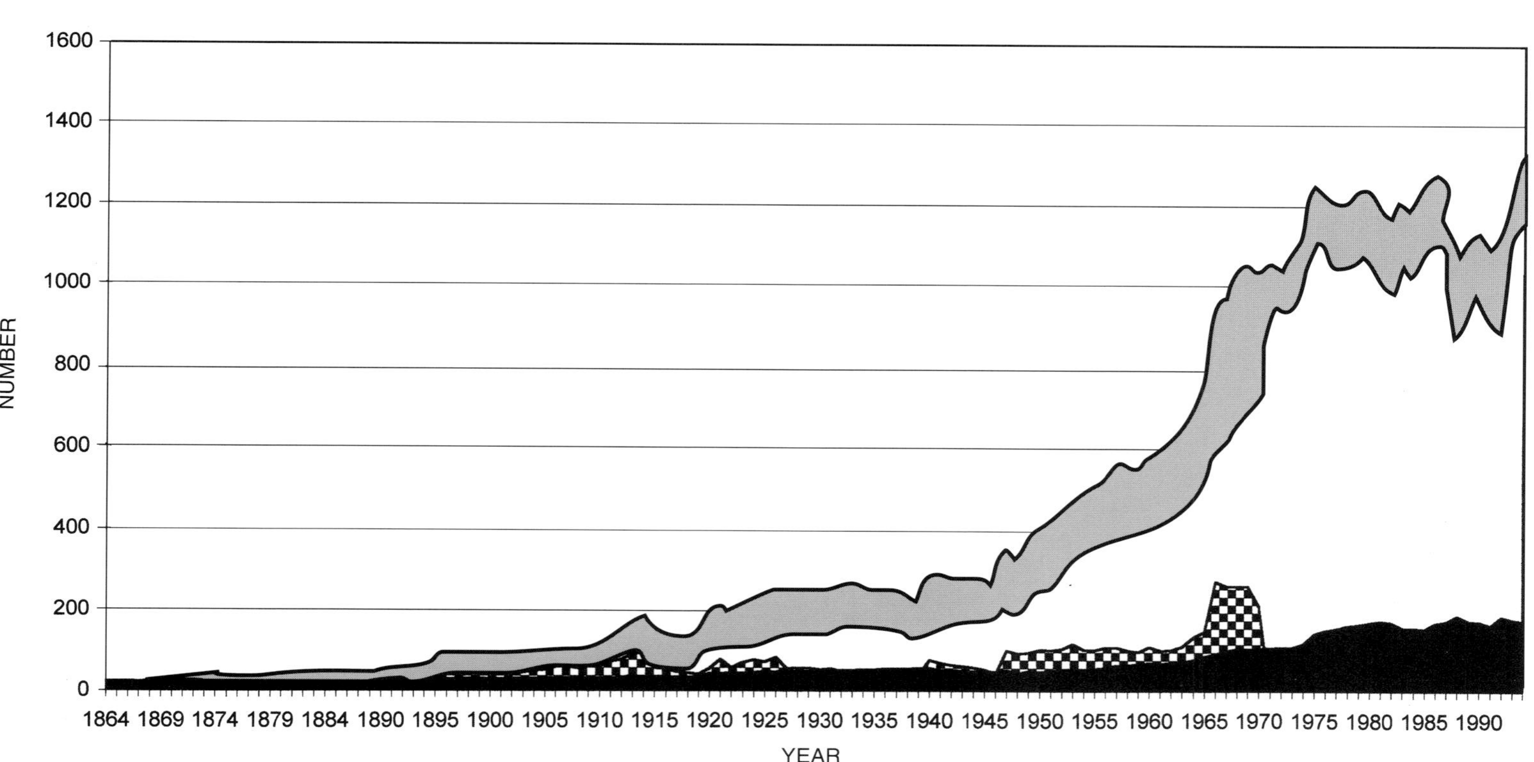

Table 1
Student Matriculations by Gender 1994/95 – 1998/99

Academic Session	*Sex*		*Total*
	Male	*Female*	
1998–99	9,156	11,470	20,626
1997–98	9,969	12,520	22,489
1996–97	9,991	12,336	22,327
1995–96	9,608	10,790	20,398
1994–95	9,369	10,288	19,657

Includes Associated Institutions: Glasgow School of Art, Royal Scottish Academy of Music and Drama

Table 2
Matriculations by Faculty 1994/95 – 1998/99

Academic Session	*Med* %	*Vets* %	*Eng* %	*Science* %	*Law* %	*Div* %	*Soc Sci* %	*Arts* %
1998–99	14	3	9	28	8	1	13	24
1997–98	14	3	9	27	8	1	13	25
1996–97	14	3	10	26	8	1	13	25
1995–96	14	3	10	27	7	1	13	25
1994–95	14	3	11	26	7	2	12	25

Dentistry Matriculants included in Medicine

Table 3(a)
Percentage of Male Matriculations – Arts, Social Science, Divinity and Law 1994/95 – 1998/99

Academic Session	*Arts* %	*Social Science* %	*Divinity* %	*Law* %
1998–99	34	43	53	45
1997–98	37	43	50	45
1996–97	35	43	55	48
1995–96	36	46	53	49
1994–95	38	46	57	56

Table 3(b)
Percentage of Male Matriculations – Medicine, Dentistry and Veterinary Medicine 1994/95 – 1998/99

Academic Session	*Medicine* %	*Dentistry* %	*Veterinary* %
1998–99	40		37
1997–98	43	44	35
1996–97	41	43	38
1995–96	42	45	39
1994–95	49	45	37

For 1998–99 session Dentistry included in Medicine

Table 3(c)
Percentage of Male Matriculations – Science and Engineering 1994/95 – 1998/99

Academic Session	*Science* %	*Engineering* %
1998–99	50	85
1997–98	51	85
1996–97	52	89
1995–96	53	88
1994–95	55	87

Table 4
Degrees Awarded by Faculty 1994/95 – 1998/99

Academic Session	*Arts*	*Divinity*	*Edu*	*Eng*	*Law*	*Med*	*Science*	*Soc Sci*	*Vets*	*Total*
1998–99	1,248	58	165	453	304	584	1,230	469	108	4,619
1997–98	1,316	46		452	312	549	1,298	535	85	4,593
1996–97	1,389	47		485	288	505	1,076	527	08	4,425
1995–96	1,538	59		494	312	623	1,007	506	25	4,564
1994–95	1,556	42		521	308	449	1,012	514	73	4,475

Includes first degrees and higher degrees. Dentistry and Nursing Degrees included in Medicine

Table 5(a)
Percentage of Ordinary and Honours BSc Degrees 1994/95 – 1998/99

Academic Session	*Ordinary* %	*Honours* %
1998–99	22	78
1997–98	23	77
1996–97	25	75
1995–96	23	77
1994–95	25	75

Table 5(b)
Percentage of Ordinary and Honours Arts Degrees 1994/95 – 1998/99

Academic Session	*Ordinary* %	*Honours* %
1998–99	20	80
1997–98	24	76
1996–97	24	76
1995–96	28	72
1994–95	24	76

Table 5(c)
Percentage of Arts Honours Class Results 1994/95 – 1998/99

Academic Session	*First* %	*Second* %	*Third* %
1998–99	9	90	1
1997–98	10	88	2
1996–97	11	87	2
1995–96	9	87	4
1994–95	10	88	2

Table 6
Home Residence of Full Time Students 1994/95 – 1998/99

Academic Session	*Radius of 30 miles* %	*Rest of Scotland* %	*Other UK* %	*Overseas* %
1998–99	45	27	16	12
1997–98	46	28	16	10
1996–97	46	27	16	11
1995–96	46	26	17	11
1994–95	45	26	18	11

Table 7
Academic Staff by Category

Academic Session	*Professors*	*Lecturers*	*Total*
1998–99	255	1,362	1,578
1997–98	247	1,209	1,447
1996–97	242	1,207	1,449
1995–96	238	1,182	1,429
1994–95	216	1,131	1,386

Number of Professors are from 1 Aug to 31 July each year, Professors do not include Clinical Professors

Sources and Bibliography

Primary Sources

(a) University Records and University-Related Records, the University Archives

These represent the principal body of original material underlying this work. The most commonly used category of records were:

Court minutes and papers (including Finance and Works Committees), C 1/1–9
Senate minutes and papers, SEN 1/1–2
    Graduation Albums, R 1
    Matriculation Albums, R 8
    Class catalogues, R 9
Extra-Mural Education Committee, minutes and papers, ACE 1–3
University Calendars, SEN 10/1–137
Papers of:
    Robert Story, Principal, 1898–1907, DC 21
    Sir Donald MacAlister, Principal, 1907–1929, GUA 73199–73420
    Sir Hector Hetherington, Principal, 1936–61, DC 8
    Sir Charles Wilson, Principal, 1961–76, DC 191
    Sir Alwyn Williams, Principal, 1976–88, DC 223

(b) Serial Publications

Glasgow Herald
Glasgow University Magazine, 1889–1972
Letter to Graduates (Principal of the University of Glasgow), 1946–53
Report of the Carnegie Trust for the Universities of Scotland, 1901–
Report of the General Council (University of Glasgow), 1860–1986.
Scottish Educational Statistics, 1970–1989
UGC Returns from Universities and University Colleges, 1919–20 to 1965–6.
University of Glasgow Newsletter, 1977–
University of Glasgow Students Handbook, 1903–1987

(c) Parliamentary Papers

'Report of the Royal Commission on Scientific Instruction', C.318 (1871)
'Report of the Royal Commission on Scottish Universities', C.1935 (1878)

'Parliamentary Return regarding assistants etc. in Scottish Universities', Cd. 365 (1888)

'Royal Commission on the Civil Service, Appendix to 3rd Report', Cd. 6740 (1913)

'Report of the UGC on the Financial Needs of the Universities of the United Kingdom', Cmd. 1163 (1921).

'Report of the Special Committee appointed in April 1937 to enquire and advise regarding an application by the University Courts of the Universities of Scotland for a Grant from the Education (Scotland) Fund', Cmd. 5735 (1937–8)

'Second Report of the Committee on Veterinary Education in Great Britain', Cmd. 6517 (1943–4)

'Report of the Committee on Agricultural Education in Scotland', Cmd. 6704 (1945–6)

'Report of a Committee appointed by the Lord President of Council' [Barlow Report], Cmd. 6824 (1945–6)

'Report of the Special Committee . . . for an increased Grant from the Education (Scotland) Fund', Cmd. 6853 (1945–6)

'University Grants Committee [UGC]: Report on University Development, 1947–1952', Cmd. 8875 (1952–3)

'UGC: Report on University Development, 1952–7', Cmnd. 534 (1958)

'UGC: Report on University Development, 1957–62', Cmnd. 2267 (1964)

'The Development of Higher Education into the 1990s', Cmnd. 9524 (1984)

(d) Other

Observations by the Principal and Professors of Glasgow College on Schemes of Reform (2nd edn., Glasgow, 1837)

Scottish Universities Commission, General Report (Edinburgh, 1863)

University of Glasgow New Buildings: Report by the Chairman of the University Removal Committee (Glasgow, 1877)

The Extension and Better Equipment of the University of Glasgow (Glasgow, 1902)

University of Glasgow Handbook (compiled for the use of overseas students and graduates) (Glasgow, 1919)

Second Congress of the Universities of the Empire (London, 1921)

Report of the Inter-Departmental Committee on Medical Education [Goodenough Report] (London, 1944)

Report of the Inter-Departmental Committee on Dental Education [Teviot Report] (London, 1945)

Higher Technological Education: Report of a Special Committee [Percy Report] (London, 1945)

Report of the Committee on Higher Education [Robbins Report] (London, 1963)

Future Strategy for Higher Education in Scotland: Report of the Scottish Tertiary Education Advisory Council on its review of higher education in Scotland (Edinburgh, 1985)

Report to the Committee of Vice-Chancellors and Principals Steering Committee for Efficiency Studies [Jarratt Committee] (Edinburgh, 1985)

Review of the University Grants Committee: report of a committee under the chairmanship of Lord Croham (London, 1987)

Secondary Sources

(a) Books and Pamphlets

Adams, R. J. Q., *Bonar Law* (London, 1999)
Alexander, W., *First Ladies of Medicine* (Glasgow, 1987)
Anderson, R. D., *Education and Opportunity* (Oxford, 1983)
Anderson, R. D., *The Student Community at Aberdeen, 1860–1939* (Aberdeen, 1988)
Anderson, R. D., *Universities and Elites in Britain since 1800* (Cambridge, 1995)
Anderson, R. D., *Scottish Education Since the Reformation* (Dundee, 1997)
Bell, R. E. and Youngson, A. J., *Present and Future in Higher Education* (London, 1973)
The Book of the Bazaar: University of Glasgow Student Welfare Scheme (Glasgow, 1923)
The Book of the Fifth Centenary (Glasgow, 1952)
Bowman, A. K., *The Life and Teaching of Sir William Macewen: A Chapter in the History of Surgery* (London, 1942)
Bridie, J., *One Way of Living* (London, 1939)
Brown, A. L. and Moss, M., *The University of Glasgow 1451–1996* (Edinburgh, 1996)
Burleigh, J. H. S., *A Church History of Scotland* (London, 1960)
Butt, J., *John Anderson's Legacy: The University of Strathclyde and its Antecedents, 1796–1996* (East Linton, 1996)
Caird, J., *University Sermons preached before the University of Glasgow, 1873–1898* (Glasgow, 1898)
Caird, J., *University Addresses* (Glasgow, 1898)
Calder, A., *The People's War: Britain, 1939–45* (London, 1969)
The Centenary of the Glasgow Veterinary College and University Veterinary School, 1862–1962 (Glasgow, 1962)
Collins, K. E., *Go and Learn: The International Story of Jews and Medicine in Scotland* (Aberdeen, 1988)
Conquering by Degrees: GU Union Centenary History, 1885–1985 (Glasgow, 1985)
Coutts, J., *A History of the University of Glasgow. From Its Foundation in 1451 to 1909* (Glasgow, 1909)
Crowther, M. A. and White, B., *On Soul and Conscience: the Medical Expert and Crime* (Aberdeen, 1988)
The Curious Diversity. Glasgow University on Gilmorehill: the First Hundred Years (Glasgow, 1970)
Davie, G. E., *The Democratic Intellect* (Edinburgh, 1961)
Davie, G. E., *The Crisis of the Democratic Intellect* (Edinburgh, 1986)
Dickson, W. P., *The Glasgow University Library: A plea for the increase of its resources* (Glasgow, 1889)
Duiguid, B., *Macewen of Glasgow: A Recollection of the Chief* (Edinburgh, 1957)
Dyhouse, C. J., *No Distinction of Sex? Women in British Universities, 1870–1939* (London, 1995)
Engel, A., *From Clergyman to Don: The Rise of the Academic Profession in Nineteenth Century Oxford* (Oxford, 1983)

Fenwick, I. G. K. and McBride, P., *The Government of Education in Britain* (Oxford, 1981)

Fisher, H. A. L., *James Bryce (Viscount Bryce of Dechmont O.M.)*(London, 1927)

Fortuna Domus: A Series of Lectures Delivered in the University of Glasgow in Commemoration of the Fifth Centenary of its Foundation (Glasgow, 1952)

Geyer-Kordesch, J. and Ferguson, R., *Blue Stockings, Black Gowns, White Coats* (Glasgow, 1994)

Gibson, G. A., *Life of Sir William Tennant Gairdner* (Glasgow, 1912)

Hargreaves, J. D. with Forbes, A., *Aberdeen University, 1945–1981: Regional Roles and National Needs* (Aberdeen, 1989)

Henderson, T. B., *History of the Glasgow Dental Hospital and School, 1879–1979* (Glasgow, 1979)

Hetherington, H. J. W., *The Life and Letters of Sir Henry Jones* (London, 1924)

Hoeveler, J. D., *James McCosh and the Scottish Intellectual Tradition: From Glasgow to Princeton* (Princeton, 1981)

Hull, A. and Geyer-Kordesch, J., *The Shaping of the Medical Profession: A History of the Royal College of Physicians and Surgeons of Glasgow, 1858–1999* (London, 1999)

Hutcheson, R. T. and Conway, H., *The University of Glasgow, 1920–1974: The Memoir of Robert T. Hutcheson* (Glasgow, 1997)

Hutchison, I. G., *The University and the State: The Case of Aberdeen* (Aberdeen, 1993)

Illingworth, Sir Charles, *University Statesman: Sir Hector Hetherington* (Glasgow, 1971)

Introductory Addresses Delivered at the Opening of the University of Glasgow, Session 1870–1 (Glasgow, 1871)

Jacyna, L. S. (ed.), *A Tale of Three Cities: The Correspondence of William Sharpey and Allen Thomson* (London, 1989)

Jarausch, K. H. (ed.), *The Transformation of Higher Learning* (Chicago, 1983)

Jebb, C., *Life and Letters of Sir Richard Claverhouse Jebb O.M. Litt.D.* (Cambridge, 1907)

Jones, D. R., *Origins of Civic Universities: Manchester, Leeds and Liverpool* (London, 1988)

Jones, Sir Henry and Muirhead, J. H., *The Life and Philosophy of Edward Caird* (Glasgow, 1921)

Jones, Sir Henry, *Old Memories: Autobiography* (London, 1922)

Kemeny, P. L., *Princeton in the Nation's Service: Religious Ideals and Educational Practice, 1868–1928* (New York, 1998)

McAlpine, C. J., *The Lady of Claremont House: Isabella Elder, Pioneer and Philanthropist* (Glendaruel, 1997)

Macfarlan, D., *University Tests in Scotland* (Glasgow, 1846)

MacKenna, R. O., *Glasgow University Athletic Club: The Story of the First Hundred Years* (Glasgow, 1981)

Mackie, J. D., *The University of Glasgow, 1451–1951: A Short History* (Glasgow, 1954)

MacLehose, J., *Memoirs and Portraits of One Hundred Glasgow Men* (Glasgow, 1886)

Malloch, D. M., *The Book of Glasgow Anecdote* (London, 1913)
Medicus, *University Pamphlets III: Personal Experiences* (Glasgow, 1888)
Members of the University of Glasgow and the University Contingent of the O.T.C. who served with the forces of the Crown, 1914–19 (Glasgow, 1922)
Memoir of Robert Herbert Story D.D., LL.D. by His Daughters (Glasgow, 1909)
Moore, L., *Bajanellas and Semilinas: Aberdeen University and the Education of Women, 1860–1920* (Aberdeen, 1991)
Morgan, A., *Scottish University Studies* (Oxford, 1933)
Murray, D., *Question of a degree in commerce – a minority report* (Glasgow, 1918)
Murray, D., *Memories of the Old College of Glasgow* (Glasgow, 1927)
Oakley, C. A., *The Fleeting Years* (Glasgow, 1950)
Oakley, C. A., *Union Ygorra. The Story of the Glasgow University student over the last sixty years* (Glasgow, 1951)
Primrose, C. M., *St Mungo's Bairns: Some Notable Glasgow Students Down the Centuries* (Glasgow, 1990)
Record of the Ninth Jubilee of the University of Glasgow, 1451–1901 (Glasgow, 1901)
Robb, J., *The Carnegie Trust for the Universities of Scotland, 1901–1926* (Edinburgh, 1927)
Robertson, W. S., *Glasgow Engineering: Achievement and Potential* (Glasgow, 1974)
Roll of Honour: Roll of members of the University of Glasgow who lost their lives in the service of their country, 1939–45 (Glasgow, 1952)
Rothblatt, S., *The Revolution of the Dons: Cambridge and Society in Victorian England* (Cambridge, 1968)
Sanderson, M., *The Universities and British Industry, 1850–1970* (London, 1972)
Shattock, M., *The UGC and the Management of British Universities* (Buckingham, 1994)
Shearer, J. G. S., *Town and Gown Together: two hundred and fifty years of extra-mural teaching at the University of Glasgow* (Glasgow, 1976)
Shinn, C. S., *Paying the Piper: the Development of the University Grants Committee, 1919–46* (Lewes, 1986)
Sir Donald MacAlister of Tarbert, by His Wife (London, 1935)
Sloane, W. M., *The Life of James McCosh* (Edinburgh, 1986)
Smith, C. and Wise, M. N., *Energy and Empire: A Biographical Study of Lord Kelvin* (Cambridge, 1989)
Southgate, D., *University Education in Dundee: A Centenary History* (Edinburgh, 1982)
Story, J. L., *Later Reminiscences* (Glasgow, 1913)
Students' Jubilee Celebrations Committee, *A Book of the Jubilee: In Commemoration of the Ninth Jubilee of the University of Glasgow* (Glasgow, 1901)
Thom, A. S., *From the Days of the Horseless Carriage: Centenary of the Glasgow University Engineering Society* (Glasgow, 1991)
Thomson, R. Y. (ed.), *A Faculty for Science: A Unified Diversity* (Glasgow, 1993)
Tweed, J., *Biographical Sketches of the Honourable The Lord Provosts of Glasgow* (Glasgow, 1883)
University of Glasgow: History and Constitution, 1977–78 (Glasgow, 1977)

Walker, D. M., *A History of the School of Law* (Glasgow, 1990)
Warr, C. L., *Principal Caird* (Edinburgh, 1926)

(b) Articles and Book Chapters

Anderson, R. D., 'Scottish University Professors, 1800–1939: Profile of an Elite', *Scottish Economic and Social History*, 7 (1987)
Anderson, R. D., 'Sport in the Scottish Universities, 1860–1939', *International Journal of the History of Sport*, 4 (1987)
Anderson, R. D., 'Ideas of the University in 19th century Scotland: Teaching versus research?', in M. Hewitt (ed.), *Scholarship in Victorian Britain* (Leeds, 1998)
Bradley, J., Crowther, M. A. and Dupree, M., 'Mobility and Selection in Scottish University Medical Education, 1858–1886', *Medical History*, 40 (1996)
Brock, C. H., 'Dr William Hunter's Museum, Glasgow University', *Journal of the Society for the Bibliography of Natural History*, 9 (1980)
Caird, E., 'Memoir of Principal Caird', in J. Caird, *The Fundamental Ideas of Christianity* (Glasgow, 1899)
Collier, A., 'Social origins of a sample of entrants to Glasgow University', *Sociological Review*, 30 (1938)
Hamilton, S., 'The First Generation of University Women', in G. Donaldson (ed.), *Four Centuries: Edinburgh University Life, 1583–1983* (Edinburgh, 1983)
Hetherington, Sir Hector, 'The British University System, 1914–1954', *Aberdeen University Review*, 36 (1955–6)
Kendall, C. M., 'Higher Education and the Emergence of the Professional Woman in Glasgow, c. 1890–1914', *History of Universities*, 10 (1991)
Lloyd, C. F., 'The Search for Legitimacy: Universities, Medical Licensing Bodies and Governance in Glasgow and Edinburgh from the late 18th to the late 19th Centuries', in R. J. Morris and R. H. Trainor (eds), *Urban Governance: Britain and Beyond since 1750* (Aldershot, 2000)
Marwick, W. H., 'The University Extension Movement in Scotland', *University of Edinburgh Journal*, 8 (1936–7)
Matthew, W. M., 'The Origins and Occupations of Glasgow Students, 1740–1839', *Past and Present*, 33 (1966)
Morgan, N. J. and Trainor, R. H., 'The Dominant Classes', in W. H. Fraser and R. J. Morris (eds), *People and Society in Scotland: II, 1830–1914* (Edinburgh, 1990)
Nenadic, S., 'The Victorian Middle Classes', in W. H. Fraser and I. Maver (eds), *Glasgow: Volume II, 1830–1912* (Manchester, 1996)
Robertson, P. L., 'The Finances of the University of Glasgow before 1914', *Higher Education Quarterly*, 16 (1976)
Robertson, P. L., 'Scottish Universities and Industry', *Scottish Economic and Social History*, 4 (1984)
Robertson, P. L., 'The Development of an Urban University: Glasgow 1860–1914', *History of Education Quarterly*, 30 (1990)
Trainor, R. H., 'The Elite', in W. H. Fraser and I. Maver (eds), *Glasgow: Volume II, 1830–1912* (Manchester, 1996)
Withrington, D. J., 'The Idea of a National University in Scotland, c. 1820–1870', in J. J. Carter and D. J. Withrington (eds), *Scottish Universities: Distinctiveness and Diversity* (Edinburgh, 1983)

(c) Theses

Hamilton, S., 'Women and the Scottish Universities, c. 1869–1939: A Social History' (Ph.D., University of Edinburgh, 1987)

Lloyd, C. F., 'Relationships between Scottish Universities and their communities, c. 1858–1914' (Ph.D., University of Glasgow, 1993)

Myers, C. J., 'Give her the apple and see what comes of it.' University Coeducation in Britain and America, c. 1860–1940 (with special focus on the University of Glasgow . . . and the University of Wisconsin at Madison)' (Ph.D., University of Strathclyde, 1999)

Wakeling, J., 'University Women: Origins, Experiences and Destinations at Glasgow University, 1939–1987' (Ph.D., University of Glasgow, 1998)

LIST OF ABBREVIATIONS

ADC	Academic Development Committee
B.Sc	Bachelor of Science
BDS	Bachelor of Dental Surgery
BL	Bachelor of Laws
CM	Master of Surgery
CMN	Court Minutes
CNAA	Council of National Academic Awards
CVCP	Committee of Vice-Chancellors and Principals
DD	Doctor of Divinity
DNB	Dictionary of National Biography
ERCC	Edinburgh Regional Computing Centre
FD	*Fortuna Domus . . . Lectures delivered in commemoration of the fifth centenary* (Glasgow, 1952)
GCMN	General Council Minutes
GH	*Glasgow Herald*
GMC	General Medical Council
GUA	Glasgow University Archives
GUM	*Glasgow University Magazine*
HEFCE	Higher Education Funding Council for England
LL.B.	Bachelor of Laws
MA	Master of Arts
MB	Bachelor of Medicine
NAB	National Advisory Board
NHS	National Health Service
OHGM	J MacLehose, *Memoirs and Portraits of One Hundred Glasgow Men* (Glasgow 1886)
OTC	Officers Training Corps
PCFC	Polytechnics and Colleges Funding Council
PhD	Doctor of Philosophy
PP	Parliamentary Papers
QMC	Queen Margaret College
QMU	Queen Margaret Union
RAE	Research Assessment Exercise
RC	Royal Commission
RCST	Royal College of Science & Technology
RDM	Resource Distribution Model
RSAMD	Royal Scottish Academy of Music and Drama
RSI	Regional Strategic Initiative
RTC	Royal Technical College
SHEFC	Scottish Higher Education Funding Council
SMN	Senate Minutes
SRC	Students' Representative Council
STEAC	Scottish Tertiary Education Advisory Council
UFC	Universities Funding Council
UGC	University Grants Committee
WWG	*Who's Who in Glasgow in 1909*

INDEX

Note: Page numbers in *italics* refer to illustrations, and are placed at the end of entries.